Racial Asymmetries

Racial Asymmetries

Asian American Fictional Worlds

STEPHEN HONG SOHN

New York University Press
NEW YORK AND LONDON

NEW YORK UNIVERSITY PRESS
New York and London

www.nyupress.org

© 2014 by New York University

All rights reserved

LIBRARY OF CONGRESS CATALOGING-IN-PUBLICATION DATA

Sohn, Stephen Hong.
Racial asymmetries : Asian American fictional worlds / Stephen Hong Sohn.
pages cm
Includes bibliographical references and index.
ISBN 978-1-4798-0007-0 (hardback)
ISBN 978-1-4798-0027-8 (pb)
1. American literature—Asian American authors—History and criticism.
2. First person narrative—History and criticism. 3. Point of view (Literature)
4. Race in literature. 5. Subjectivity in literature. 6. Equality in literature.
7. Lee, Chang-rae. Aloft. 8. Foster, Sesshu. Atomik Aztex. 9. Murray, Sabina.
Carnivore's inquiry. 10. Nunez, Sigrid. Last of her kind. I. Title. II. Title:
Asian American fictional worlds.
PS153.A84S54 2014
813'.5409895—dc23

2013027468

References to Internet websites (URLs) were accurate at the time of writing. Neither the author nor New York University Press is responsible for URLs that may have expired or changed since the manuscript was prepared.

New York University Press books are printed on acid-free paper, and their binding materials are chosen for strength and durability. We strive to use environmentally responsible suppliers and materials to the greatest extent possible in publishing our books.

Manufactured in the United States of America
c 10 9 8 7 6 5 4 3 2 1
p 10 9 8 7 6 5 4 3 2 1

Also available as an ebook

A book in the American Literatures Initiative (ALI), a collaborative publishing project of NYU Press, Fordham University Press, Rutgers University Press, Temple University Press, and the University of Virginia Press. The Initiative is supported by The Andrew W. Mellon Foundation. For more information, please visit www.americanliteratures.org.

Contents

	Acknowledgments	vii
	Introduction: The Many Storytellers of Asian American Fiction	1
1	White Flight, White Narration: Suburban Deviancies in Chang-rae Lee's *Aloft*	25
2	When the Minor Becomes Major: Asian American Literary California, Chicano Narration, and Sesshu Foster's *Atomik Aztex*	63
3	The Incomplete Biography in the Post–Civil Rights Era: Narrating Imagined Lives in Sigrid Nunez's Fictions	101
4	Comparative Colonial Narration: Conquest and Consumption in Sabina Murray's Fictions	136
5	Impossible Narration: Racial Analogies and Asian American Speculative Fictions	171
	Coda: Fiction Unbound	209
	Notes	213
	Works Cited	235
	Index	275
	About the Author	289

Acknowledgments

Let me begin with my deepest apologies for any oversights or omissions.

My journey into the labyrinthine world of Asian American literature was initiated by Shirley Geok-lin Lim; this book could not have been possible without her tireless mentorship and her galvanizing presence. Gavin Jones, Michele Elam, Andrea Lunsford, and Paul Robinson were patient enough to read through the complete manuscript and to offer incisive critiques; they became what I might call the perfect postgraduate school "first book committee." In the early and formative stages, I was lucky enough to be a part of an amazing writing group with Juliana Chang and Celine Parreñas Shimizu, who gave me the courage to go down this manuscript path. I look forward to many more years of collaborating with you both. I also could not have survived book writing without the occasional study hour and intellectual companionship offered by Yvonne Yarbro-Bejarano. To the winners—Jennifer Ann Ho, Betsy Huang, Paul Lai, and Sue J. Kim—your generosity and kindness always inspire me and humble me. Glen Mimura: thank you so much for your mentorship during my postdoctoral period.

Other colleagues and friends have generously given their time and support by reading, commenting, and advising me on chapter drafts; these include Ramón Saldívar, erin Khuê Ninh, Stewart Chang, Jerry Miller, Aimee Bahng, Jean Kim, Sau-Ling C. Wong, John Bender, Nancy Ruttenburg, John Peterson, Melissa Colleen Stevenson, Donald C. Goellnicht, Shelley Fisher Fishkin, Yanoula K. Athanassakis, Jeanne Sokolowski, and Anne Anlin Cheng. I give thanks to the faculty of

Stanford's English Department, who have been so welcoming and collegial, especially Arnold Rampersad, Ken Fields, Eavan Boland, Jennifer Summit, Paula Moya, Ursula Heise, Patricia Parker, Judy Richardson, Alice Stavely, Roland Greene, Franco Moretti, Claire Jarvis, Vaughn Rasberry, Peggy Phelan, Sianne Ngai, Mark McGurl, Michelle Karnes, Adam Johnson, Hannah Sullivan, Blair Hoxby, Toby Wolff, Roland Greene, Nick Jenkins, Franco Moretti, Hilton Obenzinger, Shimon Tanaka, Saikat Majumdar, Subhasree Chakravarty, Chris Rovee, Alex Woloch, Denise Gigante, Shimon Tanaka, Blakey Vermeule, Terry Castle, and Helen Brooks. Elizabeth Tallent: thank you for the pleasure of tea time. Stephen Orgel: thank you for the generosity of your friendship. Across the campus, I am grateful for the presence of the many who have supported my teaching and research: Russell Berman, Harry Elam, Gordon Chang, David Palumbo-Liu, Heather Hadlock, Helen Stacy, Stephen Murphy-Shigematsu, and James Sheehan.

The anonymous reviewers during my fourth-year review were also incredibly helpful in improving the quality of this manuscript.

There has been a large community of scholars, writers, and others who have read and helped to advance my work: Michael Benveniste, Alexander Chee, Tina Chen, Floyd Cheung, Cheng Lok Chua, Kandice Chuh, Hyeyurn Chung, Martha Cutter, Robert G. Diaz, Enda Duffy, Diane C. Fujino, Dorothy Fujita-Rony, Catherine Fung, Geneva M. Gano, Donald C. Goellnicht, Christine Hong, Terry Hong, Hsuan L. Hsu, Linh Hua, Adria L. Imada, Allan Punzalan Isaac, Wen Jin, Laura Hyun Yi Kang, Claire Jean Kim, Elaine H. Kim, Ju-Yon Kim, Seong-Kon Kim, James Kyung-jin Lee, So-Hee Lee, George Lipsitz, Catherine Liu, Colleen Lye, Anita Mannur, Victor Roman Mendoza, Marshall Moore, Venus Nasri, Greta Ai-yu Niu, Susie Pak, Jane Chi Hyun Park, Josephine Nock-Hee Park, Sarah Park Dahlen, Jeffrey L. Partridge, Arlene Phillips, Martin Joseph Ponce, David Roman, Jeffrey J. Santa Ana, Cathy Schlund-Vials, Lindsey Smith, Min Song, Fatimah Tobing-Rony, Elda Tsou, Linda Trinh Vo, Karen Tei Yamashita, Caroline H. Yang, Timothy Yu, and Xiaojian Zhao. I must also acknowledge the writers who were so kind as to respond to my queries during the writing of this book and to whom many of these chapters are devoted: Jessica Hagedorn, Tony D'Souza, Sigrid Nunez, Sabina Murray, Chang-rae Lee, Sesshu Foster, Brian Ascalon Roley, Bhira Backhaus, Claire Light, and Ted Chiang.

I have benefited immensely from my interactions and discussions with both undergraduate and graduate students at Stanford University. I take time to mention the handful who went on to work with me in more extensive capacities, completing research projects or working with me in instructional capacities: Raechel Lee, Vanessa Seals, Steffi Dippold, Lupe Carrillo, Justin St. Germain, Kathryn Van Arendonk, Vanessa Chang, Vida Mia Garcia, James Matthew Estrella, Michelle Rhee-Weise, Karli June Cerankowski, Allen Frost, Long Le-Khac, Stephanie Otani-Sunamoto, Johaina Crisostomo, Kathryn Marie Frank, Emma Clare Trotter, Thanh Nguyen, Cynthia Liao, Christian Ngo, Alok Vaid-Menon, Sarah Chang, and Lilian Thaoxaochay. My research was supported by a phalanx of diligent and productive research assistants, including Haerin Shin, Trac Dang, Nicole E. Chorney, Allison Sarah de Gorostiza Bayani, Jennifer Hsin-Ting Liu, Samantha Tieu, Stephen Hilfer, Tenyia Iris Lee, and Charles (Charlie) Syms. I have also been lucky to work with those who helped direct and promote Stanford's first Asian American writers' group, including Iris A. Law, Henry Leung, and Victoria Yee. The guidance of Stanford's incredible staff helped propel this book forward in a timely fashion: Dagmar Logie, Alyce Boster, Nelia Peralta, Judy Candell, Katie Dooling, Nicole Yun Bridges, Colleen Boucher, Monica Moore, Cindy Ng, Shelley Tadaki, Chris Queen, Tania D. Mitchell, Michelle Zamora, and Mariatte Denman.

I wanted to take the time to acknowledge the tremendous efforts provided by the editors over at NYU Press—Eric Zinner, Ciara McLaughlin, and Alicia Nadkarni—as well as my anonymous manuscript reviewers in helping me hone this manuscript. Tim Roberts: thanks for your flexibility and making the production process streamlined and transparent.

To my close family and friends—Richard Hong Sohn, Joan Chyun, Henry Oh—I very much appreciate your patience, as you all know how long the process of book writing has been. Shawn Lynn Keeler: this book could not have been completed without your love and unquestioning belief in my work. C.S.: thank you for the gift of balance and, of course, for the oranges. John Hong Sohn, it was awesome to have spent my first years up in the Bay with you! My sisters—Julianne Hong Sohn, Krystal Young, and Gina Valentino—you know I could not have made it without your support—I am the luckiest brother ever. My parents, Soon Ho Sohn and Yunpyo Hong Sohn, deserve a special note of gratitude for all that they have given and for all that they have modeled.

Introduction: The Many Storytellers of Asian American Fiction

Asian American literature is traditionally understood as a body of texts written in English that depicts a specific social history in which individuals of various ethnicities have faced discrimination due to perceptions and laws that designated them as aliens.[1] Common narratives involve the troubling acculturation process of the Asian immigrant, the intergenerational ruptures between Asian immigrant parents and their more Americanized children, and the challenges of defining identity when an Asian American travels back to a land of ethnic origin.

Critics tend to further delineate Asian American literature through "maximal ideological inclusiveness" (Lye, "Introduction" 4). This "inclusiveness" appears in the way critics embrace particular cultural productions, based on factors such as ancestry, the author's residency status, and textual content. Most of the works that have achieved canonical status tend also to depict Asian or Asian American contexts. Certainly, critics understand that American writers of Asian descent are often inspired by their personal experiences of racial oppression and racial difference in the creation of their cultural productions, both fictional and otherwise. Bounding Asian American literature in part by the writer's ancestry leads not merely to a biologically centered notion of textual classification but to an understanding that race produces material effects on bodies, lives, *and* corresponding acts of creative expression. The most acclaimed texts exemplify these definitional boundaries. Maxine Hong Kingston's *The Woman Warrior* (1975), reputed to be one of most frequently adopted books in college-level curriculums, focuses on the challenges connected to Chinese American immigrant assimilation and acculturation. Carlos Bulosan's *America Is in the Heart* (1946), Bharati Mukherjee's *Jasmine* (1989), and Chang-rae Lee's *Native Speaker* (1995) respectively explore similar issues from the viewpoints of Filipino American, Indian American, and Korean American narrators. John Okada's *No-No Boy* (1957) reveals the struggles faced by Japanese Americans during the postinternment period from the perspective of a young man named Ichiro Yamada. These now-classic texts, the subjects of numerous critical articles, book chapters, and required reading on many graduate qualifying exams, can reinforce an assumption that Asian American literature is defined by the overlaps among ethnoracial authorial identity, narration, narrative perspective, and cultural scripts that direct our understanding and analyses of the fictional world.

Racial Asymmetries reconsiders this approach. It challenges the tidy links between authorial ancestry and fictional content, and between identity and form, to expand what is typically thought of as Asian American culture and criticism.[2] This book is inspired by a persistent phenomenon: works of fiction that trouble critical methodologies through the storytelling perspective. Take Jessica Hagedorn's novel *Toxicology* (2011) as one clear example. Hagedorn employs first-person narration to offer readers unobstructed access to the mind and the life of Eleanor Delacroix, an eighty-year-old writer and avowed lesbian who is of Caucasian-Mexican descent. The novel is set in contemporary New York and involves an eclectic set of characters in addition to Eleanor, including a budding filmmaker named Mimi Smith and her daughter Violet. Hagedorn (with Irish, Filipina, Chinese, and French ancestries), like Eleanor, is of mixed-race background, but Eleanor could hardly be called her fictional counterpart or imaginary double. In *Toxicology*, we see Eleanor Delacroix's fame dwindling in light of the new modes of art and authorship being promoted in the age of digital cultures and the ubiquity of social media technology. Strikingly, the novel does not contain any characters clearly marked as Asian or Asian American. *Toxicology* hence moves away from the Filipino American–centered content of Hagedorn's first three fictional publications and provides us with a meditation on the shifting morphology of cultural production in a media-saturated new millennium. Hagedorn's novel demonstrates the "racial asymmetry" at the heart of my book: the author's ethnoracial status is not easily or directly mirrored within the fictional world. A central aim of *Racial Asymmetries* is to recenter works such as *Toxicology* within Asian American cultural studies, to challenge the standard narrative perspectives,

INTRODUCTION / 3

plots, and devices of the field and to further encourage the development of more expansive social-context methodologies.

Toxicology is assuredly not the only text that pushes the bounds of Asian American cultural criticism through narratorial construction. Indeed, this novel is part of a wide-scale emergence of fictional narratives produced roughly within the past two decades.[3] I specifically concentrate on first-person narration to show how Asian American writers engage the invention of dynamic fictional worlds.[4] My book reveals that the construction of narrative perspective encourages cultural critics to engage a highly comparative mode of analysis, which opens up a whole range of texts heretofore facing marginalization. *Racial Asymmetries* examines a selection of such texts, which include Sesshu Foster's *Atomik Aztex* (2005), Chang-rae Lee's *Aloft* (2004), Sabina Murray's *A Carnivore's Inquiry* (2004) and *Forgery* (2007), Sigrid Nunez's *For Rouenna* (2001) and *The Last of Her Kind* (2006), Claire Light's "Abducted by Aliens!" (2009), and Ted Chiang's *The Merchant and the Alchemist's Gate* (2007). Such fictions ask readers and critics to develop reading practices that move away from an autobiographical or autoethnographic impulse attuned to authorial ancestry. By doing so, readers and critics remain more open to a range of storytellers including a merchant from the Islamic Golden Age, an American antiquities dealer who travels to Greece in the post–World War II period, a Chicano slaughterhouse worker agitating for union reform in the period following civil rights, a sixty-year-old Italian American man, an African American female prisoner, and even a man who purports to be an alien abductee. This analytical approach pushes critics to consider why these storytelling perspectives are featured, why certain geographies and historical periods are represented, and who gets written out of the plot, among other such issues. While the unconventional narrators employed by these Asian American writers might seem to reject the foundational issues of race and racism that first propelled the field into existence, this study reminds us that aesthetic choices are not somehow free from political ramifications. Thus, we must attend to the ways that a given story is told and how the telling unlocks fictional worlds that radically widen the social contexts of Asian American cultural productions.

It would be premature, however, to suggest that Asian Americanist and ethnic literary critique, as they have traditionally been defined, is no longer needed.[5] We understand that the writer's racial identity still matters and can be used to categorize a literary body. Nevertheless, if a strategic essentialist approach persists as one of the primary modes for defining Asian American literature, what then of thinking about the strategic antiessentialism of fictional worlds? I borrow here from George Lipsitz's conception of strategic antiessentialism as a kind of disguise "on the basis of its ability to highlight, underscore, and augment an aspect of one's identity that one cannot express directly" (*Dangerous Crossroads* 62).[6] Given the potential propensity to assume that Asian American writers depict only narrative perspectives that overlap with their ethnoracial backgrounds, the aspect of "identity" that cannot be expressed directly is that of the writerly imagination, which cannot be tethered to a single ancestry or origin point. My deployment of strategic antiessentialism thus shifts Asian American cultural criticism outside of its more traditional topics and themes. In this way, strategic antiessentialism offers a paradigm that moves beyond the limits of cultural nationalist models and forefronts a deconstructive critical methodology in which the Asian American writer and his or her nonautobiographical narrator stand at the center.

Narrative Perspective and the Constitution of Asian American Literature

One element we need to consider further is the relationship between authorial descent and narrative content, as this link conditions the emergence of specific literary forms. Indeed, twentieth-century narrative texts by American writers of Asian descent generally fall into two aesthetic and formal categories: autobiography/memoir or the ethnoracial bildungsroman (or some variation that melds those two literary genres). The dominance of these two forms is clearly connected to the expansive opportunity both forms provide for telling stories of the Asian American subject, whether in a nonfictional configuration, such as autobiography, or in its fictional valences, as in the ethnoracial bildungsroman. Despite the apparent differences between these two forms, their connection lies in the importance of the narrating subject and corresponding narrative perspective. In the Asian American autobiography and Asian American bildungsroman, narrative cohesion typically results from the maintenance of *one* narrator or main character, whose life readers follow from the beginning to the end and who *can* or *could be* conflated with the author. Given the centuries-long hostile and dehumanizing caricatures of Asians as yellow perils, model minorities, dragon ladies, and kung-fu masters, self-representation is of paramount importance. One might call this developmental narrative, as figured in both autobiography and in the ethnoracial bildungsroman, a "racial form" (Lye, *America's Asia* 1), precisely because sociohistorical circumstances exert influence on modes of literary expression. The ability of the minority writer to explore his or her life (or someone's not too dissimilar) in autobiographical or fictional form has thus consistently provided a valuable means to nuance and diversify what we understand as the American experience.

Asian American literature's emergence through the development of autobiography and the ethnoracial bildungsroman must also be considered alongside its connections to the literary and commercial publishing markets. Especially in the first half of the twentieth century, ethnic writers played the part of the native informant, providing depictions of the so-called authentic Asian American experience.[7] While some authors faced difficulty in reaching a wide audience, commercial interest in the ethnic experience helps explain the appeal of writers such as Etsu Inagaki Sugimoto, Younghill Kang, Jade Snow Wong, C. Y. Lee, and Lin Yutang in the period prior to Maxine Hong Kingston's monumental work, *The Woman Warrior*. Indeed, as guides to the American minority experience, these writers negotiated a complicated milieu where literary value was often tied to authenticity. Interest in Asian cultures and oriental objects had been circulating in the United States from as far back as the late seventeenth century, helping create a reading audience receptive to the increased popularization of such writers in the early twentieth.[8]

This authenticity paradigm circumscribes Asian American writers by assuming unification among the author, narrative perspective, and narrative content. For instance, a Chinese American might be presumed to write from the narrative perspective of a Chinese American character. In addition, the corresponding representational terrain is then expected to primarily elucidate Chinese American social contexts. Narrative perspective is therefore often under incredible pressure to exhibit ethnoracial authenticity. An alignment among the writer's ethnoracial descent, narrative perspective, and content is not in and of itself impoverishing and restrictive, but I am most interested in exploring how and to what ends Asian American writers travel outside and can be read outside of this model.[9]

While American writers of Asian descent have not always remained confined within fictional worlds that mirror their ethnic and racial backgrounds, deviations prior to 1989 are few and far between.[10]

The most well-known writers to flout a more autoethnographically inflected practice are Winnifred Eaton, of Chinese British heritage, who took on an ethnic pseudonym to pen her many Japanese-themed novels, and Diana Chang, author of six novels, many of which do not contain major characters of Asian descent.[11] Eaton and Chang both provide interesting but historically isolated cases for contextualizing the commercial and critical response to ethnoracial narratives at different historical points in the twentieth century. Eaton composed her fictions roughly between 1899 and 1925, while Chang composed hers between 1956 and 1978. Hence, it is difficult to read Eaton and Chang as part of a sustained movement constituting an expansive, nonautoethnographic fictional literary tradition.[12] At the same time, the emergence of such fictions spotlights the complicated relationship between Asian American writers and textual content, especially as themes of racial oppression, migration, and assimilation do not always ground their cultural productions.

While the commercial pressures that reduce Asian American writers to native informants have been in place for at least a century, the contemporary period is exceptional. The commodification of Asian American writers unquestionably continues. The incredible success of Amy Tan in the late 1980s, for instance, inaugurated another sustained wave of literary marketplace racialization, in which the publishing industry codified the Asian American writer as a native informant. But for a number of reasons, the current moment differs from when Eaton and Chang were first published, precisely because of processes related to institutionalization. Asian American studies programs and departments are now found across the United States. In addition, the Immigration Act of 1965 enabled Asian immigrants to enter the United States in considerable numbers for the first time since 1924. This influx set the stage for a new and larger generation of writers. It is no coincidence that nonautoethnographic fictions began to appear en masse in the 1990s, roughly a generation after the Immigration Act. During this latter period, Asian Americans have also been understood as model minorities, a shift in racial formation that must be taken into account to consider the changes occurring in fictional worlds.

Thus, three general historical and sociocultural circumstances frame this project: the emergence of postracial discourse in the model minority era, issues of literary commodification, and the development of critical trends in relation to Asian American writers.

Asian American Fiction in the Postrace Era

The archive of Asian Americans fictions explored in this study, all which were published after 2000, collectively appear in a period in which conversations concerning social inequality have dramatically shifted, especially in relation to the issue of racial oppression.[13] According to Linda Trinh Võ, the "postracial narrative" involves the assumption that the United States has moved "beyond its racist past"; she argues further that this viewpoint "reaffirms the palatable and celebratory multiculturalism, which is devoid of historical context and ignores the complex ways in which racism is embedded in our society. It reflects, in some respects, the way a color-blind society would supposedly operate, by flattening out racial difference" (332). Subsumed within the postracial narrative, Asian Americans appear in a complicated position precisely because they are held up as model minorities, a group that has transcended social inequalities. The model minority myth suggests a narrative of development. Indeed, it upholds the racial minority as evidence of a color-blind democracy and as an example that all Americans can follow. Despite the challenges of immigration, acculturation, and assimilation, Asian Americans, according to this script, somehow still succeed and achieve. This reductive formulation further shows how ethnic and racial difference is not necessarily a barrier, thus showing up (and perhaps even shaming) other racial groups perceived to be underperforming.

THE POSTRACIAL AESTHETIC

Because the Asian American writers in this study take on narrative perspectives or characters that do not mirror their own ethnoracial ancestries, these works might be taken as examples of what the literary critic Yoonmee Chang has called a "postracial aesthetic." Chang defines the postracial as "literature written by Asian American writers that does not contain Asian American characters or address Asian American experiences" (201–02). Chang engages a lengthier reading of Nam Le's opening short story from *The Boat* (2008), "Love and Honor and Pity and Pride and Compassion and Sacrifice," to show how the postracial operates through an "ethnic abnegation" (202), as writers turn away from their Asian ethnic backgrounds as direct sources or inspirations for their creative work. Chang asserts that "this rejection frees the author from the ostensible shackles of ethnic particularity and difference to examine transcendent universal themes, like 'love and honor and pity.' For Asian American authors, the postracial more specifically frees them from writing orientalist caricatures and reductive ethnographies—from the 'Chinatown' book" (202). Le himself cannot be defined so strictly as Asian American due to his Australian national origin, but the story's setting in Iowa and its thematic content is more broadly applicable to minority writers. As read by Chang, the main character from the opening short story, presumably modeled on Nam Le himself, is an example of a writer seeking to break free from the bonds of autoethnographic and autobiographical fiction. Le's collection as a whole seems to follow the pattern of the writer who has broken free from the expectation that he write from his own ethnoracial viewpoint, as many of the stories take on perspectives of racially unmarked characters or those of different ancestral backgrounds from Le (who is of Vietnamese descent). At the same time, the final story, "The Boat," adheres to a Vietnamese context and engages one of the more common concerns of that ethnic experience by relating the harrowing refugee flight from the homeland in the wake of war. The inclusion and the sequencing of "The Boat" suggests that the postracial aesthetic is itself a questionable fantasy and that some established forms and themes of ethnic-minority writing cannot simply be disregarded as unoriginal or superficially pandering to an audience hungry for the ethnoracially authentic narrative voice.

But the larger problem with any postracial aesthetic is the assumption that constructing "universal themes" ultimately enables a writer, Asian American or not, to ever be free from the "shackles of ethnic particularity and difference." Even as a writer seems to move beyond narrating a particular story from the viewpoint of a character who strongly mirrors his or her own ancestry, deeper analytical inquiry reveals a fictional world imbued by the often brutalizing forces of power based on material realities and external referents. In other words, universal themes might appear in the fictional world, but always and only alongside very specific social contexts that have always been the concern of cultural critics and scholars involved with race and ethnic studies.

For one concrete example within the realm of Asian American fiction, let us turn to Tony D'Souza's novel *Whiteman* (2006). The narrator and titular "whiteman," Jack Diaz, travels to Côte d'Ivoire as a volunteer for Potable Water International (PWI), an international humanitarian aid organization that helps tribal villages find reliable sources of clean drinking water. D'Souza, a biracial Asian American writer, does not situate the first-person narrative through a storyteller whose ethnoracial background overlaps with his own but rather focuses it through the main character's challenging journey surviving in the rural backcountry of West Africa. *Whiteman* might be seen as exemplary of postracial Asian American fiction.[14] One could say that D'Souza has freed himself from the bonds of his own "ethnic particularity" as it relates to the fictional world, giving him the potential grounds to explore more universal themes. On one level, the novel is very much about the practical application of universal themes, especially in relation to human rights. Article 25 of the United Nation's Universal Declaration of Human Rights, for example, drives the goals of many international relief and humanitarian organizations. D'Souza's fictional organization, PWI, has some clear real-world analogs such as Global Water, water.org, and Water Health International, all with similar aims.

But, on another level, even as Jack seeks to advance the aims of universal human rights, these lofty goals collide with the social contexts of Côte d'Ivoire. For instance, D'Souza's construction of the fictional world demands to be read alongside racial tensions involving the northern and southern tribes within the nation-state. The regime of biological essence and racial difference exported into Côte d'Ivoire through the colonial process is central to the country's regional tensions, as elucidated by Ruth Marshall-Fratani (13). Key to Marshall-Fratani's theorization is that Ivoirians ultimately appropriated colonial ideologies of race to try to define what an authentic and essential national subject could be. Because Côte d'Ivoire is one of the most diverse countries in West Africa, the attempt to define the authentic Ivoirian subject has been bloody, intense, and conflicted. Within *Whiteman*, D'Souza represents this complicated milieu through the religious tensions existing among various populations. Not long after settling in the Worodougou region, Jack details the rift between Côte d'Ivoire's Muslim northerners and Christian southerners as emerging in part through French postcolonial influence; the resulting clashes over citizenship set the stage for violence over issues of belonging and racial difference. For the local individuals, national disenfranchisement occurs in multiple ways, including lack of access to health care and the unequal distribution of federal funds for vital infrastructure projects (15). At the same time, Jack's anger is obvious, and he places his political investments with those who reside in the Muslim-majority north. Thus, his commitment to social justice extends far beyond the desire to install new well pumps and provide clean water. However, given the chaotic national and international situation, Jack never gets to fulfill his main goal as a member of PWI. By the time the novel concludes, Côte d'Ivoire's civil war has begun, and the eight remaining members of PWI must make a perilous journey to a neighboring country to be evacuated.[15] We see how the institution of universal human rights finds unstable grounding in the midst of chaotic nation-state formation.

The novel's structure further enables one to consider the link between formal conventions and social contexts. *Whiteman* can be considered a "dissensual bildungsroman," specifically detailing the challenges of developing any "egalitarian imaginary" in a postcolonial and neocolonial Ivoirian context (Slaughter 28). While Jack begins the novel as an ostensible adult, every chapter illustrates how much he must learn in order to adapt to and understand the Ivoirian cultures that surround him, suggesting that he still requires maturation. Despite some acculturation to Côte d'Ivoire over the course of the novel, Jack's experiences leave him unfulfilled, especially as evidenced by his journeys after he is forced to leave the country. He "wandered another half year around the far reaches of the continent" and "tried, and mostly succeeded, to enter every war-torn nation there was: Burundi, Angola, Congo, Zimbabwe" (D'Souza 278). But Jack finally divulges that he never found what he was "looking for" and finally came "home" (278). This last sentiment reveals the interruption of Jack's identity quest, a reflection perhaps of his limited power as an individual to effect positive change. If the novel's setting in Côte d'Ivoire brings with it the residues of its French colonial past, the war-torn nations that Jack later visits gesture to the larger history of European colonization, as Burundi, Angola, Congo, and Zimbabwe were respectively colonized by Germany, Portugal, Belgium, and England. The constructed narrative perspective, the "I" of Jack Diaz, is one haunted by his individual failures and the larger scope of political instability on the African continent.

As race relations collide catastrophically within the postcolonial milieu of Côte d'Ivoire, the novel depicts, without romanticizing, how Jack's persistent attempts to portray life there are indelibly marked by social inequalities. Though D'Souza does not necessarily choose to narrate the novel from the perspective of a mixed-race South Asian American character, *Whiteman* offers us a storyteller who realizes the shortsightedness of his humanitarian mission in the face of the racial and ethnic tensions embroiling Ivoirian society. If the foundational motivations for social-context methodologies within Asian Americanist critique have been to elucidate the experiences of those who are facing oppression and historical erasure, *Whiteman* certainly fits this purpose, even with its use of a fictionalized narrative perspective. But my larger point is that D'Souza's novel is not anomalous. It belongs to a vast archive of Asian American fictions that emerged in what has been called the postrace era, yet it must still be read with an attentive eye to issues of social inequality.

The "Model Minority" in the Postrace Era

Like Hagedorn, D'Souza, and Le, the writers included in this study might be read as pushing for a postracial aesthetic as they take on narrative perspectives of non–Asian American or racially unmarked characters. However, on deeper inquiry, these cross-ethnoracial storytelling viewpoints direct us to consider social inequality in relational, refractive, and comparative formations. That is, Asian American characters or experiences may seem marginal to the plotting, but this marginality is advanced in the service of exploring the multifocal configurations of power. This move away from the autobiographical and autoethnographic storyteller is explained in part by timing: these writers have emerged during a period in which their racial status can be hailed as a marker of privilege. As I mentioned earlier, Americans of Asian descent have been labeled as the "model minority." This designation distinguishes this racial group from others (such as African Americans, Native Americans, and Chicanos/as) and grants us a way to understand why authorial ancestry still remains a vital component to cultural criticism. The connection between racial formation and literary expression cannot always be directly ascertained, yet contemporary Asian American writers must attend to their creative work in an era in which their status as a minority can be levied as a kind of cultural capital. While many scholars cast light on the problems with the logic of the model minority myth, it still remains a pervasive way to conceptualize Asian Americans.[16]

The model minority narrative emphasizes closure, uplift, and, most of all, the Asian American subject who achieves and succeeds. In this construct, the Asian American becomes, most importantly, a docile minority, one who does not protest and instead obeys the formulation that he or she models for others to follow. The term "model" itself suggests a prototype that can be seamlessly replicated among all the different Asian American ethnic groups, flattening out an incredibly heterogeneous population in terms of class, religion, language, and other such differences. Further still, the model minority mythos is funneled through a particular form of achievement. As the legal scholars Miranda Oshige McGowan and James Lindgren note, Asian Americans are "said to be intelligent and highly educated, though a large number of them are dismissed as math and science geeks" (335). A number of other scholars such as Frank Wu (40), Jean Yonemura Wing (462), Guofang Li (70), and Debora A. Trytten, Anna Wong Lowe, and Susan E. Walden (440) echo the stereotype that Asian Americans only excel in certain academic areas and occupational fields. As the model minority paradigm functions within a reductive homogeneity, Asian American writers at the center of this study directly undermine this racial formation through the construction of such diverse storytelling perspectives. The practice of decentering the ethnoracial autobiographical voice actively challenges the homogeneity and the inherent prototyping that the model minority myth foregrounds. And of course, as Asian American writers create narrators whose ethnoracial ancestries do not match their own, they make an imaginative artistic leap in the creation of these fictional personages. In this sense, we must attend to the Asian American writer not only as a figure whose works may be read for their multifaceted political valences but also as an artist who can be studied for the mastery and deployment of literary craft.

Emergence of Mixed-Race Studies

It is important to note that the postrace era also overlaps with the development and rise of mixed-race studies, a field that casts attention on the nature of descent. With changes in the US Census that offer individuals the chance to mark one or more boxes to denote ancestry, theorizing racial formation becomes all the more challenging. A number of scholars show that mixed-race Asian Americans face thorny issues related to community inclusion and ancestral ties.[17] Does one identify strictly as Asian American or as a mixed-race American? What does it mean when one attempts to identify only with one ancestral background and not another? These questions generate particular friction with respect to mixed-race Asian American writers, who do not always create narrative perspectives that mirror their manifold ancestries. In the following chapters, I focus on a number of authors—Sesshu Foster, Claire Light, Sigrid Nunez, and Sabina Murray—who hail from mixed-race backgrounds.[18] Like D'Souza's *Whiteman*, their fictions cannot be easily tethered to their ancestries. Without an obvious autobiographical center to influence analytical inquiries, such works encourage critics to engage a diverse set of character-narrators and corresponding sociohistorical circumstances.

INTRODUCTION / 13

THE FALLACY OF POSTRACE DISCOURSE

The fictions briefly touched on—Hagedorn's *Toxicology*, Le's *The Boat*, and D'Souza's *Whiteman*—and the ones analyzed at length later in this study ultimately expose postracial discourse as a fallacy, but not in such a way as to celebrate racial difference in some sort of superficial multiculturalism.[19] Indeed, such cultural productions engage cross-ethnoracial perspectives that allow us to consider both the relational and the asymmetrical nature of social difference and associated inequalities. In *Whiteman*, Jack Diaz's attempt to identify with the local Ivoirians does not simply come about through his work with PWI, and though we see him struggle to attain a measure of acceptance, his personal problems are effectively contrasted with those of his hard-won friends as they find themselves mired in a bloody civil war. And while Le's *The Boat* engages various narrative perspectives and characters located all over the globe, unveiling a veritable multicultural tapestry—with stories set in the United States, Vietnam, Australia, Japan, Iran, and Colombia—these depictions target rather weighty topics that do not exalt the richness of ethnic differences. The various stories probe into issues such as refugee flight in the wake of war, systemic poverty in shantytown communities, and racial ideologies that fuel international and local conflict. Finally, Hagedorn's *Toxicology* draws up a fictional world in which art's value finds dubious social import in a city focused so much on celebrity sightings and superficial capitalist consumption. At the same time, the novel includes an important minor figure named Agnes, the cousin of one of the main characters, who reminds us that the glitzy veneer of New York City also includes an immigrant underclass of domestic workers and laborers.

Despite my focus on such an idiosyncratic archive, one that has not been the center of much critical attention, let me be clear: I do not believe that the ethnoracial bildungsroman and autobiography have become obsolete as forms employed by Asian American writers, nor do I believe that a direct connection between authorial background and narrative perspective somehow results in an impoverished fictional world. For instance, the recent surge of Cambodian American autobiographies relating the experiences of Khmer Rouge survivors clarifies the importance of certain literary forms as a way to give voice to personal histories that have been profoundly altered by trauma and violence. The period following the terrorist attacks on 9/11 saw a substantial rise in cultural productions from South Asian American and Anglophone writers seeking to expose the rise of racial profiling, especially as anti-Muslim sentiment flared. The years following the Tiananmen Square massacre have also seen the emergence of a new generation of Chinese expatriate writers who have detailed the challenges of living under communist rule. Such developments reveal a field that continues to grow in manifold directions.

Touristing in Asian America

Despite the proliferation of postrace rhetoric, one arena—the contemporary literary marketplace—continues to aggressively promote a form of racial authenticity. As I stated earlier, Asian American writers have often been circumscribed by the expectation that their fictions are composed with their personal and communal histories in mind. Amy Tan's *The Joy Luck Club* (1989) exemplifies how an Asian American fiction can be both commercially viable and reductively marketed as a kind of authentic narrative. *The Joy Luck Club* remained on the *New York Times* best-seller list for approximately thirty-three weeks, debuting on April 16, 1989, and finally falling off the list on November 26, 1989. It garnered rave reviews, became a runaway best-seller, and possessed enough popular momentum to be adapted into a mainstream Hollywood movie of the same name directed by Wayne Wang, himself a Chinese American. While the sales figures for *The Joy Luck Club* have varied, most scholars and critics agree that the book has sold more than four million copies (Dong 1205).[20] Tan's popularity is singular, in spite of comparisons to Maxine Hong Kingston and other prominent Asian American writers, as evidenced by sales figures from comparable periods.[21] To this day, Tan remains one of the few American-born writers of Asian descent to have successfully landed at the top of the *New York Times* best-seller list.[22]

In the second chapter of *Beyond Literary Chinatown* (2007), Jeffrey F. L. Partridge investigates the consequences for writing in the post–Amy Tan era by comparing the book descriptions included on hardcover dust jackets or paperback covers of nine different narrative fictions produced by Chinese American writers, four of which are by Tan.[23] Partridge concludes by arguing that literary marketers engender "the tour guide function" (73) promoting an ethnic authenticity. Yet Partridge chooses not to go beyond the Chinese American authors in exploring the tour guide function, which could demonstrate not only an ethnic commodification but a racialized one. Despite Partridge's focus on one ethnic group, his approach persuasively shows how narratives are marketed in relation to authorial identity. Book-jacket descriptions, back-cover plot summaries, and Internet editorial blurbs describing the Chinese past as "hidden," "tangled," and "terrible" (73) call attention to an unassimilable origin point. This narrative heightens the inscrutability long attached to Asian American subjects as the yellow peril. While the American present is embraced and in some cases celebrated within these novels, the Asian ethnonational past is far more treacherous to navigate, so much so that many include various first-generation subjects who die. American identity then depends on a jettisoning of the hazardous past. The success of this kind of narrative demonstrates how Chinese American literature becomes commodified through marketplace practices. Such marketing approaches, of course, target what publishers consider a broad audience who will not likely have much familiarity with ethnic-minority contexts. Thus, the appeal of the tour guide narrative unfolds in the context of readers who look to begin a new and dynamic journey offered, apparently, only by the authentic storytelling voice.

This process can be elaborated more broadly within a racial context, as evidenced by the marketing approaches to several other novels not specific to the Chinese experience. The back-cover description to the paperback version of Lan Cao's *Monkey Bridge* (1997), for example, illustrates how racial authenticity is rehearsed: "Lan Cao's narrative traverses perilously between worlds *past and present, East and West*, in telling two interlocked stories" involving, among other things, a mother-daughter relationship and "*family secrets.*" The summary goes on to note that "the *haunting* and beautiful terrain of *Monkey Bridge* is the 'luminous motion,' as it is called in Vietnamese myth and legend, between generations, encompassing Vietnamese lore, history, and dreams of the past as well as of the future" (emphases mine). The binary that structures East and West is telling, despite the different ethnic context, in which Vietnam stands in for the threatening Asian past. As Partridge details in the case of Chinese American literature, so many of these mother-daughter descriptions are leveraged on a "secret" often detailed or existing in conjunction with an Asian ethnic heritage. The revelation of the secret enables the main character to undergo a kind of healing (73). In *Monkey Bridge*, the daughter, Mai Nguyen, one of two narrators, must confront her mother's past to find out why her grandfather did not join them in the United States. This "secret" propels the novel forward and requires readers to delve into the traumas of the Vietnam War. *Monkey Bridge* is one of numerous examples external to the Chinese American context wherein the writer is marketed as the tour guide.[24] The writer leads readers into the Asian past and then delivers them safely away from it.

The tour guide construct resides in the expectation that the Asian American writer represents his or her ethnic background through the narrative perspective and thus directs the story's content through his or her position as the storyteller. This parallel is essential because, as Partridge states, "to go into the past to make sense of the present, the Chinese American author must be a part of that past and an emblem of that history" (73). However, if the Asian American author is likened to an "emblem of history," one is already in danger of conflating the author specifically with historian, autoethnographer, or autobiographer—roles that do not grant the possibility of Asian American creativity and artistry. The storyteller's ancestry in a novel such as Tan's *The Joy Luck Club* or Cao's *Monkey Bridge* aligns with the author's racial and ethnic background. In some cases, the novel's events can even be corroborated by the author's own life, therefore invoking elements of autobiography. On another level, the Asian American writer can be called on to provide an account of the past as a sort of layman's historian. At the same time, the author's creation often details a larger ethnic community's characteristics and struggles, with the narrator serving as our gateway into the appropriately authenticated fictional world.

The success of Tan's *The Joy Luck Club* and other blockbuster Asian American works that followed, including Lisa See's *Shanghai Girls* (2009), Abraham Verghese's *Cutting for Stone* (2009) and Jamie Ford's *Hotel on the Corner of Bitter and Sweet* (2009), helps to strengthen the link between the writer's Asian ancestry and narrative perspective, thus continuing to fuel the assumption that fiction is a mask for historical, autobiographical, and autoethnographic documentation. What Partridge calls the "literary Chinatown" can be seen as a burden distributed across different ethnic groups that constitute the racial category known as Asian American. I am thus interested in how the literary marketplace helps articulate some of the forces that render the Asian American writer as a native informant and as a hazy double for the narrator and/or protagonist within the fictional world. As we can see, the Asian American fiction writer exists at a complicated historical and cultural nexus. On the one hand, postrace rhetoric implies that the Asian American subject is a mobile entity, free from the bonds of racial prejudice and therefore ostensibly just as free to imagine fictional worlds as devoid of social inequality as his or her own life apparently is. On the other, we have a literary marketplace that openly commodifies the racial ancestry of the Asian American writer as a way to authenticate the fictional world. In the space between the restrictions of the authorial native informant and the apolitical freedoms of the postrace artist, the writers at the center of this study imagine fictional worlds that push cultural critics to expand the scope and methodologies of their analyses. I next consider the ways that the field of Asian American cultural criticism has developed and further outline the unique interventions offered by my book.

The Rise of Asian American Literary Criticism

With the publication of Asian American writing gaining more steam throughout the mid-twentieth century, race and ethnic literary criticism began to surface in the 1970s. In the period following the civil rights movement, Asian Americans enjoyed widespread legislative inclusion for the first time. As ethnic minority histories and cultures gained more social visibility, questions arose as to why American literature syllabi so commonly lacked any representation from people of Asian descent. After all, had there not been Asian Americans living in the United States for more than a century? Had Asian Americans not already been publishing their works? These questions propelled writers such as Frank Chin, Jeffery Paul Chan, Lawson Fusao Inada, and Shawn Wong to put together *Aiiieeeee! An Anthology of Asian-American Writers* (1974), one of the first works devoted to collecting Asian American literature as a panethnic grouping. The book's foundational theorizations dovetailed with cultural nationalist discourses that favored domestic-centered narratives, racial resistance, and masculine perspectives, found in novels such as John Okada's *No-No Boy* and Louis Chu's *Eat a Bowl of Tea* (1961). At that time, Chin and the other editors limited the bounds of Asian American literature to works produced by three ethnic groups: Filipino Americans, Chinese Americans, and Japanese Americans. Any conflations among Asian American writer, narrator, and the fictional world did not necessarily pose an interpretive problem for these editors or for early critics, precisely because the initial project was heavily invested in the archiving of erased sociohistorical and cultural contexts.[25] In other words, it was important in these initial stages to read these texts as forms of nonfictional documents, representational mirrors reflecting particular social inequalities experienced by Asian Americans and perhaps even the lives of the writers themselves, occasionally over and above the qualities of such writings as aesthetic creations.

Academics did not take up such literatures as the grounds for full-length book studies until Elaine H. Kim's *Asian American Literature* in 1982. Kim was already grappling with the complexities of what constituted Asian American literature in her introduction by adding Korean Americans as an ethnic group to the taxonomy. As critics such as Kim, Shirley Geok-lin Lim, and Amy Ling wrestled with defining boundaries, the field underwent a significant metamorphosis, moving from the identity-politics model popularized under cultural nationalism to an analytical methodology influenced by fluidity, decenteredness, and poststructural and postmodern theories.[26] Sunn Shelley Wong elucidates some of the changes to critical genealogies in her reading of Theresa Hak Kyung Cha's mixed-genre text *Dictee* (1982).[27] According to Wong, the cultural nationalist leanings of the field in its earliest period would have been incompatible with an interpretive apparatus equipped to consider the multifocal nature of Cha's mixed-genre work (63). The "politics of difference" (63) certainly has propelled the scholarly field forward, especially in the way that it allows a host of different types of Asian American literary studies to negotiate the intersectional, fragmented, and comparative nature of racial identity. The entire field constellates around this foundational methodology: scholars make apparent what Lisa Lowe, building off Kim's foundational book, calls the "heterogeneity, hybridity, and multiplicity" (66) of Asian American lives, whether related to issues of gender, sexuality, class, diasporic trajectory, age, disability, generational dynamics, or psychic structures, among other such markers of difference and social rubrics.

The field is thus characterized by its commitment to examining Asian American racial formation from as many different perspectives and approaches as possible, so much so that the term "Asian American" often seems incoherent. Susan Koshy's "The Fiction of Asian American Literature" clarifies these incongruities: "'Asian American' offers us a rubric that we cannot not use. But our usage of the term should rehearse the catachrestic status of the formation. I use the term 'catachresis' to indicate that there is no literal referent for the rubric 'Asian American' and, as such, the name is marked by the limits of its signifying power" (342). The "limits" of the "signifying power" can be seen in the litany of monographs that illuminate the inconsistencies that define Asian American literature, including but not limited to Viet Thanh Nguyen's *Race and Resistance* (2002), Kandice Chuh's *Imagine Otherwise* (2003), Tina Chen's *Double Agency* (2005), and Christopher Lee's *The Semblance of Identity* (2012).

Even with these many critical interventions, the field faces an incredible challenge with respect to theorizing what constitutes the Asian American fictional world. As the earlier example of *Whiteman* suggests, must the Asian American fictional world contain Asian American characters? Must it possess a narrator of Asian descent or a narrative perspective that primarily follows an Asian American character?[28] Fortunately, a large number of recent book-length publications devoted to the study of Asian American literature, genre, aesthetics, and formal impulses tackle such conundrums.[29] This book adds something new in its concentration on first-person fictional narratives in which the narrator's and writer's ethnoracial descent do not explicitly match.[30] By focusing on the storyteller, we can push cultural critique rooted in race and ethnic studies in unpredictable directions and ultimately agitate for more interdisciplinary and syncretic analytical approaches. Rajini Srikanth argues that an autoethnographic reading practice "can insulate and isolate us from the very people among whom we wish to become more visible, from whom we desire greater understanding, and with whom we perhaps seek greater intimacy" (201). Such a call to reconsider South Asian American literatures informs my project, but I address the desire for "another kind of narrative" in relation to Asian American literature at large, considering those texts that take us to the "frontiers of our consciousness" (201). While Srikanth specifically directs her appeal to creative communities, she also pushes critics to challenge their analytical practices and to move out of the zone that requires Asian American cultural studies to be specifically formulated through Asian American subject matter (however that might be defined). The fictions I focus on lead us exactly into the "frontiers" of our consciousnesses as literary studies and ethnic studies scholars by questioning the place of the author in relation to the fictional world. What do these fictions tell us, not only about Asian American identity politics and culture but also about comparative subject positions, whether elucidated through ethnic, racial, or other social differences? *Racial Asymmetries* shows that the answer is bound up with the Asian American writer's move to create storytelling perspectives that undermine an autobiographical or autoethnographic reading practice and, by doing so, to craft expansive possibilities for fictional worlds.

In this era of postracial conversations and viewpoints, Asian American cultural criticism stands at a fascinating crossroads. The critical methodologies employed by scholars within the field undoubtedly remain important to analyzing the representations of Asian Americans. At the same time, the deployment of strategic essentialism that constitutes the field through a coalitional framework based on authorial descent and its connection to the representational landscape can, however unintentionally, marginalize fictions that do not focus only or specifically on Asian American experiences or contexts. Even as Asian American cultural criticism gains more visibility at the institutional level, it must remain ever vigilant to the ways that analytical inquiries should embrace the egalitarian ethos that characterized the field when it first emerged and cultivate more expansive interdisciplinary methodologies that can attend to the rich morphologies of fictional worlds.

Giving Voices to Asian American Fictional Worlds

The archive at the center of this book does beg the question of what makes such Asian American fiction *fictional*. Here, narratology provides a set of tools to advance my critical inquiries, as theorists have looked at narration as a site to consider how fiction operates in contradistinction to other genres more stringently tethered to external referents, such as historical studies and biographies. The narratologist Kalle Pihlainen reminds us that "in historical narratives ... the viewpoint that we have is consistently that of the extradiegetic narrator— equatable, and indeed equated, with the author, the historian who has access to the material and who is critical toward the material as well as makes it clear to readers when he or she does not know something" (53).[31] Pihlainen's consideration of the writerly subject position has wider ramifications for the truth-telling characteristics of certain narrative forms such as lifewriting, memoir, and autoethnography. Per Philippe Lejeune's definition of the autobiography/memoir (5), the author's name is synonymous with the narrator-character. Autobiographical and autoethnographic narration have similar valences, where the storyteller, extradiegetic or not, overlaps in some way with the author.[32]

In contrast, fictional narration does not have the same constraints. Speaking of heterodiegetic narrators, Dorrit Cohn spotlights one element integral to fictionality: the narrator's unobstructed access to characters' minds, a process akin to telepathy: "This penetrative optic calls on devices—among others free indirect style—that remain unavailable to narrators who aim for referential (nonfictional) presentation" (*Distinction of Fiction* 16).[33] I extend Cohn's proposition beyond heterodiegetic narrators (typically third person) precisely because there are homodiegetic narratives (typically first person) that cannot be attached to an external referent (such as an actual person), and such narratives cannot be placed in parallel with the author in the way that an autobiographical text, memoir, autoethnography, or historical study might.[34] In other words, the "I" doing the narrating may be of an entirely different ancestral background than the writer, and in these cases, the author must imagine what this other constructed entity sees, thinks, and feels. The majority of narratives critiqued in *Racial Asymmetries* are told through the first-person mode, as the American writer of Asian descent employs the voice and narrative perspective of a character whose racial and ethnic background do not match his or her own.[35] For writers, severing the link between the author and the narrator is part of an "exercise," per Richard Walsh's rhetorical theory of fiction, that enhances how the representational terrain can be read as make-believe ("Fictionality and Mimesis" 119). However, when the "tour guide function" collapses the Asian American author with certain narrators and with certain narrative perspectives and then commodifies this collapse, fictionality is imperiled.

Fully engaging Asian American fictionality requires a serious reconsideration of narrative perspective. By depicting the lives, viewpoints, emotions, thoughts, and voices of imaginary characters, Asian American fiction writers in this study create anthropomorphic storytellers who encourage cultural critics and readers to engage why the story is told from this particular perspective. Because we cannot assume that the writer is sympathetic to or identifies with the storyteller he or she constructs, we must analyze how the storyteller functions as one nodal point within a larger representational power matrix. With such great responsibilities given to the narrator who directs our access to the fictional world, other issues begin to emerge: which characters become central and which are placed at the peripheries, what historical circumstances frame the plot, and what spatial contexts ground the construction of fictionalized settings, to name a few.[36] Here, the narrator's telling of a story arcs out into a variety of concerns that must be considered to explore the extensive bounds of the novel's racial asymmetries.

I use the phrase "racial asymmetries" to describe two interlocking levels of this book: the first to describe a particular phenomenon and the second to describe a critical reading practice. "Racial asymmetries" first describes the incongruities that emerge between the Asian American writer and narrative perspective, where the writer undermines the alignment between ethnoracial background and the narrator. This first level grants an explicit space for thinking about Asian American literature through its fictional qualities, as a writer's ancestry does not directly mirror that of the narrator's. The first-person storyteller is an imagined life, one that might have existed but actually does not and should not be assumed to be the double for the Asian American author.

In this way, the fictional landscape is bound up with the second level of racial asymmetry, which involves the aesthetics and the politics engaged within and offered by the representational terrain. *Racial Asymmetries* thus finds traction at the complex juncture between fiction and nonfiction. On the one hand, Asian American writers enhance the imaginative aspects of their creative publications by locating narrative perspective in characters whose ethnoracial backgrounds differ from their own. On the other, these characters travel through a fictional world enmeshed in larger social contexts and historical frameworks. These characters thus find their individual lives entangled amid structural inequalities, such as colonial conquest, class immobility, racial oppression, sexism, and homophobia, among other systemic issues. Asian Americanist critique offers a unique intervention at this intersection because the field has been so highly influenced by historicist and materialist analytical methodologies. As I attend to the dynamics of narrative perspective, I also employ the data and research offered by many disciplines, including history, anthropology, sociology, urban studies, and American race and ethnic studies, to closely examine the fictional world's complex relationship with external referents. While this book clearly pushes the Asian Americanist critique into radically new territories, it also parallels developing scholarly trends within cultural studies.[37] Here, I refer to calls to make American studies increasingly intersectional, whether through the framework of globalization, hemispheric approaches, or analytics of comparative race and ethnicity.[38]

Charting Our Racially Asymmetrical Course

I begin my study with texts that reflect some of the more traditional concerns of the field but move increasingly toward those that seem to have little to do with Asian American racial formation. Chapter 1 explores how Asian American-ness might be structured in relation to the psychic interiority of a white narrator. I focus my reading on Chang-rae Lee's *Aloft*, in which the Italian American narrator disrupts any clear overlap between author and narrative perspective. The novel attends to the racial asymmetries of Asian American fiction by forefronting how a white narrator perceives the issue of racial difference as it unfolds in an exclusive Long Island community. In chapter 2, I shift from analyzing a white storytelling perspective to a Chicano viewpoint. In Sesshu Foster's

Atomik Aztex, the narrative models how a Chicano narrator comes to terms with a broadened class consciousness, one that involves a multiracial union of his slaughterhouse-factory workers. Foster also employs a speculative alternate reality that becomes a useful analogy to convey the Chicano subject's fractured self, as a political organizer and social activist as well as a potential agent of destruction.

The second half of the book focuses on writers whom critics have almost completely ignored because their fiction remains difficult to categorize. While Sigrid Nunez's first novel, *A Feather on the Breath of God* (1995), contains clear autobiographical valences, two subsequent publications do not. Chapter 3 critiques Nunez's *For Rouenna* and *The Last of Her Kind*, both of which complicate any clear link between the author's ethnoracial background and the novels' protagonists. But this chapter progresses the book further by emphasizing the process of narrative construction. In each novel, the storyteller is an individual who looks to reconstruct the life of another character but in the process calls attention to other individuals on the peripheries and pushes the biographical form to expand. Though neither novel employs the narrative perspective of an Asian American character, each shows measured attention to pressing social issues, whether related to the plight of female veterans who fought in the Vietnam War or the failures of the American prison system.

Directing *Racial Asymmetries* to its most transnational dimensions, chapter 4 investigates a selection of Sabina Murray's publications, concentrating on *A Carnivore's Inquiry* and *Forgery*. The narrators of these cultural productions open up perspectives that convey how violence and brutality advance various colonial projects. They trace the paths of international conquest through various countries—the United States, Mexico, Spain, the Philippines, Greece—and, in this regard, illuminate racial formation as a comparative colonial construct. The final chapter explores the ways two speculative fictions function through racial analogies. Claire Light's "Abducted by Aliens!" and Ted Chiang's *The Merchant and the Alchemist's Gate*, though narrated by characters who exist in fantastical landscapes filled with alchemy, time traveling, or alien invaders, can be interpreted through their oblique relationship to external social contexts and historical archives. "Abducted by Aliens!" demonstrates how the alien-abduction narrative can be analogized to the experience of Japanese American internees, while Chiang's novelette shows how an oriental tale set in the Islamic Golden Age can be analogized to American foreign policy in the post-9/11 era. Both works provide dramatic examples of the Asian American writer who makes imaginative use of narrative perspective but whose fictional worlds can be firmly tethered to material and historical contexts.

Though this study primarily focuses on a select number of fictions, another aim is to cast light on the larger archive of works penned by Asian American writers in which narrative perspective and its connection to authorial ancestry cannot be clearly linked. In this respect, *Racial Asymmetries* seeks not only to supplement the critical methodologies that we employ in the analysis of Asian American cultural studies but also to complicate and to expand the kinds of social contexts and historical circumstances that characterize the field as it continues to burgeon in the new millennium. In this process, we find that an incredible multitude of subjects and storytellers constitute this so-called subfield of literary study, thus revealing the elastic bounds of the fictional world.

1 / White Flight, White Narration: Suburban Deviancies in Chang-rae Lee's *Aloft*

Racial Asymmetries begins with one obvious starting point for Asian American studies: the experience of racial exclusion under the guise of white hegemony. The large-scale racial rubric constituting the Asian American as an outsider has been in place at least since 1917, when the US Congress passed some of the first major federal laws restricting immigration.[1] The exclusion period officially ended in 1965 when Asian immigrants were allowed to enter the United States under the quota system. Under the "model minority" designation that emerges in 1966, Asian Americans occasionally assume a different racial status, something that Mia Tuan provocatively terms as "honorary whites" (31). Yet racial exclusion retains an insidious influence for contemporary Asian Americans. This chapter explores the complicated nature and effects of that influence for both Asian Americans and whites in the post-1965 era through the way that it is depicted in Chang-rae Lee's novel *Aloft* (2004).

Aloft, like Lee's earlier novels *Native Speaker* (1995) and *A Gesture Life* (1999), is narrated in the first person. However, while those two novels are narrated from the perspectives of Korean American men, *Aloft*'s narrator is an Italian American named Jerry Battle. Racial asymmetry thus appears first in the dissonance between Chang-rae Lee and Jerry Battle: by positioning Jerry as the storyteller, the novel refracts the Asian American experience through the lens of a white character rather than presenting it, presumably more directly, through a figure assumed to be a fictionalized double for the author. A second level of racial asymmetry emerges as the novel exposes the blind spots in liberal individualist thinking; that is, Jerry conceives of his suburban life through a specific set of norms and regulations that place whiteness at the center and racial minorities as deviant bodies on the periphery. In such ways, *Aloft* dynamically spotlights narrative perspective and mode to erase a clear definition of racial authorial authenticity, to show how issues of race and identity unfold in specific formal and contextual registers.

This chapter first explores the uses of whiteness in Asian American literature; I theorize select fictional texts that, like *Aloft*, employ white narrators and narrative perspectives. These perspectives serve as an aesthetic tool for writers as they complicate figurations of Asian American characters as inescapably foreign, as the yellow peril. This same tool also allows the writers to illuminate how whiteness operates with respect to minority racial formation. I then consider the complicated reception of *Aloft* by book reviewers and critics, many of whom draw on the dissonance between Chang-rae Lee and Jerry Battle for their analyses. As these reviews show, the novel continually invokes questions of storytelling authenticity, as many reviewers note a presumed similarity between Lee and the narrator. After considering the reviewers' reactions, I focus on Jerry's point of view as a mode of unreliable narration in which racial minorities suffer a subtle marginalization. Lee's representation of his narrator's beliefs is complex: Jerry cannot be easily understood within a binary that labels him as either racist or not. Instead, the novel presents the intricacies of his white consciousness, which exhibits a coded and perhaps more sophisticated form of racism.

I conclude my analysis with a focused reading of *Aloft*'s fourth chapter, which presents an egregious case of Jerry's liberal individualist thinking. This chapter fleshes out Jerry's first marriage to Daisy Han, which ends tragically with her suicide, an event that he attributes to her bipolar disorder. I explore how Jerry fails to interpret his wife's life within a larger immigrant context. Specifically, he does not take into account how his wife's bipolar disorder might stem, at least in part, from complex environmental triggers in which the suburban Long Island racial milieu plays a major role. Jerry's belief system thus recalls the postracial discourse that disavows the pervasive nature of social inequality as it emerges in the post-1965 period, an era in which the Asian American is considered to be a kind of model citizen. Daisy's eventual disintegration exposes postracial viewpoints as a fallacy, especially as her decline unfolds in the perfectly manicured lawns and lushly decorated homes of one affluent, regional suburb. I employ a variety of academic resources that help to explain the social contexts invoked by Lee's fictional world, specifically in relation to the depictions of post–World War II Long Island and to the development of Daisy's mental illness. Here, the novel imagines how the issue of race can still bear a tremendous impact on the psychic life of the white American subject, despite the fact that race may not be explicitly acknowledged in daily conversations or everyday experiences. Lee's choice to narrate the novel through a white character's perspective cannot be seen simply as an aesthetically imaginative decision; this refractive storytelling technique ultimately pushes us to reorient our critical gazes to the ways in which a white narrative perspective functions to politically frame the fictional world.

The Whitenesses of Asian American Literature

As I discuss in the introduction, the construction of storytelling perspective by American writers of Asian descent complicates and undermines the possible expectation that the narrator match the author's ethnoracial background. For instance, many such writers employ racialized narrative perspectives to query the binaries that structure whiteness as the norm against what is foreign, different, or culturally alien.[2] While whiteness is typically understood to be a racial construct imbued with power and privilege, Asian American writers are well aware of other contingent representations. That is, Asian American writers do not portray all white characters as inevitably racist; rather, they are invested in revealing how whiteness becomes mapped as a literary site of racial, cultural, and spatial normativity.

Rattawut Lapcharoensap's short-story collection *Sightseeing* (2005) offers an innovative example. The marketing department at Grove Press makes sure to include biographical information on the inside of the hardcover's back flap: "Rattawut Lapcharoensap was born in Chicago, raised in Bangkok, and now lives in New York City," reinforcing the author's status as someone authorized to write about the Thai experience. Fittingly, the majority of his short stories are set in or around Thailand, many of them specifically in Bangkok. However, in "Don't Let Me Die in This Place," Lapcharoensap tactically filters the expected view of Thailand through a non-Thai character. Mister Perry, after suffering a stroke, is placed in the care of his son Jack, who relocates to Bangkok for a job and later marries a Thai woman. Mister Perry faces the everyday challenges of living with his new family, which includes two young children. Lapcharoensap's decision to narrate from the first-person perspective of this elderly white character precludes the possibility of reading this story as explicitly autobiographical. This approach enhances the entire collection's fictionality and directs the critic (and reader) toward a comparative perspective, where Thai culture and community is observed through an outsider's eyes. "Don't Let Me Die in This Place" cannot be read only as an expression of Lapcharoensap's double consciousness, for it is less about Thai American identity and more a study of reverse assimilation and white transnationalism. The story masterfully constructs whiteness without ever naming it, suggesting its presence through inference and deductive reasoning. In Mister Perry's narrative monologues, he labels his daughter-in-law "foreign" and his grandchildren "mongrels" (125), placing his Thai familial counterparts as toxic and alien forces, something distinct from his own racial genealogy. Mister Perry could be of a minority racial background, perhaps Chicano or African American, but Lapcharoensap does provide cumulative significations to indicate his whiteness. For instance, Mister Perry notes the lighter eye color ("brown-speckled blue") in one of his grandchildren, a characteristic he connects to his son (138).

Lapcharoensap also interrupts the main narrative to include a flashback with Mister Perry's friend and fellow senior citizen Macklin Johnson, who was once married to an African American woman, with whom he fathered a son, Tyrone (132–33). In this temporal shift, Mister Perry and Mac (as Johnson is more familiarly called), who seems to be suffering from some form of dementia, are traveling to an Orioles game; this rather innocuous narrative subplot has the added effect of elaborating on Mac's fetish: "He nattered on about his own live-in [nurse] and how much he liked her, how much better she was than the last one, how she was real beautiful and tall, like an African princess, and how irritated she'd gotten that morning when he said she looked like Nefertiti" (133).[3] Mac's confusion over why his nurse would be annoyed by being called Nefertiti and later his claim that he had not called her "Aunt Jemima" (133) elucidates a racist viewpoint that Mister Perry does not negate or challenge. That Mister Perry "nodded along" with Mac's tirade suggests his approval of the compliment and disdain for the nurse's overreaction. These racially coded responses suggest that Mister Perry is white. Later, Mister Perry laments in relation to his own Thai daughter-in-law and grandchildren, "But at least Mac can see himself in Tyrone and the grandchildren. At least he can call them by name. At least they all speak a common language" (139). The phrase "at least" situates a gradation of racialization in which Mister Perry locates blackness as closer to being

American, especially through a common linguistic connection.[4] This story reveals how whiteness is coded in racially unmarked characters who speak out about the strangeness and difference of other ethnic and minority figures populating the fictional world.

Lapcharoensap's shift from Thai narrative perspectives to a white narrator in "Don't Let Me Die in This Place" serves many purposes. First, it subverts readerly expectations of a native-informant perspective since the informant in this story is an individual quite foreign to Thai culture. This move foils readers' tendency to conflate the points of view of the author and the narrator. This appropriative aesthetic choice reveals the Asian American artist's willingness to push the bounds of storytelling perspectives offered to the minority writer, especially as conditioned by literary marketplace pressures and by the traditions of autoethnographic fictions. Further, "Don't Let Me Die in This Place" presents one depiction of white racial formation in the context of transnational movement, setting the grounds for the narrator's difficulty in acculturating to his new homeland. This perspective is important because Lapcharoensap exposes an instance of inferential racism, showing how racial Othering can appear through daily interactions. While it seems clear that Mister Perry possesses a disdain for Thai individuals, he never directly calls his daughter-in-law foreign, nor does he use racist epithets in regard to the children in direct speech. Only through narration are readers given access to racist thoughts (e.g., when he thinks of his grandchildren as "mongrels"). As a result, the relative coldness aimed at his daughter-in-law and grandchildren is not surprising, but the reasons for that coldness cannot be gleaned from dialogue or direct speech. His son and daughter-in-law can surmise his attitude, but unlike readers, they are not given information that elucidates his racist psychic life. Lapcharoensap grants us an invaluable viewpoint, illustrating subtle ways in which racism exists without its explicit avowal in direct speech or action.

Lapcharoensap's depiction of Mister Perry in relation to his daughter-in-law and grandchildren does at first parallel the many antagonistic connections that form between white and Thai characters throughout the collection. In the opening story, "Farangs," for instance, Lapcharoensap imagines a number of tourist and military figures engaging in problematic relationships with local Thai populations and villagers. The story's narrator is a mixed-race Thai teenager whose father, Sergeant Henderson, is an American *farang* (foreigner) who breaks a promise to bring the teenager and his mother to the United States. Lapcharoensap's first story presents "whiteness" as possessing a transpacific circuit routed through global capitalism in the form of sex tourism and through the military-industrial complex (Sergeant Henderson not only is in the military but also engages in a sexual relationship while stationed in Thailand).[5] In this initial story, we discover that the narrator's mother manages a local motel, but the vacationing season causes much frustration for her. At one point, she tells her son, "You give [*farangs*] history, temples, pagodas, traditional dance, floating markets, seafood curry, tapioca desserts, silk-weaving cooperatives, but all they really want is to ride some hulking gray beast like a bunch of wildmen and to pant over girls and to lie there half-dead getting skin cancer on the beach during the time in between" (2). This tirade clearly assumes that white foreign men primarily travel to Thailand to engage in sex tourism and with little respect for the richness of the cultural traditions. Despite this unsavory opinion, the story goes on to highlight some of the truth behind the mother's exasperated statements. The plot revolves around the narrator's love for *farang* women from the United States; the prospect of such a relationship motivates him to court Lizzie, an attractive high-school-aged female vacationing in the local area. Her boyfriend, Hunter, is another *farang* and found sleeping with a Thai prostitute, much to Lizzie's ire. In response to Hunter's infidelity, Lizzie takes up with the narrator in order to incite jealousy. Later, Lizzie is confronted by Hunter in a local restaurant, where he is described as "dressed in a white undershirt and a pair of surfer's shorts. His nose is caked with sunscreen. His chest is pink from too much sun. There's a Buddha dangling from his neck" (16). Hunter perfectly exemplifies why the narrator's mother expresses such disdain toward *farang* men, that these white foreigners only come to Thailand in search of Thai women and with a superficial understanding of the culture. Because Hunter is only visiting the country, his trajectory inevitably parallels Sergeant Henderson's; they are both white men who are involved in transitory sexual relationships with Thai women.

Yet, for Mister Perry, the luxury of a transnational movement is not predicated on brief sexual encounters, a business venture, or military might, as it appears in some of the other cases of white representation. Lapcharoensap instead grants Mister Perry a character arc that troubles a simple understanding of his racial politics. Mister Perry is in Thailand reluctantly because, as a widower who recently suffered a stroke, he must live with his son who has moved to Thailand to work in textiles. In the chapter's climax, Mister Perry joins the family for a day of festivity at a local temple where a carnival has been set up; he watches his son and daughter-in-law take to the dance floor. Mister

Perry observes: "I look around and see some of the men under the tent snickering in Jack's direction. I notice, too, that the women are talking to one another sternly, peering at Jack and his wife. I can tell by the way they look at her that they think Tida's some kind of prostitute and suddenly I'm proud of them both for being out there dancing, proud of my boy Jack for holding his wife so close" (152). Though readers cannot be sure that Mister Perry is accurately explaining why the men and women are reacting negatively to his son and daughter-in-law, this moment reveals his willingness to begin to embrace his multiracial and multiethnic family. Lapcharoensap's representation of Mister Perry expands how whiteness is depicted and offers readers a more sympathetic figuration of such racialized characters. Finally, "Don't Let Me Die in This Place" presents an imaginative assertion of the Asian American writer's ability to depict a storyteller whose ethnoracial background does not overlap with his own.

A similar refractive narrative aesthetic is seen in the work of Jhumpa Lahiri, another Asian American writer who uses white narrative perspectives to consider poles of normativity and difference. Lahiri's white characters can seem almost peripheral in relation to her numerous Indian American protagonists, but excluding their "outsider" perspective may lead to the critical danger of flattening the stories' inventive narrational mobility. In "Mrs. Sen's" from *Interpreter of Maladies*, for instance, Lahiri employs a third-person narrative perspective to consider the attachments that can be made across ethnic and racial lines. The short story revolves around a white eleven-year-old boy named Eliot who develops a friendship and emotional connection to an Indian immigrant woman, Mrs. Sen. She is married to an untenured mathematics professor who has just started teaching at the local university, and Eliot has been put in her care after school until his mother can pick him up. Much of the story includes Eliot's observations of Mrs. Sen's life, especially her difficulty adjusting to the United States. In particular, Mrs. Sen has an inordinate fear of learning to drive, an obstacle that serves as the story's central trope for her assimilative troubles. Toward the story's conclusion, Mrs. Sen attempts to drive herself and Eliot to the coastal fish market, but before traveling very far, she gets in a minor car accident. Although no one is seriously injured, Eliot's mother withdraws Eliot from Mrs. Sen's care, and the plot concludes with Eliot becoming a latchkey kid who must look after himself until his mother comes home. While critics such as Noelle Brada-Williams (458) and Laura Anh Williams (73) have concentrated on the alienation Mrs. Sen experiences while living in the United States, Lahiri's use of narrative perspective suggests that it is equally important to consider other subject positions that refract the Asian immigrant experience. In this way, Lahiri expands how we read narrative perspective, making issues of isolation relevant for both Asian immigrant and white characters. Mrs. Sen seems resigned to living in the United States while her husband works diligently to secure his professional future and provide stable finances for himself and his wife. At the same time, the story explores an intriguing connective point in that Eliot stands in for the child whom the Sens do not (yet) have. Although the Sens make clear how important community and relatives are to their lives, their childlessness leaves them particularly receptive to Eliot's presence. In some sense, Eliot becomes the sensitive surrogate son that the Sens clearly desire.

Lahiri takes an elliptical approach in racializing Eliot and his mother. When Eliot first meets Mrs. Sen, he notices how different she looks in comparison to his mother. As he reflects, "it was his mother, . . . in her cuffed, beige shorts and her rope-soled shoes, who looked odd. Her cropped hair, a shade similar to her shorts, seemed too lank and sensible, and in that room where all things were so carefully covered, her shaved knees and thighs were too exposed" (112–13). In this fascinating moment of cultural, racial, ethnic, and gender comparison, Eliot finds his mother lacking in some particular way, especially as it relates to her manner of dress. In addition, he mentions his mother's hair color, "a shade similar to her shorts," just noted as "beige." Though Eliot and his mother remain racially unmarked for the entire story, Eliot's ability to note the difference between Mrs. Sen and his mother provides oblique cues that delineate their status as white characters. In contrast to the Sens, who are grounded by their ethnic culture and family, Eliot and his mother do not seem to possess an extended community. There is no sense of who Eliot's father might be or if they have any relatives or even friends. Mrs. Sen serves to highlight the pedestrian cultural and domestic life that Eliot's mother pursues. Eliot's mother passes this alienation, however indirectly, onto her son. Lahiri's choice to present the narrative through Eliot's point of view configures the quiet tragedy of this child's upbringing. However, the question must then be asked: what does "whiteness" signify more broadly as an element in the story? While literary critic Ruth Maxey focuses on the negative registers that designate the "white Americans" (536), she does not fully consider what it means for the narrative to be told from Eliot's perspective. Here, Eliot acts as an observational mediator who can intimate how the Sens face multiple forms of exclusion and rejection in everyday life; but he also offers a sympathetic gaze, signifying the possibility of strong, intimate interracial contacts.

But ethnic and cultural differences sometimes seem unbridgeable, in spite of Eliot's mediating presence. It is only to Eliot that his mother admits she does not always enjoy Mrs. Sen's cooking: Eliot "knew [his mother] didn't like the tastes; she'd told him so once in the car" (118). That Eliot's mother does not "like the tastes" registers her failure to recognize the symbolic value of Mrs. Sen's cooking as an act that establishes community between them. However, Mrs. Sen is not privy to this negative reaction, and so readers are offered this perspective only through Eliot's viewpoint. Another fraught interracial encounter occurs when Mrs. Sen and Eliot are traveling back to her apartment by bus after having purchased a fish. Eliot notices that "on the way home an old woman on the bus kept watching them, her eyes shifting from Mrs. Sen to Eliot to the blood-lined bag between their feet. She wore a black overcoat, and in her lap she held, with gnarled, colorless hands, a crisp white bag from the drugstore." Later on, this woman "stood up, said something to the driver, then stepped off the bus" (132). The bus driver then asks Mrs. Sen about the contents of her bag and whether she speaks English, suggesting that next time, Eliot should "open her window or something" (133). As Maxey notes, Lahiri makes a point of marking the old woman's racial difference through her "gnarled, colorless hands." The old woman's shifting vision signals that she is disturbed by the smell emanating from the bag, but Lahiri's choice to emphasize her skin color accentuates this moment as racially charged. Whereas Mrs. Sen remains unaware of the problem, Eliot, the white character, notices the old woman's cold response. This rather minor encounter symbolizes the larger struggles that Mrs. Sen faces as an immigrant. She is someone who possesses a potentially rich cultural and ethnic life but nevertheless finds herself the object of subtle racism. In this case, she is unaware of what is going on, which makes Eliot's viewpoint vital precisely because it alone clarifies how other white characters see Mrs. Sen as an inassimilable foreigner tied to offensive smells. That Eliot registers this scene at all reveals his awareness of racial prejudice, and yet, even given all of these tense interactions, he finds a way to appreciate Mrs. Sen in her difference. He identifies with her despite her racial and ethnic background, her cooking and the associated odors, because he understands that they share a sense of loneliness. Further still, Mrs. Sen offers a sense of home and family life that Eliot cannot find elsewhere. In this regard, whiteness signifies in multiple ways. Eliot's perspective provides an insider's gaze into a white culture that can either marginalize or embrace ethnic and racial alterity.

Taken together, Lapcharoensap's "Don't Let Me Die in This Place" and Lahiri's "Mrs. Sen's" exhibit forms of refractive narration that Asian American writers employ to complicate constructions and discourses of racial normativity and deviancy. Of course, these stories also undermine the assumption that the Asian American writer exists as a ghostly double to the narrator in the fictional landscape that he or she creates. In "Don't Let Me Die in This Place," Lapcharoensap figures whiteness in relation to an individual instance of forced migration, as Mister Perry must go to Thailand due to his fragile health and despite his desire to remain in the United States. This representation contrasts with the other white characters in the collection, who are more typically presented as mobile figures with little regard for local history and communities. Lahiri's "Mrs. Sen's" complicates the commonplace theme of Asian exclusion through the sympathetic eyes of a young white character, suggesting the possibility of interracial identification, however fleeting and cursory. Analyzing the whitenesses of Asian American literature entails lengthier considerations of the tactical deployment of cross-racial narrative perspectives and helps resolve what is at stake in Chang-rae Lee's choice to narrate in the first-person mode. Here, authenticity is again a concern when the writer creates a fictional narrator of a racial background he or she cannot claim. This narrative perspective also shows how constructions of whiteness in the ethnic literary imagination can question what is normative and what is not, what is racially deviant and what is racially acceptable.

Readerly Reception and the Ghostly Double of Chang-rae Lee

Since *Aloft* presents an intricate narrative, a short plot summary seems in order. Jerry Battle, the Italian American narrator, is about to turn sixty, and much of the plot revolves around his introspective musings concerning his mixed-race family and his relationships to women. His first wife, Daisy, a Korean immigrant, died tragically decades earlier in what is believed to have been a drowning accident following a period of mental instability. Daisy and Jerry's two children, Jack and Theresa, are grown. Jack runs Battle Brothers Brick & Mortar, the family's landscaping and construction business; he is married to a German American woman named Eunice, and their two children are a girl named Tyler and a boy named Pierce. Theresa, Jerry's younger child, is an English professor who is engaged to an Asian American writer named Paul Pyun.

At the start of the novel, Jerry is flying an airplane, and we discover his deep interest in aviation. He has retired from Battle Brothers and has taken a job as a travel agent. The novel's meditative opening sequence is interrupted when his coworker and former girlfriend, Kelly Stearn, overdoses, and he must rush to the hospital. Coincidentally, the emergency-room nurse on duty when Kelly arrives is another of Jerry's ex-girlfriends, a Puerto Rican woman named Rita. This scene, then, offers us a spirited introduction into the rather complicated social life that Jerry leads. Other chapters explain the strained relationships that Jerry maintains with everyone else in his life, including his pregnant daughter, who also suffers from non-Hodgkin's lymphoma. To increase the baby's survival chances, Theresa forgoes chemotherapy, much to the consternation of her family. In the midst of dealing with these issues, Jerry also struggles to care for his father, Hank, who is in an upscale nursing home due to his deteriorating health.

The concluding arc features a number of revelatory events. Hank flees from the nursing home; Jerry successfully reconciles with Rita; Jack bankrupts the family business; and Jerry flies Theresa to Maine for lobster. During the plane ride, Theresa reveals a pivotal memory related to her by Jack, who observed his mother on the day she died. Theresa explains that Jack saw his mother plan her suicide; prior to drowning herself, she took all flotation devices out of the pool. Jack had never told his father because he did not understand at first what was going on; later, he believed his mother's death was his responsibility. After telling this story, Theresa goes into premature labor; the plane makes an emergency landing, but complications from childbirth lead to Theresa's death. In the final chapter, the grieving family is reunited under one roof.

Aloft's critical and commercial success may be attributed in part to the groundwork Lee laid with his first two novels. Having published two ethnic-themed works that gained him a larger critical, commercial, and popular following, Lee takes on a fictional terrain that markedly diverges away from Korean American contexts and characters. Relatedly, *Aloft* signals an important methodological shift in the way that an Asian American writer might be marketed. The reading guide found on *Aloft*'s portal on the Penguin Books website reads, "Now, with *Aloft*, Lee has expanded his range and proves himself a master storyteller, able to observe his characters' flaws and weaknesses and, at the same time, celebrate their humanity" ("Reading Guide"). The description claims that Lee has pushed himself artistically but does not define how exactly he has done so. *Aloft*'s "range" is explicitly articulated in a handful of reviews that followed the book's publication. For instance, Tom Kagy states that "Ishiguro fans would argue that if a Nagasaki-born Japanese Englishman can write faultlessly about the regrets of an Oxfordshire butler, then Seoul-born Lee can write about an Italian American Long Island contractor full of the failings most amusingly lampooned in thick Tom Wolfe novels." Ed Park's headline also compares Lee's novel to Kazuo Ishiguro's *The Remains of the Day* (1989) and adds, "Now it's Lee's turn to upend the ethnic p.o.v. *Aloft* is a leisurely novel—some laughs, some tears—in the voice of Jerry Battle, Caucasian of Italian descent, fiftysomething part-time travel agent, widowed father of two, recreational Cessna pilot, and former head of the family business, which over time has morphed from masonry to landscaping to a high-end home furnishings outfit." For both Kagy and Park, Lee's expansion in range reveals itself in the narrative shift that moves the novel away from an Asian American context and narrator. The comparison with Ishiguro is sound, given that he also penned two novels that are ethnically specific to his Japanese heritage prior to embarking on a set of novels that make little or no reference to that background. Not surprisingly, Lee has admitted to being a fan of Ishiguro.[6]

Despite such praise for Lee's imaginative approach to narrative perspective, his novel was simultaneously challenged for its authenticity of voice. In the *New York Times*, A. O. Scott deems that "Jerry has absorbed some of his daughter's theory-talk, insouciantly dropping words like 'modality' and 'imbrications' into his regular-guy diction. Still, this does not quite explain the self-consciously lovely writing-school language through which his consciousness is awkwardly filtered." Scott's insistence that Jerry's linguistic mastery does not match up with his character's background is repeated in other instances. Tom Kagy writes, "Poet-contractors undoubtedly exist, but having one for a narrator overlays the novel with an uneasy consciousness of Chang-rae Lee the Princeton writing professor." Here Kagy points out that Jerry's incredibly lyrical eye does not resonate plausibly with his background as an Italian American landscaping business owner. In a review for the *Asian Reporter* regarding the narrative perspective, Polo queries, "But is it the voice of the 60-year-old stiff who took over Battle Brothers Brick & Mortar, or that of a 38-year-old graduate of Phillips Exeter Academy and Yale University and, of course, Duck U"?[7] In contrast to Scott, who takes a more New Critical approach to the faltering of authentic voice, Kagy and Polo take aim at Lee's status as a literature professor. Lee's occupational experience apparently intrudes on the narration by granting the character abilities and viewpoints he should not necessarily have. Of course, such seemingly disingenuous narrative stylings are moot because the notion of an authentic narrative voice is based to a certain extent on speculative assumptions, and yet the ramifications of these perceived aesthetic incongruities stand out particularly in relation to Lee's background as a Korean American and Asian American writer. Valerie Ryan asserts, "Lee writes in the voice of the quintessentially American Jerry, Eastern seaboard variety, but waxes about race and ethnicity throughout." However, Ryan ultimately argues, much in the same vein as Kagy and Polo, that various narrative tracks "are less Jerry-like than Lee-like," again suggesting that Lee's authorial voice intrudes on Jerry's storytelling.

In the passage that generates Polo's critique of authenticity, Jerry describes his son-in-law Paul and the challenges he faces as an Asian American writer. Jerry explains, "I guess if you put a gun to my head I'd say he writes about The Problem with Being Sort of Himself—namely, the terribly conflicted and complicated state of being Asian and American and thoughtful and male, which would be just dandy in a slightly different culture or society but in this one isn't the hottest ticket" (74). By including Paul Pyun as a character within the novel, Lee anticipates and invites the leap Polo makes as a reviewer.[8] That is, readers will ultimately conflate Paul Pyun with Chang-rae Lee, but Polo takes it a step further by articulating that the inclusion of such a character legitimates the critique that Lee invades the text as a shadow narrator. The strange overlapping of Jerry Battle, Paul Pyun, and Chang-rae Lee exists at the core of a racial authenticity abyss, where Lee's desire to move outside the Korean American and Asian American paradigm is still challenged based on his ghostly narratorial presence, what Kagy calls an "overlay" of Lee's voice directly onto Jerry's. Kagy contends that "Battle's son-in-law Paul Pyun is the author's effort at relegating his Asian identity to a conscientious, academic footnote," but this assertion reduces both the writer's ability to fictionalize and the ability of the minor character to call attention to larger issues (focused on race, ethnicity, and Asian American identity) that do not necessarily take up as much narrative space as, say, Jerry's daily ramblings.

I target these book reviewers because they focus on the "real" at the expense of the metaphorical significance that Paul Pyun plays in the novel. Ed Park writes that Paul Pyun is Lee's "wry self-critique, not without longing," and while this description is accurate to a certain extent, the dilemma that Paul opens up as a writer is experienced not only by Chang-rae Lee but by Asian American artists more generally.

In an interview with Terry Hong, Lee admits, "[Paul is] someone I wrote to make fun of myself and to make fun of the image of the 'Asian American writer' working out his anxieties"; Paul exists simultaneously as a "self-critique" and as a reference to a larger discourse ("Flying Aloft" 23). These "anxieties" are perhaps related to the native-informant status of the Asian American writer, what Jerry calls "The Problem with Being Sort of Himself," but this rather murky predicament hinges on the phrase "sort of," denoting "not fully." Can an Asian American writer not fully be him- or herself, at least in relation to race and ethnicity? The reading practices and responses to the book suggest that this challenge still exists despite the fact that *Aloft* has been so widely and positively reviewed.

The limits of authenticity for Lee do not lie in the fact that he is Asian American and therefore cannot try to imagine what it would be like to be Italian American. Scott's seemingly more insular (read: New Critical) review is probably the one that Lee himself would have most appreciated, as Scott is suspicious of Jerry's voice but does not link it to Lee's background, as Kagy and Polo do. Kagy's and Polo's critiques are speculative at best and do not address the foundational issue related to how literary characters are constructed. Scott relates how Jerry's professor daughter fails to be a convincing source of Jerry's scholarly knowledge, but in Lee's own estimation, Jerry's characterization belies another impulse. In an interview with Kenneth Quan, Lee admits that Jerry is not a "realistic portrayal" but explains his choice for Jerry's unique storytelling skills: "It's an articulation of what I think a person like Jerry thinks and feels and wants to feel and that's why I wrote it the way I wrote it because he has the same kind of feel and reach and depth that anyone else has. One of my first ideas was what kind of language should he have—then I thought I've met a lot of Italian-American guys who have a lot of learning and lot of depth and sensitivity." Lee flouts mimeticism as a model for character creation, but more than that, he directs his construction to challenge stereotypical conceptions of Italian Americans. In other words, there is a rhetorical impulse behind Jerry's linguistic idiosyncrasies that cannot be simply justified through the explanation that Lee's voice invades Jerry's. Although there is an obvious disarticulation between the author and the narrator-protagonist, not only on the ethnoracial level but also with regard to occupational difference, some reviews continually refer to Lee's spectral presence in the novel, without more directly engaging the meaning produced by the specificities of narratorial identity and voice. Analyzing character construction rather than discerning authenticity, then, might be directed toward thinking about, for instance, what giving Jerry such a voice does to our understanding of the novel and how he views the fictional world he inhabits.

If we bracket Lee's background as both a creative-writing professor and a Korean American, how do we read Jerry's incredibly imaginative and lyrically inflected observations? If we take his authenticity of voice as a concern, where does Jerry's voice, rather than Lee's intrusion, fail us? If we accept Lee's thesis that such sensitivity in Jerry's character reflects a larger consciousness that flouts stereotypes and assumptions, then how do we investigate the nature of racial difference as it appears in Jerry's storytelling? Such questions animate my reading of *Aloft*, in which I consider the nature of inferential racism at play within the novel, a form of subtle prejudice made explicit through Lee's use of refracted narration.

Refracting Whiteness

The interviews and reviews on *Aloft* tend to gloss over the political ramifications of Lee's imagination of the Other, in this case the Italian American character. Astutely, many note the suburban ennui, the upper-middle-class crises, and the relatively meandering plot, but the question of Jerry's identity in relation to race and as a form of critical whiteness is absent. What does whiteness signify, and how does Lee's figuration of Jerry refract and recontextualize minority subjects? The definitions offered by whiteness studies scholars begin to answer such a question. The anthropologist Melanie E. L. Bush explains that "being white has generally been associated with ancestry from the European continent and the denial of African blood. The borders of whiteness have shifted during different periods in history to include or exclude various groups." But Bush clarifies that "the claim to European heritage is often less significant than whether one is identified as white in everyday interactions" (15). While there are various branches within whiteness studies, I am most concerned with how whiteness has been constructed as a racial identity posited through exclusion.[9] Absent an actual definition of "whiteness," this racial formation appears to solidify only against those bodies and lives deemed deviant or foreign (Babb 43). Pamela Perry offers a definition of white identity that undergirds many such studies in the field, articulating importantly how white identity is seen "*as* universal, the signifier of perfect human rationality and morality" (380, emphasis in original).[10] In these various considerations, whiteness operates on a superstructural level that is ultimately linked to a position from which to draw power.¹¹ Critical race theoreticians and historians such as Ian F. Haney-López, Cheryl I. Harris, and George Lipsitz contend that the politics of white exclusion can be traced to property laws, while Abby L. Ferber argues that white supremacy developed out of the regulation of human sexualities.¹²

These definitions for white identity seem at first to contrast with Lee's *Aloft*, especially since Jerry is keenly attuned to the minorities that populate his Long Island community. Jerry's sexual relationships with various women of color demonstrate that he does not necessarily wish to maintain some vision of white purity, nor does he abhor the possibility that a person of color might own property within the seemingly exclusive suburbs in which the majority of the characters reside. *Aloft*'s construction of white identity and white exclusion functions with much more subtlety. Jerry, as a "sensitive" Italian American, epitomizes the complexities of race and race consciousness in the post–civil rights moment. He knows precisely what to say to appease certain parties but does not necessarily comprehend why he must say it. In this respect, his failure to acknowledge his own white privilege and its place within a wider spectrum exposes the inferential racism operating within the novel. A discreet form of white supremacy is also at work, which emerges in a paradox: Jerry espouses multicultural viewpoints while overlooking his elite status as a white, upwardly mobile subject. Jerry views his suburb as a location that cannot remain homogeneous, yet at the same time, he reads the racial and ethnic subjects as anomalous bodies, potentially subject to being expunged. Jerry's narration constantly asks: how do these minorities fit into the frame of a changing Long Island suburbia? He does not ask the same of the white characters. Instead, in Jerry's view, whiteness becomes the norm against which all racial Others are measured. Jerry's supposedly more self-conscious narration does not suggest that he understands how suburban racial Others must contend with the very social fabric undergirding the phalanx of Long Island tract homes and upper-middle-class living, for which whiteness is a dominating racial force. Jerry focuses on the singular; that is, he situates his life within a liberal individualism that absolves him of personal guilt and from fully confronting his white privilege.

Jerry's observations paint the Long Island suburb within a multiracial paradigm, but his insights still fail to point out how whiteness remains his universal point of reference. While criticism on *Aloft* is still relatively sparse, the literary critic Mark Jerng provides useful methodological springboards for expanding the critical conversation on the novel. Jerng employs phenomenology to demonstrate how Lee uses Jerry's perception to establish the normative and the foreign, a perception that always orients Jerry at a racial center, while minorities orbit him as deviant bodies ("Nowhere in Particular"). Whereas Jerry positions himself within the lens of a universalizing gaze, those who cannot conform to that gaze are denoted as particular—different and potentially strange. My own argument draws some inspiration from Jerng's approach, as formulations of whiteness within the novel are typically depicted as a subject position against which all other characters might be compared. Yet I consider the paradigms of universality and particularity not through phenomenological approaches but through the aforementioned critical race theories, which argue that racial inequality can be advanced through the tactical deployment of liberal individualism. In other words, whiteness can be both universalized and particularized in different narrative instances that cover over the systemic nature of racial inequality. *Aloft* plays with both poles of whiteness, in the sense that Jerry's gaze occasionally demonstrates an expansiveness to its scope but nevertheless finds its grounding within the white upper-middle-class and segregated Long Island suburbs he knows best.

The novel's opening sets up the importance of narrative perspective quite clearly as Jerry pilots a private plane. In this instance, Jerry's distance above the earth provides an entry into what is supposed to be first-person narration, in which Jerry is consistently a part of the story he is telling. However, in the following passage, the narration seems to border on a third-person viewpoint, as Jerry does not reveal his narratorial "I" in his observations: "There is a mysterious, runelike cipher to the newer, larger homes wagoning in their cul-de-sac hoops, and then, too, in the flat roofs of the shopping mall buildings, with their shiny metal circuitry of HVAC housings and tubes" (1). The altitude flattens out the landscape, providing Jerry with a panoramic view of the communities below. This opening vista embodies the quintessential fantasy of upper-middle-class American suburbia, replete with air-conditioning, the requisite commercial districts, and the immaculate landscaping. Here, we must carefully attend to the repeated phrase "from up here," a vantage point that allows Jerry to escape and ruminate on landscapes that look aesthetically pleasing, if only because they are reduced to pleasantly illuminated, geometrically shaped objects, whether these are "flat roofs," "tubes," or "simple, square houses" (1). The insularity of Jerry's solo flying expeditions is further augmented by the "light reflecting" off the asphalt terrain and "shiny metal circuitry" (1). In a certain sense, while the scene is cast in this romanticized glow, Jerry idealizes a form of partial blindness. The description of a "mysterious, runelike cipher" implies that the language of suburbia requires decoding and cannot be translated from so far above the earth. One wonders, though, whether Jerry wishes to unlock the linguistic intricacy of the space below him. If there is a central mystery, it emerges directly from the space of Long Island tract housing and shopping malls. His observation that the landscapes look to be "fretted over by a persnickety florist god" (1) reflects a simplistic view of the labor that would have gone into the making of this suburban space. This moment is rather ironic, as readers will find out that Jerry has worked in the construction business for many years. That is, he should understand how much physical toil goes into the maintenance of any space, but he ignores it here in favor of his fanciful viewpoint.

Jerry's plane flight continues to reveal his feelings concerning difference within Long Island. In contrast to the suburban perfection he views from above, Jerry admits to the cracks that surface when one moves closer: "And I know, too, from up here, that I can't see the messy rest, none of the pedestrian, sea-level flotsam that surely blemishes our good scene, the casually tossed super-size Slurpies and grubby confetti of a million cigarette butts, the ever-creeping sidewalk mosses and weeds" (2–3). Jerry alerts his audience to the ways in which the homogeneity of suburban life cannot be maintained, impressing on them a sense of affiliation with his usage of the pronoun "our." Thus, the opening scene establishes *Aloft* as essentially a monologic narration that masquerades as a conversational interplay. Jerry immediately understands the distortion of his gaze as he avoids these "blemishes." Fearing judgment, he asks, "Is that okay?" (3) and, as if hearing a positive response from someone listening, corroborates with an "Okay" (3). Since the novel establishes itself more or less within a realist tradition, the narrative mode suggests a disruption: the narrator is always already aware that he is being judged, breaking the wall with his implied but unseen audience. But if there is a critique to be made of Jerry, it is that even in his self-conscious awareness, he not only glosses over the particulars but takes pleasure in doing so.

The narration that begins the novel verges on a kind of omniscience where Jerry molds the suburban framework to his liking, choosing to filter all that he sees prior to telling it to the audience. But if he seemingly wishes for an unchanging, static conception of suburbia, do we understand the vagaries of "cigarette butts" and "dead, gassy possum" (3) to be the sole determinant of his disdain for facing the reality of his life? In describing such unseemly suburban detritus, Jerry grants us more information that recalls other processes of erosion. First, he explains to his unnamed audience what one can expect to eventually pass over: "older, densely built townships like mine, where beneath the obscuring canopy men like me are going about the last details of their weekend business, sweeping their front walks and dragging trash cans to the street and washing their cars as they have since boyhood and youth, soaping from top to bottom and brushing the wheels of sooty brake dust, one spoke at a time" (2). At first glance and without having perused paratextual materials such as a book-jacket blurb or reviews, the phrase "men like me" is hard to parse at this point in the novel. The passage suggests that men like Jerry, who have lived in the area all their lives, go about their day completing mundane tasks and errands. Despite the pedestrian nature of the activities, this depiction of suburban bliss conveys a tradition handed down from generation to generation. This moment firmly establishes Jerry within a longer tradition of the suburbs, where maintenance of family yards and vehicles becomes ritual.

The first chapter, as I have mentioned, revolves around Jerry's decision to buy a plane, which requires him to travel to the owner's home. Jerry describes the residence this way: "an attractive cedar-shingled colonial, built in the 1960s like a lot of houses in this part of Long Island, including mine, when the area was still mostly potato fields and duck farms and unsullied stretches of low-slung trees and good scrubby nothingness"; this contrasts to the current activity in the area, where "now the land is filled with established developments and newer ones from the '80s, and with the last boom having catapulted everyone over the ramparts there's still earthmoving equipment to be seen on either side of the Expressway" (9). At this point, the deliberate character construction reveals why Jerry is so focused on buildings, homes, structures, and spaces. The more rural and smaller townships that he recalls are becoming ever more populated, to the extent that any traces of a more bucolic lifestyle are being expunged. The alterations he observes are all part and parcel of postwar hypersuburbanization. Jerry's fetishization of his flying "aloft" and above the statically framed vista is an attempt to harness what seems to be a chaotic location, one where meaning cannot easily be pinned down.

Not surprisingly, it is not soon after this moment of suburban superconstruction that Jerry drops what I would call his first racialized thought bomb. His meeting with Hal, the owner of the Cessna, leads him to muse on racial difference in his community and his life:

> He was a nice-looking fellow, with a neatly clipped salt-and-pepper mustache and beard. And I should probably not so parenthetically mention right now that Hal was black. This surprised me, first because Shari wasn't, being instead your typical Long Island white lady in tomato-red shorts and a stenciled designer T-shirt, and then because there aren't many minorities in this area, period, and even fewer who are hobbyist pilots, a fact since borne out in my three years of hanging out at scrubby fields. Of course, my exceedingly literate, overeducated daughter Theresa (Stanford Ph.D.) would say as she has in the past that I have to mention all this because like most people in this country I'm hopelessly obsessed with race and difference and can't help but *privilege* the *normative* and *fetishize* what's not. And while I'm never fully certain of her terminology, I'd like to think that if I am indeed guilty of such things it's mostly because sometimes I worry for her and Jack, who, I should mention, too, aren't wholly normative of race themselves, being "mixed" from my first and only marriage to a woman named Daisy Han. (11–12)

A number of elements can be teased out of this passage. At no point does Jerry share his observations about Hal's racially anomalous presence in the Long Island suburban region with Hal or his wife, Shari. Instead, he admits this information only to his implied audience. Jerry possesses enough presence of mind to explain why he would be "surprised" by Hal's racial background, including an important reference concerning the status of his children as being "mixed" and of his marriage to Daisy Han. It is here that readers are finally given the first indication of Jerry's own racial background. At no point, of course, does he state that he is white, or even Italian American, but rather identifies race through a paradoxical absence and presence, making his own visible only through contrast with others. Like Lapcharoensap's figuration of Mister Perry and Lahiri's depiction of Eliot, Jerry is racialized only through deduction, as the reader meditates on what is "normative" about Shari as a "white lady," what is nonnormative about Hal as "black," and finally, what it means when Jerry has "mixed-race" children from a marriage to a woman with an ethnic surname. Whiteness, which does not need to be named, exerts a tremendous force on creating racialized narrative meaning.

Jerry maintains a defensive posture in his contemplation of racial difference, as he attempts to forefront his sensitivity to these minority figures. Rather than disdaining Hal for sullying the Long Island suburb as the "flotsam" that can be found in every neighborhood, Jerry notices Hal's phenotypic difference but does not use this difference to denigrate him. Nevertheless, the divulgence of racial identity is enough to suggest that Hal's presence, whether Jerry cares or not, is one that can incite "worry." Difference, as Jerry implies, can make one a target for further scrutiny. What bears most significance is Jerry's awareness that Hal could belong in this Long Island but does not.[13] But Jerry's narration does not elucidate the way in which Hal, as an individual, can be placed into a structural context of suburban racial politics and histories. While it might be a lot to expect that Jerry give the readers a sense of the larger forces that exist behind Hal's marginalization, he invites such a critique, especially by his eventual divulgence concerning his worry over Theresa and Jack as mixed-race individuals. In other words, he begins to point to the systematic nature of exclusion, one that targets Hal, Theresa, and Jack, but he still fails to express fully how this exclusion manifests itself. Jerry's narration encourages us to ask, why are there so few minority "hobbyist pilots" living in the area, and what are the ramifications for not being "wholly normative"?

Lee does not specifically name the city or town where the scene with Hal takes place or, for that matter, where the majority of the scenes within the novel take place; but the emphasis on whiteness is everywhere, and the Long Island that Jerry knows is predicated on racial homogeneity. While explaining his first encounter with Rita, his ex-girlfriend, he recounts how individuals seek others like themselves: "In this middle of the middle part of Long Island we're no different, nearly all of us on that boat descended from the clamoring waves of Irish and Italians and Poles and whoever else washed ashore a hundred or so years ago, but you're never quite conscious of such until somebody shows up and through no intention of her own throws a filter over the scene" (50). Once again, whiteness, despite the different ethnicities within that umbrella designation, functions as a racial collective. Jerry thus narrates how Irish, Italians, and Poles eventually have assimilated into one racial group. Such figures constitute the norm against which minorities are compared, as Jerry reveals their majority status in the area through the phrase "nearly all of us." Rita's arrival at a party held on a boat plays a disruptive role; she acts as a "filter" in the sense of a device mounted over a camera lens, which alters the shading of photographs. In this case, Rita's presence as a Latina literally colors the party. Again, Jerry does not name the exact Long Island location where this scene takes place. Instead, he describes it vaguely as the "middle of the middle part," a reference to a homogeneous center that glosses over the suburban segregation in the area.[14]

Because Jerry's storytelling never squarely confronts the nature of white spatial supremacy as it emerges in his locality, it must be placed in conversation with the sociohistorical conditions that have engineered Long Island into one of the least racially integrated locations within the continental United States and how Lee explores such issues through Jerry's perspective. The novel occasionally refers to areas such as Farmingville (26), MacArthur Field (20), Walt Whitman Mall (4), Old Westbury (12), and Nassau-Suffolk (315) that directly provide evidence of the general Long Island geography that Jerry discusses and traverses. It is, most notably, home to Levittown, one of the model housing communities that induced the white-flight phenomenon.[15] According to the urban studies scholar Paul Knox, "Without doubt the most famous was the original Levittown on Long Island, begun in 1947 by Abraham Levitt and his sons William and Alfred. They were the first large-scale developers to apply a highly rationalized, assembly-line approach to residential development" (26).[16] With the support of both the Federal Housing Administration (FHA) and the Veterans' Administration (VA), the construction and success of Levittown was predicated on racial segregation.[17] As the sociologists Melvin L. Oliver and Thomas M. Shapiro note, "the most basic sentiment underlying the FHA's concern was its fear that property values would decline if a rigid black and white segregation was not maintained" (18), thus paving the way for suburban homogeneity constructed around racial divides.[18] The cultural critic Robert Sickels explains that preferential treatment to white veterans also compounded the problems of suburban racial integration in the post–World War II period: "The government instituted the G.I. Bill of Rights, which offered 'qualified' veterans job training, money for schooling, and, perhaps most importantly, money to buy their own homes. While this was a wonderful opportunity for white soldiers, many minority veterans were excluded from the process" (68). Not only did suburbanization create "white" havens, but the impulse to exclude racial minorities in Long Island also functioned through systematic removal of such populations already living in areas desired for more development (Wiese, "Racial Cleansing" 61, 63). Although great numbers of racial minorities have always resided in Long Island, the centralization of racial populations in distinct areas raises major questions concerning the racial-steering and fair-housing laws.

Racial minorities who did attempt to integrate were often met with incredible obstacles and overt racism. As one scholar explains, "*Look* magazine ran an article in August 1958 of the first black couple, William and Daisy Myers, to move into Dogwood Hollow (a section of Levittown, Pennsylvania); they were subject to vandalism, physical threats, a flaming cross on the lawn, and 'KKK' painted on their friendly neighbour's house before state authorities could intervene" (Halliwell 34). The class studies scholar Robert E. Weir adds that "as late as 2000 Levittown, New York, was over 94 percent white, and fewer than 1 percent of its residents were African Americans" (454). Major New York City publications have reported on the racial tensions within the area.[19] Bruce Lambert writes, for example, that "the federal census shows that Long Island continues to be among the most segregated areas in America": "eighty-four percent of whites on Long Island live in white neighborhoods, it said, while nonwhites are concentrated in other neighborhoods" ("Long Island Has Failed"). Another report summarily calls Long Island "the nation's most segregated suburb" (Lambert, "Study Calls L.I.").[20] The autoethnographer Lorraine Delia Kenny asserts that despite the growing heterogeneity of places like suburban Long Island, "many communities are still, for the most part, the lily-white enclaves that the post–World War II generation settled and consolidated in the decades after the war" (6). In light of these contexts, one can reconsider Jerry's gaze, flying above the suburban communities, as glossing over the complicated milieu of Long Island's local race relations. As he views the houses as repetitive geometric shapes below him, the question of who gets to reside within those homes is conveniently ignored. His viewpoint is timeless, enabling him to leave social issues behind.

These social contexts allow us also to revisit and reconsider Jerry's interactions with Hal and how his thoughts do not explicitly engage racial prejudice as it has long affected the area. Hal connotes an anomalous presence that, when cast in the historical trajectory of racist housing policies, suburban segregation, and the potential bodily harm that integration could incite, suggests that Long Island's structural perfection comes at a price. Jerry's concern for his children also implies that he is aware that his mixed-race children are not the norm, but he does not make an unequivocal connection between their racial status and Long Island's spatial politics. As such, when racism appears as a masked tension in the conversation between Hal and Jerry, readers understand how white exclusivity functions through coded language. Before Jerry purchases the plane, Hal asks him whether he is serious: "because sometimes guys realize at the last second they don't want to buy a *used* plane. You know what I'm talking about, Jerry?" (12, emphasis in original). Prior to responding, Jerry grants the readers this perspective, concerning a couple trying to sell their "mansion in Old Westbury": "They had lots of lookers, but no offers, so they lowered the price, twice in fact. So the listing agent suggested they consider 'depersonalizing' the house, by which she meant taking down the family pictures, and anything else like it, as the owners were black" (12–13). At no point does either character mention race in direct conversation, but Jerry implies that the homebuyers are prejudiced. At the same time, this event is narrated in isolation and thus obscures the larger issue of suburban housing policies and cultural practices that function to exclude minority sellers and buyers. Jerry's awareness of how race can be encrypted in daily conversation demonstrates the veil that covers racial discourses in this suburban area. In some sense, Jerry is uniquely attuned to such coded language precisely because he is in the business of facades. Though he and his construction company are hired to help make homes look attractive to homebuyers, this veneer is only one component of the way that capital changes hands within an exclusive suburban area. Doublespeak surfaces everywhere, as racial difference is transformed into words such as "depersonalizing," and homeowners desire more than a stunning property. Jerry's thoughts ultimately reveal no clear sense that African American residents of Long Island have faced systematic racism through property issues. Jerry thus fails to contextualize Long Island as a center of continuing racial division. While the readers can potentially make this larger correlation, the way in which Jerry presents such information individualizes it. Hal and these black homeowners exist as but two examples of what Jerry would perceive as blips on the racial minority radar. This moment also recalls the earlier definitions offered by scholars such as Ian F. Haney-López, Cheryl I. Harris, and George Lipsitz, in which property ownership was used to shore up whiteness and white identity. Even in the context of a post–civil rights moment, this novel demonstrates how white identity still emerges through, in this case, the ability to buy or sell a home.

Consequently, Jerry's supposed multicultural ethos has its limits, revealed especially at points where his daughter Theresa is concerned. Jerry uses the term "Asian American" to describe both his daughter and her fiancé, Paul Pyun; as he admits, "I'm to say, 'Asian-American,' partly because they always do, and not only because my usage of the old standby 'Oriental' offends them on many personal and theoretical levels, but also because I should begin to reenvision myself as a multicultural being" (29).

This passage hinges on the word "should," in that Jerry understands that there is pressure for him to develop a kind of race consciousness, especially in his approach to politically sanctioned terminology. Here, Jerry reveals that "he doesn't quite appreciate what all the fuss is about" (29), a statement illustrating he has much further to go in terms of becoming the "multicultural being" he feels others expect him to be. His willingness to go along with calling Paul or Theresa "Asian-American" stems not from a concerned sense of race consciousness but from what appears to be more socially acceptable. In other words, this moment reveals how much Jerry's actions and spoken words are a performance masking a racialized ideology. Jerry, who as a white, heterosexual, upwardly mobile male living in an affluent suburb of New York has never been outside the norm, does not concede how damaging the word "Oriental" has been to Asian Americans as a racial group. Further, the term "Asian-American" is notated with the hyphen in Jerry's narration, which recalls the long debates about how to designate the relationship between Asia and America. The more commonly employed usage is "Asian American," where the hyphen is absent. However, the inclusion of the hyphenated punctuation serves as a reminder of the quite minute ways that Jerry fails to exist as a "multicultural being." Perhaps there is a larger gap between Asian Americans and European Americans than Jerry would like to admit. Jerry's rhetoric in this passage is of color-blindness, in which race should not necessarily be a factor in how one views another.

As such, why should it matter what he calls his daughter or future son-in-law anyway, since he loves them? But such a question fails to frame his daughter or son-in-law (or wife and son) beyond their familial connections. In describing his mixed-race (Asian American / white) and ethnically mixed (Italian, German, Korean) family, Jerry claims, "as a group you can't really tell what the hell we are, though more and more these days the very question is apparently dubious, if not downright crass, at least to folks like Theresa and Paul, whose race-consciousness is clearly quite different from mine" (69). Jerry is aware enough to realize that his position as an "an average white guy" (69) makes any question directed toward a racial minority concerning descent and origin potentially fraught. At the same time, he seems far more dubious about Theresa and Paul's racial politics, which apparently are too intellectualized for his tastes: "They inordinately fear and respect the power of the word, having steadily drawn down the distinctions between Life and Text. Let me say that when I was growing up the issues could be a lot heavier than that, a switchblade or Louisville Slugger being the *text* of choice, and one not so easily parsed or critiqued" (69–70). Again, Jerry demonstrates a short-sighted view of the damage wrought by prejudicial language. He attempts to minimize the complications that can result from ethnoracial tension by comparing it directly to the threat of bodily violence. He asserts that it is a much "heavier issue" to deal with someone attempting to stab or beat you up rather than being called, for instance, a racist epithet. Yet predicating the terrain of violence in this manner ahistorically represents race and does little to acknowledge how ethnoracial difference has incited centuries' worth of exclusion, much of which dovetailed specifically with physical brutality. In these various examples, two returning motifs appear: the family and the home. Jerry places value on these two elements in the understanding of his place and his inclusion within Long Island suburbia, but his individualistic thinking neglects to point out the long history of American white supremacy.

Madness and Suburban Civilization

For Jerry, American-ness seems based on something as simple as the change of a name. As he tells it, "the family name was originally Battaglia, but my father and uncles decided early on to change their name to Battle for the usual reasons immigrants and others like them will do, for the sake of familiarity and ease of use and to herald a new and optimistic beginning, which is anyone's God-given right, whether warranted or not" (23). The phrase "anyone's God-given right" suggests an egalitarian view of an individual's right to self-determination, but this statement, in actuality, reveals Jerry's belief in the importance of an Anglicized genealogy and immigrant transformation. As Jerry notes, the name change reinvents the family not simply as Americans but as a specific kind of American. That is, their family name is altered to mimic that of someone of English or Anglo-Saxon heritage. The ease with which this change occurs contrasts with the other character who has an "English" name but whose transformation remains incomplete: Jerry's wife, Daisy Han. It is important to note that Daisy's name would not be an exact Korean-to-English transliteration because its phonetics, broken into "day" and "zee," would be difficult for a Korean to enunciate. There is no "zee"-sounding equivalent in the Korean alphabet, so Daisy's name would at best be a rough approximation. This attempt to reinvent through a change in the first name rather than the family name, as in the case of the Battaglias, features Daisy's more tenuous American acculturation. Even as Daisy maintains her family name in contrast to the Battles, her Korean past is routinely erased in Jerry's understanding of her life.

This oversight demonstrates that white liberal individualism's subtle appearance within the novel bears more scrutiny, especially in relation to the chapter that relates Daisy's rise from department-store perfume-counter employee to upwardly mobile suburban housewife and then to her fall as a manic-depressive suicide. The chapter, of course, is narrated from Jerry's point of view and reveals how he figures Daisy as an irrational subject based on a diagnosis of what is likely to be bipolar disorder. I say "likely" because the chapter never directly refers to this condition, and my earlier mention of it as manic depression is based preliminarily on Jerry's description of Daisy as experiencing "manic heights" (124). Although Jerry admits he "didn't know what it was to be DSM-certified, described in the literature, perhaps totally nuts" (103), he does provide enough details to suggest that Daisy is suffering from bipolar disorder. Jerry does not go on to explain the acronym DSM, which stands for *Diagnostic and Statistical Manual for Mental Disorders*, a reference manual for American psychiatry. It is difficult to know when Daisy might have gotten a firm diagnosis for bipolar disorder, as the doctor who tended to her before her death did not have a psychiatric background. Instead, Jerry comes to know this diagnosis at a later point, perhaps while reflecting on what he had observed in the instances prior to the drowning.

It is worth noting that the description of bipolar disorder has changed over the course of the five different editions of the DSM.[21] According to the medical professionals Benjamin J. Sadock, Harold I. Kaplan, and Virginia A. Sadock, "patients with both manic and depressive episodes or *patients with manic episodes alone* are said to have *bipolar disorder*" (527, emphasis mine). "A manic episode," they explain, "is a distinct period of an abnormally and persistently elevated, expansive, or irritable mood lasting for at least one week, or less if a patient must be hospitalized. . . . Both mania and hypomania are associated with inflated self-esteem, decreased need for sleep, distractibility, great physical and mental activity, and overinvolvement in pleasurable behavior" (528).[22] The psychologist Sheri L. Johnson further clarifies that "there are two major subtypes of disorder in DSM-IV-TR: bipolar I and bipolar II. Bipolar I disorder is diagnosed on the basis of a single lifetime manic or mixed episode. Despite the name 'bipolar disorder,' depression is not a diagnostic criterion" (4). In *Aloft*, Daisy's mania first appears in ways that are too subtle for Jerry to notice, except in retrospect. Notable events include the following instances described by Jerry: "she bought herself and the kids several new outfits and served us filet mignon and lobsters and repainted our bedroom a deep Persian crimson trimmed in gold leaf" (103); "she worried me a little with her insomnia and solo drinking and 2 a.m. neighborhood walks in her nightgown" (104); and, most disturbingly, she "went off to Bloomingdale's and charged $7000 for a leather living room set and a full-length chinchilla coat" (103). Jerry notes that given the depressed economy at that time (the year is 1975), the spending spree creates a definite strain in their marriage. A final mishap serves as the proverbial last straw when he arrives home to find Daisy "going through a couple hundred fabric swatches piled on the kitchen table, she had four or five different room chairs, some Persian rugs, several china and silver patterns, she had odd squares of linoleum and porcelain floor tile; she had even begun painting the dining and living room with sample swaths of paint, quart cans of which lay out still opened, used brushes left on the rims dripping" (106). After this scene of domestic chaos, Daisy strangely joins Jerry in the shower, but they are interrupted in the middle of sexual intercourse when food left on the stove catches fire. Although Jerry finally gets the fire under control, the potential danger to the children caused by Daisy's inattention, coupled with her earlier spending spree, leads him to take drastic measures. Heeding his father's counsel, Jerry severely restricts Daisy's access to money, effectively cutting off her purchasing power. She therefore cannot continue decorating the house (instead of watching the kids) or go on extravagant shopping trips.

Daisy manifests the strain of the fire and her restricted monetary conditions in a variety of ways. Her diet changes markedly: "Daisy set down my dinner and she sat, too, but wasn't eating. After serving all of us seconds she took our plates and began cleaning up. The kids chattered back and forth but Daisy and I didn't say a word to each other" (113). Her insomnia worsens: "We usually went to bed at 11 or so, after the news for me and maybe a bath for her, but she started getting up at 5 in the morning, and then 4 and 3 and 2, until it got to the point when she didn't even get *ready* for bed, not bothering to change into a nightgown or brush her teeth or even take a soak" (118). The climax of Daisy's manic episode begins with a nude nighttime walk she takes to the local school. When she is brought back home by a police officer, her nonchalant attitude infuriates Jerry and provokes a shouting match. Jerry demands that Daisy see the family's general practitioner, but Daisy refuses; she further incenses Jerry when she does not seem concerned about waking up the children (122). But when Daisy lunges at Jerry with a knife, missing his "throat . . . by a mere thumb's width" (123), this act finally pushes her to agree to see Dr. Derricone, who prescribes her a course of Valium. After taking a dose, Daisy drowns. Later, when Jerry recounts this event, he comes close to realizing the duress she must have been under: "For who really imagined that there could be a state grayer than that for our mad, happy Daisy, lower than low, beneath the bottom, when suddenly it was all she could do to lift herself out of the bed in the morning and drag a brush through her tangled unwashed hair?" (124). Yet what is uncanny about this entire chapter, which finally provides an account of Daisy's death, is the way in which Jerry resists acknowledging his awareness that Daisy had been under considerable stress prior to her mania. Rather, he explains away Daisy's mania as something biological, coded in her very being, even as his descriptions betray the possibility that there were indeed signals and hints of her undergoing a significant crisis. Jerry fails to fully interpret his wife within the context of a suburbia in which her racial and ethnic difference marks her as a kind of outcast. Jerry's misreadings and misinterpretations are evidence of a blindness to the challenges Daisy faced attempting to assimilate into a white suburban culture. His liberal individualist thinking positions Daisy as a singular anomaly, a woman surprisingly gone mad, rather than as an immigrant facing a significant adaptive challenge due to a racially segregated setting.

Jerry's cursory reference to the DSM encourages readers and critics to reconsider psychiatric and psychological approaches in relation to Daisy's mental condition and to interpret her manic acts in other ways. The psychologist David Jay Miklowitz summarizes what is at stake: "Can bipolar disorder be caused by environmental factors, such as a highly conflictive marriage, problems with parents, life changes, a difficult job, or being abused as a child? These are extremely important questions that are not fully answerable" (90).[23] The aporias that Miklowitz calls "not fully unanswerable" bear more scrutiny. Various disciplines ranging from feminist studies to philosophy provide important corollaries and cautionary warnings to psychiatric diagnoses, especially as they can potentially elide complex trigger points for bipolar disorder.[24] Although bipolar disorder commonly is understood as having a strong genetic component,[25] psychiatrists form a consensus that environmental factors do play some role in the onset.[26] These findings strongly suggest that one must consider the nature of the individual's relationship to his or her surroundings.[27] The psychiatrist Gerald Grob, for instance, emphasizes how supportive communities can help to deter the onset and the development of mental illness (219).[28] In *Aloft*, it is unclear whether Jerry understands the challenges Daisy might have faced as a Korean American immigrant and how she might have responded to living in a relatively racially homogeneous suburb. We can only guess whether Daisy had any measured support systems to enable her to express her frustrations or to confront her psychic traumas.[29] Daisy therefore becomes part of the glossy suburban landscape that Jerry constructs, and we are tasked with pushing past his storytelling to continually revisit how she is represented through Jerry's narration.

In *Aloft*, even though madness, like race, is only inferentially referenced by Jerry, Daisy's mania is clearly exacerbated by external stresses and triggers. Sadock, Kaplan, and Sadock help explain Daisy's various signs and symptoms: "A long-standing clinical observation is that stressful life events more often precede first, rather than subsequent, episodes of mood disorders" (533).[30] A study conducted by Sheri L. Johnson and her fellow psychologists Ray Winters and Björn Meyer links sleep disruption with a dysregulation that appears in the BAS (behavioral activation system) that monitors the response related to stressful life events ("Polarity-Specific Model" 157). The researchers discovered that, in combination with insomnia, "controlling for manic symptoms in the month before an event occurred, the partial correlation between the intensity of the goal attainment event and the increase in manic symptoms over the next two months was significant" (160).[31] If we are to accept psychiatric findings that the manic subject ultimately suffers from a dysregulation of the BAS, which is intensified through the successive intensity of the "goal attainment event" and an inability to get proper rest, then Daisy fits this model in relation to her insomnia and her subsequent attempts to create domestic perfection conditioned by the suburban culture that surrounds her. In this way, *Aloft* gestures to the ways in which domestic and community ideals structure gender and racial power dynamics. For Daisy, the "goal attainment event" fuels her desire to furnish the home with expensive furniture, to repaint and redecorate the entirety of the interior, to cook appropriately decadent meals, and to outfit the family in the class-appropriate attire. As her obsession with becoming the perfect, deracinated Long Island wife and mother becomes all consuming, she cannot still her addled mind and find modes of relaxation and rejuvenation. Jerry's myopia prevents him from broaching the possibility that Daisy's mania might be connected to her adjustment to upper-middle-class suburban living. Indeed, the chapter's conclusion illustrates Jerry's feelings of relative guilt, not over having been an inattentive husband, one quite blind to the challenges his wife experiences as a Korean American working-class immigrant, but rather at having placed Daisy in the care of a general practitioner instead of a doctor more fully sensitive to the development of mental disorders. Inasmuch as this sentiment demonstrates Jerry's remorse, he still neglects to see other potential pitfalls in the way he treated and supported Daisy during their marriage. This failure is not simply interpersonal but reveals that his narrative perspective is not as expansive or nuanced as the novel's opening might suggest.

The Not-So-Korean American Housewife

For Jerry, Daisy is so individualistically imagined that her appearance in his life almost seems too good to be true. Their first encounter is a picture-perfect moment, a Hollywood meet-cute in which they randomly connect at a department store, where Daisy playfully sprays Jerry with cologne. Their relationship, however, is skewed from the start. Here, Jerry is not only a suitor but also a customer, while Daisy, an employee, aims to serve his every need. He never considers the class and race differential in relation to her. Moreover, we are never told what sort of life Daisy had prior to coming to the United States or why she immigrated; Jerry provides only very veiled references that Daisy has contacts back in Korea.

For Daisy, attaining suburban inclusion requires ethnic, racial, and cultural erasure in which her Korean heritage is almost entirely segregated from her daily life. Crucially, the extent to which her husband and her new social circles fail to move outside their own cultural frameworks is evidenced at numerous points leading up to her demise. Daisy is routinely infantilized, misjudged, and underestimated in her intelligence and comprehension of her surroundings, much of which are conditioned by her difference in ethnoracial and class status. Jerry, for instance, sees Daisy's culinary skills as exceptional, though he hardly shows cultural literacy relating to her Korean background. He recalls what Daisy would often prepare: "her homemade egg rolls and some colorful seaweed and rice thing that we didn't yet know back then was sushi, which people couldn't *believe* she had made, and maybe some other Oriental-style dishes like spicy sweet ribs and a cold noodle dish she always told us the name of but that we could never remember but which everyone loved and always finished first" (101, emphasis in original). While Jerry certainly recognizes Daisy's ethnically specific talents as a cook, he likely misidentifies the food she has been preparing by calling it "sushi," which is specifically connected to a Japanese cuisine, instead of referring to it as *gimbap*. The misidentification is somewhat understandable given that both cuisines employ seaweed wrapped around rice and other foods. The difference is that *gimbap* does not have raw fish as one of its major components. The "Oriental-style dishes" are not so much oriental as specifically Korean; the "spicy sweet ribs" are *kalbi,* and the "cold noodle dish" that they "could never remember" is likely *jap-chae.* The fact that he or anybody else would be so forgetful about the name of a Korean food dish or would confuse it with Japanese cuisine might be forgivable except that this insensitivity becomes part of a larger pattern. Jerry's ethnic misidentification could be troubling for someone whose relatives lived through the Japanese occupation of Korea. Jerry carries his lack of food-related cultural awareness into the present day. Rita, in a conversation about her new boyfriend, Jerry Coniglio, explains her preference for his companionship in this way: "Around the house, he likes to garden and read. He practices tai chi. He's also a very good Asian cook, Thai and Japanese," to which Jerry responds, "I always took you to Benihana's" (59). The comedy in this response results from the fact that Jerry's attention to ethnic foods is only on the level of identifying a popular restaurant chain, which is not widely considered exemplary of traditional Japanese fare. Daisy's experiences therefore can be contextualized as a subtle but nevertheless destructive form of alienation. While people in her immediate social circles appreciate Daisy's ethnic cooking, they never attempt to move beyond a superficial understanding of her immigrant and racial background.

Jerry's communication with Daisy further miscasts her difference, again demonstrating the shallow nature of their relationship. As he divulges, "pure talk was never that important to us anyway, even at the beginning, when it was mostly joking and flirting, for though her English was more than passable it was just rudimentary enough for us to stay clear of in-depth and nuanced discussions, which suited me just fine" (119). Jerry's avoidance of "in-depth and nuanced discussions" is more evidence of Daisy's impoverished suburban life, in which her ethnic background is nothing more than local color. The linguistic barrier proves to be a way that Jerry can avoid confronting the deeper problems in his marriage. Since Daisy calls Korea frequently enough to occasionally rack up large phone bills, she clearly has quite a lot to share, but Jerry is not the recipient of such conversational attention. At the same time, Jerry is more than willing to objectify Daisy's Asian body. Despite his self-reflexive admission that he is "fetishizing once again," he admits, "I'm not sorry because the fact is I found her desirable precisely because she was put together differently from what I was used to, as it were, totally unlike the wide-hipped Italian or leggy Irish girls or the broad-bottomed Polish chicks from Our Lady of Wherever I was raised on since youth, who compared to Daisy seemed pretty dreadful contraptions" (107–08). Ultimately, his self-awareness is undermined by his unwillingness to see beyond Daisy's externalities. He cannot acknowledge that she possesses a culturally specific life that cannot be limited to her domestic suburban household interactions among husband and two children.

Suburban Long Island thus becomes the perfect venue for exploring the prospect of performance and masquerade. While Jerry admits that much of his dealings with Daisy involve basic strategies that are motivated by his desire to control her (e.g., the restriction of her cash allowance following her spending spree), he all but ignores the possibility that her daily mood fluctuations and instability might also result from her suburban resettlement. He does not ask how Daisy's seemingly incongruous moods are influenced by the sociopolitical peculiarities of this setting. Such a question is essential to consider in light of her mental instability because Jerry assumes from the beginning that everything is quite stable before her mania begins. However, Jerry's narration subtly reveals instances when he underestimates both her difference in status as a Korean immigrant woman and her compliancy (before the onset of her mania) to accommodate their suburban lifestyle. For instance, when Jerry first begins the backstory to Daisy's demise, he explains the relatively stable position of the household at the time: "I was working a lot then, having just been made second-in-command at Battle Brothers by my father and uncles, and Daisy was like a lot of young mothers around the neighborhood, meaning she took care of the house and the kids and the cooking and the bills and whatever else came up" (101). This mundane description is juxtaposed, however, with another that bears more scrutiny: "When you got right down to it she was an old-fashioned girl in matters of family, not only because she wasn't so long removed from the old country but also because her nature (if you can speak of someone's nature, before she changed and went a little crazy and ended up another person entirely) preferred order over almost all else" (101). As Jerry rationalizes it, Daisy is fit for such domestic duties not only because of a particular character trait but also because she was an "old-fashioned girl in matters of family," something that he connects with her life back in Korea. One wonders, considering her recent travels from that country, how much she could have in common with the other "young mothers around the neighborhood" in matters related to class, culture, race, and ethnicity. In fashioning Daisy as so similar to her neighbors, without exploring how different she could be, Jerry idealizes his wife's entry into the suburban landscape as if she has already successfully assimilated. Her different ethnic dishes are rendered exotic yet palatable, and her physical exterior, although distinct from the many women Jerry has known, can be sexually circumscribed. Perhaps the most dangerous element of Jerry's characterization of Daisy occurs when he describes her as someone who "preferred order over almost all else," attributing this quality to something in "her nature." Jerry already affixes Daisy within a rigid frame, imposing the suffocating expectation that she maintain a perfectly ordered household. Even as Daisy's mania worsens and Jerry attempts to curb her spending habits, he places acutely high expectations on her to maintain the "order" that he sees as an inherent part of her personality, forcing her to remain indoors, without access to a car or credit cards and with a weekly allowance of twenty dollars (111).

While Jerry believes that his wife is not so different from other young mothers living in Long Island, Lee includes a pivotal interaction that complicates Daisy's supposed adaptation to the suburban life. During a mishap in which Jerry must help put out a pan fire caused by Daisy's inattention, Jerry rushes outside with the pan in the midst of their neighbors' dinner party on a back patio. Though he had invited Mr. Lipscher and his wife over a "couple of times" for a "barbecue," they "never actually made it over." Jerry adds, "they were into tony, Manhattan-type gatherings, with candles and French wine and testy, clever conversations (you could hear every word from our deck) about Broadway plays or Israel or their favorite Caribbean islands, everyone constantly interrupting everyone else in their bid to impress, all in tones that said they weren't" (110). This notable passage reveals the division between the Battles and the Lipschers, who attain a level of cultural capital noted by their taste in wine, their theater literacy, and their cosmopolitan attitudes concerning travel. The word "tony" clarifies the nature of these gatherings, which contrast to the more informal "barbecue" settings thrown by the Battles. The performative character of these meals is evidenced by their very public setting. The Lipschers can be gazed on and heard, their place in suburban Long Island thus cemented by their ability to lay claim to their posh surroundings.

The neighbors' relationship to the Battles appears to be less than congenial, as the dismissed barbecue invitations suggest. Such an implication is made even more explicit when the fire is finally extinguished. Because Jerry is showering when he is first alerted to the fire, he runs outside nude. Daisy later appears, in a towel, with children alongside her. In response, Barry Lipscher yells over, "Hey there, Battle, you want to end the show now? We're still eating here if you don't mind." Daisy retaliates against this snide remark, as she "unhooked her bath sheet and wrapped it around [Jerry's] waist, then turned to the Lipschers and guests in all her foxy loveliness and gave them the finger" (110). This scene bears considerable weight because it is the only one that establishes any sort of external relation between Daisy and her neighbors. Rather than a benevolent connection, she shows derision and scorn for them. The only instance that Jerry recalls in which their suburban counterparts loom large occurs when Daisy and Jerry are literally and figuratively exposed. Indeed, their home and their children were both put in peril. The Lipschers' dinner party serves as a stark contrast to the kind of domestic perfection that is precisely and constantly imperiled for Daisy.

What Jerry does not mention in relation to the neighbors is their racial or ethnic backgrounds. While such information might not seem necessary for Jerry to point out, the novel's opening chapter foregrounds exactly how pivotal race and ethnicity is in Jerry's situating himself in relation to his environment and with respect to these social relationships. The Lipschers are unmarked and therefore coded within the novel as white, and we see again how Daisy functions as the racially disruptive force, her "foxy loveliness" that could still be perceived by her white suburban counterparts to be polluting Long Island. Whereas Daisy cannot change her phenotypic features to fit seamlessly into the suburban racial makeup, her tacit willingness to undergo ethnic erasure and cultural assimilation speaks to the challenging milieu in which she finds herself. As such, she never speaks Korean, and her children do not seem to be fluent in the language; Daisy, at least from what we can tell, does not attempt to educate Jack, Theresa, or Jerry about her ethnic heritage or background. Jerry is, of course, complicit in this radically assimilative process, precisely because he does not need to change the way he views the world; instead, she must evolve, while he remains moored within a familiar cultural and racial frame.

As a result, Daisy focuses on her goal-attainment event. Recall that mania is characterized by a BAS malfunction that is tied to some important achievement trajectory. For Daisy, the event that catalyzes the major tension in the chapter revolves around the restriction of her finances and discretionary spending. Without such monies, she cannot engage the various home-improvement projects she has initiated. The home becomes the symbolic location in which Daisy toils not simply to cement her status as the perfect mother but to imagine herself as the optimum Long Island suburban housewife. Recall the passage in which Jerry finds Daisy in the process of radically remodeling the family home. If she cannot refashion her racial background, she certainly can try to remake her home into something that might offer the chance to claim a spatial suburban whiteness. Daisy does not seek just a place in this community but also spatial evidence that she excels—that she, although Korean and an Asian immigrant, belongs.

In a study of suburbia and fictional representation, the literary critic Catherine Jurca notes the way white suburban novelists articulate a form of spatial victimization called sentimental dispossession, in which "white middle-class suburbanites begin to see themselves as spiritually and culturally impoverished by prosperity" (6–7). In thinking about sentimental dispossession as a form of white identity formation that emerges in relation to suburban space, one necessarily observes how the racial minority cannot always think of the home or house in this manner. Sentimental dispossession becomes the purview of white privilege. For someone like Daisy, the lie of the American Dream surfaces dramatically, in that no matter how much she purchases, how perfectly she cooks, or what outfits she acquires for her children, she might never fit in because of her ethnic heritage and racial background. She occupies a subject position defined by contradiction: how can she dispossess herself of race and ethnicity? the chapter seems to ask. Daisy's suicide, when placed in context with the opening sequence in which Jerry attempts to purchase the private plane from Hal, reminds us of the power of suburban contexts to structure whiteness as a norm. Daisy and Hal are both evidence of the possibilities—and impossibilities—of racial integration; their experiences illustrate the tenuous nature of suburban inclusion.

Racism and Narration: What Is Directly Said, What Is Indirectly Said, and What Is Performed

If Jerry rarely discusses race explicitly or in direct speech, his daily interactions reveal a mismatch between what he seems to believe about himself and what he will say. Despite prevailing stereotypes about racial minorities, he wants the reader to know that his life with Daisy moves beyond such prejudicial viewpoints. But if Jerry expects this imaginary audience to sympathize with him, then, on account of his representation of Daisy's mania, he categorically fails. When Jerry finally pushes Daisy to see Dr. Derricone, he recounts the event in this way: "'He's a *complete fool*,' she said, with a perfect, and faintly English, accent, as though she'd heard some actress say the phrase in a TV movie or soap. Daisy was a talented mimic, when she got the feeling. *'They are complete and utter fools'*" (121, emphasis in original). Of course, Jerry does not pay attention to what Daisy is saying in that moment, assuming that she has simply "gone crazy," and replies with this racially insensitive remark: "I don't care if you think he's the King of Siam. Dr. Derricone has been around a long time and you'll show him respect. He's seen it all and he's going to help you" (122). In some respects, both the doctor and Jerry are "utter fools" in their inability to properly diagnose and provide care for Daisy. Dr. Derricone prescribes Valium, a drug that, by itself, cannot be used to treat manic depression over the long term. Jerry's reference to the "King of Siam" paints the doctor as the foreigner, perhaps unconsciously directing us to consider how this medical professional understands very little about Daisy's condition. The use of the word "mimic" to describe Daisy emphasizes her performative capabilities. If she can speak like anyone else, if given "the feeling," how might such talents translate to her life and actions more broadly? Such a question spotlights how her position as the organizer of the domestic household is, in essence, the pinnacle of Daisy's masquerade, her way to cast attention onto something other than her racial difference.

Toward the novel's conclusion, Jerry's daughter, Theresa, rebukes him for his response to Daisy's death. "I'm talking about how you managed everything so quickly after that. I mean, come on, Jerry. It was a world speed record for goodbyes. I didn't think it then but it was like a freak snowstorm and you shoveled the driveway and front walk all night and the next day the sun comes out and it's all clear, all gone" (321). The speed with which Jerry casts Daisy off is perhaps the most spectacular example of his ability to cover up a sense of guilt, perhaps not for having given Daisy inadequate medical care but for failing to recognize and address the psychosocial conditions that could have triggered her mania. After discovering that his son, Jack, had observed his mother's actions before her suicide, Jerry admits, "you'd have to be a complete innocent (or maybe a kid) to imagine such a thing *not* happening, that her drowning in the pool wasn't somehow foreseeable, given the way she was raging and downfalling and the way I was mostly suspended, up here before I was ever up here" (321). This moment is perhaps proof that Jerry was aware of a significant problem but that he could not find a way to address the issue. We should pause, though, on the word "suspended," as it connotes his relative position not only to the events that befall his wife but also to his racial status. Somehow, he cannot move past his racial privilege to come to terms with his wife's position as the deviant racial minority, one whose "downfalling" and "raging" perfectly encapsulates how out of place she finds herself in Long Island.

While *Aloft* is not centered exclusively on the Asian American experience, it is nevertheless a work about race and race relations, as well as the subtle means by which white privilege can operate. Lee plays a role beyond that of native informant, destabilizing the relationship between narrator and author; Daisy's supposed madness challenges the post-1965 stereotype of the Asian American model minority citizen. With a loving husband, two beautiful and healthy children, and a palatial Long Island suburban home, what more could Daisy want? Jerry implies that, given everything Daisy seems to have, no possible reason except a genetic component gone awry could explain the development of her mental disorder. If we are suspicious of Jerry's explanation, it is only because Lee creates a narrative perspective in which a man's ability to see the world with such lyric sensibility encrypts a significant aporia. According to the sociologists Joe Feagin and Eileen O'Brien, "most white Americans are resistant to the idea that they have major privileges over other racial groups. To acknowledge such privileges means recognizing significant racial disparities in the societal fabric—which recognition ... is frequently considered socially unacceptable in this era of assertive color-blindness" (72). As Daisy unravels, what Jerry fails to see is how that unraveling might be intimately woven into a suburban "fabric," which is simply impossible to purchase and to own.

2 /   When the Minor Becomes Major:
      Asian American Literary California,
      Chicano Narration, and Sesshu Foster's
      Atomik Aztex

This chapter shifts from the white-Asian paradigm discussed in the first chapter to an investigation of how and why Asian American writers include other racial minority groups in their fictional worlds. Chapter 1 called attention to a racial paradigm that substantively undergirds Asian American studies: white consciousness in relation to immigrant exclusion. As scholars such as Lisa Lowe, Ronald Takaki, Sucheng Chan, and numerous others have revealed, whiteness signified the ultimate racial criterion of American citizenship and was defined in part through its opposition to the Asian, the forever foreign subject. Despite the early barriers that Asian immigrants and their children faced in America, the economic opportunities that emerged consistently encouraged successive populations and generations to make the arduous journey across the Pacific Ocean through whatever methods possible. The post-1965 period ushered in a new era for Asians and Asian Americans as immigration restrictions were lifted, but chapter 1 also reveals the ways in which racial minorities still suffer from different and perhaps subtler forms of prejudice. I employ Chang-rae Lee's *Aloft* to illustrate how a white narrative perspective can occlude the significant adaptive challenges faced by people deemed to be minorities; this novel reminds us that our attention to racially inflected social inequalities must continue and exposes the pitfalls of postracial ideology.

Examining these social, cultural, and interracial contexts rightly forms one critical basis of our discipline, but race and ethnic studies scholars continue to reveal the complicated contours of exclusion, especially as it occurs with respect to multiple minority groups. In a special issue of *PMLA* on comparative racialization, the literary critic Shu-mei Shih encourages scholars and critics to consider racial formations as inherently interconnected but not necessarily symmetrical or equatable in their constructs. In this chapter, I am most interested in the representation of one comparative minority racial axis—that of the relationships forged and the antagonisms that erupt between Chicanos and Asian Americans.

As one of the states closest to Asia, California consistently beckoned to Asian migrants as a robust center for numerous industries, ranging from agriculture to technology. At the same time, California's economic history cannot be constituted solely from the perspective of Asian labor, as historians such as Tomás Almaguer and Kevin Starr have shown. Indeed, California's vexed past includes the colonial exploitation and enslavement of indigenous populations, the systematic restructuring of the agricultural industry through the recruitment of transnational Mexican guest workers, and the influx of African American workers during the Second Great Migration. In relation to these multiracial contexts, Asian American writers do engage with such intricate social and historical formations within their representational terrains. I am particularly attentive to writers such as Carlos Bulosan, Brian Ascalon Roley, Bhira Backhaus, and Sesshu Foster, all of whom explore the connections and complications that arise between Asian American and Chicano characters. These writers present an exceptional subset within the Asian American literary archive in that their fictions conspicuously depict characters of other racial minority populations.

As I discuss in the introduction, Asian American literature has often been presented, read, and marketed as both autobiographical and autoethnographic in scope. The writer's Asian ancestry often seems directly reflected in the use of narrative perspective and can lead critical readings to focus primarily on a single ethnoracial context. The appearance of other racial minorities in the course of the narrative offers one way to begin disarticulating the writer's ethnoracial background from analytical practices. This chapter first examines how representations of California coincide with external social contexts and how some Asian American writers imagine a literary California imbued with a comparative minority race aesthetic. I present short readings of Carlos Bulosan's *America Is in the Heart* (1946), Brian

Ascalon Roley's *American Son* (2001), and Bhira Backhaus's *Under the Lemon Trees* (2009) to show the links between fictional worlds and external referents: in these novels, Chicano presence, although seemingly marginal to the plotting, evidences a cross-minority hybridity that gestures to dynamic aesthetic possibilities and political reading practices. Yet these Chicano figures remain minor characters and, as such, are ultimately excluded from the narrative, revealing the necessity of different formal approaches to engage a comparatively racialized fictional world.

I spend the bulk of this chapter on Sesshu Foster's *Atomik Aztex* (2005) because it presents an instance of Asian American literature becoming Othered to itself from the vantage point of Chicano/a characters who narrate their own experiences and who exist at the center of the plotting. In *Atomik Aztex*, Foster's decision to take on the voice of another racial minority undermines the assumption that only one racial or ethnic group can claim ownership over the representation of the minority experience. While there are perils in appropriating an ethnoracial perspective, Foster's novel helps articulate why the Chicano experience is germane to Asian American studies. While Asian American characters do not always appear as major figures, the novel nevertheless exhibits a larger racialized underclass that exposes the inequities produced by global capitalism. By granting more narrative space, attention, and voice to a Chicano character, Foster provides an explicit political vision behind his imaginative fictional world by linking slaughterhouse work so firmly to external social contexts, where Chicanos have currently become the most prominent laboring pool engaged in this physically dangerous occupation. Though this chapter certainly deviates from chapter 1 with respect to the storyteller and his situatedness in time and place, the introduction makes clear that these narratives exist in a larger historical continuum. Indeed, as *Aloft*'s depiction of postwar suburbanization of Long Island functions to fragment racial populations and to encourage a subtler form of racial segregation, Foster's *Atomik Aztex* details a postwar urban Los Angeles in which minority laborers find themselves part of a disposable and often invisible underclass powering global capitalism. Each novel, though often deviating from an identifiable Asian American narrative perspective, cannot be categorized as advancing a postracial aesthetic. Instead, such works provide cultural critics with fertile terrain to consider both the artistic and political concerns undergirding narrative perspectives as imagined by American writers of Asian descent.

The Promise of Interracial Coalitions: California Social Contexts and the Borderlands of Asian American Literature

This chapter invokes what Vijay Prashad calls the politics of the "polycultural" ("Bruce Lee" 53).[1] Prashad employs his polycultural critique within a historical methodology, specifically highlighting points of intersectionality among various communities and racial populations.[2] A polycultural critique can also be extended to fictional worlds, but my argument diverges from Prashad's conception in thinking also about sites of rupture that make polycultural formations so challenging and so fragile. In thinking about race at the borderlands of Asian American literature, I follow the articulations of Linda Martín Alcoff (7), Nicholas De Genova (11), Crystal Parikh (16), and Rodolfo Acuña (132), who have theorized the linkages between Asian American and Latino/a populations. While these four scholars acknowledge the differences in the racial formations of the two populations, a unifying point among the scholars emerges in the ways they each conceive these two racial populations as being labeled as inescapably foreign.[3] In considering the historical connections between Asian Americans and Chicanos, I also assert how California's regional location remains of paramount importance to comparative racial formation. As two states that are geographically close to Asia, California and Hawai'i were logical settlement choices for Asian migrants. The need for cheap labor during America's industrialization opened up economic opportunities that became major factors for migrating populations. In California, some of the strongest draws were railroad building, gold mining, and domestic service. In addition, from the late nineteenth century and through the early decades of the twentieth, Chinese, Japanese, Koreans, Asian Indians, and Filipinos migrated to California in roughly successive waves to join the agricultural sector of the economy. The Asiatic Barred Zone law of 1917 eliminated almost all Asian immigration except for Filipinos, who possessed special status as US colonial subjects. However, with the 1934 passage of the Tydings-McDuffie Act conferring independence to the Philippines, all Filipino migrants were reclassified as aliens ineligible for US citizenship, thus furthering the massive and widespread restrictions on Asian immigration. The gradual elimination of Asian bodies once again created a labor vacuum, one that was filled primarily by itinerant Mexican transnational populations.[4] It was this temporary worker status, situating Mexicans as sojourners, that conditioned their twentieth-century racial formation through semipermeable US-Mexico border dynamics. Labor would be extracted, but citizenship status would not necessarily be conferred. Such histories begin to show the mutually constructing relationships among Asian immigrants, Mexican immigrants, and the labor required for the economic development of the western United States.[5]

While the post-1965 era has altered the dynamics of Mexican and Asian immigrant labor, the need for low-cost workers continues in many sectors, especially in the retail, food service, and manufacturing industries.[6] The geographic centrality of such migrants within the Southern California area continues to demonstrate the importance of regional locations for studies of comparative racialization. The garment industry, for instance, draws on a large population of immigrants from Asia and Latin America, many of whom end up in Los Angeles (Y. Espiritu, *Asian American* 87–88).[7] But these migration patterns result in a class structure in which many Asians appear to rise more quickly to middle-management positions. As a result, Latin Americans often take on the most physically demanding jobs in dangerous working conditions (Budde 46).[8] This class asymmetry often distinguishes the Asian and Latino working classes, but such distinctions must also be tempered with attention to their comparative racialization. Both Asian Americans and Latinos are essential for California's economy, and together they help drive the massive engine of global capitalism. In the specific case of the garment industry, the movement of bodies into the United States helps generate the labor required for a service sector that is itself involved with the movement of goods within and beyond the nation.[9]

In citing the work of sociologists, urban studies scholars, and historians, I provide the social contexts that often inform Asian American writers and their constructions of California-based fictional worlds. The presence of minor characters demonstrates how attuned particular writers are to an aesthetic process inspired by comparative racial formation. For example, Carlos Bulosan's *America Is in the Heart* is a foundational work within the Asian Americanist canon, but most scholars do not fully consider the text's interracial elements.[10] While the vast majority of the criticism on *America Is in the Heart* rightly concentrates on the intricacies of Filipino immigrant subjectivity during the early twentieth century, Bulosan takes care in presenting the Filipino migrant laborer experience alongside Mexican American populations.[11] Allos, the fictional protagonist of Bulosan's autobiographically inflected novel, constantly travels to Mexican American districts and interacts with Mexican American characters. The importance of Mexican American geographical sites is made palpable by the fact that many Filipino migrants employ such spaces to meet friends and family and to find potential sex partners. Allos later travels to Los Angeles and expresses this particular kernel of belonging across collective colonial histories and mestizo consciousness: "I went to Main Street, turned to the north, and found the Mexican district. The sound of Spanish made me feel at home, and I mingled with the drunks and the jobless men" (127). The linguistic connection elucidates a common colonial heritage between the Philippines and Mexico, highlighting the historical significance of the Filipino-Mexican interethnic and interracial axis. However, Allos finds his Mexican companions to be lacking in quality, punctuating how community building can be far more tenuous than simply traveling to an ethnic enclave to hear a familiar language.

America Is in the Heart thus also chronicles the tensions and antagonisms between characters of Filipino and Mexican descent. The novel often depicts Filipino men's inability to sustain long-term relationships with Mexican women, and these examples show the gendered and sexualized nature of such interracial interactions. On the one hand, they elucidate the gender disparity that characterized the Filipino migrant experience in which men outnumbered women by a large margin, spurring Filipino men to seek sexual liaisons with women who were not coethnics. On the other, given the limited occupational trajectories available for Mexican women during this period, their bodies became commodities, exploited by pimps and endangered by unsafe sexual practices.

In terms of the text's historical moment, individuals of Mexican descent would be the primary populations to labor alongside Filipinos. As more Mexicans moved northward due to the labor vacuum generated by the Immigration Act of 1924, this shift also altered social relations more broadly. Indeed, the increased numbers of male Mexican workers offered tantalizing prospects for unionizing. Allos's working-class politic is partially derived from his sense of collective oppression: "The sugar beet season was in full swing in Oxnard, but the Mexican and Filipino workers were split. The companies would not recognize their separate demands, and although there were cultural and economic ties between them, they had not recognized one important point: that the beet companies conspired against their unity" (195–96). Allos recognizes how interracial solidarity is subverted, despite common working conditions and perhaps what Allos calls the "cultural" and "economic" ties between the populations. While the attempts at unionization ultimately fail, this rupture occurs because of the charismatic and undermining presence of a strikebreaker named Helen, who has been hired by the companies to create dissension and to spy on unionizing activities. Bulosan's text hence reveals the structural nature of this failure: corporate power functions to maximize profits at the expense of coalitions agitating for workers' collective rights.[12]

America Is in the Heart explores the potential of interracial interactions between Mexican American and Filipino American populations, but the text does not merely celebrate hybridity. Indeed, a sustained interracial coalition never appears; the narrative gestures to a representational landscape where the seed of comparative race activism exists but never fully germinates. The novel further foreshadows the projects of contemporary Asian American writers. Brian Ascalon Roley's *American Son*, for instance, can be partially read through its representation of the interracial tensions between Asian American and Latino minor characters. Early on in the novel, the protagonist, Gabe, and his brother Tomas are traveling through Los Angeles on their way to sell some attack dogs that Tomas has been training. Gabe makes a striking observation, noting "the wetbacks who stand in golden shafts amid the shadows waiting to get picked up for work, short little men who smoke cigarettes and talk in groups" (38). Gabe's racist terminology explicitly shows the problematic ways in which racism occurs between different minority groups. This scene is also notable in that Gabe uses the word "pass" in two variations: first in the word "overpass" in relation to where the workers are standing and second in relation to passing them as he and Tomas drive by (38). Because at this point in the novel Gabe's brother is passing for Chicano as a way to appropriate a form of racialized masculinity, this stylistic repetition amplifies our attention to racial performance and to masquerade. We see that the Mexican laborers stand amid a mix of "golden shafts" and "shadows," partially obscured from view. The presence of these Mexican subjects reminds us that such laborers help support the Los Angeles economy. Inasmuch as Tomas wants the machismo that comes with being a Chicano thug, these male figures standing under the freeways call attention to his rather superficial racial masquerade. The laborers are not simply racial Others who can be denigrated by Gabe or have their racial backgrounds so easily appropriated by Tomas. Instead, the scene finds footing in historical contexts invoking comparative racial and ethnic formations: as we saw with Bulosan's work, in the early twentieth century, Filipino Americans often migrated to the United States to work in canneries, agricultural industries, and other service capacities that are now sometimes filled by people of Mexican and Latino descent.

This scene speaks to the ways in which interracial and class tensions so often ground California literary representations, and this passage is one of many throughout the novel in which minor characters of Mexican descent appear. While Gabe often disparages Mexicans and Mexican Americans through racial epithets, the novel also illuminates how Gabe's disidentification with them stems from his insecurity over his own class standing, as the biracial Filipino child of a domestic service worker. Indeed, Gabe's mother functions in a service capacity similar to that of many of the minor characters of Mexican descent in the novel. *American Son* pushes literary critics to consider the influence of region, class, and comparative minority race relations on the construction of the fictional world.

Bhira Backhaus's novel *Under the Lemon Trees* also explores the comparatively configured racial formation of Asian American and Chicano populations. Like Bulosan's *America Is in the Heart* and Roley's *American Son*, *Under the Lemon Trees*' comparative race aesthetic is expressed through minor characters who appear within the fictional terrain. The novel explores the life of a fifteen-year-old Indian American girl, Jeeto, who attempts to navigate the tricky world of traditional Punjabi value systems, especially as they relate to romance, love, and marriage. Jeeto's notions of romance develop due to the circumstances that involve her older sister, Neelam, who is spurned by her first love, Hari. Neelam later enters into an arranged marriage, despite her reputation having been sullied by her earlier indiscretion. But Neelam and Hari's star-crossed romance is part of a longer lineage of doomed interracial relationships. In flashbacks, readers discover that Hari's father, Uncle Avtar, as a young man working as an agricultural laborer and farm hand, falls in love with a young Mexican American woman. Uncle Avtar, who is impoverished, is unable to win her over after a series of misfortunes that cast both of them in a bad light.

Uncle Avtar's background and life are pivotal to the novel's representation of interracial relationships. Readers are introduced to a highly specific social context in which Punjabi immigrants, most often of peasant origins, immigrated to the United States in the early twentieth century. As Karen Isaksen Leonard notes, the ratio between Punjabi men and women was highly imbalanced (we recall a similar situation with Filipino migrants). To remedy this situation, Punjabi men often turned to one of the populations found toiling alongside them, the Mexican American community.[13] Backhaus's novel moves away from being a kind of fictionalized autoethnography through key narrative and temporal shifts. While most of the novel is narrated in first person, in a temporally linear fashion, the flashback sequences depicting Avtar's work as an agricultural laborer in the early to mid-twentieth century appear in omniscient form, moving the narrative to a radically different sociohistorical context in which restrictive immigration laws had not yet been lifted on Asian populations. Readers are led to believe that Jeeto might be narrating these sections in some sort of retrospective fashion, but readers are unable to determine this storytelling standpoint with full certitude. This more impersonal voice contrasts with the tone of Jeeto's youthful first-person narration, creating the sense that she (and readers) must place Avtar's life in multiple frames of reference.

In one of the chapter sequences that moves from first-person narration to the omniscient third-person storyteller, Jeeto first begins to imagine through her own perspective what Uncle Avtar's past life might have been like, even though she could not have experienced such events herself. As part of this fanciful reconstruction, Jeeto explores his past through photographs. Jeeto describes one photo: "My uncle stood beside two Mexican men in front of an old Hudson. He appeared even younger here. I pressed my thumb along his image, as if the motion would make him come magically alive" (70). Uncle Avtar's life as an agricultural laborer then begins to emerge, specifically a part of his past in which he routinely encounters Mexican American populations. The physical movement of Jeeto's thumb over Uncle Avtar represents her desire to cross time and space, to make that moment "come magically alive" again.

As we see, Uncle Avtar's movement out of suspended animation is initiated first through Jeeto's first-person narration, but she later admits the limits to her understanding of his life. Thus, Jeeto's perspective cedes to another storytelling entity, one who reveals that during Uncle Avtar's earliest years in the United States, he constantly sought work: "He'd ridden as far as Merced with [a Mexican named Armando] and four other Mexican laborers. Green fields stretched as far as the eye could see on either side of the road going north: alfalfa, beans, cotton plants frosted with white bolls, orange groves sequestered in more sheltered valleys" (89). Again, Backhaus's novel places Asian Indians alongside Mexican migrant workers, demonstrating here how Uncle Avtar completes a collective migratory commute. At the same time, this passage is followed by an indirect thought that cannot fully be attributed to Uncle Avtar: "What had blessed this land, this soil, to make it so bountiful?" (89). To understand how Uncle Avtar can "magically come alive," we can reread this section as an attempt by Jeeto—perhaps the entity behind the third-person narration—to understand what Avtar might have been thinking in this moment, a telepathic move that shifts her into another's frame of mind. Even as this passage illustrates the amazing capability of the land to produce so many crops, it also shows how this fertility so heavily depends on the labor of migrant workers. As Uncle Avtar is reanimated through third-person narration, this active engagement with his past is not simply a celebration but a reminder of the toil engaged in by so many Asian and Mexican immigrants in California's agricultural industries.

If Bulosan's *America Is in the Heart* presents us with the possibility of comparative race labor coalitions, contemporary Asian American writers such as Bhira Backhaus and Brian Ascalon Roley continue to employ the fictional world to contour further the nature of interracial bonds with respect to these economically interwoven social relationships. This subset of Asian American fictions demonstrates the importance of regionalism to the understanding of ethnic literatures, triangulating Asia, Mexico, and the western United States. These works show us how writers employ fictional worlds to engage complex comparative race linkages beyond a white–Asian American binary. Further, these fictional worlds push Asian Americanists to consider the minor characters who appear within the textual landscapes as central to the formation of literary meanings. In this way, even the most canonical of texts can be revisited to produce new interpretive valences. Alex Woloch's typology of minor characters in the nineteenth-century realist novel reveals that these marginal figures perform a vital kind of narrative labor. In their jobs as the narrative's proletariat, they help move the protagonist in a particular direction and act as antagonistic or supportive forces; minor characters are hence understood as "eccentric" or "worker" figures, respectively (25). Woloch further asserts that the emergence of these minor characters appears in concert with the Industrial Revolution in England. In this respect, Woloch clarifies how social contexts inevitably inform and influence certain aesthetic forms and genres. Extrapolating from Woloch's thesis to the realm of California's labor history enables us to consider the widespread appearance of Chicano minor characters in Asian American fictional worlds. On the one hand, these novels call attention to the ways in which California's economic needs consistently pull in a broad range of migrants of varying racial and ethnic backgrounds. On the other, *America Is in the Heart*, *American Son*, and *Under the Lemon Trees* do not offer the possibility of sustained interracial coalitions or relationships.

America Is in the Heart's subtitle, *A Personal History*, is suggestive of its aim: it is a social realist novel that helps to explain why interracial coalitions cannot flourish. Given the power of farmers to control the wages of laborers, any union organizing would have been difficult. People at the highest level within the agricultural industry could also recruit strikebreakers to further undermine interracial solidarity. Backhaus's *Under the Lemon Trees* shows us how mixed-race marriages do not necessarily yield culturally hybrid families. Indeed, Punjabi-Mexican families typically would model domestic cultural life on the father's ancestral lineage, which is almost invariably South Asian. In Roley's *American Son*, minor characters of Mexican descent often appear relegated to service positions, such as laborers, busboys, and cashiers. While such figures remind Gabe of his own racial and class difference, he actively denies his connection to them.

In these three novels, characters of Mexican descent ultimately die, disappear from the narrative quickly, or become expelled due to their status as antagonistic forces. Many of these figures do not even receive full names. Finally, they are subordinated to the development of the Asian American protagonist's identity formation. All three novels also make consistent use of the first-person perspective, in which the narrator's ethnoracial ancestry overlaps with that of the author's. As I explore in the introduction, this connection between authorial descent and narrator often reduces the ways we analyze fictional worlds; they can primarily appear as or be interpreted as veiled autobiographies and autoethnographies. This overlap can further obscure the importance of minor characters to the readings of Asian American fictional worlds by pushing critics to focus on one racial or ethnic group rather than on multiple groups and their relationships to each other.

When Minor Becomes Major

Atomik Aztex intervenes in the potential erasure of the minor character of Mexican descent by repositioning him as the protagonist and the narrator. Though written in part as a speculative fiction,[14] *Atomik Aztex* helps reconfigure Asian American literary California as a site constituted by a multiracial laboring force. *Atomik Aztex* shunts readers between two competing parallel universes; Foster uses italics and bold type at different points in the text to aesthetically represent these colliding realities. In the first, we meet Zenzontli, Keeper of the House of Darkness. He is a leading military figure in an alternate reality in which the "Aztex" defeated the Spanish invaders in 1521, thus creating a different trajectory for modern American and European history. Accordingly, in the novel, the "Aztek" civilization generates much of its power through the sacrifice of human beings, specifically offering up the hearts of the conquered to the cosmos in order to increase the empire's grandeur. As a leader of the empire, Zenzontli suffers from constant headaches and soon hopes to receive surgery in order to relieve him not only of the pain but also of disturbing visions. These visions, though, are the portal into another reality, one in which a similar figure exists who is meant to be read as a double for Zenzontli. This other reality is modeled on our own, in which the narrator, referred to as Zenzón, works in a Farmer John slaughterhouse, where his job involves hog butchering.

As the novel progresses, we discover the various challenges that Zenzón and Zenzontli face in their respective positions. In particular, Zenzón works under a difficult foreman, Max, who seems to want Zenzón fired. Likewise, in the Aztek reality, Zenzontli faces the antagonism of Maxtla, a fellow Aztek warrior and military figure who heads the House of Mist. Maxtla seems to be working to hasten Zenzontli's retirement from his military duties by pushing him to complete dangerous and potentially fatal missions. The novel moves toward its climax when Zenzón is approached by a beautiful woman, Nita, who encourages him to rally the slaughterhouse laborers to support a union-ratification vote. At the same time, Zenzontli begins to realize his own limited power as the Keeper of the House of Darkness, a position that figuratively keeps him in the dark about the Aztek Empire's reliance on barbaric methods for world domination. As the narrative unfolds further, Zenzón and Zenzontli make difficult choices about the power that they each wield. In the case of Zenzón, he agrees to organize the laborers to sign the union contract, despite possible retribution from Max and other higher-ups. In the alternate dimension, Zenzontli appeals to the highest governmental officials to rule the globe in a different way, one that does not depend on human sacrifice and ritual violence. Zenzontli attempts to reform the Aztek economic practices, and he is forced to shift his goals when those same government officials try to kill him. Here the narrative worlds seem to collapse together, as Zenzontli's battle takes him into the world occupied by Zenzón; it is suggested that they might be the same person. By the novel's conclusion, Zenzón has become aware of his Aztek-warrior consciousness, which now inspires him to continue with the mission of advocating for his fellow slaughterhouse workers.

Given the plot and character focus of the novel, a reductive appropriation of Chicano cultural nationalist tropes could present a potential danger for Foster as an Asian American writer. Certainly, critics should confront Foster's motivations and inspirations for representing a Chicano experience, especially because he does not and cannot identify as a Chicano. The author's background discloses some of the intentions behind his aesthetic choices, as he reveals in an interview with poet Eileen Tabios. Foster's upbringing in East Los Angeles during the Vietnam era brought with it a sense of coalitional politics that went beyond his identification as a mixed-race Asian American. Speaking of his prose poetry collection *City Terrace Field Manual* (1996), Foster explains, "*CTFM* has a personal basis," adding, "I have a white Dad and Nisei mom and grew up in a Chicano barrio" (229). He later reveals, "And because I grew up in a Chicano barrio, part of my coming of age was the Chicano movement, reflecting a change in consciousness among the community. The Chicano movement came in part from anti-Vietnam activism" (231).

This personal information clarifies some of the obvious influences on Foster's writing, which has always possessed a strong interracial aesthetic impulse. It would be too cursory, however, to consider Foster's writing process as one marked by disidentification with his Asian American background. Instead, this interview shows how Foster's definition of community could not be tethered to one ethnic or racial group and that his understanding of community also emerged alongside political activism. Accounting for his aesthetic approach to *City Terrace Field Manual*, Foster says that "there is a deliberate blurring of which war is being addressed by some of the poems—whether Vietnam, El Salvador, Nicaragua, urban renewal or community-related wars—because many activists became involved with one war and then another, right on up to the Gulf War" (231). Especially interesting here is the concept of "blurring" that Foster introduces directly into his writings. Despite the awareness of the difference in context and situation for each war, Foster's work takes inspiration from an activist model that forges links between ethnoracial groups and explores interrelated histories. This approach dovetails with the author's negotiation of racial identity, where the continuum between the Asian American experience and the Chicano experience finds productive "blurring" within *Atomik Aztex*, both in its content and in how the represented realities blend into each other. The novel can be read as a cautionary critique of world domination, whether advanced by the Aztek Empire (in one reality) or the American Empire (in the other).

Speculative Futures: The Logic of Aztek Sacrifice

Foster provocatively unmoors himself from an autobiographical narrative perspective by taking up two different viewpoints, which offer competing visions of post–civil rights Aztlán, the legendary location repurposed in part to help galvanize the Chicano activist movement.[15] In the introduction to Alicia Arrizón's reading of Chicana feminist cultural productions, she explains that the "birth of the Chicano nation Aztlán is a continuation of the indigenous past, affirming that the conquest of space does not necessarily lead to the extinction of a people's cultural identity, memory, and vernacular traditions" (25). While articulations of Aztlán have various nuances, the significance does not necessarily lie in a literal reclamation of a physical location but in an oppositional and resistant political stance that could unite Chicano/as.[16] Although initial conceptions of Aztlán were predicated on this political positioning, its practice has been considerably more complicated, especially as this cultural nationalist model has ultimately marginalized in-group particularities.[17] For instance, cultural nationalists overlooked women and queers as figures who might be central to envisioning what this new activist project might be.[18] Influenced by poststructuralist thought, Rafael Pérez-Torres reconsiders the term "Aztlán" by arguing that "Aztlán remains relevant to Chicano discourses because of its status as an empty signifier" (104), allowing it to become "overdetermined" (104) so it can be constantly configured, reconfigured, and redeployed.[19] Aztlán has thus been reformulated as a "traveling culture" whose "identity depends upon its social construction, in which memory and forgetting are as much a part of the history as the myth" (E. Pérez 79). By thinking of Aztlán as a "traveling culture," artists and cultural producers who do not identify as Chicano/a may imagine it within their representational terrains. While this approach entails dangers of ownership and appropriation that perhaps cannot be categorically avoided, the significance of such a cross-racial aesthetic move is important to analyze.

Foster's unique conceptualization of Aztlán illustrates both the productivity and the limitations in representational forms of Chicano cultural nationalism. The novel suggests that the project of imagining Aztlán is ongoing and that its unifying power must be tempered by a continued self-critical and self-conscious stance. It is clear that within the Aztek Empire's alternate timeline, Zenzontli is proud of his cultural and racial heritage: "It's up to us, the Aztex, the Mixteks, the Yanomamo,

Warani, and other indigenous allies of the Mexika to come in & prove to the Nazis that they aren't as tough as they probably like to think!" (62). In this instance, Zenzontli links the Aztex to other indigenous populations resisting the global takeover by the Nazis, who function here as a speculative representation of a group promoting racist ideologies. Zenzontli's idealistic vision of his empire surfaces in his belief that his people are "more completely developed, trained, tempered, hardened, sharpened. We invented the krucial teknological advances of Ritual Offering of the Heart During Human Sacrifice" (65). The emphasis in this passage is not on inherent racial qualities but rather on a process of refinement, a process that is not necessarily inborn. But the bellicose emphasis on the most efficient mode of violence suggests that the Aztek value system requires reform.

Indeed, Foster's satirical tone shows the ridiculousness of denoting one mode of violence as being more civilized than another. Hence the politics of the Aztek Empire come to be fundamentally questioned by Zenzontli as the body count generated by the global conflict continues to rise: "We Aztex also gotta admit we have things to learn from the peoples whose hearts we're cutting out. We have to control our own science, teknology and power when we subjugate primitive kultures and cut their hearts out in the most cost-efficient, legal manner possible. That's all there is to it. I know this is not a popular position" (109–10). The novel imagines how the current socialist vision focuses solely on one functional value of conquered peoples. These spoils of war are treated as sacrificial objects without any consideration of cultural value. Zenzontli reveals how socially and communally accepted methods of warmongering must be tempered by the "minority" (110) viewpoint, the locus of a different and potentially enlightening perspective. Zenzontli's "minority" viewpoint seems to bring up the peril and the promise of individualist thinking within "the New Ekonomic Policy of free market socialism" (110), suggesting that warfare may not be the best way to motivate and to defend the Aztek peoples. The use of first-person narration in the singular is complicated here, as a collective mentality is denoted by the "we." The interplay between the Aztek "we" and "I" thus signals Zenzontli's struggles as he attempts to forge his own path toward political and ethical insight. Zenzontli eventually argues that even the highest-minded and most egalitarian Aztek ideologies must finally be overturned. He later laments that *"they were attending to the economik health of the State & of the entire land & its Many Races of people while they were being fooled, entranced, or confused by their own Existential Stupidity and*

Korruption" (145, italics in original). Zenzontli's individually situated opinions contradict the collective "they," the dominant point of view in his alternate reality. Over the course of the novel, he struggles to retain a perspective that can be distinguished from what he deems to be a politically corrupt oligarchy.

The novel illustrates how the Aztek Empire employs a governance system not unlike one founded on capitalism, colonialism, and racialization. Zenzontli's military duties enrich the coffers of only a select few, revealing a socialist system defined ironically by class differences. While Zenzontli records his "objection to the whole strategy" (19), he nevertheless exposes his own troubling notions of racial and ethnic difference in which the Mayas and the Spanish are described as "people who didn't have the heart(s) to appease the Sun and therefore never had a batshit chance in a hurricane wind of surviving as a kulture" (26). Lamenting the degradation of the empire, he states, "Now everywhere you go you find Kakchikels, Tzotzils, Mams, Pokomams, Kiche, and Kekchi. Even now, there were Spanish slaves among the passersby watching my every move" (26). Rather than the "white man's burden," we have a version of the Aztek man's burden, in which the domestication of supposedly savage and inferior peoples is carried out not by a historically situated world power such as Spain or Britain but rather by this fictitious Aztek Empire. Foster thus exports the violence wrought by capitalism, racism, and colonialism and maps it onto an alternate Aztlán reality. In this way, the novel decenters how race and oppression surface, demonstrating how systematic inequities can be produced and reproduced outside of white supremacy.

Foster's vision of Aztek "sacrifice" deviates from the social context of that culture, in which cosmological grounds legitimated the offering up of bodies to appease the gods. As the historian Alison Futrell explains, the Aztec cosmos was ordered by a god with a large appetite: "Huitzilopochtli demanded continual expansion of the Aztec Empire because of his ever-growing need for the nourishment provided by human sacrifice, the majority of victims being prisoners of war" (172).[20] Human sacrifice was not simply employed to kill people in capriciously violent ways but followed a cultural logic that promoted the continued supremacy of the Aztec Empire. According to the criminologist Christina Jacqueline Johns, in addition to the maintenance of divine balance, sacrifice was "an effective form of state terror that assisted in the intimidation of surrounding Indian groups into accepting a position of political and economic subordination" and "was an important symbolic representation of the centrality and power of the Aztec state, an act which graphically stated the importance of the Aztec empire as a political entity" (95–96). The practice of human sacrifice hence offered the empire a way to publicly address its status and its intent to govern. While Futrell notes that the Aztec Empire did indeed function through a "continual expansion," the translator Michael Richardson, via critiques by Tzvetan Todorov and Georges Bataille, illustrates the key differentiation with respect to the colonial expansion as characterized by the invading Spanish: "For we can see here a very clear distinction between the expansionism of the Aztecs, which was not done for territorial gain but to strengthen the centre and maintain its social cohesion, and the imperialism of Spain, which was a response to the breakdown of social cohesion in a feudal society" (81).[21] Richardson's exegesis of Todorov's and Bataille's writings on the Aztecs advances a separation between conceptions of massacre and sacrifice. The concept of sacrifice highlights rituals involving the subject who must publicly be killed for another, whereas deaths associated with massacre occur when violence is "hidden away" (83). Richardson cites the conquistadors as an example of figures who engaged in massacre, as they moved across the Americas claiming lands, fighting and killing indigenous populations. Such systematic brutality emerges at the edge of the empire, away from the minds and lives of colonial elites in Europe (83).

The refiguration of the Aztek Empire within Foster's novel becomes more compelling with respect to the differences between sacrifice and massacre. The novel suggests that Aztek sacrificial rituals are compromised by the desire for increased profits. If Zenzontli's superior craves more slaves for his stock portfolio, the notion of a socially invested, religiously grounded, and culturally enlightened empire is shown to be an illusion. Zenzontli's various adventures unmask the capitalistic secularism that has become the new Aztek "religion" and places the moralistic economics of the empire, supposedly free-market socialism, in doubt. When the novel opens, Zenzontli possesses a far more optimistic view of his surroundings in the open urban space of Teknochtitlán, relating that "every neighborhood retains an appearance of lively tranquility, thriving pedestrian community interspersed with animals of all types who are our brothers, our nahual spirits, feedstock and pets" (22). And yet the bustling cityscape betrays certain problems, including overcrowding, with "multitudes on raised causeways, jam-packed subways and crowded avenues" (10). Further, the locations where sacrifices take place are revealed to be "immense-pyramids," which are further described as structures that "hovered above the smog" (10). While civilians navigate a dense city, the sacrificial apparatus cannot be seen unless one passes through the polluted atmosphere. When Zenzontli chooses to approach the people in power about changing governmental and military policies concerning sacrifice, he must travel to the top of a pyramid of immense height, a structure removed from the public eye. The lack of transparency concerning these sacrifices accentuates how violence is "hidden away." Zenzontli hopes, *"when **I got to the top**, I'd just speak to whoever was in charge and everything would be all worked out in a jiffy"* (132, italics and bold in original). Foster rarely employs bold type, and its presence signals the irony that Zenzontli's physical movement to the top will result in his downfall. His inquiry into corrupt governance practices is met with derision, and warriors are dispatched to assassinate him. Zenzontli thus confronts the possibility that sacrifice has been transformed into massacre. From the perspective of those who have been conquered, the difference between sacrifice and massacre might seem negligible, but the novel gestures to the ways that Zenzontli seeks to clarify how power, even in its most destructive manifestations, must have a significant purpose and must finally be justified in its brutality.

The critique of cultural nationalism that the novel stages is based on the corporatization of the Aztek Empire, a governmental system that further solidifies its power through an ideology of racial supremacy. The Aztek Empire operates to maximize profits only for a hallowed few and discourages the organization of its workers and its military service members to agitate for rights. This speculative representation of cultural nationalism gone awry seems far from any actual social contexts, but Foster's narrative points to a shift in America's multicultural character. While Chicanos cannot necessarily claim to have transcended the particular burdens that come with being marked and read as racial minorities, they will likely end up, along with Latinos more broadly, achieving a demographic majority within the United States. The timing of Foster's publication dovetails with numerous articles and sources predicting this eventual shift in the US racial makeup. Such population changes bring with them the possibility that Chicanos and Latinos will become a bigger force for social, economic, and legislative reforms. According to the sociologist Rogelio Saenz, "although Latinos represented hardly a blip on the national radar screen only a few decades ago, demographic processes have made Latinos critical to the future social and economic direction of the United States." In book-length studies, Lisa Bedolla and Kim Geron both show the increasing presence and clout of Latinos within the political system. The historian Albert M. Camarillo further explains the centrality of Chicanos and Latinos to the changing demographics of California urban locations, which have become "burgeoning minority-majority cities" (15). The demographers Kenneth M. Johnson and Daniel T. Lichter also reveal the increasingly diffuse population patterns of Hispanics all across the United States, casting an especially attentive eye to the surprising growth "outside traditional gateway states" such as California and Texas (327). And in a sentiment that parallels Foster's cautionary novel, the legal scholar Ian Haney-López writes that "the increasingly nonwhite population brings real pressure to bear on the advantages previously reserved for whites. Observe electoral politics, where the major parties increasingly see their futures bound up in attracting Hispanic votes" ("Race on the 2010 Census" 42). Chicano and Latino population growth, increasing political participation, and cultural dissemination all contribute to an America undergoing a rapid and undeniable transition. To a certain extent, then, it would seem that Foster's novel speculates on the dangers inherent when a particular racial or ethnic group in power, Chicano or otherwise, employs a corporate model to govern. With more power, *Atomik Aztex* reminds us, comes greater responsibility.

Atomik Aztex points us to the malleability of what the political scientist Claire Jean Kim calls a "racial order" (10). In Kim's *Bitter Fruit*, she describes how various racial groups collide with each other on two different axes based on these dyads: superiority/inferiority and insider/foreigner (10). *Atomik Aztex* shows us a speculative reality in which individuals of Mexican descent achieve the highest position in the racial order, making all below them fit for enslavement or massacre. While this alternative reality seems purely conjectural given the current social situation of Chicanos and Latinos,[22] racial orders are constantly in flux, and the novel strikes a cautionary note regarding the standing of minorities as they make gains in legislative, economic, and political arenas. Given the representations of minor characters of Mexican descent in other Asian American fictional productions, Zenzontli offers a case of an individual who continues to agitate for social reforms in spite of the fact that his own ethnoracial group remains in power. This speculative reality also reminds us that a given racial group's dominance requires continued vigilance toward maintaining justice and social equality. Foster's choice to focus narration through this character of Mexican descent widens the so-called Asian American fictional world to include, in this case, the continued importance of activism even in a fantastical realm where the Aztex achieve a tenuous racial supremacy.

The Refracted Self: The Emergent Oppositional Consciousness

As we recall, in *Atomik Aztex*, Zenzontli regards his Aztek culture as one that is unnecessarily violent: "*Blood and skreams of agony lubrikate the steel wheels of progress*" (144). This belief applies to the American Empire as much as it does the Aztek one. The overlay between the graphic and unadorned reality of Zenzón's work at a slaughterhouse with the bloody Aztek Empire is, of course, two variations on constructed "realities" in which bodily subjugation is part and parcel of the quest for world domination. Zenzón's work to help unionize the Farmer John slaughterhouse laborers is not quite the same as Zenzontli's middleman military role as he attempts to challenge the empire's policy concerning the desire for increased human sacrifices, but there are parallels. If the Aztek Empire ultimately seeks to sacrifice its own subjects for capital gains, the figurative parallel in Zenzón's life is the way in which he is constantly put into danger, despite serving a clearly vital function as a worker of the American Empire. How different, then, is ancient sacrifice from capitalism? According to the cultural critic Susan Mizruchi, the two systems can be intimately related: "A capitalist system, like an ancient sacrificial one, tends to justify inequities through structural differences that are made to appear natural. Where a traditional kinship system stresses blood identity, a modern capitalist might stress merit or industry. But both factors are meaningful across contexts" (26–27). In the context of the Aztek Empire, the logic of human sacrifice might seem to preserve the cosmos but instead supports only the select few already in the highest positions of power.

In the context of the slaughterhouse, kinship rather than "industry" or "merit" offers the best path to promotion. The two foremen, Max (Zenzón's rival and primary antagonist) and Bob Handler, for example, possess very different lineages. As Zenzón explains, "Bob could care less about the details of your particular crew assignment or work details, as long as you got the job done without problems. His major concern was not to be made to look like a fool before his superiors, who were, of course, his father and his uncles, the owners" (126). In contrast to Max, who is bogged down by his work as the foreman, Bob "took an active interest learning the operations of the plant. Handler knew that in the long run he'd reap all the benefits of his labor, real or perceived, while Max, well—Max would just remain a foreman for a long, long time" (126). As Zenzón implies, it does not matter how hard Max works; he will always remain below Bob as long as the system operates through nepotism and blood ties rather than meritocratic advancement. Max's career limitations are in part linked to his status as a racial minority and the fact that his class background is similar to Zenzón's.[23] But Max also happens to be the major Chicano character in the novel who avoids any explicit link with union organizing. Given his distaste for Zenzón's growing reputation among the workers, Max is more than an individual antagonist. He symbolizes the Chicano who seeks individual success and achievement without considering the situation of others in his racial community. He is the racial minority who buys into a form of the slaughterhouse's corporate logic, which assumes the myth of liberal individualism. Zenzón must therefore approach any promotions with skepticism and with an eye toward the many others who work alongside him. If, as Mizruchi posits, capitalism proliferates by making inequities appear natural, Zenzón's growing awareness serves to unmask these power differentials and incites him to do something about them. Within the structure of the transnationally connected corporation such as the Farmer John meat company depicted in *Atomik Aztex*, the politics of biopower come into play to regulate the lives of minority workers. The Chicano bodies toil, but without the possibility of significant advancement, and the corporate structure downplays the essential part played by racialized laborers in contrast to the elites who continue to garner promotions due to their connections.

As Zenzón gains more work experience, he details the importance of his developing border subjectivity. He reveals the perils associated with labor migration and the many costs associated with such transnational movements. As he confesses, "I wasn't born working in a slaughterhouse. I crossed deserts to get here. I traversed the mountains of the Rumorosa & the Coast Range, skirting secret borders of forgotten history & identity. I sacrificed the Past, relationships & dreams of community. I tore open blisters & stubbed my toe on rocks. Empires lay in ruins along the way" (40). The tenuous nature of the "crossing" narrative is elucidated as Zenzón realizes how exceptional his own trajectory has been. Zenzón reveals that the numerical odds of even getting the chance to work in the United States were already low; he is only "one of a select few" to have survived the arduous journey (40). The crossing of borders is so dangerous, Zenzón explains, because it is always relationally linked to the violent process of international conquest. He realizes that his migration occurs alongside empires that "lay in ruins," referencing perhaps the many indigenous cultures that have already disappeared. Zenzón also details the physical dangers in border crossing: natural geographical barriers, police surveillance, and human traffickers render undocumented migrants endangered. To add more turmoil to his transnational migration, Zenzón's wife loses her interest in social activism and the arts. Further, his children do not respect his incredibly "lucky" trajectory (40); they instead "disdain" him, despite the hardships he has endured (41). As the graphic descriptions of hog butchery that appear throughout the novel suggest how American Empire relies on the violent destruction and consumption of other living beings, the border subject is also implicated in this process of brutality through self-sacrifice. One recalls the very use of the word "sacrifice" as Zenzón "sacrificed the Past, relationships & dreams of community." For Zenzón, butchery takes on a figurative construct, as he cuts off his attachments to the homeland and communal culture.

Zenzón's vision of sacrifice is significantly impoverished in that it focuses so specifically on a model of biological kinship. His transnational movement across the border is rationalized through a future he imagines will nurture only his most immediate family. This model of sacrifice functions too provincially, as it does not generate an expansive conception of work and labor across the slaughterhouse floor. As such, the novel's parallel realities question the desire to continue to labor under exploitative systems and to what ends this labor is offered up. If Zenzontli's Aztek alternate reality is imperiled by having to assert his individuality within a morally bankrupt political economy, then Zenzón's problem is the opposite. He is too invested in the concept of the personal and the familial. Foster makes this issue clear in the previously mentioned passage of the border crossing, in which the narrator's "I" becomes a litany of the first-person pronouns alongside an action verb: "I crossed," "I traversed," "I negotiated," and so on. The novel generates a sustained critique concerning the logic of sacrifice, as each competing reality explores how the characters negotiate what it means to give of oneself and to give in order to advocate for others. For Zenzontli, the Aztek Empire's desire for more victims denotes a culture of excess, in which the ritualistic killing of conquered people serves only to increase the profit margins of governmental and military elites. This speculative terrain critiques cultural nationalism as a political model that, even in fantastical circumstances, can perpetuate social injustices. Zenzontli must assert his individuality at great risk, the possibility that he may be assassinated for his ideas. This danger finds a distinct contrast in relation to Zenzón's occupation as a slaughterhouse worker. He sacrifices physical safety without linking such toil to the larger systematic exploitation of racial minority laborers. The challenge that Zenzón faces is one in which he must contextualize his own experiences alongside those of others, which will enable him to confront the power differentials that structure a hostile workplace environment.

The novel thus illustrates how the laborer must be open to developing what the Chicana studies scholar Chela Sandoval calls an "oppositional consciousness," a resistant subject position that takes into account the many ways in which oppression functions (1). Foster engages this process specifically through Zenzón's collisions with other realities, in which he confronts other possible futures, other selves, and other collectives, in order to refashion himself into a more politically progressive entity. Foster employs a streamlined first-person narration to advance a more fruitful version of sacrifice, one revealed by the novel's ending. The resolution of *Atomik Aztex* requires Zenzón to acknowledge the alternate reality offered by Zenzontli, and Foster concludes by privileging only one narrative viewpoint. Zenzontli's alternate reality is sacrificed—reminding us that this process can have positive valences—when Zenzón is able to understand the nature of his own physical labor as a slaughterhouse worker. In this way, the novel takes on a more linear trajectory, suggesting the possibility of union coalitions, collectives informed by a Chicano cultural nationalism intent on organizing and activism. Zenzontli's bellicosity as an Aztek warrior and his desire to advocate for his subordinates is not simply excised from the narrative; rather, his character informs Zenzón's new spirit of resistance.

If much of the first half of *Atomik Aztex* depicts the empty sacrifices offered by both the Aztek Empire and by Zenzón as an individual, the novel later moves toward a reconciliation of the individual and the collective. I accordingly shift my analysis to those passages that suggest the emergence of another self, a figure who begins to appear in reflective surfaces early on in the novel but whose importance to Zenzón only becomes clear as he develops a more nuanced race and class consciousness. In these moments, Foster includes flashes of images and objects suggestive of alternative realities and alternative subject positions that push Zenzón to see that his life means more than his individual sacrifice for his family. That is, he is part of a larger community of racial minorities who have been struggling collectively to make ends meet and to achieve better futures. Whenever Zenzón sees his image refracted in windows or on shiny exterior surfaces, these moments visually multiply his presence, showing us that he must be read from many metaphorical angles and that he himself must be willing to take on new responsibilities and acknowledge his complicated subject position. He is at once an overworked slaughterhouse laborer, a father and husband, an undocumented migrant, a border crosser, an activist organizer creating coalitions to create better working conditions, and a kind of warrior struggling for social justice.

Zenzón's growing awareness of social inequalities in the workplace coincides with new observations concerning his position alongside his rivals. For instance, Zenzón must contend with Max's seemingly irrational attempts to get him fired. As the two antagonize each other, the novel suggests how difficult it can be to define who the enemy actually is. In a sequence of visual collisions, Zenzón first observes, "Max glared at me from the other side of the frosted glass, malevolent eyes widening darkly as I brought my face to within an inch or two of my side of it. For a heartbeat, my face reflected over his like a photographic double exposure. Then his face vanished from the little window" (86). Again, Zenzón must attempt to acknowledge his complex relation to labor. If Zenzón can be mistaken for Max, the very person who reacts so negatively to his presence, he must take care not to replicate Max's cutthroat attitude and naively believe that only a hard work ethic might lead him to rise in the company. Zenzón's charisma eventually leads him to become a significant figure within the factory workforce, and Max's dislike of Zenzón may have its source in Zenzón's capacity to make constructive associations with others. Furthermore, Max cannot see beyond his duties as the slaughterhouse foreman. As a result, an individual such as Bob Handler, gifted with the appropriate lineage and education, will rise to a higher place within the company despite the hours and efforts Max might put into his work. Zenzón must confront the potential enemy within himself, these "double exposures" suggest, to give up or, more pointedly, to sacrifice an upward mobility predicated only on his own advancement.

As Zenzón seeks to avoid becoming someone like Max while developing his oppositional consciousness, he also faces up to the dangers of hog butchering. In this case, the more explicit connection between butchery and sacrifice surfaces as he finds himself once again confused: "I figured it was just some mistake on my part, just some trick of the light as I pushed one of the tubs back into line with a bang against the wall, the bad fluorescent lighting on a pool of bloody water rippling in the stainless steel tub full of intestinal tubing and meat scraps. I went and got the signatures of the warehouse workers" (86). Like previous instances of optic disorientation, this one forces Zenzón to think of his physical labor in relation to its political ramifications. Only after seeing something disturbing in the meat-processing vats does he go to get the necessary signatures for the union-ratification vote. He later muses about what he has seen inside the "stainless steel tub": "*It can't be. It looked like a face, a human face—eyeless mask of a skinned face floating underwater, terrible white bloodless skin wrinkled by the pink bloody water as the water moved, but it had to have been a pig's head, maybe a small pig's head*" (87, italics in original). As Zenzón must remain alert to the power he wields as a union organizer, there is always the suggestion of imminent danger, registering on multiple levels. First, Zenzón's sacrifices metaphorically return here, where the "pig's head" recalls his own position as the unacknowledged and invisible slaughterhouse worker. His daily toils go unnoticed once the meat products are shipped out and digested by customers. Zenzón's resistance to identifying the "pig's head" as human reveals the difficult process of seeing himself and his fellow workers from a new viewpoint. It is not just "a trick of light," as Zenzón first believes, but rather that their lives as workers remain submerged and "underwater." The turbid reflection emphasizes the material perils of working on the kill floor, in which the possibility of severed limbs and other such accidents looms. The association being compounded is one in which the laborer's body is always figuratively and literally on the chopping block. Finally, this scene speaks to the jeopardy Zenzón faces simply because he is one of the leaders of this union-organizing movement, who will no doubt be subject to intense corporate scrutiny and possible retaliation.

As Zenzón begins to observe himself from multiple perspectives, other characters help push him to widen his lenses even further. Nita Yahui, for instance, gets Zenzón to think coalitionally. While the novel stresses Zenzón's charisma and ability to rally his fellow workers, only through Nita's involvement do we understand Zenzón's commitment to the cause. As a result, Foster's vision of political progressivism is invigorated, in large part, by major female figures and thus diverges from the initial conceptions of cultural nationalism marked by a heterosexist, masculinist ethos. Following Nita's exhortations, Zenzón grapples with the larger stakes in organizing his fellow workers into a union: "How were we to know that they hired illegal Mexikans by the truckload to run the meat processing & packing industry for the entire city, the entire southland region? The whole ekonomy was built upon the backs of our people, so-called illegals. Lucky for us" (75). Zenzón's identification of the relationship between Mexicans and the Los Angeles economy's reliance on immigrant labor affirms the development of his political views. His sarcasm, seen in the phrase "so-called illegals," draws out how the undocumented migrant's labor power is desired, while his ability to claim America as home is denied. He also indirectly references how parts of California were once geographically part of Mexican territory, thus raising questions about the nature of legality and land ownership for contemporary Chicanos.[24] Zenzón further observes the concentration of Mexicans in labor industries, enabling union organizing. Here Zenzón's work is placed in conversation with a larger group of toiling subjects. The phrase "backs of our people" shows how Zenzón's sacrifice comes through his willingness to expose a collective injustice rather than a singular one. This communal awareness is further emphasized by a brief change in the narrative mode. While much of Zenzón's observations are rendered through the narratorial "I," the passage shows how he shifts to the plural "we," evidencing a developing minority and activist consciousness absent from earlier sections of the novel. The structural inequalities that characterize the slaughterhouse are delineated by the phrase "they hired," implying a collective movement to subjugate the "we" and the "us" that embodies the labor required to generate income for the company.

The novel concludes with a guarded hope for a new future stemming from an acknowledgment of collective class solidarity, one that is spurred by, of course, the critical support of Nita. At the same time, Zenzón's position within the slaughterhouse is made tenuous in a number of ways. For instance, he is put under investigation and is unjustly interrogated by the local police department after Max, who had been harassing Zenzón, disappears. This unexpected development coincides with the emergence of another power structure employed to monitor laboring bodies. In the absence of the foreman, Zenzón is elevated to this position, which grants him more power but also more responsibility to act judiciously to his fellow workers. Zenzón remarks, "Sometimes you could glance in the mirror surprised to find out you got a brand new look, your face might be re-arranged, not always for the better since stitches stick out like hog's whiskers & confused looks flit nervously across a bruised & blackened, squinting face; other times you look in the mirror in the cramped restroom at the end of the hall and see nothing but smoke" (200). This passage reminds us that Zenzón must continually be mindful that he and other workers can still be placed in dangerous situations, with their bodies "bruised & blackened" and their lives likened to that of animals about to be slaughtered. Cognizant of other perspectives and other future trajectories, Zenzón embraces a cautionary reorientation toward labor politics to advocate for fair wages and safety regulations.

Atomik Aztex does not obviously foreground an Asian American protagonist and experience but primarily considers issues of racial formation and social inequality through Chicano cultural nationalist tropes. The use of a Chicano narrative voice also calls attention to the connection between Foster's fictional world and California's (and the nation's) social contexts, in that Zenzón's struggles parallel those faced by Los Angeles immigrants of similar ethnoracial backgrounds. But the novel does not offer us only historical or ethnographic information. The novel continually uses a refractive aesthetic technique that appears in the collision between the Aztek Empire geotemporality and the temporality of the Farmer John slaughterhouse episodes. As Zenzón's reality appears slightly out of focus, he, toiling in a world much like our own, finds both inspiration and cautionary messages from parallel universes. Class consciousness and oppositional politics finally merge to generate a sustained resistance to the seemingly all-consuming forces of global capitalism. In these localized sites of activism, Foster's *Atomik Aztex* places its modest hopes. Recalling Foster's interviews, we see how an attentive eye to Chicano culture and contexts does not derive from a desire to appropriate without cause. Indeed, Foster's goals align with the very ideals of a comparative race aesthetic, as he employs the fictional world to depict how the struggles faced by people of Mexican descent in the United States can be placed into conversation with other minority groups. *Atomik Aztex* refocuses the fictional world by constituting the minor Mexican figure as the central storyteller and thus helps illuminate the multiracial nature of California's labor history.

Yellow Chicanismo

As I advanced in the introduction, the marketplace impulse, along with the rise of autoethnographic fiction, can encourage audiences to conflate the authorial ancestry with narrative perspective. At the same time, the emergence of the so-called postracial aesthetic suggests that Asian American writers might be free to present stories completely unrelated to their own ethnic and racial ancestries. Foster is a writer who demonstrates a kind of middle way between the bind of authenticity and the apolitical freedoms of the postracial aesthetic. Presenting his story through a first-person narrator from a minority background other than his own allows Foster to challenge any potential expectation or desire that he should write from a position that strongly mirrors his own ethnoracial descent. Without the author being explicitly tied to the storyteller, the novel still speaks to issues of social inequality, especially in its depiction of the Chicano racial minority agitating for social reforms. At the same time, Zenzón as a narrator is occasionally attuned to a variety of ethnic and racial minority contexts. While Zenzón looks to parallel universes to inspire the development of his own warrior consciousness, these other alternate realities are a useful metaphor for the ways in which he must continue to think comparatively. That is, he must not only imagine how a path to an activist orientation imbues him with a strong fighting spirit, but he must also consider how that path intersects with other life experiences that do not necessarily or only involve other Chicanos. As I will show in this section, his growing interracial consciousness reveals his knowledge of the exploitation of Asian women within the workplace, the injustice of Japanese American internment, and the vitality of Chinatown ethnic enclaves. The novel therefore illuminates another level of racial asymmetry with respect to the narrational perspective. Zenzón's storytelling demands to be read from this expansive framework, in which other racial groups and contexts, despite a more marginal status within narrative plotting, attain greater significance. I now shift my discussion to the ways in which the novel includes references to Asian American and Asian bodies, lives, and cultural signifiers and offers up an explicit comparative race aesthetic.

One of Zenzón's first descriptions of the kill floor of the Farmer John slaughterhouse implies a multiracial cast of workers. He explains that the "USDA inspectors came thru checking the line once in a while, four signs on the wall say, 'this department has worked 154 days without lost time. avoid accidents on the job. safety begins here' in English, Spanish, Chiu Chow & Vietnamese" (6). The reference to the USDA inspectors calls attention to the particularly dangerous working conditions faced by laborers. The journalist Eric Schlosser considers meatpacking "the most dangerous job in the United States. The injury rate in a slaughterhouse is about three times higher than the rate in a typical American factory. Every year about one out of three meatpacking workers . . . suffer[s] an injury or a work-related illness that requires medical attention beyond first aid." Schlosser adds that it is very likely that injuries sustained while on the job are underreported (172). While the novel's revelation that there have been "154 days without lost time" suggests the slaughterhouse's admirable adherence to a protocol that protects the health of its workers, the underbelly of the industry surfaces when we see the constant stress and fatigue Zenzón experiences. The reference to safety within the meatpacking plant paints a façade over the constant hazards and diverts attention away from improvements that still need to be made.

The novel helps illuminate a particular social context that reminds us that only certain populations would be responsive or attracted to the meatpacking industry.²⁵ Novels such as Upton Sinclair's *The Jungle* (1906) reveal that at the turn of the century, slaughterhouse work often involved Eastern European immigrants. The following decades saw the meatpacking industry rely increasingly on African American workers. But the industry underwent a seismic shift after World War II as unions lost bargaining power and wages dropped dramatically.²⁶ To combat this shift in labor supply, the Chicano studies scholar Dennis Nodín Valdés explains that "employers found replacements principally among Mexicans, along with smaller numbers of other Latino and Asian workers, whom they initially lured to the small towns on the prairies and plains through employment agents and contractors in larger Texas cities and in communities along the United States–Mexican border" (230).²⁷ Valdés unveils the current asymmetrical nature of the meatpacking industry, which now hinges primarily on Mexican, Latino, and Asian immigrant labor as other ethnic laboring communities gradually left the slaughterhouses and animal pens for better opportunities and occupational tracks.²⁸ While Valdés situates his study in the Midwest, his findings are broadly applicable to the Southern California region, which attracts similar minority populations.²⁹ As I wrote earlier in the chapter, numerous labor historians and sociologists show how the United States—and California in particular—rely on specific immigrant populations to staff the various unskilled labor positions in a range of industries, from garment construction to meatpacking.³⁰ In connection to these studies, *Atomik Aztex* refracts both Asian and Latino migrants into the fictional world as the major laboring pools that toil within the slaughterhouse. Because there are no characters in the novel who seem to be conversant with the languages and dialects of Teochew and Vietnamese as referred to on the many signs posted on the wall, this brief reference to Asian immigrants plays a major role in indirectly elucidating the presence of a multiracial and multiethnic group of workers. Thus, the plight of the immigrant laborer extends beyond one ethnoracial context, a fact that Zenzón increasingly understands.

As the novel concludes, there is a clear shift in the way that Zenzón observes the slaughterhouse. In particular, he takes note of other raced bodies that are present, making more legible those who would speak the languages found on the signs and warnings posted on the walls: "*Between you & me, they didn't have to notify **me** safety begins **here** by the door the Chinese & Vietnamese women go in & out of, Safety is practically* *my middle name, I know there's dangerous machinery in operation at all times caution is advised, it's a big plant with several tall buildings sporting steaming towers in the industrial nite*" (196, italics and bold in original).[31] Whereas the Chinese and Vietnamese women do not directly participate in the union-ratification vote as represented through the novel's explicit plotting, the "secret armies of the night who make" the "city run" (197) are a multiracial and multiethnic coalition of many different industries and occupational positions. Recall that the Chinese and Vietnamese women are not even named in the novel's opening sequence but are only implicitly referenced through foreign languages found on warning signs. Here, Zenzón addresses the impact of their actual and tangible presence. The emphasis on these toiling bodies highlights the understanding that he must support an environment that protects the safety of the laborers on multiple fronts. There are, of course, the day-to-day dangers of working directly on the kill floor, but the panoramic viewpoint advanced in the passage implies that larger and more ambitious organizational plans are necessary so that unions can advocate for higher wages and better health-insurance plans. Again, this passage is important not only for its content but for its key shift in narrative mode. Whereas Zenzón begins his statement in first-person-singular narration, he later widens this perspective, as in the line "we pull the graveyard shift." This moment demonstrates a subtle but nonetheless important instance when his literary subjectivity courageously speaks for other individuals, including those of Asian descent. Of course, we can briefly link this moment back to the larger project that Foster engages through the construction of the Chicano storyteller, an aesthetic choice that recasts an appropriative act as one that perhaps might be considered admirable rather than culturally exploitative.

In another instance of the intersections between Chicano and Asian American populations, Zenzón travels through Los Angeles's Chinatown district on his commute home. Zenzón underscores his sensitivity to the complexity of the ethnic and racial urban geography by pointing out specific locations within the enclave: "Chung Mee's was closed as I went up Alpine Street (they told me the card games in the back went on till morning, I don't know, I can't play Chinese poker), but the lights were still on. In front of the open door, a guy in a white apron swept the sidewalk as I went by and I caught a whiff of rice porridge that roused a sharp hunger" (29). As with other references to different cultural and racial contexts within the novel, the question can be posed: why include what seems to be such arbitrary information? How might the novel change without this passage? On its own, the excerpt shows Zenzón's acknowledgment of other ethnic and racial urban communities. While he "can't play Chinese poker," he has been told about the card games that go on and is cognizant of other cultural and ethnic registers within the city. This understanding is juxtaposed against the figure of a man, presumably Chinese, sweeping, and thus we are always reminded of Asian immigrant labor. Chinatown is central to Zenzón's observations, as it is a location that exudes "fresh air" (29), a welcome atmosphere after the long hours of hog butchery. The hunger that arises literally from a Chinatown dish reveals Zenzón's openness to incorporate other ethnoracial cultures and contexts into his life. This passage thus disrupts the ethnoracial hermeticism that has often been associated with the most conservative forms of cultural nationalism. This moment again reflects how Zenzón's interracial and interethnic awareness must extend outside the factory space.

While Foster's part-Japanese heritage does not seem to inspire or influence much of what appears in the novel, there are glimpses into this other ethnoracial context. In one scene, Nita Yahui and Zenzón are sitting in a cafe when he is struck by a series of strange thoughts about California: "Celebrities like Bugsy Siegel called it home, thanks to friends in the mayor's office. Japs had been carted off to concentration camps out in the desert, which was too bad, cuz I could have used some raw fish and tofu right about that time, wasabi horse radish on my sashimi, tempura and curry over rice, chop chop" (70). The rather flippant attitude toward the internment of Japanese Americans appears in the context of the collision between the two realities that Zenzón and Zenzontli are each navigating. At this point, it seems as if Zenzón observes the Southern California area through Zenzontli's eyes, thinking that, rather than a home, it is "some 3rd-class city called Los Angeles, something to the north. Kalifornia or some fucking thing, Western civilization, the New World, they called it" (70). In other words, Zenzón, who has considered Chavez Ravine his home for quite some time, would not think of Los Angeles as a city "to the north" unless he was accessing the Aztek alternate reality in which Los Angeles would be north of Tenochtitlan. Further still, Zenzón misspells "California," calling attention to this alteration in mind-set. As Zenzontli's consciousness asserts itself in Zenzón's psyche, critiques of this passage must shift to consider this change. One might rationalize Zenzón's response as conditioned by Zenzontli's disillusionment over the Aztek Empire, where the Japanese American internment would perhaps not register so starkly (perhaps the event never even happened), except in relation to the loss of food options. Zenzón's tone satirically amplifies and affirms the injustice of that event, in which the reduction in culinary diversity is the very least of the issues that one might want to protest against. It is important that these two passages occur in the context of his meeting with Nita to discuss the possibility of generating a union-ratification vote. The oppressions that laborers endure in relation to long hours on the killing floor amid deplorable working conditions must be linked relationally to the injustices faced by other minority groups. In this case, the fact that Japanese Americans languish in "concentration camps out in the desert" reminds us of the ways that the slaughterhouse workers also find themselves in inhospitable conditions. Certainly, these situations are not the same, but Zenzontli's presence allows Zenzón to think historically and comparatively, enabling him to consider how American minority populations find themselves at the mercy of larger structural systems and social institutions.

Speculative Hybridities

Zenzón's reality demonstrates that Asian Americans are still important to the narrative, despite their status as minor figures who do not merit specific names. These Asian American presences invoke the multiracial nature of California's labor history. Despite the more chimerical aspects of Zenzontli's alternate world, his observations and experiences are also still central to the novel's comparative race aesthetic. Earlier in the chapter I spoke of speculative fiction as a genre offering Foster the imaginary terrain on which to explore how social inequalities might be produced outside of white-supremacist societies. Zenzontli's reality shows us a fantastical Aztlán with an economic system reliant on the indiscriminate massacre of those who have been conquered. Thus, Foster's depiction of that world outlines a malleability in racial orders that requires anyone in power to be constantly vigilant of systematic inequity.

In an earlier conception of the Japanese American internment, Zenzón, thinking from the perspective of Zenzontli, remarks that the tragedy of this event can be explained most vulgarly in terms of the loss of culinary options. At a later point, Zenzontli reflects on what might occur in other realities:

> Worlds collide, *The Day When Time Stood Still*, war leaders say somebody must die, notice to all persons of japanese ancestry, somebody attacked, fuck it, civil rights are suspended, cities on fire,

National Guard tracers fired from machine guns into buildings in Watts, you might want to live some kind of quiet life working at a slaughterhouse in Los Angeles, go home to sleep in your stucco bungalow in El Sereno in East L.A., you might suddenly find out something completely different. (116)

By changing the title of the film *The Day the Earth Stood Still* to *The Day When Time Stood Still*, Foster again emphasizes temporality and alternate realities to reveal how the narrative juxtaposes the Chicano storyteller alongside other ethnoracial contexts. The plot from *The Day the Earth Stood Still* clearly advances the novel's comparative race aesthetic. One of the central events from the original 1951 film involves an alien visitor who travels to Earth, instructing its citizens to live peacefully, or else the aliens will destroy the planet with atomic weapons. The film's release date suggests an oblique reference to Hiroshima and Nagasaki. In a similarly roundabout manner, the Japanese American internment is referenced only through the phrase "notice to all persons of japanese ancestry," which, if taken literally, cannot be fully understood because it does not provide any explanatory references. This phrase calls attention to fliers alerting Japanese Americans that they would be evacuated and sent to assembly centers just prior to internment. The passage implies that the Japanese American internment and the atomic bombings can also be placed in relation to other problematic historical occurrences, such as the 1965 race riots. The concatenation of these various events does not equate them but rather explains why US minority subjects might seek to alienate themselves from history, if only to exist in a state of blissful ignorance. Such violent circumstances allow Zenzontli to understand the desire to stay insulated within a "stucco bungalow," seemingly safe in his apolitical isolation. We recall that the film's retitling—in which time "stood still"—refers to a kind of respite from having to confront the nature of systemic social inequalities wrought over the historical continuum.

Zenzontli's decisions to challenge the Aztek economic and bureaucratic system increasingly come with more complex understandings of the multiple realities that he knows do exist. He continues to contemplate the various ways that Mexican and Asian lives are intertwined, suggesting how such individuals become targets for exploitation. For instance, he discusses the ways in which capitalism might exert pressure on the body as a literal site of commodification in some imagined future: "Maybe they will invent organ transplants so people can get vital organs from prisoners executed in places like China & Indonesia or imported from some dude driving up to a shed on a ranchito outside of Juarez to deliver an ice chest duct-taped closed for the exchange, all this for probably like the equivalent in today's money of $150" (115). The magical realist character of *Atomik Aztex* appears most prominently in these moments, as Zenzontli's ruminations expose the injustices of actual social contexts. In this passage, China, Indonesia, and Mexico can be plundered for black-market organ donations in some "future" time period, but a number of scholars have revealed actual circumstances in which illegal organ harvesting and trade proliferate.[32] Nancy Scheper-Hughes, in particular, clarifies the economic gradient that often pits elites against individuals desperate enough to sell their organs to the highest bidder (65).[33] Jean and John L. Comaroff further argue that the black-market organ-donation trade might be called an occult economy, in which richer nations "[siphon] off the essence of poorer 'others' by mysterious means for nefarious ends. All of which gives evidence, to those at the nether end of the global distribution of wealth, of the workings of insidious forces, of potent magical technologies and modes of accumulation" (312). If one is to think about the possibility of the "occult" economy based on resource inequality, *Atomik Aztex* outlines the racial character of this international market. The bodies that populate the slaughterhouse, primarily those of Latino and Asian descent, are implicated on the transnational level; they come from the geographical locations in which organ harvesting tends to occur with more frequency. On a more symbolic level, references to organ harvesting from a location such as China, Indonesia, or Mexico can be pushed further into the context of meatpacking. Although no human organs are literally being harvested, the workers in the Farmer John facility do face a kind of harvesting of their labor, as they fuel the enormous demands of a multinational corporation. Of course, this occult economy reflects the nature of the commodity fetish, as various meat products magically appear in supermarkets and grocery stores all across the world, without explicitly revealing the labor that went into the making of such items.

Zenzontli's ability to simultaneously perceive the fantastic and the awful points us to the most insidious features of a global economy that can unfairly take advantage of particular racial Others. The proliferation of the "occult" economy as depicted by *Atomik Aztex* constellates Latino and Asian signifiers, such that, as Zenzontli tells us, "Tokyo could be destroyed by UFOs, chupacabras, Godzilla, a craving for ramen noodles. Anything could be possible in the future" (116). Foster's inclusion of both

Godzilla and chupacabras reinforces a comparative race aesthetic that points to the collective fragility of the global economy. Latino and Asian "monsters" serve as spectacular myths that cover over or distract individuals away from social inequalities wrought by transnational capitalism. As these powerful and otherworldly beings wreak havoc on what the urban studies scholar Saskia Sassen has called the "global city" (1), the impossibility and ludicrousness of the scenario threatens to overpower the importance of what these figures symbolize. The Mexican economic crises that followed the presidency of Carlos Salinas de Gortari and the ratification of NAFTA coincided with a rise in chupacabra sightings, as many farm animals were found dead at the time (Gallo 18). In an exploration of folktales and bloodsucking organisms, the literary critic James Tobias provides a reading of the chupacabra, placing it within a global economic context. Influenced by the work of Guillermo Gomez-Peña, Tobias explains, "the absurd aspect of the chupacabras might perform as folkloric ridicule of the advanced technologies of extraction that were supposed to inject new life into the Mexican economy, especially near the northern border, which has only grown more polluted and dangerous with the economies of 'free' trade" (167).[34] Tobias's assertions clarify how American Empire, global economies, and occult phenomena such as the chupacabra can be combined together into a murky, fantastic form that attempts, however strange or otherworldly, to account for scarcity and destruction. Likewise, critical considerations of Godzilla have explored not only the monster's birth from atomic energy but also the economic valences of his existence. In the context of the challenges Japan faced after World War II, Godzilla comes to embody the fear of yet another national collapse, but not necessarily coming from within (Kalat 162). Indeed, Godzilla's birth from atomic energy commonly underscores his metaphorical relationship to American deployment of weapons of mass destruction, the human cost and the economic ramifications of another catastrophic nuclear event. In the social contexts indirectly invoked by each "monster," the perils of America's global economic power appear in various forms, whether in military conflicts or in transnational trade agreements. As Godzilla or the chupacabras descend on Tokyo and Mexico City, respectively, these racialized fiends symbolize the monstrosity of a voracious global capitalist appetite.

While Zenzontli muses on organ harvesting and mythical beings, there are also other speculations to consider, especially concerning his own ethnoracial identity. Prior to Zenzontli's confrontation with his Aztek superiors, Maxtla states, "Look Zenzontli, forget about breakfast.

You are a Party member, full-fledged Aztek warrior (tho there's some rumor about Japanese infiltration of your bloodlines someplace, it's none of my business, I don't care, as long as you don't sit by me at official functions or anywhere we might be seen together in public), all I wanna say is you're a good guy" (88). While the conception of *mestizaje* has typically involved the mixing between Europeans and American Indians, this passage presents the interesting possibility that Zenzontli might possess some Japanese heritage.[35] Though we cannot know for sure, this information nevertheless raises questions about who might be able to claim Aztlán. Maxtla's own position suggests the limits of a Chicano cultural nationalism promoting ethnoracial purity, as he will not "sit" or "be seen" with Zenzontli in public. At the same time, Zenzontli's rumored Asiatic heritage does grant a small space for thinking of Aztlán beyond the racial framework offered by the typical figuration of *mestizaje*. The literary critic Daniel Cooper Alarcón reminds us that "we should also ask who is being excluded when Chicanos stake a claim to the Southwest based on Aztlán, whether that claim is legitimated through myth, history, or genealogy. Obviously Native Americans must be included in these debates, as must the Asian Americans and African Americans living in the region" (30). According to the cultural geographer Patricia L. Price, "Most Native Americans in the Southwest did not consider themselves to be modern-day Aztecs, Chicanos, or Mexican Americans. Discussion did not even begin to mention Asian Americans and African Americans, who could also potentially assert historical claims to the region" (74). In introducing Alarcón's and Price's viewpoints, I do not look to undermine the point of Chicano claims to Aztlán but rather to consider how Foster's novel opens up Aztlán to a wider framework in which multiple racial identities might take part in the construction and the deployment of the borderlands.

If Zenzontli's potentially mixed-race background presents problems for any interracial coalition within the Aztek reality, we also see how hybridity can unfortunately be advanced for the sake of warmongering. In the battle scene that takes place on the Aztek sacrificial pyramids, one of Zenzontli's adversaries is described as "a tall skinny kid with all sorts of Asian tattoos like a Yakuza" that include "dragons fulminating in Hiroshige klouds on both shoulderblades, Zapotek calaveras with horns grinning down his arms," and a "Virgin of Guadalupe emblazoned with skroll ('Brown Pride') on his stomach" (147–48). The inclusion of Japanese signifiers (such as the references to the Japanese ukiyo-e artist Utagawa Hiroshige, as well as the Japanese crime syndicate Yakuza, alongside a clear invocation of Chicano nationalism as evidenced by the phrase "Brown Pride") serves again to disrupt any unitary understanding of Aztlán. Even people within the empire boasting significant military positions take on and perhaps even identify with different racial backgrounds, ones not traditionally associated with conceptions of the *mestizaje*. In this respect, Foster's novel consistently defines an Aztlán that binds together Chicano and Asian cultural elements, such that even the phrase "Brown Pride" fails to fully encapsulate the warrior's description. Zenzontli's later description of him as the "Yakuza Vato" perfectly fits the multiracial rendering of Aztlán in the Aztek reality. While the Yakuza Vato challenges the purist standpoint offered by Maxtla regarding the bloodlines of Aztek warriors, this hybridity is deployed in a violent way. The Yakuza Vato illustrates an example of Chicano–Asian American mestizo that opposes the egalitarian politic that Zenzontli seeks to uphold within the Aztek Empire. Thinking back to Bhira Backhaus's *Under the Lemon Trees*, we recall that Chicano-Asian interracial unions did not necessarily yield culturally hybrid households, nor did marriages lead to sustained interracial bonds between Punjabi and Mexican immigrant workers. Indeed, one of the Punjabi-Mexican characters, Anna, even ends up dying in childbirth, perhaps a tragic symbol of the challenges facing mixed-race individuals in the early twentieth century. We should read *Atomik Aztex* in a similar way, in the sense that mixed-race characters do not necessarily act as evidence of a harmonious multiracial future. Instead, as Zenzón discovers at the novel's conclusion, much work still must be done to rally the workers together and to solidify the multiracial union.

The Racial Asymmetries of Asian American Literary California

As this chapter highlights, a number of Asian American fiction writers represent a multiethnic and multiracial cast that speaks to the heterogeneous populations that have historically been drawn to and have resided within California. My readings of these fictions attend to an interracial and interethnic axis that has not yet been fully considered—that of Chicano and Asian American coalitions. Given California's proximity to both Asia and Mexico, it is not surprising to see the influence of these two "borders" on fictional worlds. While novels such as Brian Ascalon Roley's *American Son* and Carlos Bulosan's *America Is in the Heart* include representations that allude to the multiracial nature of California's laboring history, *Atomik Aztex* recenters characters of

Mexican descent, moving them from status as minor figures and making them major players in the narrative, with one even functioning as our narrator and hero.

As narrators, Zenzón and Zenzontli grant us a space to consider the aesthetics of Chicano representation and cultural production. The novel revises cultural nationalism such that Chicano characters must reconfigure their own position with respect to class politics and, further, to their relationship to a multiethnic and multiracial cast of slaughterhouse workers. There is always peril in appropriating cultural, racial, and ethnic contexts with which an individual cannot claim to identify. Yet Foster risks such danger to advance a nuanced construction of Chicano narrators who expose the sacrificial economy and social inequalities produced out of transnational capitalism, in which racialized bodies toil for endless hours. While the novel often concentrates on issues related to Chicano culture and contexts, the work must also be mined for its racial asymmetries, as the narrative continually advances a comparative race aesthetic focused on minority union activism. The slaughterhouse laborers, whether Chicano or Asian, suffer from similarly dangerous conditions and collectively experience a kind of capitalistic erasure, as the products they create are shipped out and conveniently consumed at dinner tables all across the country and the globe. Foster's novel foregrounds how slaughterhouse workers figuratively butcher themselves—and perhaps even literally in the case of workplace accidents—to find whatever place they can to survive in California's economic structure.

3 / The Incomplete Biography
in the Post–Civil Rights Era: Narrating
Imagined Lives in Sigrid Nunez's Fictions

In this chapter, I take a slightly different direction from those that appeared earlier by focusing on one writer, Sigrid Nunez, and her deployment of biographical representation. Nunez undermines any expectations that might arise, for example, due to marketplace pressures or from the increased recognition of the ethnoracial bildungsroman, in relation to the narrative perspectives she employs in her novels. In this case, her storytellers do not always match up with her own multiracial ancestral background. Even as such aesthetic choices suggest that a writer is free from the bonds of rehearsing a kind of ethnoracial authenticity, her fictional worlds still reveal the pervasive and systemic nature of social inequality and oppression.

Chapters 1 and 2 focus on Asian American writers who also represent their fictional worlds through characters of ethnoracial backgrounds that differ from their own, but in contexts that respectively address issues such as white liberal individualism and comparative minority labor politics. Chapter 1 reads Chang-rae Lee's *Aloft* and complicates the rubric of Asian American literature in its conception of a white protagonist and narrator, Jerry Battle. While he shows sensitivity toward racial difference, Jerry also subtly disavows the nature of oppression experienced by minorities in his rendering of an affluent but nevertheless segregated New York suburb. The novel further emphasizes the distance between author and narrative perspective, as Lee's narrator is Caucasian, thus pushing critics to consider the aesthetic construction of whiteness and how it becomes used to negotiate deviations from racial norms. Chapter

2 analyzes Sesshu Foster's *Atomik Aztex*, a novel that highlights the asymmetrical but interconnected histories of labor, class, and racialization faced by individuals of Mexican and Asian descent in California. Like Lee, Foster complicates any autobiographically inflected reading of the narrative perspective, as *Atomik Aztex* is told from the first-person viewpoint of a Chicano character. In this case, the storyteller's ethnoracial background directs cultural critics to explore the struggles of Chicano workers in the context of hog butchery. As the progression of these two chapters indicates, the rough trajectory of *Racial Asymmetries* deviates from the more traditional concerns of Asian American studies as posited through themes such as racial exclusion to other social issues such as comparative minority racial formation.

I now concentrate on groups that have posed other interpretive challenges for critics and scholars. This chapter and the next, for instance, concern the work of mixed-race Asian American writers and consider how their publications can be read through their racial asymmetries. In the introduction, I mentioned the career of Diana Chang, one of the best-known writers to emerge prior to Maxine Hong Kingston; she offers one example of the complications that arise when classifying and analyzing the work of mixed-race Asian American writers. In a foundational bibliography on Asian American literature first published in the spring of 1985, the literary critic Amy Ling lists only Chang's first novel, *The Frontiers of Love* (1956).[1] This work most strongly adheres to an autobiographical narrative, in the sense that Chang's biracial background could be reflected in some of the main characters and narrative situations. The bibliography, however, overlooks Chang's many other novels, such as *A Woman of Thirty* (1959) and *A Passion for Life* (1961), which cannot be rooted within an explicitly Asian American context. In a headnote entry to the *Encyclopedia of Asian-American Literature*, the scholar Bennett Fu asserts that "in Asian-American literary criticism, the importance of Diana Chang and her work has been downplayed, partly because of the absence of conspicuous 'Asian-American' themes in the major body of her work, and partly because of Chang's attempt to delineate universal themes in her narratives" (36). Fu clarifies how the mixed-race Asian American writer tends to be embraced by cultural critics if his or her fictional work fits more neatly within the field's traditional areas of inquiry. The omission of Chang's works without overtly Asian American themes spotlights the question Ling likely wanted to avoid: does literary classification require narrative content that mirrors the author's ethnoracial descent? Ling's sole inclusion of Chang's *The*

Frontiers of Love would suggest so, but I argue that such labeling unduly privileges the alignment between the author's mixed-race background and the way it can be mapped onto the narrative perspective. Chang is just one of a small handful of mixed-race Asian American writers to gain prominence prior to 1965. The contemporary period boasts numerous such figures, and the classification and interpretation of Chang's fictions prefigures issues that the discipline of literary studies now faces. Now more than ever, critics need to attend to the questions yielded by the cultural productions of writers who do not fit neatly within a monoracial frame.[2] Significantly, many of these writers do not imagine Asian or Asian American contexts within their fictions, nor do they all present their narratives through the perspective of a character of Asian or mixed Asian descent. As a grouping, the fictional works produced by these mixed-race writers push critics to further develop interdisciplinary methodologies, to engage exactly how and why such works should be embraced as an important branch of ethnic cultural studies and specifically Asian American studies.

While many definitions for "mixed race" exist, I use the term with respect to a particular author's biological descent. As with previous chapters, I am also interested when authorial background cannot be directly connected to the first-person narrative perspective.[3] The relationship between a writer's mixed-race background and the representational terrain he or she depicts has typically been vexed. The cultural critic Michele Elam notes this fact in *The Souls of Mixed Folk* through various critical readings focused on mixed-race African American writers.[4] This chapter draws on Elam's thesis by showing that mixed-race Asian American writers do not engage in critical avoidance of their identities when fictional worlds fail to correspond to their exact blood quanta.[5] Indeed, such a conclusion suggests that these writers advance a kind of postracial aesthetic, in which the fictional world becomes an unbridled, apolitical landscape. But an attentive look at the representational terrain reveals fictional worlds in which the variations in the storytelling perspective provide us with specific entry points to consider depictions of social inequality. As these imagined landscapes forefront the dynamics of power and oppression on a multitude of characters, we see that issues related to racial mixing do not necessarily hold center court but can be relationally and elliptically connected to those concerns.

To specifically illustrate these claims, this chapter primarily reads two of Nunez's novels, *For Rouenna* and *The Last of Her Kind*, and explores how the fictionalized biography functions in each work.[6] Nunez's biographies are fictionalized insofar as neither the biographer nor the life being archived is tied to actual living figures. But these life-writing ventures also include the emergence of characters and contexts that require the reader to cast aside the very object of the biographer's fascination—to look beyond the one life that the biographer seeks to highlight—in order to also consider what is obscured or who is in danger of being eliminated. Nunez's fictional publications exhibit a creative use of narration that exceeds the boundaries of what traditional biography offers, pressing the form to expand. While mixed-race characters remain largely absent in both novels, the fictional worlds engage the larger problems of societal hybridity especially in relation to the political issues that arise in the post–civil rights era.

I focus on Nunez rather than other mixed-race writers because her novels so effectively model how mixed-race authorial ancestry cannot be explicitly tied to narrative perspective. These fictionalized biographies shift narrative concerns from singularity to pluralities, showing us the struggles of people attempting to renew their lives in various sociohistorical circumstances—specifically, the female military service personnel who served during the Vietnam War and the inmates mired in the American prison system. Nunez's fictions depict a historical moment in which social inequality seems to have abated, especially as racial prejudice and racial difference appear to be less pressing concerns. In *For Rouenna*, the narrator-biographer reminds us of the ways in which gender equity has offered females more options for military service. At the same time, her quest to archive the life of a Polish American army nurse leads the narrative to explore how Vietnamese civilians become casualties of the war. In *The Last of Her Kind*, the unnamed narrator seeks to recount the intriguing life of an activist-convict who had hailed from an affluent white family but who later languishes in the American prison system. As with *For Rouenna*, the narrative moves beyond the exploration of this single life; as I demonstrate, key perspective shifts push the novel outside the range of a traditional biography, delineating the larger multiracial community that suffers from the failures of the carceral institution. Both novels involve a narrator-biographer who cannot be explicitly tied to Nunez's personal ancestry, severing the explicit connection between writer and storytelling perspective. The works discussed in chapters 1 and 2 engage specific post–civil rights contexts, and Nunez's novels expose a similar interest in that era; but they forefront the metafictional quality of representing events and circumstances during this period through the form of life-writing.

Nunez's novels make concrete what the literary critic Kandice Chuh articulates in *Imagine Otherwise* as "subjectless discourse." This phrase, while potentially misunderstood given the materialist methodologies that undergird Asian American studies, directly pertains to racial identity as it is represented and refracted within the fictional world. Chuh leaves us with the sentiment that the term "Asian American" is "a *metaphor* for resistance and racism" (27). By opening up Asian America to its metaphorical connotations, Chuh enables a wide variety of interventions to be made. This liberating conception of identity is inherently comparative, as the phrase "resistance and racism" implicates a wide number of communities, individuals, and social rubrics that do not necessarily or only relate to Asian Americans. In the porous membrane between fiction and nonfiction, *For Rouenna* and *The Last of Her Kind* effectively invoke the asymmetries of Asian American fiction and remind us of the diverse inspirations that influence mixed-race writers. I move this chapter forward by offering a critical review of biography as a genre—specifically detailing how Nunez appropriates the form and fictionalizes it—I then move to readings of the novels and suggest that biography's form produces a narrative inequality that is challenged by the inclusion of other narrative perspectives, characters, and social contexts. The biographer's quest to archive one life is perpetually in flux, as the form's uneven features allow for more inclusive lenses.

Fictionalizing the Biographer's Quest

Nunez is the author of six novels; she is of Asian descent, with a Chinese Panamanian father and a German mother. Her oeuvre is difficult to locate in a conventional Asian American context. Her first novel, *A Feather on the Breath of God* (1995), deliberates on the complexities of the mixed-race experience. This debut emphasizes the protagonist's estrangement from her father, as his Chinese-ness becomes utterly foreign to her despite their kinship ties. The novel treads closely to the form of an autobiography. The protagonist's mixed-race background mirrors Nunez's exactly, as the protagonist recalls the difficulties connecting to her Chinese Panamanian immigrant father while bonding more closely with her German immigrant mother. However, despite the novel's depiction of this estranged Chinese father and the complications of growing up as a mixed-race Asian American, it is difficult to label. As Josephine D. Lee argues, "Its spare yet evocative prose depicts experiences familiar to many readers of fiction by Asian Americans—the harsh conditions of immigrant urban life, language barriers, and the symbolic emasculation of the Asian American male. Yet the kinds of differences that the novel delves into cannot simply be divided into what is 'Asian' and what is 'American'" (Review 109). Lee's observations stem from the immigrant identity formation that Nunez explores, in which the protagonist's Chinese heritage (and hemispheric trajectory) must be placed in dialogue with the mother, who emigrates from Germany and is more communicative about her own ethnonational past. The novel further includes an entire section based on the protagonist's fascination with ballet. Finally, the last portion focuses on the affair the narrator initiates with a Russian immigrant. As the content demonstrates, traditional ethnoracial rubrics cannot be used to map Nunez's text.

We can push Lee's evaluation further by considering the strongly European cast of Nunez's first novel. As Petra Fachinger asserts, "*A Feather on the Breath of God* has become part of the Asian American literary 'canon,' as indicated by its inclusion on the reading lists for courses on Asian American literature" (261), but she later adds that "the mother-daughter conflict in Nunez's text also differs significantly from that between Chinese mothers and their Americanized daughters as portrayed in contemporary Chinese American novels by women" (263). Fachinger specifically reads the novel through the intergenerational relationship in which culture is imbued and extended through the mother's German heritage. The narrative's deviation from the mother-daughter trope prominent in Asian American literature demonstrates how the novel can be studied through a different lens, one in which whiteness and European culture fundamentally influence the protagonist's upbringing and identity formation. Despite the narrator's stronger attachment to her European ancestry, the overall embrace of *A Feather on the Breath of God* by those who teach Asian American literature demonstrates the flexibility that characterizes literary boundaries, reminding one of the continued importance of Lisa Lowe's conception of "heterogeneity, hybridity, and multiplicity" (67) within Asian American cultures. However, Nunez's subsequent novels—*Naked Sleeper* (1996), *Mitz: The Marmoset of Bloomsbury* (1998), *For Rouenna*, *The Last of Her Kind*, and *Salvation City* (2010)—rarely if ever touch on recognizably Asian American subject matter. The narrative perspectives do not follow characters who are identifiably of Asian, Asian American, or mixed-race backgrounds.

In Nunez's first novel, the one that most clearly aligns the narrator with the author, we can already begin to see her interest in the form of biography as life-writing.[7] The first two sections are titled "Chang" and "Christa," after the narrator's parents. Accordingly, the narrator becomes the biographer of her parents in an attempt to piece together their lives. One major aporia, though, is that the narrator's father never offers much information about his past. Further, his inability to assimilate into American culture as readily as Christa makes him even more difficult to read for the narrator. The section devoted to Christa is much more detailed and shows the narrator's greater connection with her mother. The failure to catalog her father's past causes the narrator guilt and reveals that the biographer's project is riddled with uncontrollable parameters and unexpected setbacks. She determines the general shape of her mother's life, but not so much her father's. It is the lack of fatherly connection that, in part, will influence her later affair with a Russian immigrant who, not coincidentally, is trying to learn English. The biographer's inability to exert complete control over the subject matter that she seeks to recover is the major thematic undertaking of Nunez's subsequent novels.

Before fully delving into *For Rouenna* and *The Last of Her Kind*, I consider theories of the biographical form to show how Nunez moves beyond traditional genre elements. Nunez's engagement with a fictional form of the biography provides a schematic through which to question the position of the Asian American writer of mixed-race background, as one of the genre's fundamental characteristics is the connection between the narrator and the writer of the biography.[8] While the literary critic Michael Benton argues that there is no narrator in the most traditional sense in biography because the author enters the text as the storyteller, both he and the biographer Diane Wood Middlebrook agree that a central feature of the form involves the biographer's explicit presence within the representational terrain.[9] In most cases, the biographer simply takes the place of something akin to a third-person narrator. In relation to Nunez, however, the issue of narration is murky because the biographer functions as a fictionalized character within her novels. For instance, in *For Rouenna*, the unnamed narrator, who happens to be a writer, seeks to create an account of Rouenna Zycinski. Though this storytelling figure might seem to be a kind of double for Nunez, this connection is never finally clarified. The narrator-biographer is never racially marked, making it problematic on the level of ancestry to verify her as a stand-in for Nunez. At the time that the narrator-biographer decides to write about Rouenna, the narrator-biographer—like Nunez up to the point of *For Rouenna*'s publication—had already published two books, but the narrator-biographer does little to reveal what those books are about. Nunez thus continually plays with the desire to authenticate her presence in the fictional world through this narrator-biographer but never confirms this association. As I argue in the introduction, the Asian American writer must contend with the expectation that his or her fictional narrative is actually a veiled nonfictional document. Nunez's artful sleight of hand reminds us that we must approach *For Rouenna* not as an actual biography but ultimately as a fictionalized one.

The fulcrum of the biographical genre is its obsession with a single life, on a figure that can fulfill a particular readerly expectation. In the biographer Nigel Hamilton's estimation, "the truth is that real-life depiction—in myriad forms, from comic strip to essay, from obituaries to dramatized TV epics, from films to operas, from museum exhibitions to books, from radio profiles to film documentaries and blogs—is today the mark of our continuing fascination with individuality" (287).[10] Following the spirit of "fascination" offered by Hamilton, the fictionalized biographer seeks to explore the life of an individual, one who, at least in the eyes of that biographer, is worth more deliberation. In *For Rouenna*, the life in question is that of the titular Rouenna, the former Vietnam War nurse, a figure who, with her compelling story of military service, might be of interest to a wider audience.[11] Biography further assumes that the life story to be told belongs to someone who is, or was at some point, an actual person. While such an assumption seems reasonable, in Nunez's novels, this individual also turns out to be a fictional character, a person who could have existed but whose existence cannot be verified against the real-life world. Focusing on these said figures, these novels do accede to some biographical conventions, namely, those that assume a reading audience willing to engage the possibility that the life being highlighted is compelling.[12] These novels further spotlight the malleable boundaries between fiction and nonfiction, biography and the novel, and the individual self and his or her connection to structural inequalities.[13] The literary critic Hermione Lee points out that the biographical form envisions "a version of social politics, whether it is the nationalist agenda behind the collective biographical encyclopaedias of nineteenth-century France and England, or the post-Apartheid-era reactions which led to the biographical idealization of Nelson Mandela, or the changes in black cultural history in twentieth-century North America" (*Biography* 14). The combination of "social politics" and the lives referenced by them bring Nunez's fictions back into the orbit of cultural studies, as the individual life sought out by the biographer appears within a wider sociohistorical framework. That is, by calling attention to lives and events beyond that of a single biographical subject, Nunez's fictions lead readers continually away from one perspective and one experience. In these social multiplicities, Nunez's fictions come to emphasize and remind us of the individuals who must be included in a more flexible biographical form.[14]

Whose Vietnam? The Occlusions of Biography in *For Rouenna*

For Nunez, the fictionalized biography becomes a gateway to explore other contexts and characters beyond its traditional conventions. The life being retrieved is only one point among a larger mapping of social interactions that constitute the breadth and heft of the fictional terrain. As I mentioned earlier, the novel is told from the first-person perspective of a successful writer—readers are never given her name but understand that she has published two books and that she enjoys some measure of renown. As the narrator gains more notoriety for her work, she is inevitably contacted by individuals she knew in her past, including the titular Rouenna. Although both the narrator and Rouenna grew up in the Staten Island public housing projects, the narrator fails at first to remember Rouenna. The tension between the two immediately begins as the narrator finds Rouenna too abrasive; she is blunt, unapologetic, and lacking in the narrator's sense of decorum and social graces. The narrator discovers that Rouenna possesses ulterior motives for contacting her: Rouenna hopes that the narrator will help her write a book about her life as an army nurse in Vietnam. In response, the narrator simply says no. Although the subject never comes up again, Rouenna remains open about her past and divulges much about her varied life experience, including her service in Vietnam. Tragically, Rouenna kills herself, leaving the narrator contemplating Rouenna's life and impact. In the wake of Rouenna's suicide, the narrator also finds herself unable to write, and only when she begins to pen her recollections of Rouenna, the narrator's block lifts. In this way, the novel continues, elaborating on the challenging life that Rouenna led growing up in the Staten Island public housing projects and then shifting to her experiences in Vietnam as an army nurse. *For Rouenna* explores the writer-narrator's initial preoccupation with one life and the ways in which this nodal point extends to include a larger field of individuals affected by war.

Based on how central the narrator-biographer and her relationship to Rouenna are to the plot, the novel may seem only tangentially related to Asian American characters or contexts. It is entirely possible, for instance, to advance a reading that focuses specifically on the novel's construction of white racial formation and class mobility, especially as detailed in Rouenna's upbringing. The novel's pertinence to Asian American studies becomes clear in the wake of Rouenna's suicide. As the narrator-biographer seeks out the source of Rouenna's psychic dilemmas, the recounting transports readers to Vietnam. The narrator-biographer chronicles how Rouenna, in the dark terrain of war, finds purpose and how, later on, she succumbs to the sentiment that she could have done more to address the conflict that adversely affected so many lives.

The focus on Rouenna offers an intriguing but typically overlooked social context—the experiences of female veterans. The novel dovetails with the discourse of second-wave feminism that appeared during and after the civil rights era, which advanced the importance of gender equity for women in all career branches, including the military. In this way, *For Rouenna*'s status as a purely fictional book is already asymmetrically presented; the narrative can be compared to the documented real-life experiences of US military women serving during the Vietnam era. The book offers a fictional account of the challenges that confronted these female military personnel, injecting a feminist perspective into conceptions of military duties. Precisely because of the sexist gender dynamics inextricably linked to the legacy of the Vietnam War, scholarly works based on women's experiences in the armed forces are still relatively few.[15] Of this oversight, Keith Walker explains, "According to military policy, women are not supposed to be in life-threatening situations in a war zone, and therefore we have never developed an image of that in our minds. We think of men in combat, and women safely in the rear echelon in offices and hospitals" (2).[16] Despite the dangers for nurses, upward of approximately ten thousand did serve. Although most were expected to "volunteer" for such duty, it was routine for many nurses, as they were training in the United States for various field positions, to discover that they had been deployed to Vietnam without their understood consent.[17] In Kathryn Marshall's estimation, "between 1962 and 1973, some 7,500 American women served on active military duty in Vietnam. The Veteran's Administration, however, puts the number of military women at more than 11,000" (4).[18]

Many Vietnam War nurses lacked proper training and preparation for the conditions they would face, which included caring for soldiers with disastrous wounds resulting from increased efficiency and technological innovation in the area of weaponry.[19] Gendered and professional expectations added to these challenges: "The cultural ideal of woman as healer and the occupational expectation of a nurse to act as a healer could not be fulfilled in Vietnam. It was simply impossible. Therefore, the woman veteran feels she failed not only as a nurse, but as a woman as well. Her silence can now be understood" (S. Alexander 17). Female veterans, like many of their male counterparts, returned to the United States with a diminished sense of self, enhanced by their inability to save all those who had come into their care.[20] Such self-estimations were further compounded by the changing tide in public opinion against American involvement in the Vietnam War, which resulted in a backlash against those who served.

If historical and sociological studies of Vietnam War–era nurses are limited to a rough handful of publications, the corresponding attention paid to women in literary representations of the war is similarly limited. Bettina Hofmann succinctly describes this omission: "The canon of war literature, however, does not grant women writers a place" (18), especially with respect to writers who focus specifically on gender politics during armed conflicts. Vietnam War literature can promote what Susan Jeffords calls the "'remasculinization' of American culture" (xii), augmenting the invisibility of women in war contexts.[21] Nunez's novel, through its characterization, clearly intervenes in the masculinist bias of Vietnam War representations in its multifaceted depiction of nurses (Beidler, "Enlarging" 706–07).[22] *For Rouenna* does not glorify nurses as saintly heroes; instead, it spotlights the complicated gender politics that emerged as women tended to catastrophic injuries while struggling to maintain their equanimity. The narrator-biographer explains the challenges faced by Rouenna in this way: "Though nurses did get hurt and even killed in Vietnam, it was not this that Rouenna prayed to be spared but the worse eventuality that she herself would do harm—the Young Nurses' Prayer" (120–21). Under extreme working conditions and faced with the fact that, as an army officer, she outranks many male military personnel, Rouenna acknowledges the dangers of the power she has been given. With limited medical training stateside, she still operates on and treats patients with significant and critical injuries.

The sexist nature of military service continually confronts and affronts the various nurses who populate the novel, despite their great responsibilities for caretaking. The narrator-biographer, for instance, reveals the disdain with which Rouenna and other nurses were often treated, as "some of the army doctors were against having any women in the war zone" (90). Nurses were "constantly being goggled at, being followed around, constantly having [their picture] taken" and subject to "hoots and hollers, whistles, applause" (134). The narrator-biographer recounts Rouenna's friendship with "Pretty Polly," a nurse who eventually succumbs to a nervous breakdown in a Vietnam PX after discovering that the location carries lingerie and fishnet stockings but no tampons. For the army nurses to counteract the constant stresses bombarding them, they come together as a group. The narrator recalls Rouenna's experience: "Certainly [Rouenna] had never known anything like the closeness she would find in the Army Nurse Corps, nor would she ever find such closeness again. Home from the war, she would be struck by how hard it was all of a sudden to make friends with other women" (138). The novel thus also details the strange but welcome female camaraderie that Rouenna finds among the crushing circumstances of war.

For very long stretches, the storytelling focuses acutely on Rouenna's experiences in Vietnam, and readers can occasionally forget whose viewpoint directs their readerly access. That is, Rouenna's life is shared secondhand, but with such meticulous care and detail that the narrator-biographer seems completely absent. When the narrator-biographer does insert her viewpoint at critical moments, she reveals the arc and aim of her creative investments. For example, the narrator-biographer's friend, a male Vietnam veteran who later becomes a creative writer, states his viewpoint on nurses: "He did not see them as having had much of a role in the great Vietnam epic. A footnote, he said. Whenever we were together and I started talking about Rouenna, he would stare off" (183). This passage occurs in the context of the novel's final stretch, as the narrator-biographer reflects on the ways individuals sometimes dismissed Rouenna's experience. Making Rouenna—and the nurses who served with her—more than a "footnote," the narrator-biographer redirects the narrative back to female war veterans, challenging her friend's assertion.

At the same time that the novel models how biographical storytelling intervenes in the dominant depictions of the Vietnam War, *For Rouenna* must also be considered in relation to its representation of civilians. To explore this issue, I turn to the work of literary critic Viet Thanh Nguyen. In a critique of Peter Bacho's *Entrys* (2005), Nguyen argues that the novel reenacts the problematic erasure of Vietnamese bodies and faces found in depictions of the war.[23] Nguyen further challenges Bacho's simplification of the Vietnam War "story." Although a minority writer—Bacho is an American of Filipino descent—he is preoccupied with how a veteran's torment must be staged (V. Nguyen, "Speak of the Dead" 19). Nguyen highlights the complicated position inhabited by minority writers, who "can inflict various kinds of harm with the symbolic power they wield"

(11). In this case, Bacho's failure to nuance his representation of Vietnamese characters ultimately reinscribes the common failures of the Vietnam War "story," in which the veteran's troubles are highlighted at the expense of any other characters. Nguyen thus charges the minority writer with a lofty task: "From an ethical point of view, the horizon of our vision must be expansive, precisely because minorities have rarely been recognized, except as objects of horror or fascination. The ethical recognition of an other thus has a direct consequence for the aesthetics of narrative, through characterization" (21).[24] The slippery slope of this argument appears in the question of the Other. For Bacho's narrative, as Nguyen rightly points out, the minority veteran's experience has not been sufficiently investigated in light of the most recognized Vietnam War novelists and fiction writers, such as Tim O'Brien, Larry Heinemann, Philip Caputo, and Robert Olen Butler. In this respect, the "horizon of our vision" that Nguyen expects depends on the way in which the Other is defined. The importance of "characterization" to the "other's" constitutive emergence within the minority writer's narrative stems from the creation of a representational terrain that includes underrepresented subject positions.

In drawing out Nguyen's reading of Bacho's novel, I also could advance similar critiques of Nunez's *For Rouenna*. The novel does not flesh out any Vietnamese characters but rather concentrates on one Polish American army nurse's life and tragic death. However, the novel differs quite significantly from Bacho's representation in that Bacho focuses on an American war veteran whose primary trauma is the result of friendly fire; Rico Divina accidentally kills his American military buddy. Our narrative attention in *Entrys*, at least in relation to the war, extends prominently only to the untimely and senseless death of one other American serviceman. In relation to *For Rouenna*, Nguyen would ask, what, then, of the Vietnamese civilians? Nunez's narrator employs biography to depict a female veteran who is aware of her occlusions. For instance, Rouenna understands that one of her major failures as an army nurse was her inability to fully care for Vietnamese civilians who suffered as war's collateral damage. The biographer's quest to delve into Rouenna's life offers a forum that exposes the social context for female veterans during the Vietnam War but also draws attention to the perceptual limits of individuals who served.

Though the novel depicts Rouenna as a figure who cannot imagine the Vietnamese fully as major characters, with bigger roles than war bystanders, they are not entirely erased; they do engender key disruptions to narrative flow and to narrative resolution. These narrative asymmetries clarify the unevenness of the fictionalized biography, as the spotlight occasionally shifts to other individuals. For instance, the narrator-biographer recalls that she does not personally know anyone of Vietnamese descent, except for one aunt whom she juxtaposes against the representations offered by Graham Greene in his classic novel *The Quiet American* (1955). In Greene's novel, the main character, Thomas Fowler, falls in love with an alluring Vietnamese woman named Phuong. In *For Rouenna*, the narrator-biographer's college roommate finds much to fault in Greene's imagination of Phuong, whom she sees as a reflection of a sexist, colonial gaze: "Fowler's Vietnamese girl, his twittering bird. Passive, childlike, undemanding, rarely speaking, always serving, interested only in fashion, gossip about royalty, getting a husband, pleasing her man. 'The quintessential male fantasy: the one-man whore.' Everything my roommate was fighting against" (85).

The narrator's recollection of her Vietnamese aunt, however, unsettles the literary fantasy offered by Greene's novel. In the narrator's description, her aunt is a different kind of enigma, at once playful and crude, someone who does not conform to an imagined oriental exoticism: "Coming home from school, I would find [my aunt] watching television, a pair of chopsticks in one hand, a jar of hot chili peppers in the other. When I tasted just a shred of what she offered me, a blister rose immediately on my tongue. I did not dare to swallow. She laughed. 'For you like eat napalm, right?' Right" (84). In this description, the narrator finds the food-specific humor literally hard to swallow, as the aunt resignifies the inflammable liquid known as napalm in a grotesquely humorous gesture. Note the rather casual scene as well: the aunt eats alone without the use of any plates or bowls, rendering this moment as comic. In another instance, the narrator recalls of her aunt, "Even pregnant she could squat with both feet flat on the edge of the bathtub and without losing her balance lean all the way over to wash her never-cut hair. When she was pleased with her little boy, she held up her thumb: 'You number-one son!' She gave me manicures. Not much talk but plenty of giggles: two teenage girls" (84–85). The image of the aunt in a functional but awkward "squat" deconstructs the Vietnamese woman as the "twittering bird," gesturing to the mismatch between representation and reality. The greatest difference between the narrator's aunt and Phuong occurs in the strong personality that the aunt exudes. She is not the "passive, childlike" woman who defines the gendered and sexualized nature of an oriental female. Further, the aunt's status as a young mother moves beyond the flirtatious and carefree rendering of Phuong, who remains untethered to the burdens of childrearing. Instead of being disappointed by her aunt, the narrator finds a way to identify with her, describing them as "two teenage girls."

The narrator's memory of her aunt enables her to further reconsider a relationship she had with an American journalist who once worked in Vietnam. While the narrator at first believes that the journalist had engaged in an affair with a Vietnamese woman who was much like Phuong from *The Quiet American*, she later wonders whether her assumptions were valid: "Now I don't know whether to believe my own story about the journalist and the Vietnamese love of his life" (85). Recalling her aunt, the narrator implicitly suggests that her visions of the transnational love affair between her journalist ex-boyfriend and an anonymous Vietnamese lover were created as an orientalist fantasy. *The Quiet American*, too, will lose its exoticized hold and power over the narrator once she rereads it: "Now Phuong, Pyle, even Fowler the narrator and main protagonist—none of them quite comes to life. They are like people one has heard about rather than people one knows, and with the best novels the reader always feels as though he or she had known the characters, and known them thoroughly, in real life" (86). While the Vietnamese American aunt takes up little narrative space, she exerts a tremendous influence on the narrator as a racialized figure who takes fuller form in the United States. The aunt is a young mother, a joker, a squatter, and a teenager all at once, and she is married to a war veteran. The aunt offers the narrator a way to challenge impressionistic literary idealizations that can perpetuate stereotypes. The narrator-biographer thus illuminates the intricacies of narrative reconstructions, such that representations and their external referents might be placed in relational perspective.

The narrator's diversion from Rouenna's biography is pertinent to the question of the Vietnamese Other because Rouenna's ability to push past her own experiences requires her (and the narrator) to see the Vietnamese culture and people in a different way. Without the project of Rouenna's biography, it is unlikely that the writer-protagonist would have ever been critical of her own understanding of Vietnamese representations. In Rouenna's case, the struggle to understand her Vietnamese counterparts unfolds at different points in her life. It is clear, for instance, that Rouenna grew up in an era when anti-Asian prejudice was the norm; her father espoused such racist sentiments. It is implied that he served in World War II, where his mantra was, "*All I want is to kill every slant eye I meet and go home*" (118, italics in original). While in Vietnam, Rouenna is stationed at hospitals where she is required not only to train Vietnamese nurses but also to tend to both Vietnamese civilian casualties and prisoners of war. Her view of the potentially ungratifying task of healing the so-called enemy is explained in this way: "She might not have wanted to treat NVAs [North Vietnamese Army] or VCs [Vietcong], but when she had to she did it right, giving the same treatment she would have given anyone" (132). In one encounter, the narrator recalls, "The burn on the NVA's thigh was a bad one. Rouenna had been very gentle changing the dressing and scrupulous about minimizing the risk of infection. She had respected the soldier's dignity and privacy and tried to avoid eye contact to make the whole business less hard on him. And the goddamn motherfucking gook bastard had spat on her" (132–33). This instance vividly illustrates Rouenna's difficulty performing her nursing duties. In this case, the wounded NVA soldier is exactly who the American combat troops would be attempting to subdue out on the battlefield, but Rouenna's task is to tend to her patient, regardless of military affiliation. Notably, the racist epithet "gook" is not articulated through direct quotation, revealing an elision between narration and perspective. Is this a moment when the narrator shifts into prejudiced language, or do we understand it to be a rough translation of Rouenna's own sentiments? Without a direct answer, this scene marks how prejudice germinates in the field of war. This unnamed NVA soldier challenges Rouenna's so-called egalitarian medical ethics and presents an ethnic subject who cannot be dismissed as an inconsequential minor character.

As a caregiver, then, Rouenna engages a profoundly provocative liminal space where a more nuanced intersubjective viewpoint must emerge, especially as it relates to forms of collateral damage. In another instance, Rouenna laments her wartime encounters with young Vietnamese children, figures who, although always nameless, are not simply erased over time:

> Home for more than a year, dealing every day with patients who behaved like small children, Rouenna kept seeing those other children, from the war. She was old enough to remember the thalidomide crisis and how horrified the world had been when those several thousand children were born deformed. But the war was deforming children every day—Rouenna had no idea what the actual figure was, but she knew it had to be many times higher than several thousand. And at least no one had planted thalidomide in those women's wombs, unlike the booby traps and land mines that

were planted where everyone knew children were going to be. And of course you could never remember those wounded children without remembering what every American witness found so hard to believe: how quietly they bore their pain. (171)

Certainly, the Vietnamese are painted here as specters that haunt Rouenna despite her return from service; but their presence is evoked in comparative scope. The reproductive outrage generated by the thalidomide crisis also calls attention to the egregious oversight related to civilian-child casualties during the Vietnam War. This passage is more closely connected to a third-person perspective, as the biographer recounts Rouenna's experiences, with the narrator often giving readers access to her thoughts and feelings. At the same time, the passage is complicated by the use of the phrase "you could never remember," suggesting the invocation of an audience who must be attuned to this civilian fallout. The "you" further connects to the later phrase "every American witness," indicating that more than the nurses and soldiers observing such violence are implicated in acknowledging the pains that war produces.

The ghostly presence of the Vietnamese children in Rouenna's life increases as she gets older and finds the prospect of starting her own family impossible. Rouenna is unable to bear children due to early menopause, a condition she attributes to being exposed to Agent Orange during her military service. The detrimental effects of this toxic defoliant are made clear to her by a romantic partner: "Chuck, who said he would never dare father a child, had shown her another article that included a list of birth defects in children born to Vietnamese or American war veterans, a list that had seared itself into her memory like a brand. Babies born with heart defects, or missing parts of their brains or spines" (205). By linking both Americans and Vietnamese under the auspices of reproductive damage, the narrator grants us an opening to consider Rouenna's final admission concerning her limitations as a Vietnam War nurse. Rouenna thinks she should have adopted one of the many Vietnamese children she tended to and that her choice not to do so was a mistake: "'But maybe that was what was supposed to happen, maybe that's what God wanted me to do: save one of those babies' lives. A test, and I failed it—you know what I'm saying. So now I was being punished by never having a kid of my own.' I hated it when she talked like this, but I let her go on" (212-13). Rouenna's sympathy for the Vietnamese is consistently destabilized by racist language, as the narrator notes in direct quotations that she calls them "gook kids" (213), and yet, despite such flaws, Rouenna recognizes one of her great blind spots concerning the Other. The Vietnamese never come into full focus, but the plight of the children forces Rouenna to admit that she "failed." The unnamed narrator's choice to include this direct quotation reveals the complicated status of her biographical venture. On the one hand, she wants to convey Rouenna's tortured psyche, but on the other, she also wishes to reveal her own response to Rouenna's confessions. The narrator "hated" such talk because these admissions suggest that Rouenna believed her military service was tragically shortsighted and perhaps even morally bankrupt. That the narrator still includes this dialogue despite her power as the storyteller to edit out certain potentially unsavory details shows a desire to portray Rouenna as a flawed heroine. In this manner, the narrator persistently dispels the fantasy of the perfect, gallant veteran and brings this narrative back into the unsentimental chronicle of military service during wartime.

For Rouenna calls attention to actual historical contexts concerning the service of American women during the Vietnam War, but we must remember that the narrative itself is an adaptation—a story told to the narrator-biographer that she can re-create only as a kind of patchwork. Nunez does seem to gesture to the limits of life-writing when the narrator-biographer discusses Primo Levi's viewpoint on depictions of the Holocaust: "The fear that the more stories that get told, the more novels and memoirs and movies and TV shows about the Big Event that got put out into the world, the greater the gap between those imagined or reconstructed versions and the Big Event itself" (191–92). In the process of taking on the subject of the Vietnam War, the narrator-biographer realizes that the "gap" is a complicated area in which art and authenticity collide. To further elucidate this issue, she explains her experience of watching the movie *The English Patient* alongside Rouenna. While the narrator-biographer finds the epic to be a "great story," Rouenna finds the movie to be impossibly rendered: Rouenna "was surprised that [the narrator-biographer] had missed something so obvious: it would have been impossible for that one nurse to care for her severely burned patient all by herself" (192). This passage refers to the major plot point from *The English Patient*, in which the nurse, Hana, tends to the life-threatening wounds of a man whose backstory becomes the movie's centerpiece. This movie-watching moment clarifies the restrictions faced by the narrator-biographer in the process of life-writing: she must attempt to render another person's existence with great accuracy. At the same time, the narrator-biographer's own interest in the "great story" leads her to understand that the life being archived must be reconstructed in a compelling way. The narrator-biographer succeeds in her multifaceted quest to portray Rouenna's life precisely because she works so diligently to convey not only the many contours of her friend's military service—the pathos of her work, the heroism it entailed, and the dangers it presented—but also the larger historical and social tapestry of the Vietnam War. In taking on this "Big Event," the narrator-biographer's quest also productively unravels, revealing the limits of the life-writing project, as marginal figures bear more and more on the "great story" being told.

Although *For Rouenna* does not deliberately attempt to fully imagine the Other as Viet Thanh Nguyen might direct, we find value in its representational techniques, in the biographical re-creation of a female veteran and former army nurse, certainly limited in her worldview but nevertheless cognizant of her many myopias. In this regard, *For Rouenna* establishes a different path through which to encounter Vietnamese subjects, who exist not only as civilian casualties or enemy figures but also as the refugees who come to the United States in the wake of the war. The narrator's aunt, even as a minor character, casts one of the tallest shadows over the narrative in reminding us that Vietnamese refugees do not remain stuck in some spectral netherworld, categorically subordinated to the narrative of the war veteran. Literary critic Milton J. Bates admits in his study of Vietnam War cultural productions, "if, as [James William] Gibson has argued, we Americans lost the war because we failed to recognize and adapt to the otherness of the enemy, then we are in danger of losing it a second time by losing its lessons, unless we try to see the war as others—particularly the people of Vietnam, Laos, and Cambodia—saw it" (6–7). The lack of perspective cited by Bates is precisely the danger that Nguyen forcefully advances in his critique of Peter Bacho's *Entrys*. The self-reflexive quality of Nunez's novel, though, does suggest its political investments, even in its limited horizons. We are called on not only to address the gaps and oversights within cultural productions depicting the Vietnam War but also to expand beyond current critical inquiries that, by and large, have concentrated on narratives involving the American male veteran's perspective.[25] Steffen Hantke asserts that "the plight of the Vietnam vet speaks eloquently and concretely of the lasting significance of the Vietnam War. Here is a living reminder that, for many Americans, the war is far from being over" (66)—but what of the Vietnamese and those who immigrated here in the wake of war? Even as *For Rouenna* addresses the importance of a spectrality that moves beyond the veteran's viewpoint, we must also acknowledge the emergence of fictional representations offered by Vietnamese Americans that do depict the postwar experience with an attention to Vietnamese American lives. This list includes Aimee Phan's *We Should Never Meet: Stories* (2004), Lan Cao's *Monkey Bridge* (1997), Dao Strom's *Grass Roof, Tin Roof* (2003), lê thi diem thúy's *The Gangster We Are All Looking For* (2003), and Bich Minh Nguyen's *Short Girls* (2009), among others. These works remind us that the continued evolution of Vietnam War literature is also found squarely within the fictional imaginations of Vietnamese American writers.

This reading makes two major conclusions. The first is that the mixed-race Asian American constructs the representational terrain without linking narration explicitly to authorial ancestry and in doing so pushes cultural critics to analyze the fictional world beyond an autobiographical or autoethnographic approach. *For Rouenna* also does not address ethnicity and race through the inclusion of major characters of Asian descent. Issues of racial and ethnic Otherness are most forcefully presented through the Vietnam War context, a trajectory that further severs any clear linkage between the author's ethnoracial background and the narrative perspective. Nevertheless, the novel's content concerning the Vietnam War evokes key social justice issues that relate the text to Asian American studies as a field and to its attendant critical terrains. The second conclusion addresses the question of biographical representation. Nunez arguably perpetuates the common strain of Vietnam War representation that focuses on the American veteran, yet her novel illuminates the experience of women in combat zones. Also, though not generating a fully imagined Vietnamese American character, the novel's portrayal of Rouenna reminds us that the war cannot be discussed without attention to this erasure, this loaded amnesia.

The novel's final sequence ends not with the heroic glorification of Rouenna but instead with a character, Luther, ridiculing the narrator-biographer's project. Luther, a high school friend of the narrator-biographer, is now serving a prison sentence for an undisclosed reason. The form of this ridicule is a letter written to the narrator-biographer in anger, as the narrator-biographer had decided on her previous visit to stop seeing him. Luther writes, "*And don't get me wrong, I respect your feelings and all, but a nurse in Vietnam, excuse me, that just doesn't seem like a big deal to me. I mean it's not like she was in combat. And you want to talk about being in shit, you want to talk about a world of hurt, man, what do you think I am going through every day inside here?*" (229, italics in original). This letter structures the reader's experience of the novel's conclusion, reminding us of the quandary opened up by biography as a literary form: whose life is most worth recovering? Here, Luther does not believe that Rouenna's life makes for a compelling project and proclaims instead that his difficult life deserves to be highlighted. Luther's claim is not simply over attention but biographical ethics. That is, the person with the gift and the privilege to write faces many choices about whose lives he or she will investigate. Early on in *For Rouenna*, the narrator muses that "stories—great stories—happen to everyone. And sometimes a person has a great story that he or she is dying to tell but has no ability to tell it. What then?" (27). This last question is precisely the one that haunts the biographical writer. In *For Rouenna*, it would seem that when the narrator-biographer agrees to return to the prison to see Luther, perhaps even with the intent to reconstruct his life, biographical ethics involve the desire to continually archive. Conditioned with a talent to tell the true stories of others, the narrator-biographer cannot choose only one life over another because it becomes evident that one life leads into many more and that the biographical tale one constructs never seems to be completed. In Nunez's fictions, biography exists as an uncompleted writerly act, in which the script of one life only expands to touch on an extensive web of social relations. The experiences of the female war veteran, the prisoner, and the Vietnamese subject are placed in a complex relational structure, wherein the biographical form magnifies to track these multiple individuals.

Pessimism in the Post–Civil Rights Era: Glorified Whiteness in *The Last of Her Kind*

For Rouenna complicates biographical writing as a genre, as other narrative perspectives and other characters unmoor the importance of any single life. In this way, this fictionalized biography becomes more flexibly and unevenly structured, revealing the racial asymmetries of the narrative landscape. We see how formal structures thus enhance the emergence of social inequalities that expose the power relations undergirding the collateral damage engendered by the Vietnam War. Set in the post–civil rights moment, the novel calls attention to the ways in which racial and ethnic tensions function with the transnational valences of Cold War containment policies. *The Last of Her Kind* also explores the variability of race relations in the post–civil rights era but moves us into the context of women languishing within the American prison system. The novel's central biographical focus on a white, elite female character is undermined by narrative disruptions that continually divert the reader, allowing other characters, narrative perspectives, and corresponding social inequalities to emerge.[26] A critique of the prison rehabilitation process appears through the formal properties of the novel, as a minor character reveals the dramatic problems within the carceral institution. The novel thus moves far beyond the retelling of one privileged life, pushing us to the narrative's rich margins.

The Last of Her Kind centers on the disintegrating friendship of two characters from different class backgrounds: Georgette George (later called George), with blue-collar, working-class, white American roots and no identifiable European immigration history, having grown up in a dreary and desolate upstate New York township; and Dooley Ann Drayton, who comes from an elite, affluent, white lineage. For George, acceptance into Barnard College is itself an incredible triumph. In contrast, Dooley's life is filled with many extravagances, such as summering in the Hamptons and growing up in a resplendent home filled with domestic servants. We further discover that Dooley's maternal lineage can be traced to wealthy slave owners. The book opens with both women having been accepted to Barnard and with George discovering that her roommate will be Dooley, who eventually goes by her middle name, Ann. The time period is the 1960s, during the height of counterculture fervor and the civil rights movement. Nunez sets up the novel's tensions early on when it is discovered that Ann personally requested that her roommate come from a radically different background from her own. George later discovers that Ann had been hoping to have an African American roommate. Ann is increasingly put off by the solipsistic lives of her fellow undergraduates, finding them far too apathetic for her tastes. Ann's aggressive political activism stems in part from the injustices she witnessed as a young child when her family's African American maid was unfairly fired. Although her ire toward the indifference of her peers at first does not extend to George, their relationship begins to sour as George begins working for a trendy women's fashion magazine. The two characters eventually have a falling out, the rupture occurring due to a comment George makes about Ann's African American boyfriend, Kwame.

The novel's urgency crescendos when Ann is later convicted of murdering a police officer and injuring his partner. The crime allegedly occurs during a routine traffic stop. Ann observes from afar as her now-husband, Kwame, is detained and harassed by police officers. Fearing for Kwame's life, Ann ends up shooting both officers. In the ensuing chaos, Kwame, too, is fatally shot by one of the officers. Ann is ultimately unrepentant for her actions, and her uncompromising attitude does not generate much sympathy from the jurors or from the public at large. While in prison at the Maryville Correctional Facility, she takes it upon herself to improve living conditions, making her an object of derision from prison staff and administrators. Her outspokenness also proves reason enough for her fellow inmates to dislike her, and she is the target of extreme bullying and intimidation. During this period, George transitions from her job at the women's magazine, finishes school, and remarries; she then receives a letter from Ann requesting that the literary journal that George now coedits, *Caracara*, accept the submissions of Ann's fellow inmates about their life experiences. George is only a figurehead for the journal; her coeditor, who is also her second husband, holds the power to withdraw or accept submissions, and he does not find the pieces publishable. As Ann's health takes a turn for the worse and George's husband dies tragically, George makes a decision that she hopes will, in part, rectify her estrangement with Ann.

The biographical content in *The Last of Her Kind* is presented far more tangentially than in *For Rouenna*. In this case, it is unclear whether George is actually writing a biography about Ann, even as the novel continually reminds us of its reconstructed narration. Early on, George confesses, "as usual when I look back at the past, I am afraid of remembering things wrong" (11), and she later admits, "If I am remembering correctly that Ann had plenty of dates, for example, she was probably prettier than I have made her out to be. And what I call unattractively *sharp* features might be more generously describe as *fine*" (11, emphasis in original). The inability to remember past events and individuals with complete accuracy contributes, of course, to the hazy quality of George's first-person narration, in which Ann must be viewed from a variety of perspectives that often move beyond one storyteller to get a clearer picture of her life and how it relates ultimately to many others. Certainly, George's hesitation about her recollections of Ann models how biographical writing is itself a process riddled with potential pitfalls and inconsistencies.

The one case of explicit, biographically inflected writing appears within a creative nonfiction piece written by a woman inmate. When George receives more creative control of the literary journal after her husband's death, she decides to fulfill Ann's old request to publish inmates' writing. George has saved only a single selection, "Orphan Annie and the Hand of God," from those Ann originally had sent. The anonymous author, who requests a pen name (George denotes her Olympia Underwood), reveals toward the end of the piece that a teacher had encouraged some of the inmates to try their hands at creative writing with an assignment specifically aimed at investigating an individual: "someone you met in prison whom you admire" (378). Olympia chooses Ann. Thus, in including a memoir about Ann written by a fellow prison inmate in the final printing of the literary journal, George's narrative gives way to a first-person account written and authored by someone else. This sequence is one of the most aesthetically creative and important narrative disruptions of the novel, in which the narrative "I" shifts from George's perspective to Olympia's.[27] From this other viewpoint, other social contexts surface: Maryville's decrepit prison system with its unhygienic facilities, high recidivism rates, and AIDS epidemic—and the distressing fact that such conditions are in many cases much better than what the inmates had known prior to their incarceration. The novel therefore produces a unique formal amalgamation in that Olympia's "Orphan Annie and the Hand of God" functions doubly: on the one hand, as a biographical venture detailing the latter stages of Ann's life and, on the other, as a prison narrative.

While I examined earlier the formal and political qualities of the biography, the genre of prison writings, both fictional and nonfictional in scope, has also been the subject of increasing scholarly interest. In one of the early foundational studies on the form, the literary critic H. Bruce Franklin provides two pivotal ways for reading prison writings: first, as a longer genealogy that includes slave narratives and, second, as a way to denote the inherently carceral nature of American power structures (xxii).[28] Of course, Olympia's version of prison writing appears in the context of a novel, blurring the boundaries between fiction and nonfiction. In this regard, it is instructive to consider the work of the literary critic Jan Alber, who analyzes prisons in the fictions of Charles Dickens: "Since fictional prison narratives always transform and distort the actual prison experience, I pay particular attention to the ways in which novels and films narrate the prison experience" (2). While I diverge somewhat from Alber's more categorical positioning that fictions "always" pervert the "prison experience," I take this critical approach to be centrally invested in the rhetorical scope of representation as it is placed in conversation with external textual referents. I further follow Alber's statement that "prison narratives spread certain images of prisons and their inmates and these pictures always correlate with a certain type of ideology" (2).

The choice to include "certain images" and "pictures" is highly relevant to fictional forms, as they might construct the prison experience from a potentially more partisan standpoint. The cultural studies scholar Peter Caster argues that any analysis of the prison system must compare the "lived experience" with the "cultural imagination" (25). Taking Caster's point into account, my analyses of Nunez's *The Last of Her Kind* involve both historiographic and sociological perspectives and explore the aesthetic forms used to represent the prison experience.[29]

George's choice to publish only Olympia's piece out of the entire set submitted to the literary journal leads us to understand the piece's centrality to the novel's formal complexity as a fictionalized prison biography. Because so much of Olympia's text involves Ann, the person she most admires and writes about according to her instructor's assignment, the piece ultimately elevates Ann to the status of a virtual saint. Consequently, "Orphan Annie and the Hand of God" might better be described as hagiographic in its approach. Olympia's narrative concludes with an explanation that her ideal reader is someone who would understand her consideration of Ann's life: "I sat down and began writing for Jesus" (379). Olympia's esteem of Ann draws from Ann's tireless activist work, despite the indignation her politics often inadvertently cause. After enduring continued harassment from other female prisoners and the prison staff (especially the latter because they know that Ann had been convicted of murdering one police officer and injuring another), Ann still continues her various tasks: "She'd always be on the education committee, but instead of teaching the most advanced levels like she'd been doing for years, she went after the hard cases, the ones with no English or some kind of disability, the ones all the other teachers had given up on" (365–66). Ann demonstrates a steadfast commitment to extending the civil rights of prisoners as well as the quality of life of the inmates, efforts that certainly echo her radical politics as an undergraduate student at Barnard.

When Ann succumbs to heart disease, having moved into the AIDS ward to help tend to patients even in her debilitated state, her status as a contemporary saint seems assured. Still, Olympia's narrative should be explored specifically for what it offers in relation to her own prisoner identity, one that is in development. Olympia's prison biography provides an example of an asymmetrical narrative viewpoint, in which a seemingly minor character narrates part of the novel to advance particular questions: who should be rehabilitated—both through the biographical writing process and as an incarcerated inmate—and who deserves more attention? Olympia's prison writings seem to tell us that Ann deserves more accolades than others, but instead, this spotlight directs our readerly gaze to a larger systemic ill—that of the failures of the carceral state. Ann is, in some ways, merely one subject among many, struggling to survive and to rehabilitate herself within the prison system.

The narratologist Monika Fludernik writes extensively on what she calls "carceral topography" within the realm of fiction. Fludernik contends that representations of prisons "thematize the crucial position of the prison subject as victim of penal practices and they centrally engage with the experience, and management of, the subject's identity crisis. This identity crisis may be cast in religious terms or in terms of (moral) truth, duty (vs. betrayal), personal conviction or political/ideological commitment" ("Carceral Topography" 46).[30] Olympia's search for meaning within the prison system threatens to be overwhelmed by the focus on Ann's obstacles and her tragic death, but following Fludernik's model, we see embedded in her account a quest for literacy and access to self-representation. In a consideration of the prisoner in modern novels, the cultural critic Dennis Massey argues that "many of the characters in prison novels" possess the skill "to adapt to and even, in some cases, to thrive in this unnatural environment, [an element] that is most remarkable about these books. By the midpoint of their narratives, the fear of the unknown, which any newcomer to prison experiences, has been overcome, and the peculiar social structure of the institution has been deciphered" (45).[31] The use of the word "deciphered" distinguishes Olympia's development as a prisoner-subject, as she comes to realize that being in prison provides her with the unique opportunity to step back and reflect on her life and the lives of the people around her. At a key point, Olympia, along with a number of her fellow inmates, engages the memoir as a literary form, as the inmates join a book club and receive free copies of certain books from publishers:

> We enjoyed these books and had lively discussions about them, but some found certain stories bewildering. "Her father did it to her just that one time, and she still crying about it?" "Why on earth would she walk out on a man who gave her such fine things?" "He says here he still made it to work every day. I don't call that enough jones to write a book about." There didn't seem to be many people writing about life behind bars, and that's when I started thinking how, if I ever learned to write, I'd like to do that. (367–68)

Of course, Olympia does "learn to write," ultimately gains her bachelor's degree, and moves on to learn a whole host of other skills; by the time her piece concludes, we know she is working toward a master's in professional writing. Olympia includes the book-club members' questions here because they gesture to the question Nunez is always interested in: whose life is most worth chronicling? These female prisoners tend to find the memoirs they read to be of little consequence, narrating lives and events that seem to pale in comparison to the challenges apparent in their own lives. And yet one pauses on the phrase "there didn't seem to be many people writing about life behind bars" as a way to consider how important it is for Olympia to represent a wide set of experiences, ones that exceed the focus on Ann's trajectory within the prison system. While Olympia ends her creative nonfiction work extolling Ann's virtues by comparing her to Jesus, she also elliptically narrates the development of her own journey to literacy and the struggles that the various inmates face. In other words, the inclusion of "Orphan Annie and the Hand of God" demands to be read beyond its biographical depiction of Ann, as such an approach fails to embody the very politics that Ann fosters: self-effacement in the service of others.

As the lens through which the contemporary prison experience is refracted, Olympia Underwood offers information that clearly parallels published studies on the topic and even perhaps fictively reimagines an actual women's correctional facility. Hence, Nunez's novel demonstrates how blurry the boundaries between fiction and nonfiction can be and that despite Olympia's status as a fictional entity, her struggles find footing in actual social contexts. Although it is unclear where the Maryville prison is located, the novel's depiction does seem to refer to the Ohio Reformatory for Women (ORW) in Marysville, Ohio. The ORW opened in 1916 and currently includes more than one thousand female prisoners, as well as a handful who require maximum security and one female prisoner currently sitting on death row.[32] At one point, Olympia explains the rise in the prison population: "When I first got to Maryville, there were about two hundred inmates. Now we got more than a thousand. They keep building new housing (there's now talk about adding a Death Row), but it never seems to be enough." She further details specific statistics and observations regarding these changes: "Turns out the number of women going to jail is growing at a faster rate than the men. Average age here is twenty-five, but we are seeing more and more in their teens. Most of the drug charges are for possession, and for lots of girls it's drugs *and* prostitution, the prostitution just about always being a means to the drugs" (367). Countless academic publications note, as Olympia does here, the skyrocketing rates of women's incarceration within the past three decades as well as the reasons behind the increases.[33] One of the most recent studies on women prisoners, provided by the writer Victoria Law, opens with these sobering statistics: "Although women in prison comprise nearly 7% of the U.S. prison population, their numbers are increasing more rapidly than those of their male counterparts: between 1990 and 2000, the number of women in prison rose 108%, from 44,065 to 93,234" (1).[34] Of the rise in drug arrests, the communication studies scholar Anne-Marie Cusac details that "the most obvious and commonly discussed attitude changes have been toward drug crimes. The number of people incarcerated for drug crimes in the United States 'rose fifteen-fold between 1980 and 2000,' reports a story on the economics of imprisoning drug offenders" (177).[35] These statistical accounts demonstrate that Nunez's reconstruction of the women's prison does, at specific moments, directly reflect the ways in which female incarceration has been conceptualized, studied, and critiqued by scholars in a variety of academic fields.[36] Olympia's awareness of the changes in the prison system further shows her interest in engaging the deteriorating conditions of her environment, as women face overcrowding and possible execution. The statistical specificity of her observations also suggests the influence of anthropological and ethnographic sources and methodologies, evidence that she completed significant research prior to finishing "Orphan Annie and the Hand of God." This passage thus illustrates Olympia's trajectory from uneducated young woman to socially progressive, educated prison elder and unofficial historian.

Olympia's prison reflections further clarify the larger civil rights dilemmas that are hallmarks of the novel, thus extending the biographical focus of her writings to other social contexts. In her prison ruminations, Olympia chooses to include a verbatim excerpt from an interview conducted by a journalist with Ann, in which Ann states, "*You can't hide from the world in prison, far from it. We see the worst of America, in the form of its worst victims. I hope while you're here you won't neglect to visit the hospital, especially the AIDS ward. American prisons are terrible places, and Maryville is no exception. But I'm not unhappy to be isolated from those who are responsible for it*" (370, italics in original). Vital to Ann's critique is that the prison might be read simply as a subset of American societal ills. Olympia's prison writings clearly evoke such a sentiment in relation to issues of racial injustice and tension experienced by the prison inmates.[37] For instance, Ann's decision to help facilitate a bilingual service for Hispanic prisoners is met with much derision and opposition by the correctional officers and prison administration, who cite the fact that her work "discouraged [Spanish-speaking inmates] from learning English" (343). Ann further riles the administration with her inflammatory discourse: "She liked to point out the obvious, that just about every staff person was white (though this has changed some over the years) and just about every inmate wasn't. She said the whole American prison system was nothing but an extension of slavery" (343). Ann's point underscores the disproportionate number of minorities within the women's prison, who develop a rather segregated sense of community. Olympia notes, "We didn't have real gangs at Maryville yet, but we had clubs, which was close. A club for white ladies, a club for Puerto Ricans, a couple of rival clubs for blacks. We had families, too, with parents called Mommy and Daddy, and Big Sister, Little Sister, and so on, though often there was just one baby" (353–54). Although Olympia's prison writings tend to understate the importance of race as a factor in the incarceration of women, as has been elaborated by many prison studies scholars, racial difference appears as a common, everyday structural inequality of prison life.

The text strongly implies that Olympia is African American, although it is never explicitly disclosed. In an earlier encounter with Ann, Olympia and a fellow inmate, Winkie, are drunk and chastise Ann for her "whiteness"; they end their tirade with, "Bitch, go find the white girls. Don't tell me you wasn't raised to stay away from niggers" (349). This encounter, although brief, alludes to the three women's racial identities, which leave them segregated in their specific racial clubs.[38] Certainly, the significant proportion of inmates given proper names within Olympia's narrative are women of color, whether referring to Bharti (South Asian Indian), Chinese Lucy, Puerto Rican Lucy, Winkie, Toy Babe, or Scarecrow.[39] Given the reference to "a couple of rival black clubs" and Olympia's statement that the "Hispanic population started growing and we got all these women who didn't speak English" (328), prison life as depicted in Nunez's novel parallels the disproportionate number of female prisoners who come from minority backgrounds.[40] While Olympia does not directly engage a racial discourse to describe prison life, racial difference permeates the day-to-day life of the Maryville inmates.

The only instance in which Nunez actually includes a character who overlaps with her own Chinese ethnic background appears within Olympia Underwood's prison biography of Ann. Chinese Lucy, as she is called, generates a more contoured picture of Ann. Olympia recalls

Ann's impressions about Asians: "She said a human being needs a lot less food than most folks eat, and she said look at the Asian people" (342). Olympia further notes, "at the time, the only Asian person we had to look at was Chinese Lucy (to tell her apart from this other Lucy, who was Puerto Rican, as if anyone ever even came close to mixing them up), and Chinese Lucy was this big fat girl with a full mustache who chowed down with the best of them" (342). Although a seemingly minor character, Chinese Lucy presents a contrast to the stereotype that Ann perpetuates concerning the stature, size, and appetite of Asians. This moment is remarkable in that Olympia shows a clear awareness of the dangers of racial essentialization. As Chinese Lucy disrupts the fantasy of the diminutive Asian, Olympia's musings regarding this character further reveal how the novel complicates the notion of authorship and narrative voice. Olympia recounts how Ann comes to advocate for Chinese Lucy, who wishes to eat with chopsticks rather than forks: "How many inmates before Chinese Lucy had even made such a request for there to be a *rule* about it? Next thing you know, she's got Chinese Lucy writing letters to this person and that one (actually, Ann wrote the letters herself, Chinese Lucy just signed them), and bingo, Chinese Lucy gets her chopsticks" (342, emphasis in original). In this passage, Olympia narrates the challenges that Chinese Lucy experiences as an inmate without access to culturally specific eating utensils and reveals how Ann appropriates Chinese Lucy's problems in the form of letters that Chinese Lucy signs. Ann's education and her literacy are put to service helping others, despite the fact that we understand Ann to be a privileged subject who cannot always understand the nuances of racial difference. Ann's campaign exemplifies how one might productively take the voice of another within the realm of writing to address an inequality. Olympia's prison biography must also be read metaphorically: it recalls Nunez's writerly act of creating a literary persona of a different ethnoracial background and employing her to explore issues of social justice and power differentials. In this manner, *The Last of Her Kind* echoes *For Rouenna* in its depictions of Asian and Asian American characters; they appear as seemingly minor but nevertheless important persons who enrich the terrain of social relations and contexts.

Olympia's musings about prison life and about Ann help model how the formal and the political intertwine. Olympia's prison writings point to the multiplicities inherent to the biographical venture, in which one can direct attention to other lives besides that of the central subject. However, the novel emphasizes the predicament inherent in the project of recovering a single life, as other individuals and life trajectories surface, distributing readerly investments. Nunez's aesthetic decision to narrate the prison experiences through Olympia Underwood serves to increase the distance between authorial position and the fictional landscape. This chasm effectively allows us to interpret the racial asymmetries of fictional representations, as the autobiographical and autoethnographic valences are minimized in the service of exploring the social inequalities that emerged in the post–civil rights era.

As illustrated by the analysis of the prison system in Nunez's *The Last of Her Kind*, the novel's connection to Asian American contexts might seem to be found in the author's ethnoracial descent rather than in any one aspect of narrative content. Although the text does obliquely reference anti–Vietnam War demonstrations and contains two minor Asian American characters (Bharti and Chinese Lucy), such references and figures are fleeting. The dilemma the book poses is not so much in its categorization but in what it offers to cultural critics and to Asian Americanists in particular. Here, I return to Chuh's "subjectless discourse," which opened this chapter. Chuh reminds us of the metaphorical nature of Asian Americanist discourse, which is rooted in the exploration of "resistance and racism" (*Imagine Otherwise* 27). In this way, Nunez's novel paints a compelling picture of race relations and class consciousness and specifically features the profound limits of white activism in its depiction of Ann's steadfast politics. Ann embodies the white, upper-class elite with the privilege to be as radical as she wants to be, but when Ann is arrested and incarcerated, her radicalism is put to the extreme test. Although Ann possesses advantageous connections as an affluent white woman, she does not use them in gaining the best possible defense counsel for herself; she instead offers up a critical assessment of the systemic racist logics undergirding Kwame's death. In the admittedly challenging milieu of the Maryville prison, and perhaps to our surprise, Ann only continues to hone her activist politic. If the novel places the activist life of a white, elite character at the center, it does so as much to critique her as to privilege her tireless social work, which often alienates the very people she wants to represent and defend. Ann herself understands that her exceptional position and her racial background give her the platform to take on a political radicalism that might seem paternalistic and appropriative to others. Further, Ann's activism is put into dialogue with George's developing white bourgeois subjectivity, as George finds herself often compromising her more radical beliefs to walk a more conformist path. We recall that it is only George's connection to her high-powered editor husband and the people he once knew that allows her a final chance to see Ann while she lies dying in a hospital. George's failure is not in her inability to be a good friend to Ann but in her dangerously insular obsession to document Ann's life.

So when George chooses Olympia's piece to appear in the final issue of *Caracara*, we cannot help but think that she has missed the whole point of Ann's radical politics—that despite Ann's quest to shift attention onto social inequality, the spotlight ultimately is redirected onto her. This result foregrounds the nature of white privilege that the novel engages, so that the death of Ann's African American husband, Kwame, for instance, does not yield substantive outrage over racial profiling in police interrogations and arrests; nor does Kwame resurface significantly in any of George's ruminations after he has been killed. Instead, the novel obsesses about the "last of her kind," the title an ironic evocation of Ann's radicalism and desire to efface her white privilege in the service of reducing social inequality and advancing human and civil rights. George's final substantive mention of Kwame suggests that Ann had been selfish in shooting the police officers who had detained Kwame: "I want to know what was in Kwame's eyes. ('His *beautiful* eyes, don't you mean?'). Disbelief? Reproach? Forgiveness? Love? How often must that moment have come back to Ann. And her famous words: *If Thomas Sargente* [one of the police officers] *had said* nigger *one less time, he might not be dead*" (385, italics in original). The insinuation here is that Sargente's racial epithet pushes Ann over the edge; she herself escalates the scene, killing Sargente and placing her husband in fatal danger through her actions. Ann appropriates African American oppression for her own, acting out a form of vigilante justice that finally and ironically kills the very subject whom she was seeking to protect. The leap that George might have made is ultimately not offered: this return to Kwame during the final pages fails to generate much traction with respect to the unfair systematic detainment of African Americans, especially racial profiling, that has led to the incredibly unbalanced rates of incarceration for men and women of color within the United States. Ann's actions are at best faulty in logic and come with the incredible price of her husband's life, but the larger structural issue that places black and other minority bodies under the regime of the carceral state both inside and outside the prison appears to be obscured by a continued myopia, one that places Ann at the front and center of George's narrative perspective.

Certainly, George's focus on Ann does remind us of the occlusions of a white perspective, one I explore in detail in chapter 1 of this book.

The white narrator in Chang-rae Lee's *Aloft* purports to embrace multiculturalism, but he ultimately fails to generate a nuanced consideration of his wife's life. In a similar manner, George never looks much beyond Ann's life to find others in the shadows, such as Olympia Underwood and her fellow minority inmates. Set in the post–civil rights era, both novels show the dangers of assuming that racial prejudice and oppression have been eradicated. In *Aloft*, racial prejudice and marginalization appear masked by the pedestrian nature of everyday interactions as they occur in a Long Island suburb. In *The Last of Her Kind*, Ann's stint in prison provides a lens into the dramatic breakdown of the American prison system.

Nunez's *The Last of Her Kind* imagines, then, a more circuitous route to the political concerns undergirding Asian Americanist critique through its elucidation of white privilege. We can use this narrative as a model to understand how other events and other lives can become subsumed by concentrating only on Ann's various activities. If George grants us a perspective into white insularity—her inability to ever look through the politically invested lenses that Ann pushes her toward—we can begin to understand how someone like Kwame simply vanishes from the narrative without larger contextualization or why the Vietnam War signifies through nothing more than a Ho Chi Minh poster that hangs on Ann's wall, despite the fact that George's brother is a veteran. A singularly invested biography threatens continually to erase the social inequalities of prison life, the larger scope of the tension dramatized by black-white race relations, and the warfare extending the American military presence in the Asia Pacific. Olympia's prison writings further depict minor characters such as Chinese Lucy who call attention to the ways in which narrative voice might be productively appropriated.

Thus, the novel models how Ann's investment in activism fails to influence George, as illustrated through George's storytelling. In a *New York Times* review, Megan Marshall faults the novel on the account of George's "self-indulgence": "She goes on about pill-popping at exam time and a bad acid trip, forgetting that no one but the partaker can find such tales of interest, and she makes readers privy to a good deal of unnecessary gossip about the staff members of fictional New York publications." The "unnecessary" in *The Last of Her Kind* is precisely what should make readers most wary of George's narrative voice, rather than her admission that she might not be able to recall everything with exact accuracy. The almost complete absence of Asian or Asian American bodies or contexts serves to augment the particularity that finally occludes George's vision, a depiction of white privilege that demonstrates, perhaps tragically, how little George has actually moved in her trajectory from a poor, white country girl to a literary critic, editor, and bourgeois career woman. Both *For Rouenna* and *The Last of Her Kind*, the reviewer Claire Messud notes, "are marked with the authority of lived experience, and readily acknowledge that authority. Their scope is not large, but their effect is profound." The effect of these books is "profound" because we can identify not only with the biographer-narrator but also with the biographical subject. Yet their "scope is not large," or at least not large enough, precisely because to look past the relationship between the biography's typical concentration on one life, we must engage a self-reflexive positioning that enables other potential literary subjectivities, voices, and social contexts to emerge and to clamor for recognition.

Mixed-Race Writers and Asymmetrical Identifications

The critical practice I advocate pushes literary critics to consider the ways in which the mixed-race Asian American writer might be asymmetrically read. In considering Nunez's approach to the creation of fictional worlds, we see that we cannot categorically authenticate her narrators as autobiographical doubles. In Nunez's debut novel, *A Feather on the Breath of God*, for instance, the unnamed narrator never reveals her exact blood quantum; nor should we as readers and critics care that we cannot definitively identify her mixed-race ancestries. Despite the relative lack of prominent and identifiable mixed-race characters in Nunez's following novels, in the two analyzed in this chapter, we see the pertinence of these works to the aesthetic and political inquiries grounding cultural criticism, especially as they arise in the biographical representations that depict the aftermath of the civil rights movement.

For Rouenna grants us an extensive look at how a narrator-biographer tells the life of someone she sees as a subject in a larger historical tapestry and as the basis of a necessary creative project, one that enables her to move beyond a critical writer's block. There is a sense that she must complete this work, if only because she harbors a sense of obligation both to Rouenna and to the larger gendered ramifications of her story: the narrator-biographer's work documents the challenging lives of American women who served in the Vietnam War as nurses. She delves meticulously into Rouenna Zycinski's life and the pathos that colors it, including the guilt the ex-military nurse experiences because she was able to do so little for the many Vietnamese children orphaned during the conflict. In doing so, the writer elliptically gestures to the ways that the biographical quest is necessarily unfinished, as one life leads into many others. The novel's conclusion sees the writer ruminate on another potential writing project, directed at the life of her childhood friend Luther. As with Rouenna, the writer's interest in Luther is not merely because they know each other but because there is something quite singular about his time in prison. Indeed, Luther describes himself as being "*buried alive*" (228), a statement that he does not fully explain and that seems taken up only when Nunez pens her subsequent novel.

Though in no way a direct sequel to *For Rouenna*, *The Last of Her Kind* perhaps presents a progressive step in Nunez's fictional publications by focusing on how American prisons largely fail to rehabilitate inmates. Minor characters of Asian descent do appear as female prisoners, but they are part of a larger group that draws attention not only to one racial population but to a greater gendered collective suffering under the breakdowns of the carceral system. The novel further spotlights a variety of social contexts, extending civil rights issues to locations far outside prison walls, as when Ann concentrates on anti–Vietnam War demonstrations. While these characters and contexts only come to light at seemingly minor points, we are nevertheless drawn to them precisely because Nunez redraws her novel as a fictionalized biography. Olympia Underwood's piece, "Orphan Annie and the Hand of God," illuminates how life-writing is incredibly heterogeneous, leading our attention away from someone like Ann and letting us think for a moment about how a text focused so much on white characters could still be so relevant to Asian Americanists and ethnic literary scholars. In the context of the prison system, the novel speaks to the social justice issues that are the subject of many cultural and racial critiques.

Like the uncompleted biographical act, the terrain of Asian American fiction is not fully circumscribed, never finally delineated, and always offering new narrative perspectives in a comparative scope. Rather than rehearsing a postracial aesthetic, Nunez's work opens up the space to consider how mixed-race Asian American writers can be analyzed from an expansive frame. Though such fictions are unbound to particular autobiographical or autoethnographic tropes, these novels generate nuanced perspectives concerning the social dilemmas that arise out of war and imprisonment.

4 / Comparative Colonial Narration: Conquest and Consumption in Sabina Murray's Fictions

Racial Asymmetries pushes critics to reconsider the relationships among the Asian American writer, the narrator and narrative perspective, and the fictional world. On the one hand, each chapter explores a different facet of narrational refraction that troubles the link between the storytelling perspective and the Asian American writer. Unraveling the bind between narration and authorial background is of paramount concern in an era in which writerly authenticity can be commodified and certain narrative forms run the risk of being elevated over others. On the other hand, these Asian American fictions cannot be said to deploy a postracial aesthetic in which the writer's creative output can be read as an expression of his or her unbridled freedom to imagine a narrative apolitical in its investments. The preceding chapter, for instance, calls attention to mixed-race Asian American writers, specifically Sigrid Nunez, whose background is not always mirrored in the ancestries of her novels' main characters or protagonists. Nunez's biographically inflected fictions speak to some of the chief social justice issues of the post–civil rights period, including the failures of the Vietnam War and the deterioration of the prison system. The sociohistorical contexts invoked by her narratives matter as much to our readings of Asian American literature as do the ancestries of narrators, protagonists, and minor characters. The fictional worlds conceived by Asian American writers such as Nunez possess a dynamic heterogeneity, which can be unpacked by directing our attention to the storytelling perspective. These works encourage scholars to make their interpretive methodologies more interdisciplinary and to expand the bounds of their social context critiques.

This chapter, though also focusing on a mixed-race writer, shifts in order to more fully engage the transnational features of Asian American literature. Earlier chapters, of course, do gesture to transnationalism, especially with respect to the immigrant figure and American acculturation. Indeed, these four chapters remind us that the fictions produced within the past two decades have emerged under the aegis of increased attention to the interconnectedness the United States shares with all areas of the globe. Rather than engage in some sort of superficial recognition of American multiculturalism, these chapters reveal the rather insidious forms of systemic social inequalities and thus the myths underlying postracial discourses. Yet this chapter clarifies how Asian American writers can produce fictions set in different countries and historical eras that address and explore pressing social issues specifically interrelated by colonial and postcolonial contexts. Such works, while not always directly linked to racial oppression occurring in the United States, remind us that the Asian American fictional world extends far and wide.

This chapter focuses on Sabina Murray's fictional publications and logically progresses my larger argument in its exploration of Asian American writers who employ narrators of ancestral backgrounds different from their own. Murray's larger fictional enterprise engages the racial asymmetries of fictional worlds, as many of her publications spotlight the complex dynamics of the colonial process from the vantage points of European, American, and Japanese empire building. These fictional works address structural inequalities wrought by aggressive international ventures based on dominion. I argue that it is instructive to consider Murray's work through the lens of comparative colonialisms, as the scope of her fictions continually widens to include varied geographical terrains and temporal periods. I use the term "comparative colonialism" in concert with Augusto Espiritu's observations on developments in Filipino historiography. Drawing on the multiple colonial histories connected to the Philippines, Espiritu asserts the necessity of a "bi-national (if not multi-national) methodology" in any study of the country (181).[1] Though Espiritu reviews a subset of historical studies, the label of "comparative colonialism" applies to Murray's larger fictional project. Looking at Murray's five fictional publications together reveals a strikingly diverse set of narrators and narrative perspectives that cannot be unified under one ethnoracial lens or colonial process. Though exploring representations and residues of American colonialism is itself a challenging endeavor, Murray's aesthetic choices require a multilateral critical model that takes into account a plurality of national histories and geographical settings. Murray says, "Growing up in a place [the Philippines] that has been so powerfully colonized is what affects me. Because of that, for example, Mexico feels incredibly familiar to me even though I don't speak Spanish. These big white nations with far-reaching tentacles propelled by foreign design—you can't get away from those tentacles under the watchful eye of the U.S." (T. Hong, "Writing from a Different Place"). Here Murray admits that what often helps shape her aesthetic choices is the trajectory of colonialism as it unfolds multinationally, linking the Philippines with locations such as Mexico with respect to their collective subjugation under the Spanish. Because Murray's fictions exhibit a kind of geographical and historical expansiveness that could be mislabeled as a postracial aesthetic, these works demand that readers attend to the relational power structures arising in colonial and postcolonial contexts.

Comparative Colonialism in Murray's Early Fictions

The arc of Murray's writings is similar to that of Nunez's. Like Nunez's, Murray's first novel, *Slow Burn* (1990), contains a protagonist whose Asian descent mirrors and overlaps the author's. Also like Nunez, Murray is of mixed-ethnic background, in this case, Spanish and Filipina. After *Slow Burn*, Murray's four subsequent works, *The Caprices* (2002), *A Carnivore's Inquiry* (2004), *Forgery* (2007), and *Tales of the New World* (2011), become increasingly difficult to analyze through Asian or Asian American contexts. While it is not entirely unsurprising that Murray would abandon explicit Asian American subject matter in her works, given her obvious interest in exploring other themes (as elucidated in interviews), the problem is that critics often selectively choose to include and to study the works of mixed-race writers only when those cultural productions are deemed directly relevant to particular field inquiries. I opened chapter 3 by showing how Diana Chang's work has been only partially considered and embraced; currently *The Frontiers of Love* (1956), the only one of Chang's novels that contains multiple, significant Asian and biracial characters, is her sole work to remain in print. Murray's work suffers from a similar kind of marginalization. Though her fictions are masterful in their various considerations of postcolonial histories and circumstances, they have been almost entirely ignored by critics, both within American ethnic literary studies and without. To date, no single work of Murray's publications has been the subject of any major analytical inquiries, either in the form of peer-reviewed articles or book chapters. Yet her fictions have won acclaim in other circles. Given that *Slow Burn* was published in 1990 and that her newest collection was published in 2011, a significant consideration of Murray's work is long overdue.

Murray's creative representations include multiple geographical spaces and historical periods that expose how violence and brutality propel colonial projects, as advanced by nations such as the United States, Spain, France, and Japan.[2] She is also currently drafting a sixth fictional publication focused on the life of the Irish dissident and humanitarian Roger Casement. In addition to employing descent as one marker of Murray's affiliation to American ethnic studies, then, critics must also widen the methods by which they read her fictional worlds. Murray herself suggests how we might begin to critique her publications. In her words, "Being mixed-race keeps you slightly at a distance. No one quite identifies with your experience completely—not that you could *ever* identify completely with anyone, but one part of you always stands back looking in a distanced, ironic way of perceiving what's going on around you. That distance carries through to everything you do" (T. Hong, "Writing from a Different Place"). This "distance" finds its way into her fictional works as she explores temporalities and landscapes that move beyond a mixed-race framework. This approach informs her fictions through the variety of storytellers she employs, who together unveil the barbarities produced out of the colonial enterprise and advance the racial asymmetries of her creative productions. Murray's fictions push us to consider the bodies and lives expunged through the process of conquest, moving beyond one central narrative perspective or narrator to other figures who are often located at the margins of the fictional world. Asian American identity and diasporic trajectories can thus be analyzed alongside a whole host of other sociopolitical contexts.

Slow Burn provides an excellent example of how Murray deploys comparative colonialist narration within the fictional world.[3] *Slow Burn* might be called an anti-bildungsroman in that it shows the gradual psychic disintegration of the protagonist, Isobel Della Fortuna, a young woman from an elite Manila background. The novel depicts a superficial celebrity culture in which young, urban Filipino elites bask in the glitz and glamour of Manila. Though Isobel is a rather narcissistic storyteller, her viewpoint still points to a more complex social and historical tapestry. As such, her perspective allows us to engage oblique references to Spanish colonialism, from the influence of Catholicism as characters attend Mass to the portraits that denote a particular character's European heritage. In the novel's concluding arc, Isobel notes the presence of the communist insurgency group New People's Army (NPA) deterring travel throughout the country. Though Isobel finds that the group disrupts her personal escapades, her reference to the NPA gestures to the growing resistance in the Philippines to neocolonial influence, as the United States financially backed the Marcos regime as part of an attempt to extend the influence of the Truman Doctrine. In this case, the United States provided monetary assistance to the Philippines, encouraging Marcos and his political cronies to contain any communist influence. *Slow Burn* thus grants readers entry into the multinational valences of empire. As with many of the other storytellers analyzed in this book, such as Jerry Battle in *Aloft* (chapter 1) and George Georgette in *The Last of Her Kind* (chapter 3), we must occasionally bracket the narrator to get a sense of the history and sociocultural milieu being referenced by the fictional world.

Unlike *Slow Burn*, *The Caprices*, a short-story collection, is not set specifically in the Philippines but in a number of different geographical sites, including Japan, Indonesia, New Guinea, and Singapore. Each short story contains characters of varying ethnic, racial, and national backgrounds, thus offering different viewpoints on the Pacific Theater of World War II. The opening and title story, "The Caprices," focuses on the atrocities perpetrated by the Japanese after they invaded and occupied the Philippines. In the story, a young Filipina, Trinidad, seeks revenge on the Japanese after she discovers the local head military officer, Sergeant Shori, wearing the ring of her late father, who had been executed by the invading forces. "Order of Preference" shifts the perspective to an Anglo-English mixed-race protagonist, Harry Gillen, who is languishing in a prisoner-of-war camp located in Singapore controlled by the Japanese. "Guinea" outlines the forced companionship forged on the battlefield between Burns, an American soldier of Irish descent, and Francino, an Australian soldier of Italian descent, as they struggle to survive in the jungles of New Guinea. "Walkabout" cycles *The Caprices* back to the prisoner-of-war narrative and involves a cadre of captured Allied soldiers. "Folly" moves to Indonesia, where a former Dutch spice trader, Bouman, attempts to block the romantic relationship that develops between a "native" named Tan and Bouman's daughter, Katrina. The eruption of war coincides with Tan's involvement in the Indonesian independence movement; in the aftermath, Katrina has died by childbirth, her daughter taken captive by the Japanese and used as a comfort woman. "Colossus" explores the unshakable alliance forged between an American soldier named Jim and two Filipinos, Totoy and Clara, who nurse him back to health at the expense of their own safety but must send him to a POW camp in order to save their own lives. "Yamashita's Gold" depicts the uneasy interactions between two Japanese, Carlos Salas and Pio Balmaceda, who, after their country's defeat, pass for Filipino and wait for the proper moment to exploit an extensive set of maps leading to buried treasure. "Intramuros" details the experiences of one Filipino family during and after the Japanese invasion of the Philippines. And "Position" concludes *The Caprices* with a story that specifies the strategically advantageous position of Saipan. Only the title story and "Intramuros" prominently involve characters of Filipino descent. In this regard, the collection as a whole does not neatly meet the expectation that the work will transparently reflect Murray's mixed-race heritage. Nevertheless, *The Caprices* discloses the range of colonial encounters that have shaped Asia and thus provides a fertile terrain to consider the aesthetics of comparative colonial representation.

"Position," the collection's final story, is unique because of its constantly shifting temporal perspective. The arc moves from early colonial ventures during the Age of Exploration to World War II's Pacific Theater, where Japan suffers a major defeat in Saipan. Murray creates an omniscient narrator who is able to access wider and wider sweeps of history. The story opens with Magellan's discovery of Saipan: "In March of 1521, Magellan sights the islands. At first, his hands clawed around a telescope, he thinks Saipan to be a sleeping monster. Who else would inhabit this liquid hell where no breeze blows? The crew is starving, eating leather straps and sawdust, hunting rats through the dark, rotting carcass of the ship" (197). This passage illustrates the desperation and depravity of the colonial enterprise from an era prior to the rise of the Japanese Empire. The crew is depicted through their gnawing hunger, one that will be metaphorically related to the destructive colonial appetite. As the narrator elaborates further, "The pope has divided the earth in two. The East has been given to the Portuguese, the West to the Spaniards, and [Magellan], a Portuguese, is sailing in the name of Spain. He will learn that the West never stops, keeps winding round and round, and the earth belongs to whoever is strong enough to take it" (197). As Spain and Portugal advance their national interests in the Age of Exploration, these lines imply that domination is transitory and often changes hands. Control of Saipan, for example, would not remain with either European country. Of particular interest is the multitiered nature of colonial power, in which Magellan, despite his position as the lead explorer, does not necessarily control his own destiny.

As the plot of "Position" moves forward, the omniscient narrator unveils different historical moments connected to this island and its associated archipelago. Once colonial contact occurs, the storytelling entity calls attention to the influence of European colonialism on Saipan: "In the seventeenth century the islands are renamed the Marianas after an Austrian princess. The native population is all but wiped out by the Spaniards. Beyond this naming and slaying there is nothing remarkable about the Spanish occupation of Saipan. In 1899, Spain, facing bankruptcy, sells the Marianas to Germany for four and a half million dollars" (198). What is vital to note is the rather nonchalant way the narrator describes the eradication of indigenous populations, modeling just how insignificant this group is. Saipan continues to be traded, as if the island is a commodity independent of the communities that have long inhabited it. Germany's role in the purchase of Saipan places yet another layer of colonial intrusion onto this location. The narrator notes that the "the Germans are getting a bargain" (198), suggesting that monetary value cannot encapsulate the worth of an archipelago, as the ability to purchase an entire set of islands overrides the importance of the cultures and communities that have long resided there. By the time this short story shifts to World War II, the story has already established that Japanese imperial aggression is merely the latest instantiation of military might and international invasion, thus outlining the vicious encounters produced through conquest across historical time. The absence of these indigenous populations helps contextualize how territorial acquisition takes place alongside the production of death advanced by the colonizer and experienced by the colonized. This "necropolitical" depiction as the postcolonial critic Achille Mbembe calls it, shows that *The Caprices* is not solely concerned with the Pacific Theater of World War II, as we might have thought at first, but rather with a vast continuum in which collateral damage is the hallmark of war and global domination. This story thus acts more diachronically than any other in the collection, widening out the narrative and temporal scope to animate readers to place conquests in relation to one another.

"Position" ends in Hiroshima just before the atomic bomb is dropped, as Japanese civilians try to go about their daily lives. This scene moves the reader's attention away from the many Allied servicemen and Filipinos who dominated some of the earlier stories to the daily lives of ordinary Japanese citizens: "They are bundling letters of dead husbands, departed sons. They are bundling letters from the Japanese army that say 'Akihiro died an honorable death in Singapore,' or Gaudalcanal or

Manchuria or Burma. Mothers are wrapping babies in padded clothing despite the heat, because they must do something to protect their children" (209). The passage underscores a different representation of the Japanese soldier by associating him with domestic circles that are being radically disrupted. The narrator seems to allow for a sympathetic reading of these mother figures, leaning on specific words and phrases, such as "bundling letters" and "wrapping babies," that chip away at any absolute conviction that the Japanese imperial powers can be represented as ruthless vanquishers intent on the conquest of Asia. The sentiments expressed in this scene make one wonder about a relativism that too quickly absolves the Japanese of wartime atrocities. In the context of Japanese national identity as rendered in the post–World War II period, Marilyn Ivy argues, "The catastrophe of Hiroshima has been used, it is said, to fixate national memory, such as it is, on the moment of nuclear holocaust as a displacement from Japan's own imperial war. Thus, the national role of traumatized victim has superseded the work of coming to terms with the infliction of war death and atrocities on others" ("Trauma's Two Times" 172).[4] The collection's rhetorical message resists this conclusion, however, by suggesting that victims and victimizers are affiliated by their shared entanglement within colonial power relations. The story spotlights how a dynamic narrative perspective illuminates conquest's multifaceted terrain of damage. As the omniscient narrator moves across historical time, the story also shifts in accordance with this mercurial balance of power, and what emerges from this aesthetic is the disruption of binaries and absolutes.

Moving away from the Asian geographies in which *Slow Burn* and *The Caprices* are primarily set, I spend the rest of this chapter reading two of Murray's later novels, *A Carnivore's Inquiry* and *Forgery*, works that depict, respectively, the decimation and anthropological study of American Indian populations and the pillaging of priceless artifacts from post–World War II Greece. Both novels are narrated from the first-person perspective of a racially unmarked character who is involved in promoting various forms of postcolonial domination. In *A Carnivore's Inquiry*, Katherine Shea justifies her intellectual interest in cannibalism through the Conquest of the New World, which, according to her, dramatically emphasizes the voracious figurative appetite of the colonial powers as they subdued indigenous populations. In *Forgery*, Rupert Brigg travels to Greece in the postwar era with the intent to bring back priceless classical treasures to be sold to American bidders hungering for a piece of the ancient past. In what follows, I outline how each fictional work advances the interconnectedness of postcolonial contexts through a first-person storyteller necessarily embroiled in an exploitative form of consumption. Along with the other writers critiqued throughout this book, Murray cannot be considered as some sort of double to the storytelling figures that take central stage in the fictional world. By distancing herself from any connection to these narrators, Murray incites critics to read these works through their racial asymmetries, allowing us to reevaluate the postcolonial Asian contexts of her earlier publications in light of the American and European settings of *A Carnivore's Inquiry* and *Forgery*.

The Insatiable Colonial Appetite in *A Carnivore's Inquiry*

A Carnivore's Inquiry opens with an intriguing hypothetical scene in which Amerigo Vespucci and Cristóbal Colón (Christopher Columbus) debate whether Spain had reached a "New World" or Asia. Colón argues that his contact with Indians proves that Spain had found Asia. Here Colón conflates the native populations he had encountered in the Caribbean with those of South Asian descent (7). As the scene continues, Vespucci makes clear that he believes the geographical location does not actually matter, as long as that location is claimed for the colonial power: "'No, Cristóbal.' And Vespucci smiles and pats his friend's arm. 'I say Hispaniola is in Europe'" (10). These different contentions about the New World signify how America and Asia are both land masses claimed as property for the colonial enterprise. In this way, Murray clarifies the process by which the colonization of the Americas might be put in conversation with the colonization of Asia. In both cases, as Vespucci conveys, it is the divine right of the colonial power to claim new territories, regardless of any differences among their "native" populations. The empire builders' disregard for geographical, cultural, racial, and ethnic specificity appears as a central issue in *A Carnivore's Inquiry* and elucidates how the colonial gaze frequently renders such groups as man-eating savages to advance international conquest.

The novel is narrated in the first person by the American protagonist Katherine Shea, a mischievous young woman who revels in telling readers about the murkiness of colonial ventures. The novel begins with Katherine's return to the United States after traveling through Europe. Low on money, she seduces an aging Russian American writer, Boris Naryshkin, who provides her the means to continue her various adventures. The majority of her exploits involve seducing and sleeping with men. Otherwise, she seems preternaturally obsessed by discourses of flesh-eating and carnivorous consumption, as conveyed through historical incidents, cultural productions, and flights of fancy. The plot hinges on the revelation that Katherine is both a murderer and a cannibal. Katherine's extreme polemical beliefs, unveiled close to the novel's conclusion, reconcile her taste for human flesh as something derived from her connection to a quintessential American identity. Of her business-tycoon father, Katherine explains, "He seemed to find my motivations a mystery, that I, because of my particular appetite, was the 'other.' But here he was wrong. His need for control, for money, for power, was based on the foundation of a populace debilitated by the appetites of the strong. This was his history. My history. The history of the world." Thus, she leaves readers to understand that her man eating is no different from her father's occupation: "Were we not cannibals, dispensing with the defenseless, concerned only with our own survival?" (286).[5] Even as Katherine equates herself with her father, she challenges his emotional response: he is not entitled to the horror he experiences when he discovers that she has been murdering and eating her victims because he, too, consumes others in his entrepreneurial ventures, albeit symbolically. In Katherine, Murray creates a highly unreliable but nevertheless inventive narrator who revels in the malleability of the historical past. As Katherine details and explains her interest in artifacts, cultural productions, and myths, she also undermines the certitude with which the indigenous subject is framed as a man-eating savage. She continually disrupts the narrative plotting and creates counterfactual or speculative narratives to engage the topic of cannibalism. I concentrate on these moments to show how this novel's dynamic aesthetic links individuals to larger structural inequalities and social oppressions and encourages an interdisciplinary mode of cultural critique.

The novel's opening arc immediately engages the racial identity of the indigenous subject when readers discover that Katherine is returning from Europe on Columbus Day. In musing about the conversations Vespucci and Columbus might have had, she wonders whether they "argued and came to no agreement, or agreed that the Indians were all cannibals and worthy of condemnation, and, worse, conversion. Or maybe they ate in silence, shoveling the undistinguished food into their mouths without conversation, the hours spent waiting for an audience with the king having left them with a profound hunger" (10). Katherine's narration exudes a darkly comic tonality, especially as the "profound hunger" experienced by Columbus and Vespucci appears as her metaphorical reference to the destructive motivation behind the colonial process.

At the same time, Columbus and Vespucci's hypothetical conversation again brings up the discourse of man eating with respect to indigenous peoples. Katherine's fanciful storytelling is undoubtedly entertaining, but this scene also calls attention to the historical documentation regarding the birth of "cannibalism" as an actual linguistic term. In Sara Castro-Klarén's work on anthropophagy and modern Brazilian identity, she reminds us that "groundbreaking studies regarding the construction of Amerindians as anthropophagi have shown how this trope was deployed by European colonizers and settlers in the Caribbean from the very first days of European contact" (295).[6] Such studies include the work of Frank Lestringant, who explains, "The noun 'cannibal' derives from the Arawak *caniba*, apparently a corruption of *cariba*, the name (meaning 'bold,' it is said) which the Caribbean Indians of the Lesser Antilles gave to themselves. To their enemies, however, the peace-loving Arawaks of Cuba, the name had a distinctly pejorative connotation of extreme ferocity and barbarity." As Lestringant goes on to note, "it was from the [Arawaks] that Christopher Columbus first heard the word during his epoch-making voyage of 1492" (15). As Katherine generates make-believe scenes between famous historical figures, these conversations elliptically illuminate the historical colonial contact zone that enabled the deployment of cultural designations. The novel continually dovetails with the discourses of cannibalism, especially in relation to the controversies around how this act could frame newly discovered peoples as inherently deviant and racially perverse.[7] As such, the colonial power could deploy sensationalistic depictions of indigenous cannibalism to legitimate conquest and religious conversions.[8]

A Carnivore's Inquiry continually offers Katherine's meditations on the indigenous subject as a man-eating savage. At one point, she peruses a book on art history and pauses on a section devoted to the Spanish painter Goya. She muses on a series of Goya's paintings known as *Scenes of Cannibalism*, described as "loose vibrant sketches of the Jesuit martyrs Lalement and Brebeuf, who were slaughtered by the Iroquois in 1649" (33). Katherine is quick to note that "the Iroquois were not cannibals, despite the legend of Brebeuf. Brebeuf was a Jesuit priest, a missionary to the Indians in the Canadian wilderness, who were not interested in conversion" (33–34). Katherine further narrates that in the various "sketches" envisioned by Goya, the "cannibals seemed more of an opportunity for Goya to paint the nude, some in classical poses and some more natural. Cannibals offered more of an opportunity to paint the human figure than, say, the family of Charles IV. And Goya didn't seem bothered that his Indians looked no more like the Iroquois than they did like Spain's royal family" (33). Katherine's invocation of "Spain's royal family" implicates the colonial enterprise in a form of cannibalistic hunger. Indeed, Spain's royal family can be seen as a metonymic embodiment of a voracious colonial power that is encrypted within the painting. The power of Goya's representation enables Katherine to believe momentarily in the very myth that Brebeuf's execution is based on. She imagines how it could have unfolded: "After the flames died down, the Iroquois warriors cut down Brebeuf's body. He was a strong man, even if he was wrong-minded, even if he was an ally to the Hurons—the Iroquois' hated enemy. The Iroquois, suitably impressed, thought they might ingest some of his might. They cut out the great man's heart, and, we are told, ate it" (34). This sequence again represents the indigenous subject as cannibal, despite the fact that Katherine knows that its factual accuracy is suspect. Katherine allows readers to see how the sensationalistic power of cultural productions can influence the psychic imaginary.

Katherine's overactive mind helps articulate some of the contradictory forces that shape the discourse of indigenous cannibalism. Various historical and anthropological studies have taken the Jesuits' records of Brebeuf's torture and execution as indisputable evidence of cannibalism practiced by the Iroquois.[9] In this vein, the anthropologist Peggy Reeves Sanday, the historian Thomas Abler, and other scholars argue that Iroquois cannibalism did occur.[10] Sanday explains that "incidents of torture and cannibalism are vividly described by the Jesuits who lived among the Iroquois as missionaries and who recorded their impressions in letters and reports sent to their superior in France" (126).[11] In reference to these same Jesuit accounts, Abler writes, "It is of course possible that the Jesuits manufactured all of these stories. However, given the number and consistency of Jesuit accounts of Iroquoian cannibalism, and given the support provided by other contemporary sources, it is most unlikely Iroquoian anthropophagy is simply Jesuit propaganda" (313).[12] Abler admits that fabrication could have colored Jesuit accounts, thus granting a space for doubt, the kind of doubt that Katherine conveys to her readers. Katherine's assertion that "the Iroquois were not cannibals" echoes many scholars who are far more skeptical of the supposed flesh eating by this American Indian tribe. The most vociferous of these counterarguments comes from the anthropologist William Arens, who gives numerous reasons for doubting this specific form of indigenous anthropophagy. Arens is skeptical, for example, that "charred human remains" proves man eating.[13] While the forensic data is potentially falsifiable, more central to this chapter's concern is the "missionary reporting" (Arens 128–29) and possible reasons for its inaccuracy.¹⁴ The anthropologist Pauline Turner Strong argues that "observer bias" may have influenced Jesuit accounts, especially as these narratives involve some of the more sensational aspects of American Indian violence (344).¹⁵ Given the desire to justify Christian conversion of natives to colonial centers in Europe, such depictions could sway key populations to support these religious ventures. As Strong goes on to note, this observer bias undermines the certitude and verifiability of the Jesuit accounts concerning Iroquois cannibalism.¹⁶

Katherine's narration certainly makes the novel polemical with respect to labeling indigenous peoples as human-flesh eaters. Like the novel's opening in which she imagines a dinner-table conversation between Vespucci and Columbus, Katherine invokes sociohistorical contexts to question the nature and development of cannibalism. With respect to Goya, Katherine implies that Spain's colonial agendas highlight a kind of metaphorical consumption of indigenous populations. These brief plot interruptions create spaces in which the novel continues to gain aesthetic and rhetorical traction. Readers continually wonder why historical figures such as Spain's royal family, Columbus, or Vespucci are included in the narrative and what their presence signifies, especially in relation to native figures and native representations. Katherine's own observer bias gestures more to the emphasis on the structural inequities produced by conquest, such that indigenous bodies are viewed not as flesh-eating Others but racial minority populations without the will to survive and thus fit to be vanquished. In this way, she continually redirects us to consider the colonial enterprise as metaphorically embodied by the practice of cannibalism through its desire to take over new lands and figuratively consume the lands' indigenous peoples in the process.

The novel's longest plot sequence involving actual indigenous characters again returns to the topic of American Indian cannibalism. In it, Katherine embarks on a brief journey to New Mexico to sell her mother's property. That ancient Anasazi ruins exist within the property lines complicates the sale of Alice Shea's home, however. After befriending Johnny, a character of an undefined indigenous background, Katherine and he have a conversation about the Anasazi:

> "I've heard that the Anasazi ate their enemies. I think that's a Hopi thing, but there's all kinds of digging around here, and I guess they think the same thing."
>
> "'They' being the archaeologists?"

"That's right."

"Some people," said Johnny, "think the cannibals were rebels from Mexico. They just came up here for a while and messed around. Ate a few Hopi. Ate a few Dineh. Made some good man corn. Wrecked a civilization. Headed back south."

"And who were these Mexicans?"

"I don't know. Just a bunch of people-eating freaky Mexicans."

"What do you think, Johnny?"

"I don't know for sure, but I think it came from within. I think the Anasazi were so fucking civilized that all the animal was building up, and then it bubbled over, and took the whole nation out." (141)

The repetition of the phrases "don't know" and "I think" by Johnny points to the instability of discourses related to Anasazi cannibalism. In this case, Johnny can only hypothesize the various reasons why the Anasazi engaged in cannibalism. Nevertheless, to Johnny, the Anasazi symbolize something both mysterious and dangerous precisely because their cultural practices cannot be pinned down and fully explained.[17] Like Katherine's fanciful visions of the past, though, Johnny's postulation involves figures from long ago who become part of a cultural re-creation that cannot be finally verified. Readers must thus approach his interpretation with skepticism and careful consideration. While Katherine's narration might seem secondary to this scene, she is precisely the character who focuses our attention on troubling indigenous representation. Indeed, in these conversations, what Katherine tells us is to question: every single time Johnny speaks, Katherine responds with a question.

Johnny's hypotheses regarding what might have led the Anasazi to engage in anthropophagy not surprisingly reflect the hotly contested academic debates on the same subject. But it is Katherine's incessant desire to question that encourages a deeper consideration of these various contexts. I thus take time to outline the various positions held by scholars to highlight the incredible interest in determining the factuality of indigenous cannibalism in just one specific tribal population living in a particular historical period. One of the keystone studies on Anasazi cannibalism, *Man Corn: Cannibalism and Violence in the Prehistoric American Southwest*, by Christy G. Turner and Jacqueline Turner, examines the warlike cultures of regionally specific indigenous groups.[18] Although inconsistencies across different excavation sites and bone fragments suggest that cannibalism did not always occur,[19] certain trends still corroborate the emergence of "social pathology" that might explain why indigenous groups began to inhabit locations with better defensive positions (such as carving out habitations from cliff walls) and to build more observation towers.[20] As resources became scarce and the competition among tribes increased, outbreaks of cannibalism could have occurred. Thus, indigenous groups may have been encouraged to settle in terrain so inhospitable to child raising, food acquisition, and agriculture. These studies ultimately reveal why so many historians, archaeologists, and anthropologists now view Anasazi cannibalism as a fact.[21]

Many others have disputed the reality of Anasazi cannibalism, suggesting that conclusive evidence cannot be obtained.[22] Native American studies scholar Elizabeth Cook-Lynn (Crow/Creek/Sioux) systematically challenges the assertions that the Anasazi practiced cannibalism, on several grounds, such as the use of coded language to sensationalize academic studies and the fact that studies do not admit that cannibalism is only one of many ways to explain why certain human bones appear in the forms that they do (107). Like Cook-Lynn, the archaeologist J. Andrew Darling regards studies of Anasazi cannibalism as rife with bias, presumptions, and guesswork. Darling argues that a better explanation for the human remains found at Anasazi sites is the execution of those who were considered witches, figures believed to have been engaging in dubious practices (732–33). One of the most compelling pieces of evidence supporting Anasazi cannibalism involves the presence of human proteins in fossilized human fecal matter, suggesting that humans were consumed (Diamond 152). Nevertheless, many scholars such as Kurt E. Dongoske, Debra L. Martin, and T. J. Ferguson, as well as the aforementioned Cook-Lynn, debate the meaning of such findings.[23] In exploring the doubts related to Anasazi cannibalism, one dilemma arises: does it even matter whether the Anasazi engaged in the practice?

A Carnivore's Inquiry responds to this question by presenting indigenous cannibalism as a speculative fantasy of debatable value. As we recall, Katherine is occasionally short on money; thus she hopes that she can sell her mother's property quickly. She asks the female realtor, who is described as "Indian, but more Mexican than Navajo" (140), whether the property will fetch a good price. The fact that Katherine notes the realtor's presumed racial background reminds us of her keen attention to physical differences and especially her interest in indigenous subjects. The realtor responds, "It may not be worth much to you, but there are some Anasazi ruins about a quarter-mile north of here" (140). The realtor's comment implies that the presence of Anasazi ruins in the local area could actually increase the property's worth. The realtor's admission thus affirms the importance of the American indigenous past as one that can be marketed or even consumed as an object of study and curiosity. The value of those ruins, of course, changes in relation to a specific audience. Indeed, Katherine seems to take a rather pedestrian view of the property: "My mother's ranch was north of Gallup on Route 666. The property seemed marked off at random. To my untrained, unenlightened eye, there seemed no purpose to having claimed this particular chunk at all" (140). Her viewpoint allows us to reconsider how property value is subjective precisely because Katherine does not see the importance of the ranch's location. Katherine further keys us into a skeptical viewpoint of the ranch and whatever it might contain: "There was a log cabin of the prefabricated, Sun Valley type. The rough-hewn logs and wraparound deck were calculatedly rustic, just as the gleaming steel, heavily applianced kitchen was calculatedly convenient. I sat on the porch swing, which offered an endless view of the uninterrupted land" (140). Katherine pauses to let us know that the ranch is full of façades, made to look as if it were rustic. That is, from the exterior, the ranch seems to come from a past era, with all those pioneer trappings, but its interior tells a story of leisure and convenience. The property becomes a kind of canvas on which certain fantasies can be projected.

For Katherine, as we are reminded, the ranch ultimately signifies as a form of capital that can be used to gain money. But archaeologists and forensic anthropologists might regard the ruins found on that land as a gateway to unlocking the cultures of ancient peoples. In this respect, the property finds another form of value in its relationship to academic studies. The disciplines of archaeology and anthropology can function to incorporate and to study the cultures of indigenous subjects through the selective redesignation of specific geographical sites. Though this incorporation is focused on the distant past, academic studies of Anasazi cannibalism still significantly influence how contemporary American Indian populations are conceived.[24] Indeed, scholarly research occasionally and unwittingly contributes to sensationalizing the indigenous subject.[25] Specifically, academic studies on Anasazi cannibalism enable a kind of neocolonial violence in which ancient culture is mined in the pursuit of scholarly knowledge, but without attention to how such knowledge and findings can recast contemporary indigenous communities as primitive hunter-gatherers. Further, we can consider the fascination with indigenous cannibalism as an academically situated interest that shifts attention away from other forms of social inequality. The archaeologists' conclusions that Johnny recalls obscure the colonial process, which, as Katherine suggests, engaged in a form of metaphorical cannibalism in its gluttonous conquest of the New World. At the same time, the pursuit of scholarly knowledge or financial profit ignores the contemporary concerns of indigenous communities that assert rights to their own artifacts. In other words, this entire sequence brings to mind why so many people are obsessed with certifying indigenous cannibalism, especially when compared to other violent historical processes and events. Finally, Katherine's description of the ranch as a "log cabin" elliptically recalls one of the most common architectural structures symbolically connected with America's westward expansion under the guise of Manifest Destiny. This westering, of course, was partly brokered on the conquest and removal of American Indians from their native lands.

These various considerations of and conversations about the native spotlight the novel's political heft, despite the interruption to the central plotting related to Katherine's various romantic liaisons with men. Certainly, once we discover that her sexual appetite coincides with a desire to literally consume the men she has sex with, we see that her interest in cannibalism is an attempt to justify and to celebrate her American colonial identity. Katherine's various musings about Native Americans and flesh eating also remind us of the novel's remoteness to Asian American studies. The novel might seem more suited to people interested in indigenous cultures—until we recall that the novel opens with Katherine's fanciful conversation between Columbus and Vespucci about Columbus's efforts to locate the New World within Asia. *A Carnivore's Inquiry* therefore enacts the racial asymmetries of Asian American fiction, as the novel is told through a first-person narrator who helps reveal colonialism's complicated yet interconnected trajectories. As posited by this novel's early counterfactual scene, one could hypothetically consider the discovery of the New World as fueled by a form of oriental imperialism. Comparative colonial contexts unfold through Katherine's storytelling process, as she associates European colonial designs on both the New World and Asia.

Like Murray's other fictions, *A Carnivore's Inquiry* requires readers to question any sedimented discourse and representation; the native as ravenous man eater is one racial formation that continually requires more scrutiny and more skepticism. We thus can reconsider how the speculative fantasy of indigenous cannibalism influences the scene between Johnny and Katherine, especially as he considers whether the Anasazi tribe possessed innate bellicose tendencies (141). Describing the motive behind the Anasazi cannibalism, Johnny uses the phrase "came from within," connoting cannibalism as a racial essence, an animality at the core of the tribe. But again, we must be attuned to Johnny's own uncertainty. This speculative discourse continues as Katherine finds a box containing bone fragments. While Katherine believes the box may be a message from her mother, Johnny believes the contents may be the remains of Hopi Indians (145). He believes that observing the proper funeral rituals could appease any malevolent or restless spirits. Indeed, the possibility of Anasazi cannibalism fuels his consternation; these bone fragments might be osteological evidence of man eating. Katherine speaks of a skull with the posterior end "smashed in" along with what she surmises is "a complete set" of the other bones. If Anasazi anthropophagy surfaces as a threat, it can only emerge on a conjectural level, as Johnny attempts to convince Katherine that the bones must have an honorable burial. In this entire sequence, Katherine reveals herself as a narrator keenly interested in the historical, anthropological, and archaeological past, though, importantly, she is still unable to determine the importance of these human remains.

The many questions and mysteries that the bones signify, on the level of why the Anasazi could have engaged in cannibalistic practices or, alternatively, whose bones they really are, encourage Katherine to get a second opinion. She accordingly takes the bones from the United States to the Bellas Artes Museum in Mexico, where she hands them over to Barry Buster Parkinson, her former college professor and lover, who is stationed there for an exhibition related to his research. This transnational movement solidifies the connection between the novel and academic discourses concerning cannibalism, as Katherine employs her connections to a scholar to unravel the mystery of these bones. Once in Mexico, Katherine and Barry's conversation returns to Anasazi cannibalism:

"Take a look," [Katherine] waved the femur seductively. "That scratch looks a bit odd to me. What causes a scratch like that?"

Barry Buster took the bone and weighed it in his hands. "That scratch is nothing, but this, see?" He indicated the end of the bone. "The blunting there? That is suspicious."

"What causes that?"

"We don't know for sure, but similar blunting has been produced by using the bone as a pot stirrer." Barry Buster stirred an imaginary pot, then handed the bone back to me.

154 / COMPARATIVE COLONIAL NARRATION

> [Katherine] held up the skull. "Smashed in the back," [she] said. "And charred, to the naked eye. Maybe you do have something."
> "What does it mean?"
> "The charring? You can cook the brains right in the cranium, which makes a handy bowl." Barry Buster put the femur back in the box. (153)

Even after Barry acknowledges that his specialty is far from studies of the Anasazi, he indulges in armchair analyses of the bones. The preamble to this conversation, in which Katherine reveals that the bones came from New Mexico, is vital in establishing Barry's presumptive and speculative explanation. Without much information other than that Anasazi ruins are nearby, Barry considers the possibility of cannibalism, with Katherine even offering her own flourish, as she "waved the femur seductively." The "seduction" stems from impressing on Barry her own excitement about the prospect that the bones are archaeologically important. Indeed, her quest advances the chance that the Anasazi could have had the savage appetite that Katherine herself emulates. This conversation brings to mind the earlier one between Katherine and Johnny; she and Barry are filled with possible misperceptions and uncertainties, as bones might "look" a certain way, but, as Barry states, "We don't know for sure" and "Maybe you do have something." These suppositions also recall the ways in which Anasazi have been positioned in anthropology as man eaters, despite controversial evidence. This conversation again relies on conjecture rather than any extensive testing or analysis. Barry also advances a sensationalistic narrative: the activity of human cooking gives insidious shape to a savage repast, where a femur changes into a "pot stirrer" and a skull becomes a "handy bowl" in which to cook the brain.

Katherine's wish to discover the importance of these human remains reveals more than mere willingness to speculate about the past because she looks to find other possible cultures and peoples who engaged in cannibalistic consumption. In this process, she further contemplates the representation of the American Indian as an authentic savage. What is interesting with regard to Katherine's search for more knowledge of the Anasazi is how little certitude she possesses about this indigenous group's actual background. Her inability to access this distant past gestures to the key debates over whether the Anasazi were cannibals. In the space of instability, the novel intimates that any blanket categorization of native peoples as cannibals is dangerous and that our attentions might be diverted away from another allegorical form of flesh eating:

Katherine's desire to consume the flesh of other humans parallels the desire of one nation to dominate (and to ingest) other lands, cultures, and populations.

The conclusion to the bone-fragment saga provides one key connection between Katherine and her mother, as readers discover that the bones actually belong to a man who went missing in New Mexico. The revelation is that Alice Shea was some sort of serial killer; this information appears alongside the reader's realization that Katherine herself is engaging in cannibalism, killing her male lovers and consuming their flesh. This discovery must be considered alongside the whole discourse of indigenous cannibalism in the novel. Whereas indigenous cannibalism is consistently questioned and debated, the one person who actually engages in anthropophagy is Katherine, an individual who does not claim any native ancestry. Johnny himself is one of Katherine's victims, so in the one case in which cannibalism is linked to an indigenous subject, he is the one consumed. This tragic fate again destabilizes the existing script that represents such figures as savage man eaters. Katherine's rapacious appetite, however, is not simply homicidal, sociopathic hunger. If Katherine does embody an insatiable colonial ethos that can be satisfied only by ingesting subordinates, this analogy is one of scale, scope, and contemporaneity. That is, while cannibalism cannot be categorically determined to have occurred centuries in the past, colonialism's symbolic consumption of the indigenous subject is far more concrete and, for Katherine, far more tantalizing.

As challenging as pinning down the indigenous history is identifying Katherine's racial status. She never divulges any information about her background, though her continual affirmation of European colonial powers suggests she could be white. In that case, Murray's mixed-race ancestry is not definitively mirrored in Katherine, nor would we want to assume that a cannibal and serial killer is somehow Murray's fictionalized analog. The imaginative storytelling perspective encourages readers and critics to move beyond an autoethnographic and autobiographical reading practice linked to social contexts most firmly associated with Asian American studies. As I contend throughout this chapter, Murray's fictional trajectory employs comparative colonial narration in which her many storytellers reveal the scope of various world powers intent on subjugating other nations. Through these narrators, Murray chooses not to restrict her representational content to Asian or Asian American contexts, thus invoking the racial asymmetries in her fictional worlds. *A Carnivore's Inquiry* encourages us to consider, on the one hand, that as a part-Filipina writer, Sabina Murray cannot be tethered to narrative perspectives that mirror this mixed ancestry and, on the other, that the fictional worlds she creates cannot be assumed to focus on Filipino characters or contexts. When Katherine travels to Mexico to see Barry Buster, for example, she spends her time traveling to locations that symbolize colonial power, including the palace of Hernán Cortés. Describing the palace, Katherine notes, "There was none of that lightness, frivolity, excess here, rather the feeling that adobe walls—the very ceiling—had calcified out of crushed bone, been cemented with thickened blood. Glass cases were arranged on the walls displaying pens and inkwells, woven goods from the Philippines, leather-covered bibles from Spain, the junk of colonization" (158). This passage inconspicuously alludes to the colonial enterprise, as Spain's presence extends not only to Mexico during the conquest of the New World but also to its ventures in Asia as the colonial power that reigned in the Philippines for three centuries. As a result, the reference to "woven goods" reminds us that Asian contexts do remain connected, however elliptically, to this fictional world. Although Asian geographies do not have a major presence in the narrative, their occasional appearance reasserts the global and multinational scope of colonial domination and further reminds us of Asia's importance to the West's consumptive desire. Katherine's observation that the palace seems to be made of "crushed bone" and "thickened blood" shifts narrative attention away from purported indigenous cannibalism back onto the carnivorous appetites of powerful nations such as Spain. This reference to the Philippines is the only one in the entire novel, which challenges literary critics to read this book with a strongly comparativist eye.

 The fact that this scene also takes place in the contemporary period spotlights the unstable nature of memory. The palace is converted to something more akin to a museum, where various items are displayed as artifacts of authenticity. However, the touristic gaze reduces the complexity of the structure, allowing it to be read as beautiful and magnificent instead of as a site emblematic of bloodshed and decimation. Recall how anthropological research, although seeking to determine verifiable histories of indigenous populations, could nevertheless produce data and reconstructions that might sensationalize and reaffirm the native subject as savage. Katherine's astute gaze reconfigures Cortés's abode as a place founded on violence and the metaphorical consumption of Mexican natives. She thus redirects our attention to the systematic destruction of indigenous populations engaged by colonial powers.

In the novel's exploration of indigenous cannibalism and the historical depiction of American Indians as barbaric savages, *A Carnivore's Inquiry* possesses much relevance to the concerns of Asian American studies, on the one hand, and indigenous and postcolonial studies, on the other. If racialization can be enacted as part of the colonial enterprise, in which racial minorities must be digested for national and international gain, this experience can be placed relationally with respect to a number of Asian American immigrant populations that have, by and large, also faced subjugation under imperial designs. Although reviewers such as Carlo Wolff and Michiko Kakutani find the book too superficial for their tastes, Murray's novel exhibits a dynamic aesthetic approach to the representation of structural inequality through an unreliable narrator who is intent on justifying her cannibalism. We recall that Katherine ends the novel asserting her connection to her business-magnate father, but we should pause for a moment to think about what Katherine proposes in this assertion. One of Murray's most brilliant narrative tricks is her subtle representation of global capitalism through the shadowy business dealings of Katherine's father, who is mentioned at only four or five different points in the novel. One key moment reveals her father's almost total focus on his job: "I'd watch my father balancing the massive checkbook, scratching missives back and forth from his company (Park, Shea and Dunn) to other investment corporations that spun money out of paper. Sometimes I'd watch him for close to an hour before he noticed me sitting in the chair" (81). It is unclear what kind of investment company Katherine's father runs, but the focus on profit is obvious, as he enables his family to have a life of wealth and privilege. Despite such material advantages, Katherine reveals that her father paid her little attention except in putting her to use for the purpose of gaining more clients: "To cement the goodwill between him and his future [business partner], he decided to have a dinner party. My mother referred to the people invited to these parties as 'the living dead.' Business parties at our house acquired the acronym N.P.s, which sounded antiseptic and proper, but actually stood for 'necrophiliac prostitution'" (118). The dark humor conveyed here undergirds the larger discourse of the use and abuse of the father's occupation to dominate his family's domestic life. Katherine is forced to play the role of the dutiful businessman's daughter, despite the obvious fact that she finds her father's coworkers to be figuratively ghoulish. The emptiness that pervades Katherine's family unit is contrasted with the father's total focus on finances. Indeed, Katherine's father is rarely present in the novel precisely because he is always looking to complete the next big business deal. Katherine's father thus becomes the metonym for American global capitalist desire and its hunger to dominate populations for labor power in the service of profit. When Katherine as an individual character seeks out new flesh-eating opportunities in Canada, we wonder if she is really the so-called cannibal we should be worried about. *A Carnivore's Inquiry* leaves us in an ominous place, suggesting that the new global economy must have its appetite sated through the labor of racial Others.

Art and Crypto-Colonial Appropriation in *Forgery*

Forgery, Murray's fourth fictional publication, also involves the wide arc of imperial projects, revealing how colonialism can surface in insidious ways. Greece, although not typically associated with American ethnic studies, is the fertile ground of *Forgery*, spotlighting how the acquisition of classical art becomes a damaging form of transnational appropriation. This process is likened to a more subtle form of colonialism, detailed through the adventures of an antiques dealer traveling to Greece in pursuit of more goods. The year is 1963. Rupert Brigg, the protagonist and narrator in *Forgery*, is a thirty-year-old American man who is not racially marked. At the novel's outset, Rupert travels to Greece for both business and pleasure. Dispatched there by his father, known as Uncle William, Rupert aims to find precious classical Greek artifacts, such as ceramic jars and fragments of statues. Rupert has also been encouraged to journey abroad in the wake of a tragic drowning accident that killed his son. The strain following the child's death led to the dissolution of his marriage, and he hopes that some sightseeing in Greece will take his mind off his troubles. Upon arriving, Rupert meets an old friend of Uncle William's, a Greek man by the name of Kostas Nikolaides, who is accompanied by his son, Nikos. After settling in at an Athens hotel, Nikos and Rupert embark on various adventures, which include romancing European tourists. Rupert also manages to make another acquaintance, Steve Kelly, a journalist staying in the same hotel. Once Rupert locates a couple of leads for his artifacts search, the novel shifts to a fictional Greek island called Aspros. The plot thickens as Rupert travels with Nikos, and they stay with Nikos's cousin, Neftali, who lives near properties and areas that might yield more classical artifacts and other treasures. At that time, Neftali happens to be entertaining a motley crew of guests, including Jack Weldon, a famous American sculptor, and his wife, Amanda; Nathan, a rich American publisher, and his boyfriend,

Clive; and Nathan's dear friend Olivia, who is dying of cancer. The latter half of the novel also includes a murder plot in which Amanda ends up killing her husband, in part to retain the material wealth that Jack begins to lose as he becomes more politically involved and uses his artistic talents to aid others rather than to make a profit.

Like Murray's other novels, *Forgery*'s plot seems to have very little to do with Asian American characters or contexts. Indeed, no major or even minor characters are marked as Asian or Asian American, nor do any of the major plot elements situate Asia and the United States in some sort of dialogic relationship. Even in passages that take place in the United States, little suggests that the United States is beginning to be embroiled in a war in Vietnam. However, Asian American literature must be read through its racial asymmetries, as the storytellers directing Murray's fictional worlds encourage critical reading practices in which colonial contexts can be read comparatively. *Forgery* presents yet another case of a narrator unusually concerned with history. As opposed to Katherine's tendency to question, Rupert is much more inclined to embrace a reductive view of the past in which culture can be accessed through artifacts rather than the living people who might be able to better understand a location's peculiarities and its riches. The novel questions how individuals categorize and determine the value of objects in relation to their passage through time. Though actual man eating does not take place in *Forgery*, the novel gestures to the metaphorical ways in which one nation consumes another through the purchase and the pillaging of its cultural productions. This mode of ingestion operates selectively by promoting only goods and objects, often at the expense of that nation's inhabitants. As Rupert begins to understand his participation in this process as an antiques dealer, he begins to reconsider his relationship to art and to profit.

While Murray's earlier fictions take place in countries where colonial influence has been well documented, modern Greece is an interesting case because it was never directly colonized, although at points it was occupied by foreign powers. The anthropologist Michael Herzfeld considers Greece to be exemplary of what he has called "crypto-colonialism," defined as "the curious alchemy whereby certain countries, buffer zones between the colonized lands and those as yet untamed, were compelled to acquire their political independence at the expense of massive economic dependence, this relationship being articulated in the iconic guise of aggressively national culture fashioned to suit foreign models" ("Absence Presence" 900–01). Herzfeld's larger aim is to consider "the relationship between Greece and social-cultural anthropology: that both were products of the colonialist venture, being respectively a physical location and a discourse through which the moral segregation of the West from the rest of the world was effected" (902). Herzfeld explains how the Enlightenment project sought to identify one European origin point and targeted Greece as one possible marker for this hallowed past. According to Effie-Fotini Athanassopoulos, "Up to the eighteenth century Europeans regarded their heritage as Roman and Christian in origin. The great shift from Rome to Greece, the rise of Hellenism, began in the mid-eighteenth century. An idealized Greece was now defined as the starting point of European identity" (279).[26] In some ways, to imagine Greece is to imagine an ancient and unchanging civilization, one that could firmly root a Europe seeking a distinguished past. In a study of the ambivalence of modern Greek poets in relation to the past, Gregory Jusdanis foregrounds the historical underpinnings of artistic values: "This strong interest in Greek art established a relationship to antiquity that was unique, for it posited classical Greece as a utopia worthy of emulation. Travelers went to Italy and then to Greece with the aim of observing, recording, and removing its masterpieces" (46).[27] As ancient Greece attained this signification, archaeological excavation became commonplace.[28] The esteem placed on Greece based on its classical history was no less important for the United States, which sought to integrate classical arts and disciplines into its founding cultures, as has been documented by a variety of historians and cultural studies scholars.[29]

At the same time, Greece's relationship to the United States must be considered in relation to the novel's temporal specificity. Because the novel is set in the post–World War II era, Cold War politics offer much to ground *Forgery*'s narrative. Greece's difficult and chaotic economic recovery required significant financial support from the United States. Further, intelligence data marked Greece as a geographical nexus point; the country could function as a strong buffer between the communist East and the capitalist West.[30] In this regard, many historians argue that Greece was pivotal in the development of Cold War policies, especially in relation to the creation and deployment of the Truman Doctrine. Judith S. Jeffery clarifies the goals of the Truman Doctrine and the subsequent deviations from that initial model.[31] Moreover, Jeffery explains that though the Truman Doctrine is strongly associated with military intervention and war, "the speech on which the Doctrine was based made absolutely clear the administration's commitment to its preferred method of containment, which was through rehabilitation and reconstruction. This was the core of the Truman Doctrine, including its application in Greece" (2).[32] In addition, Howard Jones and Evanthis Hatzivassiliou both show that Greece's northern territorial integrity was consistently in question due to the possibility of an independent Macedonia as well as invasions by Bulgaria.[33] The border alongside Albania and Yugoslavia, too, became a potential haven for Greek communists engaging in subversive activities.[34] Such findings explain the militaristic nature of the Truman Doctrine, in which violence and conflict were perceived as necessary given the specter of communism. When the Greek civil war began in 1946, the United States financially and militarily supported the more right-wing government in power, to the detriment of the communist-oriented opposition, which was ultimately handed a bitter political defeat in 1949.[35]

Strengthening Greece's military clearly occurred at the expense of the social welfare programs that could have cultivated a more stable political and economic atmosphere in the postwar period. Consequently, America's hold on Greece became paramount, as the country depended on the United States to continue its economic recovery. Jon V. Kofas sums up a commonly held view that Greece was compelled to "maintain high defense expenditures, to pursue a right-wing ideological and political orientation, and to follow free trade and orthodox monetary policies. In the three decades after the Truman Doctrine, Greece struggled to forge representative institutions, to modernize its economy, to advance education and health care, and above all to improve living standards" (4).[36] Herzfeld's notion of crypto-colonialism appears most salient here, as the Greek government faced mounting expectations to remain centrist and to dilute and expel any radical leftist presence to remain in America's good graces. Complicating matters during the period directly after the end of the civil war was the territorial dispute over Cyprus that loomed between Turkey and Greece, making the postwar national environment one of ongoing uncertainty.[37]

That the novel begins in 1963 is significant, especially since Greece was then at a turning point. The right-leaning government that had been in power since the conclusion of the Greek civil war had lost recent elections to the more centrist party headed by George Papandreou. In addition, new elections gave the United Democratic Left a majority in the new parliament, a situation that alarmed many observers in Greece and in the United States due to the party's communist leanings. As Herzfeld notes, "Papandreou was no leftist—he had been the British authorities' choice for prime minister in exile during the earlier phases of the war and had refused to form a coalition with the procommunist United Democratic Left after his initial victory in 1963" (*Portrait* 186). But other sites of power, such as the palace and the military, became alarmed. Criticism of Papandreou stemmed from the perception that the country would be "under threat from communist menace within and without" (Clogg 157). Whether or not the United Democratic Left symbolized a dangerous return to the more militant tactics of the Communist Party of Greece (KKE), the implication—according to Western military intelligence—at the time was that a communist threat still existed and could overtake the country. This possibility further explains why the United States backed a Greek military-led coup in 1967, hoping to push the country firmly back toward the right. Adding to the general political turmoil during the 1960s, anti-American sentiment was high in Greece, as a result of US intervention in Vietnam and its entrenchment in the territorial disputes between Turkey and Greece over Cyprus.

Against this backdrop that merges the former brilliance exuded by Greece's classical antiquity with its postwar politics, *Forgery* treads unstable international topographies. My reading of this novel takes a cue from Constantine A. Pagedas, who states that "the study of US-Greek relations between 1952 and 1963, . . . following Greece's recovery from the devastation wrought by the German occupation and the Greek civil war, is a period often neglected by historians and has not received the attention it deserves" (91). *Forgery* enables an exploration of crypto-colonialism at work during this neglected period, in which cultural appropriation occurs in the context of economic interdependence. Rupert Brigg can be read as a narrator-character who must negotiate his own complicity in a transnationally exploitative business venture, as he seeks to find rare classical artifacts that can then be sold in the United States. We should therefore expand the conception of crypto-colonialism by considering the very word nestled in the term: "crypt," where the dead are buried. Brigg's archaeological excavations require him to literally uproot an artifact and bring it metaphorically back to life. Of course, the artifact that Brigg revives is ultimately connected to global capitalism, as art circulates in a market economy in which classical antiquities fetch exorbitant prices. This process involves Brigg's frequent interactions with Greek locals, many of whom seem unaware that Brigg has come to plunder classical artifacts, sculptures, ceramics, and pottery. Though his business operation appears harmless to the locals, Brigg clearly values inanimate objects more than he does the laborers and contemporary artists he encounters. This novel thus exposes the more inconspicuous forms of consumption that unfold alongside crypto-colonial undertakings, in which people living in the present are rendered obsolete.

Forgery also exposes other issues related to Rupert's artistic leanings, which surface based on his personal experiences of loss. At the novel's inception, Murray introduces a discussion of aesthetics as conveyed through Rupert in a monologue, which suggests that art's status might have the ability to grant humanity access to the divine: "The need to approach the inanimate bulk of solid marble and find himself within it: idealized, beautiful, immortal. Without art, we have no hope of discovering our divinity, our oneness with God" (1–2). But Rupert also reveals an ambivalent relationship to art. While he acknowledges that art can be "beautiful," he believes that it can be also "useless" (1). In the context of his son's death, Rupert finds the creation of art completely superfluous but still finds himself looking for some sort of existential fulfillment, needing to "believe in something. Maybe in science, a sort of art, and transference of energy" (2). Rupert's crisis of faith animates the novel and is resolved only amid Greece's crypto-colonial landscape, where his halfhearted journey helps him rediscover how he might put art to a range of meaningful uses.

Rupert travels to Greece, in some sense, with a skeptical gaze. As an antiques dealer, he has an attachment to the beauty of classical forms, yet he is wary of the idea that art can bring one closer to divinity. The country might contain beautiful antiquities, but this prospect still leaves him without much hope for personal healing. When Rupert arrives, he reveals this particular conception of the landscape and its people: "It was 1963, and although they'd managed to weather the last two thousand years, they had the bad form to let it show. Something in my Western education had encouraged me to view Greece as a beloved anachronism, a culture that, thus preserved, entered the modern age in England, and the space age in America, as the great baton of civilization got shuttled around" (5). Rupert conspicuously discloses his desire to traffic in the stereotype of Greece as a static landscape, akin to, we might say, orientalist depictions of the Middle East. Rather than aging, Greece should be ageless, perfectly "preserved," while other countries assume a progressive trajectory. Thus, Rupert expresses his disdain for what he sees as a flaw in the way that the country appears: "Greece should have been something I could go back and visit—Ancient Civilization Land—as if it were a pavilion at the World's Fair. But the architecture was all recent postwar-boom concrete and the music was the belch of misfiring engines and pragmatism. The people had been through a lot, and it showed in their shabby clothes" (5). These two passages establish the multiple ways in which Greece remains a landscape of oppositional conceptions. On the one hand, Greece is the "beloved anachronism," a site in which an unchanging past can be found. This perspective helps explain why Greece might be viewed as "Ancient Civilization Land" and "a pavilion at the World's Fair." The evocation of the "World's Fair" is further appropriate given the fair's historic connection to the development of anthropology as a discipline and the growing desire to classify and study what was considered foreign, primordial, or primitive. On the other hand, Rupert also realizes that Greece is not simply a location of classical ruins and artifacts, noting the "postwar-boom concrete" and other such developments. That Rupert places Greece in relation to England and America is significant because Greece, by that time, had received major financial and military support from both countries. As such, the postwar era becomes an immediately vital element to the plot, contrasting effectively with the anthropological and archaeological elements that characterize Rupert's search for classical goods and commodities. The clash between the ancient past and the contemporary moment underscores the contradictory ways that Rupert first observes Greece. Yet Rupert's critique of the Greeks' struggle to modernize—they "had the bad form to let it show"—exposes a rather dismissive attitude, especially given the nation's thorny sociohistorical trajectory.

As an antiques dealer, Rupert resituates Greece as a nation with potentially inexhaustible resources. In this quest to find precious ancient items, Rupert must authenticate such objects through two different and important characteristics tied to geography and temporality: "I had to determine the provenance and the provenience, two seemingly similar words but so much more than that to the dealer in antiques. Provenience spoke to origin; provenance to history" (41). Since Rupert can easily prove that the items he finds are from Greece, the more difficult element becomes the way he can "provide a past" for an object or artifact. The ability to categorically pinpoint an object's connection to a historical event raises that object's value. Rupert provides one example in the context of Abraham Lincoln and the pencil he may have used to compose the Gettysburg Address. On the one hand, a pencil existing at the time that Lincoln wrote the address might be considered "just a pencil from Illinois, approximately a hundred years old. Not that remarkable." But, on the other hand, "if that same pencil had been used to draft the Gettysburg Address, it would of course be priceless. The pencil would no longer be a pencil, because who would write with it? But it was something you could hold in your hand, a concrete reminder of the significant, historical, and dead" (41). Rupert explains that provenance possesses the power to transform the object, which then takes on another functional capacity. The pencil no longer would be used to write but instead accrues value in its positioning within the historical past. This shift from the pencil as a functional tool to the pencil as a priceless artifact establishes how an object's movement through time alters its signification. The reference to the Gettysburg Address further reminds readers of the tumultuous period of American history that saw the country embroiled in a bloody civil war. The historical context for the Gettysburg Address obliquely calls attention to the very moment that Rupert travels to Greece, where the tensions of that country's civil war can still be felt in the political arena.

As Rupert continues to seek out classical antiquities, he begins to understand that art's value is ultimately subjective and constructed. For instance, he realizes that his family friend Kostas can capitalize on the wish to own something related to the ancestral past: "The value of an object is whatever it can fetch at auction.... I could see how someone like Kostas, with his gift for palaver, had been able to make himself quite an empire, because provenience requires only some knowledge of regional industry, and provenance a good imagination and a willing customer" (41–42). If "provenance" can be falsified, then art assumes an unstable and arbitrary value. The word "empire" is one to pause on, as it clearly links Kostas to the economy of art production. Kostas can act as a go-between for Westerners such as Rupert who seek a piece of Greek history and the locals who might have the appropriate items that can be linked to the desired provenance. An artifactual "empire" forms through this process; Greek culture, even as it is manufactured in some cases, is appropriated, something that can be claimed from afar. Rupert will later attempt to hide the fact that a Greek sculpture he acquires is actually one of a large group of forgeries. As Rupert rationalizes it, "I knew the head was inauthentic but was not prepared to sacrifice it as such. I thought of all its sisters resting beneath the waves in Faros. If I could just get rid of them, my head would stand alone, an important find. Disputing the authenticity of a single head would be much more difficult than relating it to a known group of forgeries" (195). Rupert's quest affirms a kind of empire building that fails to account for provenience in relation to contemporary geographies. He does not fully acknowledge the bodies that work to help excavate or create these forgeries and why these forgeries would have been created in the first place; nor does he consider his privilege as a transnational elite.

In addition to Rupert's search for priceless goods and objects, *Forgery* embeds a second narrative concerning American intelligence agencies that monitor the Greek resistance and communist guerrillas. While this social context might seem peripheral to Rupert's initial quest, the novel depicts a country in political turmoil, with locals attempting to carve out their own lives, in some sense competing with all the buried treasures waiting to be found. Two local Greek characters, Tomas and Thanasi, spotlight the problematic way that Rupert views human lives in contrast to artifacts. Tomas is hired to oversee and manage the workers at the main dig. Having been hired by Rupert's cousin, Nikos, Tomas looks to this position as a gateway, opening up the "prospect of a job in Athens and maybe even New York" and thus pushing him to "find something" (162). Rupert agrees with this rationale and believes that it "was the best way of having the dig yield something real" (162). However, Tomas is a cunning tactician, maintaining close contacts with everyone at Neftali's estate in hopes of landing any opportunity to leave Aspros permanently for a more financially advantageous life. For example, he conspires with Amanda to place a sculpture at the dig site—the very one that Rupert will later discover is a masterful forgery—so that he can pretend to find it, believing that this act would cement his status as an indispensable manager and enable him to leave the island.[38] His activities also include a dalliance with the queer character Clive, despite the fact that Tomas does not seem to be interested in anything more than a platonic relationship and thus engages in a kind of homoerotic performance to keep Clive, who is particularly affluent, within his orbit. Regarding Tomas's so-called friendship with Clive, Rupert believes "not that this sort of friendship wasn't possible, it was that anything was possible as long as Tomas could get off Aspros. Behind those unblinking black eyes and heavy lashes was a calculating mind, an aware individual who knew that his only currency was his good looks and a canny intelligence capable of making the quick decisions needed to advance himself in the world" (177). Despite being persistently regarded by Nikos as "poor" (182), Tomas exploits the various Western characters who populate the novel to improve his job prospects and his upward mobility. Rather than passively let opportunities pass, Tomas establishes how the locals cannot be categorized as simple, backward, provincial, or unsophisticated. However, Tomas's very youth—his "good looks"—while granting him a certain local maneuverability, still conveys his living status, in contrast to the buried objects that Rupert seeks. These inanimate pieces are perceived to have considerably more value and mobility than Tomas could apparently ever hope to possess. In this regard, crypto-colonialism reemerges to frame the inequities faced by Greek working-class locals, who struggle to exhibit the kinds of worth already given to artifacts.

Thanasi, another local Greek, is a friend of Jack Weldon's, although the true extent of his friendship with Jack is not fully revealed until the end of the novel. Rupert and Steve Penny, the presumed CIA agent disguised as a journalist, travel to Thanasi's home on a hunch that Thanasi may know more about Jack's murder. Steve surmises that Jack had recruited Thanasi for the purpose of making forgeries that would flawlessly mimic classical antiquities. The money gained from these forgeries could then be funneled into communist guerrilla activities. However, this particular sequence also shows the difficult life that Thanasi leads as an artist. As Rupert describes it, "I assumed that Steve must have broken the news of Jack's death to Thanasi because of the dejected way he was sitting on the edge of his bed, a small one with a flat mattress and dirty sheets," adding, "I was trying to think of what Asprian things could be worth something on the black market, and all I could come up with was *myzithra*, the local cheese—one did need a license to sell it. Cheese. Chickpea croquettes. Caper salad. That's all Aspros had to offer. Thanasi's house was barely the size of my room at Neftali's and it was difficult to find a polite place to look" (194). Thanasi's meager living situation must be contrasted with the high value placed on the classical pieces that Rupert pursues. Further, the notion that so little could be of value on the "black market" in Aspros illuminates the general way in which the contemporary and the living have little relevance to an economic circuit conditioned on cultural appropriation. If Aspros has apparently so little to offer, then we understand Tomas's tactical associations with Amanda and Clive, as well as Thanasi's desire to work for someone like Jack, who clearly encourages him to engage in subversive activities.

Thanasi's life must also be considered in relation to his talents. As the sign on Thanasi's door reads "real local pottery" (191), the word "real" offers some insights into the novel's exploration of artistic production, especially in light of the way that the study of classical antiquities cast Greece as an imagined origin point for Western beauty and European identity. The "real" local pottery ends up being the forgeries, which Thanasi creates so skillfully that his inauthentic classical pieces can pass the scrutiny of expert art appraisers. At the same time, Thanasi's ability to mimic valuable artifacts generates new ways to consider the motivations behind what others could consider a dubious practice. In an earlier conversation between Rupert and Kostas, Kostas suggests that forgers could simply be recast as artists, rather than as counterfeiters: "'Forger? Is it all so simple for you?' interrupted Kostas. 'This man was an artist. A Greek! What is the difference between this artist and the man who made the bell krater five thousand years ago?'" (47). Kostas relays how the contemporary forger fails to register to outsiders such as Rupert as a skillful professional. Someone like Thanasi, therefore, becomes synonymous with the quality of his current life, specifically his squalid and small living quarters. In exploring the challenging milieu of contemporary Greece and its cultural politics in relation to their emergence in press coverage, Vangelis Calotychos argues that creating a national identity through antiquities is ultimately shortsighted (1–2). Calotychos offers a way to contextualize *Forgery*'s rhetoric as expanding what counts for a national identity: the contemporary and the classical both can and should be considered important for defining Greece. In this way, the novel intervenes in the discourse of artistic production and spotlights the importance of local communities, as they attempt to carve out livelihoods in the instability of the postwar period.

Rupert finally begins to change his opinion of Jack Weldon, especially as he further investigates why forgeries are being produced. Initially he had found Jack pompous and overblown: "[He was] a man of convictions, mostly political, and he liked to hear himself talk. He hated the Greek king and hated the current government for being controlled by the Americans. He believed that the common man in Greece lived in a state of complete oppression. As he held forth, we passed the platters of food up and down the table" (109–10). In the context of Rupert's own ambivalent relationship to art's value and his approach toward acquiring classical antiquities, he initially finds that Jack fails to practice what he preaches. And yet the plot reveals Jack's willingness to challenge his own complicity in the American agenda to control Greece's political development. His artistic talent enables him to nurture and to finance subversive political activities. That is, he uses his sculptures to generate funds for Greek resistance fighters and communist rebels. Along the way, he hires and recruits local artisans such as Thanasi to construct forgeries that fetch high prices from Western antiques dealers such as Rupert. For Jack, art becomes functional when reconfigured for a specific purpose that promotes political change. Art's value and signification lie not in its intrinsic worth but in its ability to help alter what Jack deems a corrupt governmental regime. Influenced by Jack's quest for social change, Rupert discovers a different value set for art, one not based in the historical past but in the political present.

Thus, the narrator of *Forgery* comes to comprehend the importance of contemporary artistic production. Rupert confronts his own myopia when fetishizing ancient Greece. He further comes to see the political instability and the vitality of the contemporary Greek context. Those who are living, such as Tomas and Thanasi, seek routes of escape from the class, regional, artistic, and political constraints they encounter; they desire recognition from transnational elites, such as Jack Weldon and Rupert, who offer the potential for better lives. Whereas the historical past illuminates the comparative colonialisms at play in *The Caprices* and *A Carnivore's Inquiry*, *Forgery* gives us a narrative perspective that helps to elucidate a crypto-colonial national milieu. Rupert unearths a new value for artistic objects both ancient and modern and comes to appreciate the nature of their political influence. Although *Forgery* does not directly depict colonialism through the metaphor of anthropophagy as *A Carnivore's Inquiry* does, the novel nevertheless explores the violence and brutality of artistic appropriation and consumption, on the one hand, and political domination, on the other. By situating Greece within the nexus of Cold War concerns, *Forgery* is elliptically connected to the geographical terrains so often embroiled in communist containment conflicts, such as Korea or Vietnam. As literary critic Jodi Kim points out, "although Truman's speech [later dubbed the Truman Doctrine] was immediately inspired by events in Greece and Turkey, the global battle against totalitarianism that it proposed to wage soon found its terrain in Asia" (52). Of course, Kim's reference to Greece and Turkey acts only as an introduction to her larger concerns with Asian American cultural production; but as her book *Ends of Empire* makes clear, the Cold War cannot be conceived of as a uniquely Asian phenomenon. Hence, *Forgery* finds traction as a novel that widens the bounds of Asian American studies by placing the Greek postwar period as part of the historical trajectory that later led to the containment policies enacted in countries such as North Korea and Vietnam.

Inauthentically Productive

By resituating Jack Weldon and others working with him as skillful artisans, *Forgery* recasts the contemporary forger as a cultural producer worthy of respect and attention. The novel's final scene involves Rupert admiring one of Jack's sculptures on exhibit in a museum in the United States and calling his work "'divine'" (248). We recall the novel's opening, which depicts Rupert's loss of faith in the importance of art, but

Jack's quest in Greece clearly strikes a chord with Rupert. The whole issue of forgery also brings us back to the issue of authenticity more broadly: what is the value in authenticity, and how is authenticity itself a construct?

These questions have analogous significations for the Asian American mixed-race writer who shows how authenticity might not be so transparently mapped onto the fictional worlds he or she creates. Indeed, an authentic ethnoracial narrative voice cannot be substantiated against the author's own descent, nor can we selectively privilege the work of mixed-race writers based on how their particular ancestries are mirrored in the construction of storytellers. Instead, critics must attune themselves to the ways that Asian American literature unfolds through its racial asymmetries. Whereas Murray's *Slow Burn* might be read through the direct link between the Filipina narrator and the author's Filipina heritage, Murray's later fictions are increasingly difficult to tether to this parallel. In Murray's case, her larger fictional project imaginatively illuminates comparative colonial narration in which one nation's attempt to dominate others emerges as part of a longer, repeated historical formation. *The Caprices* presents the Pacific Theater of World War II in all its murkiness, as the line between enemies and allies increasingly blurs. Here Murray employs shifting narrative perspectives to stage how violence is central to the colonial process regardless of national affiliation. The sweeping historical narration of the final story, "Position," clarifies the protean nature of brutality and conflict in conquest scenarios. *A Carnivore's Inquiry* involves a highly dynamic but troubled narrator influenced by history, but Katherine draws our attention to the colonial past to justify her man-eating habits and to commit heinous crimes. Murray sets this fictional world in America, in part as a critique of the colonial inheritance that propelled the literal destruction and the metaphorical consumption of indigenous populations.[39] Finally, *Forgery* offers us a narrator who must understand not the historical past but the present moment to find new ways to appreciate art. Colonialism emerges in far subtler form through the veiled horizon of Cold War dynamics that embroiled Greece as a buffer zone between the capitalist West and communist East.

At these rich and imaginative junctures in which colonial encounters are placed in dialogue with one another, Murray creates storytellers who help reveal that the arc and range of Asian American fictional worlds are wide and vast.

5 / Impossible Narration: Racial Analogies and Asian American Speculative Fictions

This chapter presents perhaps the most difficult epistemological questions for cultural criticism because it engages the political import and aesthetic qualities of Asian American speculative fictions. Such chimerical representations result in what the literary critic Darko Suvin calls "cognitive estrangement" (*Metamorphoses* 4), precisely because we seem unable to map our own reality onto the fictional world. Chapter 2 explored one such speculative text, Sesshu Foster's *Atomik Aztex*, which describes an alternate reality in which the sixteenth-century "Aztex" defeat the Spanish conquistadors. This narrative offers Foster the chance to reconsider the nature of conquest and colonialism and to rescript an entire global history. This fanciful depiction also enables the Chicano storyteller at the novel's center to envision the importance of a warrior consciousness. However, the novel's conclusion focuses on a fictional world more closely modeled on a realist aesthetic in that the protagonist agitates not for victory over conquistadors but for the unionizing rights of slaughterhouse laborers. Because the novel directly references contemporary social contexts, including issues related to minority migrant labor and global capitalism, the narrative finds strong relevance for scholars engaged in materialist and historicist approaches to cultural critique.

Moving away from the social realist conclusion of *Atomik Aztex*, this final chapter concentrates on what the literary critic Seo-Young Chu would describe as "high-intensity" fictions (7)—fictions that include intergalactic travel, aliens (some radically nonhumanoid in form and composition), alchemy, and time travel. This chapter presents a logical endpoint to *Racial Asymmetries* because it contemplates what cultural studies gains by embracing such phantasmagorical narratives. In some sense, speculative fictions by Asian American writers push the field the furthest toward expanding its critical lenses, precisely because these narratives are so incredibly whimsical.

I push Chu's theory of science-fictional representation, found in *Do Metaphors Dream of Literal Sleep?*, further to show how Asian American speculative fictions can be interpreted and critically engaged.[1] Chu argues that "science fiction" is "a mimetic discourse whose objects of representation are nonimaginary yet cognitively estranging" (3). In many respects, Chu reverses Suvin's foundational claims about science fiction because Chu links the genre more firmly to realism. While estrangement occurs in science fiction, her reading practices bridge that estrangement to reveal the murky boundaries between fictional and nonfictional contexts. But Chu's thesis must be expanded to encompass speculative fictions more broadly. Indeed, "speculative fiction" is an umbrella term, encapsulating a wide variety of genres that stretch beyond the bounds of realism, including but not limited to the gothic, horror, fantasy, and science fiction. Speculative fictions of all types also function to estrange readers, making us question what is believable and plausible and what is not.

Like Chu, I focus on the mimetic nature of speculative fiction, but I concentrate on the ways that speculative fictions function analogically, encouraging us to relate the fictional world to an encrypted social context.[2] According to Suvin, "the resulting alternate reality or possible world" of the science-fictional text "is, in turn, not a prophecy or even extrapolation but an *analogy* to unrealized possibilities in the addressee's or implied reader's empirical world: however empirically unverifiable the narrative agents, objects, or events of SF may be, their constellation in all still (literally) significant cases shapes a parable about ourselves" (*Positions and Presuppositions* 37, emphasis in original).[3] Suvin reminds us that there is a way to transfer meaning from science-fictional worlds and make it applicable to our lives. The importance of science-fictional analogies exists in their plasticity and slippage: the fictional world is compared, but not exactly equated, with "parable[s] about ourselves." Thus, I emphasize how one science-fictional narrative might produce multiple analogies. We can say that Asian American speculative fiction requires a critical practice that reorients our eyes toward the ways that issues of racial difference are obliquely encoded into narratives that include supernatural beings, otherworldly entities, or futuristic technologies.[4] Rather than thinking of such narratives as evidencing a kind of postracial aesthetic, instead we must be attentive to the highly metaphorical and symbolic formulations of social inequalities as they surface so idiosyncratically in these works.

The racial asymmetries of Asian American speculative fiction appear in the ways that the genre allows the writer to distance authorial ancestry from the narrator and/or the protagonist of the fictional world. This disjunction encourages readings of the fictional world that move beyond autobiographical or autoethnographic interpretations. I primarily analyze two works in this chapter: Claire Light's short story "Abducted by Aliens!" from her collection *Slightly Behind and to the Left: Four Stories and Three Drabbles* (2009) and Ted Chiang's novelette *The Merchant and the Alchemist's Gate* (TMATAG; 2007).[5] I begin with "Abducted by Aliens!" because it belongs to a collection explicitly attuned to how speculative fiction can be used to politically engage readers and invoke actual historical events, despite the cognitively estranging representational terrain. Light's use of the genre relates one Japanese American family's internment experience to a narrative of an alien abduction. Due to Light's choice to construct a fictional world with so few direct ethnic or racial markers, this story is best read alongside an accompanying afterword. I then shift my attention to Chiang's time-travel tale. Chiang's novelette, which depicts a premodern Middle East with analogs and referents to contemporary social contexts, offers a revision of the oriental tale. This genre, often set in the Middle East, illuminates a fictional world replete with caravans, harems, deserts, sandstorms, and other such images and locations. The flexibility of temporality that the genre exhibits offers us an opportunity to place this literary form in dialogue with the US War on Terror.

Though the two works are seemingly disparate in terms of their subject matter, Light's short story and Chiang's novelette both centrally explore the complicated contours of racial formation in periods of heightened fears over individuals deemed un-American. "Abducted by Aliens!" illuminates a social context in which Japanese Americans are determined to be "enemy aliens." This designation arises in part from transnational valences of racial formation. The political theorist Fred Lee reminds us that "predating America's declaration of war on Japan, the Yellow Peril figured the Japanese as a racial danger within the territory of the state as a matter of danger." If the Japanese presented a "racial danger," then so, the logic goes, did Japanese Americans on the West Coast, who might be spies. Such racist reductions were ratcheted up in the period following Pearl Harbor and clearly influenced the relocation of Japanese Americans to internment camps during World War II. As "enemy aliens," Japanese Americans lost "the protections of citizenship, at the stroke of a pen" (Bayoumi 285). Given the anti-Islamic fervor that swept the nation after the first Gulf War, many Middle Eastern Americans, Arab Americans, and Muslim Americans face increased prejudice and racial scrutiny. Many scholars explicitly reference the Japanese American internment in relation to the contemporary treatment of "anyone perceived to be Muslim" (Naber 226).[6] According to the cultural critic Amy Kaplan, the post-9/11 era inaugurates the "enemy combatant" as a "racialized category, not only because of rampant racism toward Arabs and Muslims, but also because of [a] long history" in which "stereotypes of the colonized, immigrants, refugees, aliens, criminals, and revolutionaries are intertwined with those of terrorists" (840).[7] The enemy combatant, an individual associated with and supposedly advancing the War on Terror, is considered a stateless subject, without national affiliations and therefore without protections under the Geneva Conventions. The legal scholar Natsu Taylor Saito explicitly connects the designation of "enemy combatants" to Japanese Americans in the internment era, as each group is stripped of national affiliations and the protections of citizenship (256). "Abducted by Aliens!" and *TMATAG*, both published in the post-9/11 moment, thus speak to these current social contexts in which the War on Terror marks bodies and lives for racial discrimination, increased surveillance, and loss of civil liberties. These two publications deploy racial analogies in which individuals of Japanese and of Arabic descent appear transfigured in speculative fictions: as invading aliens or wily time-traveling orientals. Each narrative gestures to the ways that conflicts and tensions in Asia— referring to both the Far East and the Near East—continue to influence the cultural imagination.

"Abducted by Aliens!" and *TMATAG* also brilliantly convey the dilemma at the heart of this entire book: the challenge facing the cultural critic analyzing Asian American speculative fictions, which warrant readings not only through racial and ethnic themes but also through aesthetic, formal, and generic registers. Finally, each work features a first-person narrator who cannot be seen as a double for the Asian American writer, but these storytellers are distinguishable from those that appeared in earlier chapters because they relate narratives that seem impossible. Light's narrator tells of extraordinary interplanetary travels, while Chiang's Arabic storyteller travels through a time-bending portal.

Alien (Japanese American) Asians

"Abducted by Aliens!" centers on a woman who is apparently retelling the fantastical experiences of her older brother, who is deemed by their family to be mentally unstable. Because of his apparent psychosis, the family further encourages the protagonist and anyone else to disregard his tales. But the unnamed protagonist disobeys this request and proceeds to reveal how her older brother was, as the title reminds us, abducted by aliens. From this point, the story meanders from one intergalactic episode to the next, as the brother travels from one strange planet to another and is basically held captive for four years. The older brother is also given a choice about whether he wants to return to Earth or end his captivity sooner, which would mean that he would have to find a place on another alien planet because the aliens are on a specific course. In the end, he endures the four-year period and returns to Earth, but even in the final pages, we are not quite sure what is happening. On the one hand, it seems as though he wakes up in a hospital, but just paragraphs later, he seems to be teleporting from a spaceship into some other location, where the "interior walls were made of unpainted, gapping wood planks" and where "the floors were covered with sand" (83). Directly following this short story, Light offers an explanatory afterword that reveals that she intends "Abducted by Aliens!" to be read as a Japanese American internment narrative.[8] Thus, Light's story and corresponding afterword present us with an analytical question: do we necessarily need an additional document or source to help analogize a speculative fiction? Light herself seems skeptical that anyone would be able to properly decode her story. In the afterword, she admits, "A childish part of me wants you to just *get it*. But I've made that impossible for anyone who is not me" (85). Without her exceedingly useful afterword, much of our interpretive activity would be focused on a fictional world that seems at the surface level about an individual who goes mad and who believes he has been abducted by aliens. Light does include certain ethnic cues: almost all proper names of the human characters sound ethnically Japanese; these include Emiko and Yuki. Further still, there are moments that interrupt the intergalactic odyssey in which words such as "camp" (75), "barracks" (78), or "war" (77) appear, suggesting that another layer of meaning is to be "decoded" (86). These various references imply that this story does contain Asian American characters and is set during a time of conflict. But such references unsettle the reader, as they are difficult to understand in relation to the alien-abduction storyline.

Given only slight implications of and allusions to Japanese American characters and the internment, Light's afterword seems an essential aspect of the story. Otherwise, the speculative fictional world takes on a level of abstraction, apparently unfolding on a depthless plane without direct connections to external referents or historical contexts. Indeed, there is never any absolute indication that the major characters are actually Japanese American; we can only guess based on proper names and some other cultural signifiers. We can turn to the literary critic Sue J. Kim to reconsider how such imaginary and cognitively estranging landscapes can be reoriented with respect to issues of racial difference and social inequality. In her reading of the fantasy film *Lord of the Rings*, Kim argues that the "racial codings" of the film "have no referent; they function at the level of pure discourse. The Uruks are big, black, savage, and dreadlocked, their faces marked with painted on designs as if tattooed. The heroes are of 'the West' and 'the White,' while Mordor is 'the Black Land.' These fantastic representations can and do exceed, while never wholly shedding, delineations of current and historical racial discourses" ("Beyond Black and White" 881). Kim shows how it would be too reductive to read the fantasy landscape as a racial binary in which evil dark races fight against the benevolent lighter ones. Instead, Kim analyzes the film through and by means of the film's production process. Most acutely, Kim reminds us that the film was shot on location in New Zealand, a country "marked by the history of colonialism and imperialism" (890). The film's speculative premise presents an ambivalent relationship to race, exporting it onto fantastical beings but obscuring the centrality of casting indigenous actors and using indigenous cultural traditions in the film. To read *Lord of the Rings*, then, is to look not only at the film beyond its self-contained depiction, but also considering the social and historical contexts in which it is embedded. For Kim, history, race relations, postcolonial politics, and global capitalism are all intertexts, which reveal how a speculative terrain can be read and reframed.

Looking at the real-world contexts that ground the speculative fictional world provides us with a way to engage Light's afterword. Indeed, I argue that the afterword is an essential intertext providing us a way to begin interpreting "Abducted by Aliens!" as it clarifies the various politicized aims of Light's speculative narration. This document gives us an insight into Light's aims as a mixed-race writer of Chinese ancestry, taking on the voice of a Japanese American woman to illuminate the predicament of cultural history and narrative reconstruction in the wake of a traumatic event. While the afterword does provide an indispensable outline of Light's aims, it is not exhaustive; thus, I use the afterword as a starting point to explore further how "Abducted by Aliens!" can be read analogically.

"Abducted by Aliens!" reveals the ways in which authorial ancestry is not necessarily mirrored within the fictional world. In published materials, Light discusses her background as a mixed-race Chinese American, revealing a fundamental difference between her life and her mother's: "I, on the Other hand, am Chinese American and multiracial. I was born an Other in the world, and have no home ground to go to where I'm not Other."[9] Her choice to write this story from a cross-minority context, in which narrative perspective is given to a Japanese American woman, requires critics to read this speculative fiction through its racial asymmetries. This story challenges the presumption that, due to Light's ancestry, it should primarily contain references to mixed-race Chinese American characters or cultures. Like Light, the narrator from "Abducted by Aliens!" is aware that storytelling can be an appropriative process: "[My brother] has permitted the sound of my voice to alter and temper his, so that I would have a voice to step into when I was grown, an authoritative male voice that could command me and that I could use to command him in turn, turning his own voice against him" (65). The passage reveals that the narrator's claims to the experience of her brother's abduction are questionable because she never witnessed the event and can only retell the fragmented memories of her older brother. In this sense, her voice gets to "command him," in that she controls what is remembered and what can be communicated. Given all these uncertainties, the narrator finally admits that she could be unreliable: "Who knows? This [story] may be entirely my own invention" (65). In this way, narrative perspective is never a transparent or an unproblematic apparatus for historical, cultural, or experiential recovery. The narrator's unreliability also reminds us that Light herself cannot be read as having produced a veiled autobiography, that the story must be considered for its "invention." Further still, this divulgence gives the storyteller a rationale for the fantastic and disjointed alien-abduction narrative.

Alien-abduction narratives possess particular generic characteristics that make Light's choice of the form quite appropriate. The form allows her to explore questions of authenticity, identity, and storytelling, as the veracity of these narratives is often questioned. The typical abductee is, according to the literary critic Adam Roberts, "a white, moderately affluent thirty-something American. Abductees are taken suddenly from their homes by aliens, restrained (perhaps shackled) and transported to the alien spaceship" (144). While captive, the victim is subjected to a variety of traumatic experiences, often including scientific experimentation, torture, and sexual assault. The ostensible motivations for such practices stem from otherworldly desires to take advantage of human subjects or to find out their weakness or biological functions to glean information that allows the aliens to carry out other tasks. These tasks might include creating an alien-human hybrid or gathering data that would help the alien species launch an attack on all of humanity. Once abductees serve out their duty, they are compelled by the aliens "to forget, or at least to suppress, memories of the experience, usually with some quasi-telepathic invasion of the mind" (Roberts 144). Only then can abductees be returned to their former lives. Thus, both body and mind are violated in the process of the alien abduction. Because these events are so traumatic, the alien-abduction narrative is formalistically fragmented, with temporal gaps and spatial discontinuities. An abductee might be faced with a blinding light on a country road, later find him- or herself on a spaceship, and then wake up in bed and realize that only two hours have passed. With the credibility of this narrative (and by extension the abductee) always in question, the alien-abduction tale, by virtue of its fanciful and speculative nature, remains without resolution. If anything, the abductees often report multiple instances of being taken by aliens, suggesting that this form is at its core all about repetition, rupture, and circularity.

Beyond some common generic features, the alien-abduction narrative invokes the binary, which first appeared during the Cold War, situating a human against an otherworldly being.[10] If Cold War tensions signaled the dangers to American global supremacy in the mid-twentieth century, the alien-abduction narrative recasts issues of national identity and authority on an intergalactic scale. As a result, many scholars read these stories of extraterrestrial captivity as analogies for transnationally configured racial tensions.[11] The literary critic Christy L. Burns argues, "aliens may tacitly be those frightening beings who drop from outer space, but this cultural phantasm operates as a thinly disguised anxiety about illegal aliens who cross national borders, allegedly abduct jobs, and create 'mutant' children through miscegenation" (197). Not surprisingly, literary and cultural critics read contemporary alien-abduction narratives as revisions to the American indigenous captivity narrative,[12] while others show how African American writers retool these stories to explore themes related to racial enslavement and bondage.¹³ These interpretive approaches suggest that any alien-abduction narrative may be considered in relation to issues of racial difference and social inequality. Indeed, the form's emergence during the Cold War and the fact that the prototypical abductee is white reveals how the alien-abduction narrative might be read as a manifestation of subconscious fears over America's hostile takeover by foreign powers, seeking to pollute the nation's racial stock.

Light's short story should also be read as an analogy for racial prejudice, as Japanese American characters are refigured not as individuals fit for captivity in outer space but as a minority population that is purposelessly exiled, exploited, and abused. In this way, the story also revises the more traditional examples of techno-orientalism in which the Asian is figured as the excessively foreign, unemotional, and calculating subject, a reductive depiction that can be found in many popular cultural productions, ranging from *Blade Runner* to *The Matrix*.¹⁴ While Light's afterword provides one vital companion document to read race into the alien-abduction narrative, we must further explore the story in relation to larger discourses of that form. My reading of Light's "Abducted by Aliens!" shows how narration and form intertwine to provide us with a speculative fiction that reveals the spatially and temporally inflected traumas of the Japanese American internment. Despite her ancestry as a mixed-race Chinese American, Light takes on the voice of a Japanese American character to convey the ramifications of a community both bonded by and in bondage to silence in the postinternment period. Light innovatively employs the alien-abduction narrative to break the taciturnity that has accompanied the internment experience.

The Space-Time Discontinuum and the Trauma of Japanese American Internment

"Abducted by Aliens!" is structured episodically with two framing narratives. These narratives are told from the first-person perspective of the younger sister of the Japanese American man who was interned. The sister narrates at the beginning; her narrative is then followed by episodic embedded narratives related by the sister but presented in the voice of her Japanese American brother. These intergalactic tales are briefly interrupted by a section again narrated only by the sister; then we return one more time to the episodic embedded narratives in which the sister seems to ventriloquize the brother. The sequences that involve the sister speaking through her brother's perspective specifically concern his alien abduction. During these portions, "Abducted by Aliens!" invokes certain aspects of the alien-abduction narrative, such as temporal gaps and spatial instability, to help stage the historical trauma of the Japanese American internment. The fanciful nature of this form offers a different and dynamic way to depict the literal confinement experienced by Japanese Americans during World War II. Further still, the alien-abduction narrative remains unclosed and without tidy resolutions, thus diverging from a realist aesthetic that, for many obvious reasons, dominates internment representations.

Both framing narratives show the unreliability of the sister's viewpoint; she is not quite sure if she is remembering what her brother told her properly. We are thus not surprised to find little order to the actual abduction experience because everything is told secondhand. But it is instructive to consider how Light does end up arranging the captivity sequence to interpret the story's analogical properties. As with other abduction narratives, "Abducted by Aliens!" includes the quintessential moment in which the unsuspecting human is blinded by light. This sequence begins with the Japanese American brother giving us the vague information that it is before "the war began" and that he had been patrolling the family farm's borders barefoot. Then, he explains, "One night as I stood in the sand of our strawberry beds, a blinding light came in over the fields. The light picked out the minerals and crystals in the sand until the albedo overwhelmed me, and I was held in a white glow, without taste or sensation" (77). Light's afterword allows us to decode the way race and ethnicity appear encrypted in this passage. Without reference to a specific West Coast location, the story still recalls the historical and cultural context for Japanese Americans in California; many were migrant workers and later became farmers in their own right.[15] Strawberries were one of the crops that Japanese Americans were known to cultivate and harvest. This particular vignette is interesting because it is sequenced just after the second framing narrative; thus, the actual tale of the initial alien abduction occurs completely out of order.

The other point of obvious disorder appears when the Japanese American brother finally returns to Earth and the abduction is supposedly over. Instead of occurring at the end of the story, this vignette appears as third to the last in order. The brother "[wakes] up in a strange, small sitting room of a city [he] didn't recognize through the window" (82). Apparently, his younger sister is just about to be born in the hospital, and he engages in a conversation with one of his other sisters, Yuki:

"'I'm back' I cried. 'You're the beauty now! I thought it would be Emiko [another sister]!' She stared at me. 'I was abducted by aliens,' I explained. She put the cup down carefully before me. 'So were we,' she said" (82). It is important to note that, like the scene with the blinding light, the older brother still remains confused. Indeed, temporal disturbance is common to abduction narratives; here, too, that disturbance is registered by the brother's surprise at the change in his sister's beauty, a marker that time has elapsed and that the older brother has been unaware of it. Compounding this issue of lost time is the fact that he does not know where he is; thus, his spatial awareness is also compromised. While the setting gestures to the sister's impending birth, it also elliptically calls attention to the brother's mental acuity, making us wonder whether he should be in a mental ward. This scene is also the only moment in the entire story when someone other than the younger sister who is narrating the frames actually acknowledges that a collective abduction might have occurred.

The final vignette appearing in "Abducted by Aliens!" directly reveals the analogy between the spaceship and the internment camp. The younger sister, speaking through her older brother's perspective, narrates, "As we entered the Zone of Manifestation, where every immaterial thing materializes, the ship grew solid. Its interior walls were made of unpainted, gapping wood planks, and the floors were covered with sand" (83). On the surface level, this scene is already quite odd: what kind of spaceship is made of wood planks and sand-covered floors? But like the vignette of the initial abduction, this scene gives us a vague historical and spatial context that moves us away from deep space. Slipshod housing and desert environments were common to many of the internment camps. As with each of the other disordered vignettes, the older brother exhibits an obvious confusion. Here, the break in the brother's mind appears in the way that he sees another version of himself: "My ghost self appeared—the pure one I lost after I started school and had to learn English—occupying almost exactly the same space, only slightly behind and to the left of me" (83). With this final vignette, readers, like the older brother, are left a bit off-kilter.

These three vignettes take on extended significance precisely because the story already meanders so much. If these are the three that allow us to discern some sort of temporal arc to the abduction process, even though they occur out of order, what do they collectively offer us? To answer this question, we should return to the final vignette, which unveils the shift from the spaceship to the internment camp. By concluding the abduction process in the Zone of Manifestation, character progression is lost and instead leaves us with the older brother seemingly subsisting in the internment camp. But the appearance of the ghost self keys us into the way this story acts to aesthetically represent how trauma functions in narrative, especially through temporal distortion. The trauma theorist Cathy Caruth reminds us that trauma is manifested "by a break in the mind's experience of time" and adds that "what one returns to, in the flashback, is not the incomprehensibility of the event of one's near death, but the very incomprehensibility of one's own survival" ("Violence and Time" 25). Caruth goes on to note in her book-length study that trauma narratives engage "a kind of double telling, the oscillation between a *crisis of death* and the correlative *crisis of life*: between the story of the unbearable nature of an event and the story of an unbearable nature of its survival" (*Unclaimed Experience* 7).[16] This ghost self showcases the "incomprehensibility" of the internment experience and its aftermath, as the older brother finds himself split into multiple time frames; he not only exists before the internment but is seemingly stuck permanently in the internment, without an expressive outlet to understand his survival. The seemingly irrational abduction tale models these temporal breaks, as the narration is not chronological.

While Caruth privileges disordered temporality as the defining marker for trauma, these vignettes also require us to be vigilant to spatial disorder as a symptom and manifestation of trauma. I follow the views of the literary critic Ruth Ginsburg, who, in a reading of Ida Fink's writings, addresses the tremendous lack of attention paid to space and place in the theorization of trauma narratives: "It is quite surprising, however, that psychoanalytic theory, which deals with lived experience in internal spaces, should, to such an extent, privilege time and neglect space in its conceptualization of trauma" (211). The "neglect" of space is particularly problematic in relation to trauma theory, precisely because a rupture in the mind's comprehension of time might also correspond with a rupture in its comprehension of space. The Zone of Manifestation in the final vignette of "Abducted by Aliens!" details how trauma functions spatially, as the spaceship morphs into the internment-camp barracks. Like the disorder in temporality, "Abducted by Aliens!" constantly shows the older brother moving from one planet to another or from space to the internment camp and then back again; he is powerless to control how space (as well as time) alters around him. These ruptures in spatial integrity help analogize the internment experience, as Japanese Americans were forcibly removed from their homes and from their places of employment.[17] The historian Brian Masaru Hayashi notes that the internment cost Japanese Americans "hundreds of millions of dollars," which were "lost in property and assets" (2). In the haste of being evacuated, Japanese Americans often pawned material goods at bargain-basement prices, knowing that they could not be stored. Japanese Americans endured living for months in temporary shelters and horse stalls, otherwise known as assembly centers, until being resettled in some of the most inhospitable locations imaginable. When they returned from the internment camps, many had permanently lost all their property and had to seek new jobs.

In the context of the short story, the reordering of the three vignettes with regard to their spatial locations provides us with other ways to think about trauma and the Japanese American internment. The older brother and his family are "abducted" from their farm and relocated to the internment camp. Apart from the internment, the only other physical location we know the older brother finds himself in is the hospital. The movement from the family farm to the internment camp and finally to the hospital suggests a progression that moves Japanese Americans from a place of stability to a place of crisis; the younger sister's felicitous birth in the hospital stands in contrast to the older brother's loss of memory and loss of self and the break with his postinternment reality. Concluding in the hospital, the short story engages an aesthetics that speaks to the spatial traumas associated with the internment. The older brother, his family, and the other internees by extension need both a metaphorical rebirth and a mental healing.

Interestingly enough, this narrative of alien abduction highlights constant travel and exploration, a seemingly boundless adventure that exposes the older brother to planets with different physical principles and aliens of varying shapes, sizes, and organic compositions. The scope and the extent of his travels suggests a kind of freedom that runs in contradistinction to the way that the internment camp confined and consolidated Japanese Americans in enclosed spaces. But his travels are not wholly about intergalactic adventure; the fact that the older brother dies on a plague planet at one point (and yet is somehow brought back to life) reveals that this mobility comes at great cost. Other planets are particularly inhospitable to human life; the older brother describes what happened when he traveled to one planet, described as a "tourist trap" (73): "I had to sign something saying that I understood that my genes might be altered by the radiation, and that it was in no way the fault of anyone but myself. The sun fried your optic nerve first. Then gusts of radiation blew your skin off you, then your muscles and bones" (73).

Despite the threat to his health and bodily integrity, the older brother expresses his enjoyment during his period there, even requesting a "souvenir" (73). His response might seem to contradict the analogy between these planets and the internment camps, but the older brother's excitement at essentially having his body "blown, particle by particle, across space" (73) speaks to the irrationality of voluntarily entering a location that could cause such incredible harm. Certainly, this moment speaks to the brother's addled mind. His odd reaction to his time on this planet also calls attention to the way in which the systematic removal of Japanese Americans from the West Coast was framed by the American government. Internment camps were designated as "relocation centers," places as radically different from tourist destinations as from what their euphemistic name attempts to suggest—that Japanese Americans might be engaged in some form of intracontinental traveling. According to the literary critic Sau-ling C. Wong, the internment "included both the indirect immobilization of coerced movement and the direct one of incarceration (first in temporary assembly centers—holding pens, rather, some hastily converted from horse stables—then in remote inland camps surrounded by large-scale concentration camps surrounded by barbed wire and armed guards)" (*Reading Asian American Literature* 126). Following Wong's observations here, I read the older brother's constant intergalactic movement as analogically recalling the contradictions related to the spatial movements of Japanese Americans during internment. Though forcibly moved from their homes and collectively displaced, Japanese Americans felt obligated to comply with governmental orders to demonstrate and prove their patriotism. The effect of this spatial disruption is not only physical but psychic. As the older brother follows the aliens from one planet to another, we can read such vast mobility as evidence of the incredible traumas induced when Japanese Americans lost claims to personal property and to the nation, traumas that did not simply heal in the aftermath of the internment. Indeed, following the war, many families struggled to gain acceptance in the communities and neighborhoods in which they once resided; others found their homes vandalized and their businesses under new ownership. At one point, the older brother reveals that his "desire was for place, not movement; place, not novelty; place, not placement. Which is to say that the spectacle of journeying— unfamiliar feels, shocks, pleas, and unexpected moral quandaries—was entirely lost on [him]" (74). For the older brother, the very rooted "place" and prison of the internment camp is paradoxically the psychic space of exile, "the spectacle of journeying" away from what he defines as a home.

The Identity of the Aliens We Are All Looking For

In employing the alien-abduction tale as an analogy to the internment experience, Light generates a hybrid narrative that, on the one hand, revises what extraterrestrial abduction might signify and, on the other, fancifully reimagines how forced imprisonment can be historically depicted. In this creative process, the short story also shows us how traumas are both spatially and temporally configured. At this point, we must also consider the importance of the aliens themselves in the story. Because so many of the planets seem truly unable to support any human life, the aliens do not seem to have a purpose in taking the older brother from one planet to another. In fact, their whole motivation for taking him (and others in his family) is never finally revealed, and we further do not understand what sorts of experiments the aliens might have been performing. Perhaps most curiously, the aliens themselves seem rather innocuous and at other moments even seem quite endearing to the older brother. One of the aliens, Ufluuuk, is described as the older brother's "interlocutor" (66) and appears to be the older brother's constant traveling companion. Thus, Light's short story deviates from some of the more common abduction narratives that detail the instrumental nature of alien contact, the desire to use human genetic components for particular and often nefarious purposes. These aliens, instead, seem almost friendly.

If the abduction scenario corresponds, at least in part, to the internment experience, who, then, are the aliens? A patent response might be that they function as a symbolic manifestation of the governmental forces that perpetrated Japanese American relocation. To a certain extent, this reading is supported by the text itself. Indeed, the younger sister in the second framing narrative explains that the abductors and the abductees spoke different languages, suggesting a fundamental difference between those who were interned and those who incited internment. In addition, the older brother's sister Emiko tells him in the hospital vignette that she and others (ostensibly, their family) were also abducted by aliens. And yet the brilliance of Light's story is that there are numerous kinds, forms, and species of aliens. Thus, the abductors may be of a particular "race" of aliens distinct from the many that the older brother later encounters while traveling on the spaceship. This reading seems important given the fact that the aliens who are accompanying the older brother seem so radically harmless and ineffectual, aimlessly wandering about the galaxy: "Was there a purpose to their wanderings?

What were they seeking? There was no such thing as a pure explorer, was there? Every sailorman and seadog who discovered a 'new world' had at least a secret hope of discovering value, something to sell or to use or see: gold, eternal youth, women, trees, things, wings, or gorges of lapis lazuli. But then my abductors were not human" (71). These traveling aliens do not possess the colonial mind-set, which seeks to extract all forms of resources from new lands. If the aliens are only understood as the structural and governmental forces that perpetrated the internment, the apparent purposelessness of their constant movement seems troublesome. Indeed, many scholars, including Brian Masaru Hayashi, Greg Robinson, and Roger Daniels, have explored the clear and meticulous rationale behind the creation of the camps and the relocation of Japanese Americans. Japanese Americans were deemed security threats and apparently required surveillance. Yet we might attribute the lack of "purpose" to the aliens' "wanderings" as evidence of the internment's ineffectual nature. Indeed, there was never any evidence to support a large-scale conspiracy perpetrated by Japanese Americans as spies or as informants for the Japanese government. At the same time, if we think of the aliens as analogs to the American government, the older brother's rather pedestrian feelings toward them suggest that a more complicated reading of these otherworldly entities is in order.

At two points during Light's story, human characters and alien beings are confused for one another. The first time this conflation surfaces is in relation to Ufluuuk and the older brother's mother: "Ufluuuk sensed my sadness. Come, he thought. The air before him glowed golden, and I put my head into it. Suddenly, I was looking into my mother's face. She placed a spoon into my mouth as my sister Emiko walked past holding a schoolbook. Behind her unfinished planks gapped showing stripes of blue daylight. A hasty job" (71). Later, the mother transforms back into Ufluuuk: "My eyes focused, my mother's eyes widened, but then I found myself asking my question to Ufluuuk's mid-region: 'Mother, where are we?'" (71). The second time the older brother experiences confusion between a human and an alien occurs in a dream: "I dreamed I was bathing with my grandfather. He stood on the concrete bathhouse floor in his socks. 'Take off your socks, grandpa!' I said and pulled him rudely onto the wooden slats. I dumped a ladleful of water on his shoulder. The skin steamed, then caught fire. 'Why did you do that?' Grandpa asked me impassively between flames, in English. I woke up and Ufluuuk was nearby. 'Why did you do that?' he asked again" (72). In both of these cases, an alien figure associated with the older brother's abduction is compared to someone directly related to his Japanese American family. This link makes us wonder how to understand the alien abductors. Was the older brother abducted by his own family? If they are aliens, is he an alien too?

Light's representation of the aliens defies any simplistic readings. Certainly, governmental forces might function as the metaphorical evil aliens, who forcibly remove Japanese Americans from their homes and make them into captives. In their systematic, legislative, and racist treatment of an American minority population, these governmental forces act without human feeling. At the same time, the government's rendering of Japanese Americans as possible spies and national-security threats constructs the latter's racial status as metaphorical beings from another planet, who might be intent on destruction and violence. These hostile, racialized aliens might be planning an all-out invasion of America. Depending on perspective, the designation of alien status alters. To complicate matters further, from the specific viewpoint of the older brother, the alien abductors might seem to be individuals in his own family precisely because they become so foreign to him. That is, he is made out to be insane by his family members because he chooses to speak to the traumas of internment figuratively through the alien-abduction narrative, while they maintain their silence about these events, as if internment never happened. In effect, his family becomes unfamiliar to him; it is they who have also become extraterrestrial. Hence, the short story offers at least three different alien figures or groups: the governmental forces, the Japanese American internees, and the older brother's family members who refuse to speak about their incarceration.

Alien-abduction narratives often include representations of otherworldly beings notable for their telepathic capabilities. The alien abductors that the older brother interacts with also have mind-reading powers; their ability to communicate solely via thought process generates a space odyssey in which spoken dialogue is absent. In other words, the alien-abduction narrative is elliptically retooled to reveal how much is actually unsaid and unremarked concerning the internment, especially among Japanese Americans. We can think of the internment as a "cultural trauma," which "refers to a dramatic loss of identity and meaning, a tear in the social fabric, affecting a group of people who have achieved some degree of cohesion" (Eyerman 160).[18] Emily Roxworthy's psychoanalytic exploration of the internment is especially useful in thinking about how silence operates as a marker of collectively experienced traumas. Roxworthy explains that "unlike the abject treatment of Vietnam veterans, who were mostly drafted into the war, the Federal Bureau of Investigation (FBI) and WRA [War Relocation Authority] coerced Japanese Americans into 'voluntary' participation with their abjection from the rest of society, demanding that they cooperate with authorities and put on a happy face for reporters and other visitors to the barbed-wire-encircled camps" (3–4). Roxworthy's study elucidates how Japanese Americans were forced to perform particular affectual roles to prove their loyalty to the United States (5). Putting on a "happy face" despite removal from homes and occupations reveals a traumatic split among what is felt, what is thought, and what is performed. To a certain extent, then, Japanese Americans become alien to themselves, unable to emotionally express their discontent in order to show complete compliance to the United States. The silence that followed the internment registers the unseen violence committed on the emotional capacities of Japanese Americans.[19] The relatively docile and unemotional status of the aliens in Light's short story metaphorically invokes the taciturnity of Japanese Americans in relation to the internment.[20]

The Japanese American Internment as Speculative Fiction

"Abducted by Aliens!" functions metafictionally in that it is all about the process of storytelling, but it also violates the regime of silence self-imposed by many Japanese Americans in the wake of internment. Indeed, the very fact that we get to read the episodic alien-abduction scenario reveals a willingness to speak out and to express disorientation and confusion. Why is it that the younger sister is able to break the silence in contrast to her older brother? What does the strangely metaphorical nature of the internment narrative say about the ways that traumatic experiences can be told? To answer these questions, we should think about how trauma functions intergenerationally. It is important, for instance, that the younger sister never directly experiences the internment herself and thus cannot draw on her own life to tell the story. Instead, everything in the story she tells is always already mediated by her brother's alien-abduction narrative. Not surprisingly, the Japanese American cultural archive of the internment is riddled with issues of representation, recovery, and recounting.

Many sansei Japanese American writers and cultural producers explore the difficulty of understanding and depicting the internment; these works are often asynchronously sequenced or told with shifting narrative perspectives in which gaps and fissures remain unfilled and unbridgeable.²¹ Light's "Abducted by Aliens!" clearly follows in this tradition. The afterword pushes us to consider further why and how the Japanese American internment narrative gets distorted: "Parts of the community itself collaborated in partially blotting out its own history by not talking openly about it to their children. Many of the children and grandchildren of the interned have had to reconstruct this key piece of their puzzle, and its meaning, outside of mainstream history and culture, and often outside of familial and oral tradition" (85). I want to elaborate on this issue of the internment experience as a kind of puzzle with multiple valences. On the one hand, Light focuses on third-generation Japanese Americans, individuals like the narrator who did not directly experience the internment, causing the narrative to remain hidden or at best highly fragmented. On the other, Light imagines how the puzzle perplexes not only those who did not experience the internment but also individuals like the narrator's older brother, who cannot make sense of the event itself so much so that his incarceration is analogized in relation to an alien abduction. According to the literary critic Patti Duncan, the Japanese American internment "fails to neatly fit any paradigms of America's language or national narratives[;] any attempt to tell is to enact an unraveling of sorts, a gesture of doublespeak, stating one thing while at the same time saying another, or perhaps stating one thing while simultaneously unsaying it" (101).²² The sister's attempt to "tell" is exactly this "gesture of doublespeak," an inability to consolidate into a lucid narrative that which has remained silenced and fragmented. With nothing but her brother's strange stories to go on, her internment narrative is itself only a part of what she knows is a larger, more complicated story: "But as I transcribe I grow more confused, for I have just caught myself, twice—no, five times now—not remembering a detail and so inventing one to bridge the gaps between ideas. I myself am the bridging of a gap, conceived before my family returned from the camps but only born after the return, bridging the time before and the time after" (75). The sister's admission reveals the partially fictive nature of her storytelling, but the "inventing" is necessary given the limits of the archives available to her. According to the trauma theorist Dominick LaCapra, "one might argue that narratives in fiction may also involve truth claims on a structure or general level by providing insight into phenomena such as slavery or the Holocaust, by offering a reading of a process or period, or by giving at least a plausible 'feel' for experience and emotion which may be difficult to arrive at through restricted documentary methods" (*Writing History* 13). If there is a connection between the narrator and the author, it appears in the way that both would have access to a very limited archive documenting the internment. Thus, fiction and speculation offer Light and the younger sister (by extension of Light's construction of narrative perspective) the chance to give a "plausible" account of the emotional and traumatic impact of that event.

But why is the sister so uniquely suited to tell the story in contrast to her other sisters, Emiko and Yuki? An answer lies in the ways that Light positions the younger sister in relation to the older brother. The brother begins to tell her the captivity narrative when she is just an infant: "He used the stories as a springboard into the life of the mind that he thereafter inhabited, and raised me to inhabit" (64). The word "raised" suggests how the brother and sister act almost as parent and child. As she did not directly experience the internment herself, the youngest sister in some ways becomes an ideal witness for her much older brother. She exists as a kind of tabula rasa, without predisposed opinions and ideas about how stories must be told. As the trauma theorist Dori Laub explains, "The listener, therefore, by definition partakes of the struggle of the victim with the memories and residues of his or her traumatic past. The listener has to feel the victim's victories, defeats and silences, know them from within, so that they can assume the form of testimony" (58). Within the bounds of this narrative, the younger sister takes on the role of the most appropriate "listener," and she is then tasked with learning how to understand her older brother's "victories, defeats, and silences."[23]

The listener must stay attuned to the story being told, while not appropriating the traumas as her own. In this vein, LaCapra argues that "secondary witnesses" to traumas should take up an "empathic unsettlement" to avoid "vicarious victimhood" and the possibility that "empathy with the victim seems to become an identity" ("Trauma" 699). According to LaCapra, empathic unsettlement distances the listener from the traumatized subject, while still allowing him or her to respond to what is being related. In Light's story, the younger sister serves as this secondary witness. Rather than a transparent identification with the interned, the younger sister admits that her storytelling only approximates her brother's experiences. She endeavors to convey the psychic damage wrought by a particular event without entirely claiming herself as a victim. Though Light herself (and other writers like her who have gone on to represent the internment) cannot identify as Japanese American, her decision to take on first-person narration suggests an attempt to engage the psychic space and emotional lives of others—a creatively configured empathically unsettled aesthetic process. Inasmuch as the short story offers Light a fictional world to overhaul the Japanese American internment imaginatively through an intergalactic space odyssey, the short story also serves a very political purpose: to reveal the many facets of structural trauma as it extends aesthetically and socially, across time, space, and generations.

Far from autobiographical or autoethnographic in the depiction of the Japanese American internment, "Abducted by Aliens!" and its corresponding afterword spotlight the political aims of the racially asymmetrical fictional world. For Light, the internment also operates as a synecdoche in that it stands for "Asian immigration as a whole" and "the simultaneous shame and anger at how one's culture is hemmed in and demonized" (Afterword 85). LaCapra might provisionally call this moment one that falls precipitously close to "vicarious victimhood." At the same time, Light is modeling the panethnic political concerns behind Asian American studies itself. That is, as a mixed-race Chinese American, she notes the racial prejudice collectively experienced by Asian Americans of all ethnic backgrounds and ancestries. Thus, her speculative fictional story, in the broadest sense, might be said to analogize the racialized history of Asian Americans. As Yasuko I. Takezawa explains concerning the collective mobility around social justice issues such as the internment, "Not only Japanese Americans but all Asian Americans found they could coalesce around this point, for all had suffered some form of racial exclusion or discrimination" (149). Takezawa's point reveals the importance of racially empathic approaches to cultural production that could occur in the period following the civil rights movement. Light appropriates a Japanese American voice to metaphorically address the suffering of "racial exclusion" through an alien-abduction narrative. This short story pushes us to revise Elaine H. Kim's foundational thesis: "As both social document and a mirror of memory, myth, dreams, and desire, Asian American literature provides unique access to understanding the social history and sensibilities of an often misunderstood American racial minority group" ("Asian American Literature" 34). Kim's point can certainly be understood given the exigency of archiving Asian American history and culture as documented through literature,[24] but "Abducted by Aliens!" is not only a mirror; it also functions through highly imaginative racial analogy. The story's central analogy encourages us to compare the experience of being taken by extraterrestrial beings and forced into intergalactic exile as akin to the experiences of Japanese Americans, uprooted and subsisting for years in internment camps. This extreme analogy, on the one hand, reveals the traumas sustained by one community and, on the other, spotlights how a distorted and fragmented narration reflects the intergenerational rupture between internees and their descendants.

From Asian America to the Near Eastern Orient

Much of my reading of racial analogy in "Abducted by Aliens!" is inspired by Light's afterword and follows the grain of authorial intentionality. Indeed, the afterword is crucial to establishing some of the pivotal connections between the intergalactic journey and the internment. However, my reading of Ted Chiang's novelette *The Merchant and the Alchemist's Gate* moves forward without the aid of authorial intentionality, as the story lacks an authorial afterword to explain how this narrative proceeds analogically.[25] Like Light's "Abducted by Aliens!," *TMATAG* is clearly a speculative fiction. With references to alchemy and time travel, the novel functions through a high-intensity cognitive estrangement. *TMATAG* centers on the misadventures of Fuwaad ibn Abbas, the titular merchant and our narrator. The novelette begins with Fuwaad recounting his incredible experiences to the Caliph. In this narrative, Fuwaad encounters a man known as Bashaarat, an alchemist who has invented the Gate of Years, a time-travel device that enables anyone who enters it to travel, depending on the direction of entry, either twenty years into the future or twenty years into the past. Bashaarat has just moved from Cairo to Iraq and set up a new Gate of Years (his son continues to run the Gate of Years in Cairo). Before Fuwaad decides whether to jump through, Bashaarat begins to tell him a series of tales involving individuals who have already used the Gate of Years. At this point, the novelette is interrupted by Fuwaad, who requests permission from the Caliph to renarrate Bashaarat's tales. *TMATAG* therefore also includes embedded narratives, told by Fuwaad in the third person directly to the Caliph. After the embedded narratives are completed, Fuwaad returns to his own story, explaining his own motivation for jumping through the Gate of Years, which involves potentially subverting the tragic death of his wife. While he is unable to save her, he does receive a key piece of information that gives him closure over her death. His adventures in the Baghdad of the past unfortunately leave him penniless, and he is later imprisoned when he breaks curfew and no one can substantiate who he actually is. He is granted audience with the Caliph only after correctly predicting that the Caliph's grandson will be born an albino. The novelette concludes with Fuwaad pleading with the

Caliph to provide him the chance to act as a political adviser based on his knowledge of future events.

TMATAG is difficult to situate within the bounds of traditional Asian Americanist frames, as the work is set in Iraq during the Islamic Golden Age (approximately between the eighth and thirteenth centuries). *TMATAG* does not clearly reference Asian American characters; nor does it seem to explore issues of racial formation. But the novelette is nevertheless set geographically within Asia, in a location that has historically been reconfigured and explored within the orientalist imagination. At the same time, it seems a curious choice to center an oriental tale in Baghdad, especially given the ongoing history of armed conflict between the United States and Iraq. Indeed, Chiang's narrator makes continual references to Baghdad as the "city of peace," which is taken from another rendering of Baghdad's name, Madinat as-Salam. The dissonance between the fictional world and the city's contemporary social context immediately bears importance for thinking about Chiang's work beyond an entertaining reenvisioning of the oriental tale. Here, Chiang exposes the fruitful possibilities of American orientalism; literary representation troubles some of the speculative imaginaries that circumscribe the Middle East as a terrorist haven and exotic landscape full of exploitable resources. While the novelette reveals Chiang's extensive knowledge of the oriental tale as a form, he subverts and estranges this form by including a pivotal piece of technology: a time-traveling portal. By envisioning a narrative in which time can move both forward and backward, Chiang's work calls attention to the importance of historical contexts in the construction and meaning of fictional worlds. As such, we are not only reading the narrative in its specific social context of the Abbasid Caliphate period but also investigating how the narrative speaks to the moment in which it is published: the post-9/11 era. *TMATAG* thus can be read analogically: the novelette helps us explore the relationship among time travel and historically informed analytical practices, the oriental tale as a didactic narrative form, and the orientalist qualities of American foreign policies aimed at advancing the War on Terror. As with Light's story, *TMATAG* reminds us that a cognitively estranging fictional world still draws out the ways that contemporary racial tensions erupt out of the complicated relationship between America and Asia. We might more creatively say that *TMATAG* is itself a kind of time-traveling cultural document, one that represents a fictional past yet comes alive and resonates alongside contemporary cultural and social issues.

The popularization of the oriental tale as its own genre offers literary critics a fertile ground to consider its formal properties, aesthetic traits, and political ramifications.²⁶ Following the geographical, cultural, and linguistic logics of the oriental tale, I focus on the framing narratives, specifically showing how Chiang authenticates his ethnoracial storyteller. Not only does the Arabic narrator Fuwaad exhibit a vast understanding of his cultural background, but he also references numerous cultural signifiers that can be connected to actual social contexts of the Abbasid Caliphate period. At the same time, Chiang complicates the traditional genre by presenting oriental geographies as slightly mysterious and resistant, even to the Arabic storyteller. This creative process reveals a writer attuned to the importance of sociohistorical circumstances in the construction of speculative fictions as well as the need to revise certain genre conceits to complicate how orientalism functions.

TMATAG contains numerous images that accompany the narrative, with ink sketches of mosques, minarets, camels, Arabic script, and palm trees, among other such details. These images recur throughout the novelette to accentuate the fact that we are in an appropriately oriental geography. That is, the writer assumes a voice or perspective that could be construed as being Near Eastern in origin; the tale might include "Persian, Turkish, or Arabic character and place names (or at least ones that sounded as such)" and contain "plot lines concerning a quest for riches, wisdom, romantic love, or magical transformation as well as elaborate descriptions of colorful processions, pomp and ceremony, utter contentment, or extraordinary beauty" (Nance 42).²⁷ The opening line of *TMATAG* places us firmly in the Muslim religious frame, with the as-yet-unnamed narrator addressing the Caliph, announcing that he has a tale "to tell" that is "strange" (7). The second paragraph quickly reveals the specific location and name of our oriental speaker: "My name is Fuwaad ibn Abbas, and I was born here in Baghdad, City of Peace. My father was a grain merchant, but for much of my life I have worked as a purveyor of fine fabrics, trading in silk from Damascus and linen from Egypt and scarves from Morocco that are embroidered with gold" (7). Chiang ingeniously introduces the narrator not only with his Muslim-inspired name and the major urban center during the Abbasid Caliphate period but also by featuring the classic trade routes that linked the Arab world with East Asia.²⁸ His trading in silk, linen, and scarves calls attention to a rich textile industry that actually flourished during the Golden Age and specifically reminds us how the genre fosters the exoticism of transnational commodity cultures.²⁹ Fuwaad is an ideal storyteller precisely because he is both Arabic and cosmopolitan. But as such a seasoned traveler, having observed a diverse range of goods and cultures, what story could possibly be "strange" to him? To find out, we can look to Fuwaad as he divulges the current state of his finances: "I was prosperous, but my heart was troubled, and neither the purchase of luxuries nor the giving of alms were able to soothe it. Now I stand before you without a single dirham in my purse, but I am at peace" (7). Again, Chiang moves us into the orientalized landscape by referencing a very specific currency, the dirham. Given Fuwaad's former life as a merchant, his contentment regarding his own insolvency seems inexplicable. Thus, Fuwaad overturns the expectation that this story will necessarily be about the acquisition of wealth and instead presents us with a kind of morality fable. He places a dubious value on the beautiful commodities he once traded, preferring to be "at peace" rather than "prosperous." Chiang thus clarifies how the narrator himself, though representative of the exotic, still introduces readers to a subtly cognitively estranging world in which luxurious goods are eschewed for personal enlightenment.

Chiang further complicates the oriental tale through Fuwaad's ability to define what is normative and what is not. Fuwaad explains how his strange tale began. While out looking for a gift, he observes that "one of the largest shops in the market had been taken over by a new merchant. It was a prized location that must have been expensive to acquire," so he enters "to peruse its wares" (8).[30] Once we enter the shop, the mystical nature of the fictional world burgeons as we discover that the shop is owned by an alchemist named Bashaarat. Though alchemy did indeed flourish during the Abbasid period,[31] Fuwaad is astounded by what he sees in the shop: "Never before had I seen such a marvelous assortment of goods. Near the entrance there was an astrolabe equipped with seven plates inlaid with silver, a water-clock that chimed on the hour, and a nightingale made of brass that sang when the wind blew" (8). This passage is notable because it requires readers to think about why Fuwaad would be so impressed with these goods. In each case, there is a form of ingenuity that distinguishes these objects from others he has seen in his travels. The astrolabe, commonly employed by astronomers and routinely used during the Islamic Golden Age, appears as more than a functional tool, as it is outfitted with precious metals.[32] The water-clock, clearly a device used to mark time, in this case shows an incredible precision by being able to mark the "hour."[33] And finally, a precious metal not only is molded into the shape of an animal but is also transformed into a wind chime. Fuwaad goes on to observe, "Further inside there were even more

196 / IMPOSSIBLE NARRATION

ingenious mechanisms, and I stared at them the way a child watches a juggler" (8). Fuwaad's description reminds us this Baghdad shop is out of the ordinary, as it is filled with strange objects and novelties.

Politicking in the Oriental Tale

In *TMATAG*, Fuwaad discloses his experiences with Bashaarat not simply to relate a series of fantastic tales to the Caliph but also because these tales act as fables. I explore the first two embedded narratives to consider what sorts of rhetorical messages they convey and how this oriental tale becomes more than a creative opportunity to depict the flexible contours of Asian American fictional worlds. We recall that Chiang's depiction of the Orient makes it a slightly unfamiliar space, full of mystery even for an apparent cultural insider such as Fuwaad. In this respect, Chiang commands an audience willing to engage the plasticity of the oriental tale and in some sense primes readers for other potentially more flagrant violations of the genre itself. Indeed, the most important element linking each embedded narrative is time travel. Chiang thus explicitly breaches the bounds of the oriental tale through the inclusion of a classic science-fictional trope in which people can move backward and forward through time.

In the first embedded story, titled "The Tale of the Fortunate Rope-Maker," the titular rope maker, Hassan al-Hubbaul, enters the Gate of Years in Cairo and takes it twenty years into the future. There, he learns of a man who has become rich who also happens to share his exact name. Piqued by this coincidence, he travels to meet the man and ascertains that he is actually a future version of himself. With information gathered from this future self, he avoids certain tragic fates that might have befallen him when he returns to the present. In the older Hassan's final advice, he instructs the younger Hassan to travel back through the portal to his own time period, go to a specific location, and dig; there the younger Hassan will find a treasure trove. The younger Hassan confronts the older about how he knew about this location and what could be found there. "'I learned it from myself,' said the older Hassan, 'just as you did. As to how we came to know its location, I have no explanation except that it was the will of Allah, and what other explanation is there for anything?'" (22). The inability to determine how the treasure's location came to be known is a temporal paradox never revealed within the narrative confines. As the tale ends, readers discover that "with the gold he was able to purchase hemp in great quantity, and hire workmen and pay them a fair wage, and sell rope profitably to all who sought it. He married a beautiful and clever woman, at whose advice he began trading in other goods, until he was a wealthy and respected merchant. All the while he gave generously to the poor and lived as an upright man" (23). Hassan's character trajectory raises a number of interesting points. First, he puts his wealth to ethical use, as evidenced by the reference to "fair wage." Second, his continued success is not simply reliant on his own entrepreneurial capability. His wife provides him with the knowledge to continue to accrue wealth, demonstrating an interesting insertion of a minor but nevertheless vital feminist standpoint. Third, Hassan shares his wealth with laborers, family, and the less fortunate. Muslim faith is rewarded not only through a financial windfall but also in the community and goodwill generated out of selflessness.

Another notable detail appears in the beginning of this tale, in which Hassan believes that as a rope maker he will never become wealthy. Later, when the younger Hassan travels to the home of the older Hassan, who he has not yet realized is actually himself, he "waited while the servant went to fetch his master, but as he looked at the polished ebony and marble around him, he felt that he did not belong in such surroundings, and was about to leave when his older self appeared" (18). Key to Hassan's character construction is his lack of class entitlement and his rather humble consideration of his life's station. This first tale more broadly suggests that one must also understand humility, while continuing to demonstrate a benevolent attitude toward others in less fortunate and less powerful positions. Financial rewards, in other words, are not the goal but the possible (though not guaranteed) byproduct of a person who cultivates a principled life.

This lesson is completely lost on the major character from the second tale, "The Tale of the Weaver Who Stole from Himself." In this story, the titular weaver, Ajib, goes through the Gate of Years after hearing about the story of Hassan. He believes that he, too, will find his future self very rich and hopes to alter his present through the acquisition of future knowledge regarding his fortunes. Unfortunately, going into the future provides Ajib with the information that he will end up being poor. Curiously, though, in searching through the meager home of his future self, he discovers a chest filled with valuables, which he then takes back with him through the Gate of Years. He uses his newfound windfall to furnish a lavish life for himself and to acquire a wife, Taahira, whom he otherwise could not have married. But his fortunes turn for the worse when his wife is kidnapped and he must pay a ransom that wipes out his finances. He then admits to his wife that he believes past misdeeds have resulted in this current insolvency. At this point, his wife confronts him about how he had gotten rich in the first place. His vague answers arouse her suspicions that he had stolen rather than earned his affluent life. She demands that he repay whoever it was that he took from, to which he assents, knowing that this agreement solidifies his love for her. They thus spend the rest of their lives saving up for the repayment that will eventually go to the younger Ajib, who will come to the future to take what they have saved for himself. The rather tragic ending for this couple, as evidenced by the fact that Ajib and Taahira's love for each other eventually "faded over time" (33), provides a cautionary tale to people who operate with avarice in mind. Unlike Hassan from the first tale, Ajib "was sure" that he "would be as rich as and generous as the older Hassan" (27). Ajib's obvious class entitlement reveals him as an individual who must temper personal desire. Indeed, the presumption is that Ajib's ambition "to taste the luxuries enjoyed by the wealthy" predetermines his later fate.

In both stories, the younger versions of Hassan and Ajib are instrumental in the process by which their future selves come into existence. In other words, it seems as if both characters must travel to the future simply to enact what will always already happen.[34] For Fuwaad, this paradox reveals the impossibility of changing his own destiny, a lesson that he otherwise ignores when he travels to the past to try to save his wife, Najya, from being crushed when a mosque collapses. While her death is tragic in and of itself, Fuwaad harbors considerable guilt because of a fight he had with her just before he left for a business trip. He believes she died bearing ill thoughts of him. Though Fuwaad is unable to alter the chain of events, he still gains valuable knowledge that helps him to realize that his wife did not harbor any resentment toward him, and thus he finds himself "at peace" (7). Without the resources to travel back to Cairo, he wanders around Baghdad and is arrested for breaking curfew and because no one can verify his identity. Thus, Fuwaad's older self is stuck twenty years in the past without a way to get back through the time portal. Fuwaad's experiences seem to corroborate the fact that the time line cannot be altered, though his knowledge of the events surrounding the past can be.

For Fuwaad, these tales take on increased significance because he is telling them to the Caliph. According to the literary critic Rosalind Ballaster, "the sequence of oriental tales is often presented as a series of political moves or manoeuvres designed to produce some change in the behaviour or perspective of the addressee" (8). Ballaster clarifies the didactic properties of the tale through the quintessential example of the *Thousand and One Nights*, as Scheherazade must use her storytelling talents to enthrall Emperor Schahriar and delay her execution (8). Ballaster's points can be directly related to Chiang's novelette. As Fuwaad narrates his plea to the Caliph, "I would be honored to relate everything I know of the future, if Your Majesty sees fit to ask" (60). This request reveals the political valences of the story. Fuwaad's fate is, in some sense, entirely in the Caliph's hands. The historian Karen Armstrong specifies that, during the early Abbasid period, "where the Prophet had always been addressed informally by his given name, like any other mortal, the caliph was styled the 'Shadow of God on earth.' The executioner stood behind him, to show that the caliph had the power of life and death" (95).[35] Fuwaad's presence before the Caliph would be an exceptional circumstance, especially given his status as a prisoner. Given the rather incredible tale he has told, it would be possible that he could face execution if the Caliph found him suspicious. Fuwaad's request to become a kind of political adviser would not be completely out of the realm of possibility, however, especially with respect to actual governance systems that placed the Caliph in contact with a stable of different attendants, including "viziers, secretaries, [and] chamberlains" (Chejne 327).[36] Anwar G. Chejne further explains that the court attendants would also include boon-companions, who "were selected from among the best talents to befriend the ruler, and were given a permanent position at the court which carried great prestige and influence" (327). In linking *TMATAG* to these social contexts, we can see that Fuwaad, with his abilities to accurately predict some future events, could become one of these important satellite figures.[37]

But going back to Ballaster's point, Fuwaad's embedded narratives are not intended simply to save his own life and grant him a new future, but they are also "designed to produce some change" in the "perspective of the addressee," who in this case would be the Caliph himself. Both Ajib's and Hassan's tales expose the dangers and possibilities of traveling to the future. Each character, though, begins his adventure with very different intentions. Hassan seems to travel to the future with an exploratory impulse, with no expectation that he will actually encounter his future self and try to change his own fortune. Ajib's avarice, on the other hand, results in a limited view of what the future can or should be and what kind of life he should lead in twenty years' time. In both tales, the past, present, and future all intertwine in seemingly predetermined ways. The inability to alter one's fate seems to fix the Iraq of the Islamic

Golden Age within a static framework, one that would augment rather than undermine a reductively configured orientalist depiction. In addition, Fuwaad's ability to divulge future events would be worthless, as one's destiny cannot be altered. This rather pessimistic reading, however, does not find traction because of one interesting narrative detail that might go unnoticed. Fuwaad, unlike Ajib and Hassan, does not return to his own time line. His presence before the Caliph signals an obvious break in what in science-fictional terms is called the space-time continuum—there is a younger Fuwaad still somewhere out there on a business trip, unaware that his wife has died. The fact that Fuwaad cannot return through the Gate of Years (because he lacks the resources to travel back to Cairo and because he is technically a prisoner) offers one major difference in relation to his trajectory as compared to the other major characters from the embedded narratives, all of whom meet past or future versions of themselves but return to their own time periods.

In leaving the future open-ended not only for Fuwaad but also for the Caliph and the corresponding Muslim Empire, the novelette ends on a rather optimistic note, portending possibility rather than foreclosure. Fuwaad's appeal to become a political adviser revises Bashaarat's approach to time travel by leaving the future unfixed. To the Caliph, such a message could strike effectively, too, on the level of his rule, which cannot look ahead with a rigid agenda in mind. That is, he must be willing to listen and be open to the many possibilities and trajectories that stand before his many Islamic subjects. What is important to remember is that *TMATAG* also converses with specific social contexts of the Abbasid period. According to the historian Antony Adolf, the Abbasid dynasty could come into being only through "overthrowing the Umayyad with a coalition of Shiites, mawali and non-Muslims," but "the cooperative spirit between them remained long thereafter, and gave rise to what is considered an Islamic golden age" (101).[38] Further still, the city of Baghdad during this period "stood for a new kind of imperial, Islamic unity that transcended the old racial connection between the Arabs and their faith to embrace people of many different races and backgrounds" (Goodwin 25). To retain "Islamic unity" across a vast geographical terrain that stretched from Cairo to Baghdad, caliphs had to work to establish coalitions at varying levels of governance.[39] These sociohistorical circumstances function to clarify the expanded political horizons of Chiang's novelette. They illuminate some of the complicated issues that arise in relation to governance and power relations. The Caliph's ability to maintain the "Pax Islamica" (Adolf 101) appears rendered through a judicious approach to despotic rule, taking into account the diversity and heterogeneity of his subjects.[40]

Analogizing the Oriental Tale

Fuwaad's fanciful storytelling, on the one hand, illuminates the aesthetic creativity of an Asian American writer who seeks to give voice to a character from another ethnoracial background, a figure who might have lived approximately a thousand years ago. On the other hand, his storytelling serves a didactic purpose by addressing individuals who attain lofty positions of power. The Caliph, in particular, with the power to determine the life or death of his various subjects, is confronted with tales that remind him to act judiciously, without avarice and with humility, and to think of the future as a landscape of unbounded possibilities. This chapter also makes a larger claim about speculative fiction in relation to the use of racial analogy. With respect to Light's "Abducted by Aliens!," we see how the alien-abduction narrative is analogized in relation to the experience of Japanese American internees. Light's creative approach revises both the alien-abduction tale and the Japanese American–internment narrative to create a hybrid form that gestures to the political power of speculative fiction. The story further offers Light the platform to create a unique storytelling perspective that ultimately helps model the panethnic investments of Asian American studies. In Chiang's work, the novelette's most explicit break from the oriental tale as a genre surfaces in the centrality of the time-travel device to the plot. The flexibility of time proves to be an important hermeneutic tool, as it pushes us to reconsider speculative fiction in a variety of sociohistorical contexts. In this case, Chiang engages an extreme form of imaginary time travel in his depiction of an era approximately a millennium in the past. This movement into the past forefronts the necessity of reading the narrative through multiple temporal frames.

Historicism thus takes on multiple vectors, as the time periods in which the novelette is set and published are both equally important considerations in formulating comprehensive literary analyses. In a reading of the *Arabian Nights*, Ballaster advances how the oriental tale could be used analogically in relation to the time of the tale's publication (14–15). As the form found immense popularity in the early eighteenth century, the oriental tale's critique of despotic rule could be elliptically applied as a warning to European audiences about the growth of tyrannical governments on their own soil. According to the philosopher Alan

Richardson, "orientalist fiction could be self-critical as well as satirically corrosive in its take on European society and culture, even if the Orient it portrayed was itself largely a European invention" (5).[41] In this respect, the tale, while set in a fictional location far from the European continent, could be placed in direct conversation with narratives concerning national identity and political power. In the context of oriental tales that were published in the United States, the literary critic Susan Nance explains, "the frequency with which Anglo-American authors adopted these purportedly Eastern forms for their own creative arts meant that in effect these colorful practices were utterly American" (44).[42] These various critical approaches to the oriental tale push us to consider how *TMATAG* can also function as a "satirically corrosive" portrayal of contemporary American society and governance.

Fuwaad's didactically informed embedded narratives consequently address not only a despotic Islamic Golden Age Caliph but also American policymakers who sought to extend governmental powers in the period following 9/11. According to the cultural critic Henry A. Giroux, "the United States is not simply governed by a center-right party supported by the majority of the populace, it is a country that is moving rapidly towards a form of authoritarianism that undermines any claim to being a liberal democracy" ("Emerging Authoritarianism" 98–99). Giroux explicitly connects this new regime to a form of state-sponsored terrorism ("Dirty Democracy" 164). The use of Guantanamo Bay to detain enemy combatants and the passing of the Patriot Act serve as two stark examples of the ways that the American government has increased its surveillance of its citizens and encroached on civil liberties. The cultural geographer David Harvey argues that the rise of the neoconservative agenda in the post-9/11 period "had as much to do with asserting domestic control over a fractious and much-divided body politic in the US as it did with a geopolitical strategy of maintaining global hegemony through control over oil resources" (195). Giroux's and Harvey's points reveal that foreign-policy interests in combating terrorism also required a shift in the way that the American populace was handled and controlled.[43] The international studies scholar Chaim Kaufmann notes that "the [Bush] administration succeeded, despite the weakness of the evidence for its claims, in convincing a majority of the public that Iraq posed a threat so extreme and immediate that it could be dealt with only by preventive war" (6).[44] The critique of the autocratic ruler, a mainstay to the genre of the oriental tale, therefore is at play not only within the fictional world but also in the contemporary social context that finds the US government imposing its growing despotic will on its own citizens. The rhetoric that energized the invasion also exploits the American populace, especially through a discourse that positions US policies as the proper and morally upright response to Islamic fundamentalism and associated terrorism.

Furthermore, we can appreciate the politicized dimensions of the oriental tale when we consider how it originally attained popularity during a period that saw the proliferation of European colonization projects. Ballaster contends that the oriental tale could be functionally integrated into the colonial enterprise (15). The oriental tale acts as a refractive representational terrain in which the Western colonial power can justify its actions in terms of its own cosmopolitan nature: the desire for the East is legitimated through what such an exotic landscape might offer its conquerors.[45] Hence I move to an exploration of *TMATAG* in relation to a contemporary oriental tale, which involves an American political rhetoric that constructs the Near East as a mystical and alluring landscape, full of riches.

If the oriental tale can be enfolded into a colonial agenda, *TMATAG* imagines a "pleasurable hybridity" (Ballaster 15) that represents the Near East as a space fit to be claimed. Let us return to the scene in which Fuwaad enters Bashaarat's shop. Fuwaad is astounded by various items he sees for sale (8). Fuwaad's gaze focuses on objects that have been adorned in some inventive way, making them seem both strange and wonderful. The reference to precious metals such as silver and brass imbue the shop with an opulent glow. These objects are not so strange as to elicit horror but rather call forth excitement and wonder. Indeed, the alchemist's shop is a physical space that promotes the logics of consumer desire. Fuwaad's observations might be analogically related to the American gaze toward the Middle East in the age of global oil consumption and the increased need for fossil fuels. In the context of contemporary Iraq, the rhetoric of the 2003 invasion was partially couched in economic terms. As the cultural geographer David Harvey puts it, "What the US evidently sought to impose by main force on Iraq was a state apparatus whose fundamental mission was to facilitate conditions for profitable accumulation on the part of domestic and foreign capital. I call this kind of state apparatus *a neoliberal state*" (7, emphasis in original). Of course, one aim in constructing this neoliberal state remains more access to oil in the Middle East and Arabic regions, as noted by a range of scholars and critics including Bradley L. Bowman, Dawn Brancati, Bathsheba Crocker, and Slavoj Žižek.[46] In this respect, Iraq, with its productive oil fields and its proximity to other OPEC countries, offers one clear motivation for

US involvement in the Middle East. Despite the fact that *TMATAG* presents the Near East as a mystical location filled with wealth and beauty, we should recall the rhetoric of Ajib's embedded tale, which relates to avarice and intentionality. As Ajib travels to the future with a single-minded expectation that he will find himself affluent, he entitles himself to wealth that he does not own to try to alter his destiny. His determination to secure one future trajectory results in his downfall. Further still, the novelette begins with Fuwaad admitting that he is penniless but still at peace. Comforted by the knowledge of his wife's love and happiness, Fuwaad is fully content without possessing material wealth. *TMATAG* can thus be read against American economic interests that seek to exploit the Middle East in the search for more resources.

If the Orient presents such attractive possibilities to the West, it also simultaneously presents hazards. The literary critic Abdur Raheem Kidwai clarifies the imperial valences of the genre within the frame of British orientalism, asserting that the tales could portray the Orient in damaging ways (27). Thus, the oriental tale directs the colonial gaze toward the East's fanciful landscapes and untold riches but at the same time acts as a cultural document detailing a heathen culture filled with religious fanatics. In the introduction to the edited anthology *The Arabian Nights in Historical Context*, the literary critics Saree Makdisi and Felicity Nussbaum elucidate that the oriental tale maintained "a sense of radical difference between West and East(s): a project that initiated in its modern form in the eighteenth century and that continues to this very day in the resurgent Orientalism that has had such influence on United States foreign and military policy after the events of 11 September 2001" (7). In readings connecting Fu Manchu and Hannibal Lecter, the international-affairs scholar L. H. M. Ling considers "resurgent Orientalism" in this way: "President George W. Bush has declared famously that the world is either with the United States (Western civilization, Christian enlightenment, law and order, progress) or with the terrorists (Oriental barbarism, Islamic feudalism, chaos and destruction, stagnation)" (377).[47] The economist M. Shahid Alam calls the growing fear of Islam a distinctly new form of orientalism in which America's gaze is "fixed, determined forever" by defining Muslims as individuals who hate American liberties (220). The radical difference being proffered in these "resurgent Orientalisms" are ones in which all Muslims are evildoers, willing to do violent harm to Americans.[48]

But rather than depicting a terrorist refuge, *TMATAG* imagines a Middle East imbued with the possibilities of progressive change. Fuwaad's own framing narrative concludes with an appeal that his knowledge of future events be put in the service of helping the Caliph, rather than attaining personal material wealth. As the Caliph's political adviser, he can influence a future that is boundless. To the Caliph, Fuwaad's message further envisions a despotic power informed by mercy and reconciliation rather than bellicosity or barbarism. Fuwaad's approach to the future must be compared against the way in which the invasion of Iraq unfolded under the Bush doctrine of the preemptive strike. Žižek notes that Bush's doctrine attempts to command "total control over future threats, justifying preemptive strikes against these supposed threats. The ineptitude of such an approach in the contemporary world, in which knowledge circulates freely, is patent. The loop between the present and the future is closed: the prospect of a breathtaking terrorist act is evoked in order to justify incessant pre-emptive strikes now" (15). The discourse Žižek relates concerning time reveals how Iraq cannot exist outside the conception of the terrorist-harboring nation-state until it is invaded. According to the cultural critics Jasbir K. Puar and Amit S. Rai, "As if projecting itself into an always already mastered future, where the risk of terrorism is neutralized before actualization, the time of counterterrorism discourse is always in a future that is continuous with a fixed and romanticized national past. . . . Counterterrorism is a technology that dreams of managing and mastering this monstrosity by targeting subjectivities, communities, countries, and, indeed, time itself" (92). If the 2003 invasion of Iraq operated under the auspices of a counterterrorist project that fixes the future into "always already mastered" military venture, then Iraq becomes a country tied to a speculative fantasy constructed by and perpetrated through American foreign policy and international conquest. America becomes the all-powerful time traveler, able to forecast into the future and apparently able to circumvent the future terrorist attack that is absolutely certain to take place. Gifted with such prophetic capabilities, American surveillance thus extends not only over the Middle East but also over time itself.

The post-Iraq-invasion context exposes a fragile American orientalist imaginary: that of Iraq as a democratically functioning nation. The terrorism studies scholar Daniel Byman reminds us that "despite having a long history as a civilization—and a once-vibrant middle class—Iraqis do not have a strong identity as a nation: British colonialists created modern Iraq, and under colonial rule the country never gained a strong identity" (49). In some sense, then, the attempt to create a democratic Iraq already stems from a colonial expectation that the modern nation-state could address the needs of a heterogeneous population comprising varying religions, tribal groups, and ethnicities. The historian Zachary Lockman further articulates that the American government expected that "the vast majority of Iraqis would enthusiastically welcome their country's occupation" (268) and would eagerly take instruction in the postwar context, but this viewpoint is what Simon Serfaty calls a "creative fantasy" (130). The key element that connects the points advanced by Byman, Lockman, and Serfaty appears in the speculative assumption that postinvasion Iraq would be a space to develop and nurture American democratic sentiment. The "pleasurable hybridity" of the Orient returns forcefully in this moment, showing how the rhetoric of Iraqi democracy is itself a misleading narrative of progress. In the dismantling of this illusion, the historian Douglas Little elaborates on the resurgence of a previous orientalism: "As in Vietnam, so too in Iraq, the longer the war lasted, the stronger all the old orientalist stereotypes about Asians and Arabs became. During the first days of the occupation, an epidemic of looting and robberies prompted unlucky American victims to liken their assailants to Ali Baba and his forty thieves." As it became clear that constructing a democratically functioning Iraq would take far more time and military support than first thought, "before long, U.S. troops came to regard their Iraqi adversaries as wily orientals, ungrateful thugs, or religious fanatics" (334). The ambivalence that structures Iraq simultaneously as a land composed of "wily orientals" and a location that should be remolded into a democratic nation-state extends around a temporal incoherence. Here, Iraq does not properly progress because it cannot fulfill the "creative fantasy" wrought in the minds of American foreign-policymakers and military strategists, but this imagined future should not have been so readily expected in the first place. In other words, we might reconsider American expectations of Iraqi democracy to exist in the time and space of a speculative fiction, one with tenuous connections to actual Iraqi social and cultural contexts.

In relation to *TMATAG*, Fuwaad's escape from the time loop that predetermines the fate of the main characters of each embedded narrative gestures to unscripted and unmapped Iraqi futures. Fuwaad concludes his story by saying that his "most precious knowledge" appears in this statement: "Nothing erases the past. There is repentance, there is atonement, and there is forgiveness. That is all, but that is enough" (60). Again, this kind of lesson appears relevant to multiple parties. Acts such as repentance, atonement, and forgiveness require one to admit one's faults and failings, to make up for them, and, when one has been wronged, to grant a pardon. The universalism ascribed to these sentiments might seem apolitical, but in the context of either an Abbasid-era Caliph with absolute powers to determine a subject's life or death or policy advisers looking to advance American democratic and economic interests in the Middle East, this lesson proves applicable in its appeal to mercy, pacifism, and humility. *TMATAG* finally reveals that the past cannot be simply disregarded and that any future course of action depends on an extended and not necessarily predetermined understanding of the sociohistorical continuum.

Unbinding Asian American Speculative Fictions

"Abducted by Aliens!" and *TMATAG* are both speculative fictions featuring a narrator who might be seen as an analogy to the Asian American writer who confounds autobiographical or autoethnographic reading practices. In Light's story, the Japanese American narrator must appropriate the story of her older brother to break the silence surrounding the internment narrative, even if that narrative can be only obliquely related through an alien-abduction story. The disorienting structure of the story also models the difficulty of representing traumatic historical events within the space of an intergenerational narrative. In Chiang's novelette, Fuwaad must appropriate the tales told to him by Bashaarat to provide the Caliph with his counsel. Like "Abducted by Aliens!," *TMATAG* speaks to external social contexts, especially in light of the contemporary discourses that have orientalized Iraq as a site harboring, on the one hand, untold riches in the form of oil and, on the other, terrorists expending their lives in the service of radical jihad. Each narrator recounts a tale already told by someone else in order to relay strongly political messages concerning issues related to social inequality and oppression. The narrators' retellings indirectly invoke the aesthetic projects of these Asian American writers, who take on ethnoracial storytelling perspectives that do not match up with their individual ancestries. Both "Abducted by Aliens!" and *TMATAG* also require a diverse set of archives and documents external to the fictional world to engage the ways that their narratives function analogically. In this way, Light and Chiang slightly estrange genres and forms such as the alien-abduction narrative and the oriental tale to reframe and to reimagine particular historical and social circumstances such as the Japanese American internment and the War on Terror.

While primarily focusing on two texts, this chapter offers a critical reading practice that applies equally well to other Asian American speculative fictions. The Japanese American older brother from "Abducted by Aliens!" tells his younger sister, "We contain a cosmos" (76), a phrase that in its reference to outer space alludes to the brother's belief that he has been abducted. But we can reconsider that phrase in light of the work of Asian Americans writers who imagine such cognitively estranging fictional worlds—fictional worlds that are unbound. These worlds are "cosmic" in scope, as they include Arabic merchants from the Islamic Golden Age who use time-traveling devices and telepathic aliens that abduct humans and take them on intergalactic odysseys. Reading speculative fictions through their analogical valences allows us to engage the large group of Asian American writers whose works may otherwise be ignored or overlooked precisely because they can journey to such unexpected places and times.

Coda: Fiction Unbound

Asian American fiction boasts a long and rich lineage, at least over a century long; its body of texts contains a multitude of unforgettable characters and compelling themes. Within this impressive archive, writers often produce narratives imbued with autobiographical and auto-ethnographic valences. And yet the parallels among author, narrative perspective, and fictional world can still result in certain presumptions about the kinds of stories Asian American writers can tell: a well-known writer such as Amy Tan might be presumed to create narrative perspectives centered only on Chinese or Chinese American characters, which in turn illuminate only Asian American social contexts.

I have worked to push past these simplifications and to unravel the bind among author, narrative perspective, and fictional world by exploring a large and equally important literary archive. This other archive contains Asian American writers whose narrators' ancestries do not overlap directly with the authors'. Literary critics must be attentive to such cultural productions, as they show a particularly dynamic approach to the creation of storytellers and their corresponding fictional worlds. This book addresses this other textual body, primarily focusing on eight writers: Jessica Hagedorn, Tony D'Souza, Chang-rae Lee, Sesshu Foster, Sigrid Nunez, Sabina Murray, Claire Light, and Ted Chiang. I concentrate on these writers at the expense of others who could have been included in a lengthier version of this book. Yet these eight writers are especially instructive as touchstones for dynamic constructions of narrative perspective that open up onto richly conceived fictional works that have all been published in the post-2000 period. These cultural productions are suggestive of what Yoonmee Chang calls the postracial aesthetic, evidence that Asian American writers have somehow freed themselves from the shackles of their ethnoracial identities.[1] Yet, rather than advancing a postracial aesthetic, each writer, despite the differences in the storytelling viewpoint and fictional social contexts, takes on cross-ethnoracial first-person narrative perspectives to spotlight particular social issues, including but not limited to human rights controversies, the plight of migrant laborers, the disintegration of prison systems, histories of colonial exploitation, Japanese American internment, and post-9/11 rhetoric concerning the War on Terror. They offer imagined landscapes that must be analyzed for their racial asymmetries, showing us the unlimited but still strongly politically engaged bounds of Asian American fictional worlds.

As I stated in the introduction, the eight Asian American writers at the heart of this study are not free from racializing effects, however individual in their experiences, ethnic backgrounds, and social positions. It is impossible to determine with full certitude why these writers create such socially conscious fictions, but the fact that they are all American minority writers is not a coincidence. This racial minority status cannot simply be dismissed offhand as tangential to what fuels their creative imaginations. In the era of the model minority, the Asian American is considered to be a privileged subject, so much so that he or she becomes an example for other underperforming minority groups to accordingly model themselves on. The model minority paradigm is inherently comparative in its racial formation, marking Asian Americans as a group that must be juxtaposed with others. Narrative perspective offers a place to reconsider the comparativity of Asian American identity, as the writers in this study reach across race and ethnicity to explore what it means to speak, think, or feel from the perspective of someone in a different social position. The model minority paradigm distinguishes and reifies Asian Americans within a position of relative superiority, a racial population that supposedly strives for social assimilation and upward mobility. But when writers occasionally disengage from the autobiographical and autoethnographic, they can resist and complicate the expectation that they should model the performance of racial privilege and a certain form of racial authenticity tied to narration. In some ways, then, these fictions are recalcitrant in their flagrant disregard for reproducing model minority narratives.

The fictions grounding this book do not retreat from the politicism that characterizes so many Asian American cultural productions. Indeed, these eight writers are extremely attentive to power dynamics and the relationship between individuals and larger social systems. Further still, we cannot always expect that racial oppression and ethnic personal histories will be the primary or sole inspiration for Asian American writers or the grounds for the constructions of fictional worlds. However, what we do learn from these books and these writers is that there is still a tremendous potential to read such texts through social justice issues that have always been important to contemporary literary studies. Such readings suggest that we must be more comparative and syncretic, brave and idiosyncratic, in the kinds of analyses we make about fictional worlds. When Michael Omi and Howard Winant made their groundbreaking theoretical formulation of race as a social construct, it became an incredibly rich paradigm for critics to use in exploring the Asian American experience as one embedded in a systematic history of oppression and exclusion. Yet the relationship among social structures and registers of difference, however defined—whether based on race, class, religion, gender, sexuality, age, disability, and so on—is as unfettered as the Asian American fictional world. In this respect, the plurality of traumatized characters with such distinct backgrounds found in these representational terrains really speaks to the quite disheartening conclusion that oppression and disempowerment remain incredibly pervasive in and intricately woven into the fabric of America and elsewhere.

Though this study remains in the terrain of make-believe, we see how these cultural productions engage the existing dilemmas that currently confound us. American writers of Asian descent are clearly not the only cultural producers to complicate narrative perspective, moving away from autobiographical and autoethnographic standpoints. Yet the circumscription of these writers under the model minority paradigm and the ways that such a racial formation might directly or indirectly influence the production of fictional worlds suggest a need to occasionally distinguish the projects and cultural representations offered by Asian Americans.

As Monika Fludernik reminds us, narration is understood to be both voice centered and anthropomorphic in quality.[2] In the case of first-person fiction, Asian American writers employ the construction of the storyteller as a gateway into a variety of social formations, geographical terrains, and historical moments. But why not just give up racial descent as a way to circumscribe a body of literary texts if the relationship between descent and the fictional world is potentially so malleable? As I discussed briefly earlier, Asian American writers may not always choose to match their ethnoracial backgrounds through narrative perspective, but their fictional worlds still speak to issues of structural inequality that energize critical inquiries. The proliferation of social contexts within fictional worlds presents problems insofar as we expect Asian American writers to write only about Asian American experiences. But to entirely give up descent would be to assume that race does not influence in any way the relationship between the writer and the textual terrain.

Cultural critics and literary scholars are keenly aware that literature can be classified and analyzed in multiple ways, but what *Racial Asymmetries* also urgently strives for is to push for scholars *outside* Asian American studies to take more effort in considering the import of racially asymmetrical fictional worlds to *their* subfields. In only a handful of cases have Asian American writers' works been widely embraced within multiple subfields and disciplines. A mixed-genre publication such as Maxine Hong Kingston's *The Woman Warrior* is one example of a text that has crossed into many different analytical terrains. Scholars situated in postmodernism, feminist theory, race and ethnic studies, psychoanalysis, and life-writing have focused much attention on *The Woman Warrior*, showcasing how one work can inform numerous disciplines and critical arenas.[3] At the same time, few books have garnered such cross-disciplinary acclaim, and *The Woman Warrior* is an exceptional case of the ways that one book can speak to multiple subfields within literary studies and beyond. Certainly, Kingston's groundbreaking work is incredibly complex, but the lack of other crossover texts since *The Woman Warrior* gestures to the lack of dialogue among subareas and subfields that currently characterizes contemporary American literary studies. In questioning the boundaries that demarcate various literary subfields, I am encouraging critics to work even more comparatively in their textual interpretations. Foster's *Atomik Aztex*, for instance, would find a fruitful place within Chicano studies as much as it has found a forum within Asian American studies. Literary taxonomies, whether organized within an Asian Americanist frame or not, must dynamically overlap such that one text might cross many borders, enriching and enlarging critical landscapes. Given the tremendous archive that I have not been able to fully consider in this book, we can optimistically say our work has only just begun.

Notes

Introduction

1. While Asian American literature typically appears within the common linguistic frame of English, recent criticism complicates this expectation as well. The addition to the Heath American literature anthology of the Chinese-language poems by those who were detained at Angel Island Immigration Center during the late nineteenth and early twentieth centuries serves as a prominent example.

2. See Shirley Geok-lin Lim's "Assaying the Gold," Sau-ling Wong's "Denationalization Reconsidered," and Kandice Chuh's *Imagine Otherwise* for some theoretical considerations of Asian American literature.

3. Rather than provide an exhaustive list of such fictions, I note a handful of the more distinctive and flagrant examples in which authorial ancestry is not paralleled in the ethnoracial background of the first-person storyteller, such as S. P. Somtow's *The Darker Angels* (1998), Sang Pak's *Wait until Twilight* (2009), Joydeep Roy-Bhattacharya's *The Watch* (2012), Da Chen's *The Last Empress* (2012), Bill Cheng's *Southern Cross the Dog* (2013), and Tosca Lee's *Iscariot* (2013). Though out of the bounds of this study, the racial asymmetries related to Asian American fiction told primarily in the third person also provide more examples of instances in which the storytelling entity cannot be assumed to be a double for the author.

4. Other branches of Asian American literature that have not received much critical attention are popular genre fiction (such as the romance novel or detective fiction) and young adult fiction (such as the paranormal romance genre).

5. Here, I take a cue from postpositivist realist approaches informing the work of Paula Moya's *Learning from Experience* and her edited collection *Reclaiming Identity*.

6. Of course, Lipsitz is himself drawing on Gayatri Spivak's foundational theory of strategic essentialism.

7. Literary critic Sunn Shelley Wong makes similar claims regarding Asian American writers and formal concerns. However, Wong restricts her periodization to the

1970s and 1980s (62). The use of autobiography and bildungsroman by Asian American writers can be tracked earlier.

8. For some useful sources on American orientalism and the commodification of Asian cultures, see Tchen's *New York before Chinatown*, Yoshihara's *Embracing the East*, and Klein's *Cold War Orientalism*.

9. I want to clarify that this model is not inherently restrictive in the sense that Asian American writers have shown the ability to explore so-called autobiographically informed fictions through a variety of aesthetic techniques.

10. I use the year 1989 as a rough marker because it is the date of Tan's publication of *The Joy Luck Club*.

11. While Eaton garnered much success for her Japanese-themed works, she simultaneously suffered from pigeonholing, at least within the publishing realm. According to biographer Diana Birchall, "her publishers kept wanting her to write Japanese novels, and the only time she had broken away, with *The Diary of Delia*, they had forced her to use the Watanna pen name against her wishes" (114). For more on this issue, see A. Ling, "Winnifred Eaton" 7; and Ferens 165. After *The Diary of Delia*, Eaton returned to fictions focusing on Japanese contexts until her final two novels. In Jean Lee Cole's estimation, critics tend to study the "works that appear to explicitly address Eaton's Asian identity" (4).

12. There are a small handful of other examples of writers such as Mai-mai Sze and Willyce Kim who occasionally stepped outside an autoethnographic fictional frame, but few have attained the level of critical attention of writers such as Winnifred Eaton and Diana Chang.

13. The development of postracial discourse is drawn, of course, from a longer one that espouses the apparent success of the civil rights movement and thus disavows the continuing and more insidious forms of racial prejudice embedded in the private sphere. For more on postrace, see Hesse; Banner; Haney-López, "Post-Racial Racism"; Bobo; Dawkins; Rachlinski and Parks; and Michelle Alexander.

14. A Chinese transnational, a friend of Jack Diaz's, appears as the central figure of one chapter, but the rest of the novel does not involve him. For more on Chinese transnational dynamics, see Ong.

15. For considerations of the political instability in Côte d'Ivoire and the recent civil war, see Mahoney; Higonnet; and Klaas. For other useful studies of the factionalism in Côte d'Ivoire, see Chirot; Toungara; and Whitaker. My readings of *Whiteman* and its representations of Côte d'Ivoire are influenced by the work of human rights scholars more generally; these include Brysk; A. Fagan; Goldberg; Ignatieff; Landman; and Slaughter.

16. See Tuan; Chou and Feagin; Stacey Lee; and Wise 93–97.

17. See Spickard; Williams-León and Brock; and Cheng.

18. Given the focus of this study on Asian American fiction at large, I cannot address the larger implications of mixed-race Asian American writers in relation to their cultural productions. Indeed, no single monograph is yet devoted to this topic.

19. For some key sources that explore both the possibilities and pitfalls of multiculturalism, see Kymlicka; James Lee; Chae; Gordon and Newfield; Obourn; and Jin.

20. By 1996, Tan's book had sold considerably more than Maxine Hong Kingston's *The Woman Warrior*, the work considered by many people to be the most widely known Asian American text, despite being published more than a decade after Kingston's work (D. Li 223n. 1). Literary critic Sau-ling C. Wong explains that "according

to Rita Holmes of the Sandra Dijkstra Agency, Kingston's agent, as of September 1996 over 900,000 copies of *The Woman Warrior* (both hardcover and paperback) have been sold" (Introduction 12n. 1). Tan's work alone has spawned numerous critical companions and single-author studies that are exceeded in number only by those about Kingston's work. In "Sugar Sisterhood," Sau-ling Wong articulates the frenetic milieu that followed Tan's success (176). For more critical studies on Tan, see Adams, *Amy Tan*; and Bloom.

21. Despite Tan's wide renown as a writer who delves into Chinese and Chinese American ethnic contexts, she disavows the term "ethnic literature" in relation to her creative work due to its connection with nonfictional forms (Huntley 39).

22. Jhumpa Lahiri's *Unaccustomed Earth* (2008) is another Asian American work to have appeared at the top of the *New York Times* best-seller list, but Lahiri was born in London. Although Lahiri's birth country does not preclude her as an Asian American writer per se, Tan does remain distinct on that particular level. Lisa See's *Dreams of Joy* (2011) also debuted atop the *New York Times* best-seller list.

23. This list includes Tan's first four novels, *The Joy Luck Club*, *The Kitchen God's Wife* (1991), *The Hundred Secret Senses* (1995), and *The Bonesetter's Daughter* (2000), as well as Fae Myenne Ng's *Bone* (1993), Aimee Liu's *Face* (1994), Sky Lee's *Disappearing Moon Café* (1991), Patricia Chao's *Monkey King* (1997), and Lan Samantha Chang's *Hunger* (1998).

24. For some prominent examples of the ways in which Asian American writers can be marketed as tour guides, see the hardcover jacket description of Julie Shigekuni's *A Bridge between Us* (1995) and the paperback plot summary of Nora Okja Keller's *Comfort Woman* (1997).

25. The masculinist approach offered by the *Aiiieeeee!* editors has been directly addressed by feminist approaches to Asian Americanist critique in book-length studies by numerous critics, including King-Kok Cheung, Patti Duncan, Amy Ling, and Leslie Bow. The psychoanalytic valences of Asian American literature established another major subset of the field, prominently in work by David L. Eng, Anne Anlin Cheng, and Juliana Chang.

26. Literary critic Mark Chiang clarifies the complexities of institutionalization in *The Cultural Capital of Asian American Studies*. Vital to his argument is the notion that much of the field of Asian American studies has revolved around murky relationships among aesthetics, politics, representation, and authenticity.

27. Even given this new approach toward Asian American identity as inherently multifocal, a text such as *Dictee* has still been read reductively. According to Sue Kim, "while demonstrating how *Dictee* interrogates the unity of subjectivity, [Lisa] Lowe, like many readers, also posits a singular narrator identified with the author" ("Narrator, Author, Reader" 164).

28. The field of African American literary criticism has already explored the ways that minority writers might complicate the relationship between narrative perspective and authorial descent, especially in Claudia Tate's *Psychoanalysis and Black Novels* and Gene Jarrett's *Deans and Truants*. Caroline Rody's *The Interethnic Imagination* is an excellent recent example of the way that Asian American literature can be read in comparative frames.

29. I follow the sentiment that Sue-Im Lee expresses in her introduction to *Literary Gestures*, when she asserts that her edited collection works to balance "sociological

and cultural materialist approaches" with aesthetic inquiries (1). Certainly, there has been some work done in combining aesthetic and contextual analyses in Asian American cultural criticism. These critical investigations include considerations of drama and performance (Moy; Josephine Lee, *Performing Asian America*; and Shimakawa), autobiography (R. Davis), the short story (R. Davis), as well as edited collections (Zhou and Najmi; Davis and Lee).

30. Jinqi Ling has already argued in *Narrating Nationalisms* that the realist tradition possesses its own narrative, aesthetic, and sociopolitical intricacies. Patricia Chu and Alicia Otano also provide more evidence that the Asian American bildungsroman is quite a complicated and rich racial form, but the Asian American realist tradition that Ling conceptualizes and the Asian American developmental narrative that both Chu and Otano investigate do not encompass the larger corpus I analyze in this book.

31. In bringing up the topic of extradiegetic narrators, Pihlainen refers to a whole set of storytelling modes that do have a narrator but that bear more attention. For more on extradiegetic narrators and other explorations of narration, see Rimmon-Kenan 94–95; Genette's foundational work, *Narrative Discourse*; B. Richardson; Chatman chap. 5; Lanser, *Fictions of Authority*; Warhol.

32. According to Lubomír Doležel, nonfictional forms are "constrained by the requirement of truth-valuation" and "construct historical worlds which are models of the actual world's past. One and the same historical event or sequence of events (historical period, life, and so on) can be modeled by various historical worlds. In a critical testing, these worlds are assessed as more or less adequate to the actual past" ("Possible Worlds" 792). For Doležel's extended study of fictionality, see *Heterocosmica*.

33. In Jonathan Culler's four-pronged critique of omniscience, he posits a similar idea concerning thoughts and feelings that a narrator should not be able to have access to: "Telepathy seems especially apposite—much more so than omniscience—for cases where an extradiegetic-homodiegetic narrator displays special knowledge" (29). Also, for earlier conceptualizations offered by Cohn on the topic of fictionality, see "Signposts of Fictionality."

34. Thomas Pavel has argued that "the narration of the inner thoughts of other individuals qua subjects indicates less the fictionality of a text than the activity of the empathic imagination, which legitimately and plausibly explores the life of other minds in both fictional and actual context" (536). Pavel's conception of "empathic imagination" stands in contrast to the work of Dorrit Cohn, who implies that fictional narration is telepathic in scope (specifically in the case of free indirect discourse). For more on cognition and narration, see also Zunshine; Flanagan; and Palmer.

35. There have been quite a few debates about the nature of narration, whether it is linguistically based, voice based, or not even relatable to anthropomorphic communication. See Banfield; Gibson 655; Gunn 36; Fludernik, "New Wine in Old Bottles?" 636; Nielson 145; Walsh, "Who Is the Narrator?" 511; and Aczel 493. For the purposes of this study, I choose to situate my critical interpretations by positing that all narratives possess narrators, following Marie-Laure Ryan's conception of audience: "The author and her audience are located in the real world, while the narrator and his audience are members of the so-called fictional world" (167).

36. My study takes inspiration from James Phelan's approach, in which he argues that "in fictional narrative, the rhetorical situation is double: the narrator tells her story to her narratee for her purposes, while the author communicates to her audience

for her own purposes both the story and the narrator's telling of it" (4). This doubling of narrative is also at work in the Asian American literature I analyze. On the one hand, I consider the importance of the narrator's perspective and what purpose emerges in the telling of a given story, but on the other, my entire study calls attention to the ways that the author's communication entails enhancing the nature of fictionality by positioning the narrative through a specific storyteller. For more on the relationship between author and narrator, see Lanser, "'I' of the Beholder."

37. By invoking the phrase "new territories," I gesture to the important place of race and space in this project. All the chapters are very much invested in aspects of space and cultural geography in the application of a social-context critique. In this respect, I focus on various different spatial formulations, including the interplay among local, regional, urban, national, and transnational depictions.

38. For some recent approaches, see Levander and Levine's *Hemispheric American Studies* and Maeda's *Chains of Babylon*.

1 / White Flight, White Narration

1. Certainly whiteness cannot be conceived monolithically. See Jacobson; Roediger, *Working toward Whiteness*.

2. One prominent example is Tony D'Souza's *Whiteman* (2006), which I discuss in the introduction. Other writers such as Alexander Chee, Bharati Mukherjee, and Jhumpa Lahiri have explored the use of white narrative perspectives in their fictions. For an example of a mixed-race Asian American writer who employs an Italian American narrator in a novel, see Prasad's *On Borrowed Wings* (2007).

3. Perhaps not coincidentally, both Mac and Mister Perry are attending a baseball game. Baseball has been long connected not only to whiteness but to white supremacy.

4. It is impossible to summarily state that the character is "white." In avoiding a clear-cut designation, Lapcharoensap plays on the desire of the reader to pinpoint definitive racial designations of characters.

5. In Susan Koshy's exploration of South Asian American racial formation and whiteness, she prefaces her work by reminding us that "studies of whiteness that are limited to a nation-state model are unable to address the ways in which global capital has used, modified, and infiltrated racial meanings in the contemporary context" ("Morphing Race" 154).

6. See the interview with Dwight Garner (1999).

7. "Duck U" refers to the University of Oregon, where Chang-rae Lee was an assistant professor. The mascot of University of Oregon is a duck.

8. Many reviewers make note of Paul Pyun as the "Chang-rae Lee" fictionalization. In addition to Kagy and Polo, John Homans writes in his *New York* magazine review that "there's a Chang-rae Lee character, a Korean-American novelist married to Jerry Battle's daughter."

9. Various disciplinary configurations of whiteness studies include working-class critiques (Saxton; Roediger, *Working toward Whiteness* and *The Wages of Whiteness*), feminist critiques (Frankenberg), cultural critique and cultural studies (Dyer; Babb; Stokes; Hartigan; Berger), historical studies (T. Allen; L. Williams), activist praxis approaches (Roediger, *Toward the Abolition of Whiteness*; Alcoff; Olson; Kendall; J. Harvey), social science approaches (Yancey; Nevels), psychoanalytic critiques (Seshadri-Cooks), among numerous others. This bibliographic listing, by no means

exhaustive, is given here to demonstrate both the emergence of whiteness studies as a distinctive discipline and its numerous branches.

10. In this regard, Jerry's whiteness can be elucidated alongside those scholars who explore the relationship between the individual and the community. The cultural critic Robyn Wiegman astutely notes the ways in which whiteness functions through a mutual constitution between two levels of racial discourse: the universal and the particular (117). Wiegman's claims are bolstered by the work of the historian George Lipsitz, who has specifically been invested in rooting out how liberal individualist philosophies uphold white privilege under the guise of color-blind democracy ("Possessive Investment" 381, 383).

11. Steve Garner provides a useful condensation: "Whiteness invokes power relations, . . . normality, dominance, and control" (9).

12. See Haney-López, *White by Law*; Harris; Lipsitz, *Possessive Investment*; Ferber.

13. For some studies of suburban development, see Lamb; Beauregard; Bonastia; Kruse and Sugrue; Freund.

14. For more on suburbanization and minority segregation, see J. Oliver 13.

15. According to Rosalyn Baxandall and Elizabeth Ewen, "Long Island, like most other suburbs, was initially developed as a bucolic haven for white upper-class families" ("Race Relations in the Suburbs" 100–01).

16. One of the definitive texts on the Levittown master-planned suburban community is Herbert J. Gans's *The Levittowners*. For other studies of Levittown, see Kelly; Lundrigan, Navarra, and Ferrer; and chapter 2 of Feder. For book-length studies that focus more broadly on Long Island suburban development, see Mahler; Baxandall and Ewen, *Picture Windows*.

17. In addition to the FHA and VA, Elaine Tyler May adds that "the highway system, the financing of sewers, the support for suburban developments such as Levittown, and the placing of public housing in the center of urban ghettos, facilitated the dispersal of the white middle class into the suburbs and contributed to the decay of the inner cities" (152).

18. Although this policy ended in 1948 with the court case *Shelly v. Kraemer*, "exact figures regarding the FHA's discrimination against blacks are not available, data by county show a clear pattern of 'redlining' in central-city counties and abundant loan activity in suburban counties" (Oliver and Shapiro 18). In addition, "to compensate for the questionable legality of discriminatory deed restrictions, the real estate industry resorted to more subtle methods; usually realtors simply refused to sell racial minorities homes situated in white neighborhoods" (Hurley 309).

19. For these news articles, see Lambert, "Study Calls L.I." and "Long Island Has Failed"; Richter; and Trillin.

20. David Halle writes, "Much of the housing in Nassau County was built immediately after World War II and excluded blacks, with Levittown on Long Island, developed beginning in 1947, a famous example. Even now, only a handful of blacks (fewer than 200) live in this community of more than 50,000" (172). Johnson, Johnson, and Farenga make similar claims regarding Levittown segregation (63). For more on Long Island segregation history, see Sellers 101–4; and Wiese, *Places of Their Own*.

21. For a useful condensation of the history of how bipolar disorder has been classified, see Nemade and Dombeck. Of particular interest is that the term "bipolar

disorder" came into wider use as the DSM-II changed to DSM-III in 1980. Given the flexible nature of the DSM, it has been the subject of wide controversy and critical study. For instance, Mary E. Wood's "'I've Found Him!' Diagnostic Narrative in *The DSM-IV Casebook*" investigates how the manual might be read in terms of its aesthetic properties, the ways in which the text might be constructed.

22. See Sadock, Kaplan, and Sadock 535–78, for more particulars related to diagnosis of bipolar disorder.

23. Isaac Galatzer-Levy and Robert Galatzer-Levy direct their critiques particularly to the DSM, which "divides mental disorder into categorical taxa, thus assuming a 'have it or don't' diagnostic rule" (162).

24. According to Charles E. Rosenberg, the trend toward biological explanation of bodily dysfunction is part of a larger structural trajectory of "medicalization" (409).

25. The genetic component of bipolar disorder, while not established completely (whether a single gene variant or a set of genes causes expression of the disorder), nevertheless predominates as the way American psychiatry views the disease. Jeffrey C. Wood offers the prevailing viewpoint: "Most scientific researchers agree that there is no single cause of bipolar disorder. However, the development of the disorder is strongly influenced by genetic risk factors" (46).

26. Paul Thagard parallels the exhortation to connect scientific and biological therapies with psychosocial interventions (350).

27. One major reason for the use of psychosocial treatment is that "first, despite the substantial efficacy of available somatic treatments, nonresponse and break-through episodes remain a major problem, with as many as 35–60% remaining chronically ill or having poor outcome" (Bauer 281). Byron J. Good also advocates a combined treatment program (231).

28. According to Grob, "many—but not all—contemporary psychiatrists recognize that chronic mental illnesses cannot be treated in isolation, and that care and management are as crucial as psychiatric therapies" (219). Andrea Nicki's exploration of trauma and feminist theories leads her to advance that "unless attention is given to the cultural or social aspects of genuine mental illnesses, we risk giving these illnesses overly personalized explanations—'bad genes,' faulty biochemistry, and so on—and viewing them as purely personal problems, in no way social" (91). Philosophical approaches have also yielded similar critiques of medicalization. In this vein, see N. Davis 183; and Zachar 179. For some recent critical considerations of disability studies in relation to mental disorders, see Wendell; Donaldson; Kudlick; Lewiecki-Wilson; and Mollow.

29. Other sociologically inflected or philosophically invested approaches to mental illnesses and disorders are explored in Laungani; Fox; Hiday; and Glannon.

30. James Whitney Hicks corroborates this point (200). For more considerations of environmental factors or psychosocial conditions that can affect or trigger manic depression, see Cohen 136; J. Allen 154–56; Basco and Rush 223–26; Miklowitz and Johnson 324–26; Miklowitz 48–68.

31. Johnson and Meyer write, "Life-stress interviews intended to address these issues have been developed, and the findings using these interview measures have consistently supported links between life events and increases in symptoms" (86). For more on the BAS and its role on mania, see Newman 247; Miklowitz 91.

2 / When the Minor Becomes Major

1. In a different piece articulating the importance of considering Asian Americans in relation to Arab Americans in the post-9/11 context, Prashad critiques ethnic studies for what he considers to be its "balkanized" organization ("Ethnic Studies Inside Out" 171).

2. The move to enrich literary criticism through a comparative race methodology has been most prevalent in the exploration of the relationship between Asian Americans and African American cultural production. For some exemplary cross-racial critiques, see D. Kim; Knadler; Maeda, "Black Panthers"; and Julia Lee, "Estrangement on a Train." There have been some explorations of Asian American studies along a north and south axis, marking a hemisphere approach to the field; see Chuh, "Of Hemispheres and Other Spheres"; E. Lee; and J. Ling, "Forging a North-South Perspective."

3. It is important to point out that the status of foreign-ness for each racial population is in many ways distinct. For Asian Americans, their designation as aliens unfit for citizenship stemmed in part from the presumed cultural, linguistic, and phenotypic differences attributed to those who had migrated across the Pacific. For Chicanos and Latinos, such differences were configured through their movement across the U.S.-Mexico border.

4. For an excellent consideration of Asian migration to the western United States, see Nomura. In a relatively early study, Lloyd H. Fisher explains that labor shortages encouraged people in the farming industry to rely on "a seasonal agricultural labor supply" (5). Guerin-Gonzales (24) and P. Martin (1128) respectively illustrate how these shortages were addressed by hiring Mexican and Asian immigrants. For more on the interrelation between Asian American and Mexican immigrants, see Dadabhay; Gonzales; and Roos and Hennessy.

5. Even within Asian American populations, Karen Leonard reminds us that historical documents have challenged a singularly posited viewpoint that "treats the various Asian 'others' as functionally equivalent to each other" (19). For another excellent account of the distinctions between Asian populations in early twentieth-century California, see Eiichiro Azuma's *Between Two Empires*.

6. While the term "Latino" might be applied in this chapter as well, I use "Chicano" precisely because of the political implications of the term, which calls attention to the civil rights discourse in which people of Mexican descent organized for more rights.

7. Evelyn Blumenberg and Paul Ong situate the Los Angeles garment industry's reliance on Asian and Latina American immigrants on the basis of migration rates: "In 1970 Mexicans and Asians comprised 28 and 12 percent, respectively, of the new immigrants to Los Angeles; by 1980 these figures had doubled, to 43 and 24 percent, respectively" (321).

8. Rebecca Budde describes the intricate divisions that characterize the Los Angeles garment industry in this way: "White Anglo-Americans are located at the peak," with Asians typically in the middle position, while the "base shoulders the burden"; the "base" typically consists of immigrants from Latin and Central America (60). For more on class stratification among different immigrant populations in the Los Angeles garment industry, see Zentgraf 60; and I. Light 88.

9. Contemporary studies of Los Angeles and interracial relations focus on Asian American and African American interactions, especially in the context of the Los Angeles race riots. Some sources on this interracial intersectionality can be found in Abelmann and Lie; Joyce; Song; Jennifer Lee; Park and Park 295–96.

10. E. San Juan makes a passing reference to the alliances that appear in the novel. Melinda De Jesús presents some readings of interracial events in "Rereading History, Rewriting Desire" but does not provide a sustained analysis of their importance.

11. I use the term "Mexican American" instead of "Chicano" in the context of Bulosan's text because the narrative was written at a time when the term "Chicano" was not yet in use.

12. The promise of stronger interracial connection seems to be one worth dreaming about, as Bulosan's *America Is in the Heart* suggests. Such a connection later came to fruition with the alliances between figures such as Cesar Chavez and Philip Vera Cruz (Fujita-Rony 149).

13. Leonard writes, "After the controversies of the first few marriages, a pattern was established, and many Punjabi-Hispanic marriages took place. Cotton was the crop that brought most couples together" (63). Beyond the agricultural connections, LaBrack and Leonard emphasize the importance of phenotypic ties, advancing that "Punjabis were frequently mistaken for Mexicans" (533).

14. Speculative fiction covers a wide range of subgenres, including horror, magical realism, fantasy, and science fiction. The form of speculative fiction offers Foster the opportunity to rethink history, if only to ask how social inequality moves beyond the scope of one hegemonic nation or racial group. In this respect, the novel strikes a cautionary note, following what Heather Urbanski cites as a pivotal function of speculative fiction: "It shows us our nightmares and therefore contributes to our efforts to avoid them" (1). For more on speculative fiction, see Gannon; and Thaler.

15. According to John Chávez, the term "Chicano" "gained popularity, but was not universally accepted by the Chicano movement until, in the spring of 1969, the first Chicano national conference, in Denver, drafted '*El plan espiritual de Aztlán*'" (141). For more on the beginnings of the Chicano movement and Aztlán, see García 95; and Rosales 23.

16. Accordingly, Arnoldo De León and Richard Griswold del Castillo contend, "It was unimportant that there existed no evidence that the Aztecs had ever actually lived in the American Southwest. What was important was that Chicanos unite themselves with their Mexican culture and brethren" (159). For more on the importance of Aztlán to the Chicano movement, see Noriega 129; Gómez-Quiñones 124; and Navarro 317.

17. For some scholarly and creative approaches to Aztlán that reveal the Chicano homeland's masculinist origins, see Price 76; Ruíz 106; E. Chávez 5; and Moraga and Mayorga. Arrizón's reliance on Cherríe Moraga in her article "Mythical Performativity" is not unexpected, as Moraga's art and creative work have been a rallying point for literary critics to conceptualize alternative cultural nationalisms. Richard Buitron notes the limits of Aztlán in relation to geography and particular urban populations (73).

18. Moraga's is just one of numerous creative reconsiderations of Aztlán; others have included Gloria Anzaldúa's *Borderlands / La Frontera*. For critical reconsiderations of Aztlán, see also Arrizón; Marez; and Gaspar de Alba.

19. Emma Pérez advances a similar claim in her conceptualization of Aztlán in relation to diaspora (78).

20. For more on Aztec mythology, see Koch.

21. For more on Aztec sacrificial culture, see Read; Knight (esp. chap. 3); Smith; and Pennock.

22. Foster's speculative reality ultimately clashes with the current and collective status of Mexican Americans and Chicanos as a group. Jorge Chapa and Belinda De La Rosa reveal that "despite the rapid growth of the Latino population, it is clear that Latinos lag behind non-Latinos" in areas such as education, occupational trajectories, and economic power (146).

23. For useful studies of America in relation to the myth of meritocracy, see Amy Liu; and McNamee and Miller.

24. This passage can be read further through the lens of the parallel universe, in that parts of California would be part of the so-called Aztek Empire rather than the American one.

25. Warren J. Wilson clarifies the class-based motives of the meatpacking industry, which sought to increase profit margins at the expense of its minority workers (67). As Trumpbour and Bernard put it, "one of the central challenges for the U.S. labor movement in the decades ahead will be the meatpacking industry, which has recruited thousands of workers from Mexico, Central America, and Southeast Asia" (134–35).

26. Dennis Valdés details this context in relation to the experiences of Mexican workers in the Midwest (229).

27. The global reach of the meatpacking industry can be seen in the variety of immigrant populations that have begun to filter into the various regional nodes and locations throughout the United States that are involved in that business. For more on the racial particularities in the meatpacking industry, see also Bacon 60; and Fink 113–14. For studies that specifically focus on the Farmer John Slaughterhouse, see Arreola 125; Coe 87.

28. Robert Zieger provides a useful account of the difficulties in union organizing between African American and "white" immigrant populations between 1910 and 1940. For other considerations of the twentieth-century meatpacking industry and the politics of race in the workplace, see Halpern; Horowitz; and Jaynes (especially 95 for the shifts in the racial demographics of the kill floor). Lumpkins offers occasional glimpses into African American unionizing in the meatpacking industry in the early twentieth century, most located in Missouri, Alabama, and Illinois.

29. For more studies on meatpacking, the American Midwest, and racial minority populations, see also Grey; Millard, Chapa, and Burillo.

30. According to Kevin F. McCarthy and George Vernez, "Not surprisingly, California's immigrants come disproportionately from those regions, Asia and Latin America, that currently send the nation the majority of its immigrants. Specifically, 78 percent of California's immigrants come from these regions versus 41 percent of the immigrants to the rest of the country" (21). For various studies of US immigrant populations and labor that focus, in some substantial portion, on California, see Min; Bonacich and Appelbaum; Ngai; and Hondagneu-Sotelo. For more general studies on the intersections of gender, immigration, and labor, see Gordon; Parks; Parreñas, *Force of Domesticity* and *Servants of Globalization*; Waldinger and Lichter.

31. In an interesting parallel, Donald Stull provides readers with an account of his experiences when touring a slaughterhouse: "The doors to the guard station were marked in Spanish and Vietnamese—but not in English" (44). Here, we see again the confluence of Latin American and Asian immigrant labor pools to the extent that English is not even a primary language being spoken.

32. Debra Satz considers the trade in human organs to be a "toxic market" in her book *Why Some Things Should Not Be for Sale*. See also Hsu and Lincoln 27 for more on human trafficking.

33. In a reconsideration of Immanuel Kant and market alienation, Ronald Michael Green provides another example of the moral component that necessarily undergirds economic transactions related to the body and to the conceptualization of the subject (259).

34. The link between President Carlos Salinas de Gortari, the chupacabras, and the Mexican economy has been detailed in other venues as well such as Joseph, Rubenstein, and Zolov 3; and Caistor 67.

35. Certainly the revelation that the narrator's descent may include Japanese ancestry offers Foster a way to partially sidestep the issue of cultural and ethnoracial appropriation.

3 / The Incomplete Biography

1. For the full bibliography, see Ling, "Asian American Literature: A Brief Introduction and Selected Bibliography." In an earlier article on Chang's work, Ling's reading attempts to articulate how Chang's mixed-race identity might still influence the production of fictional works that do not have Asian ethnic figures as main characters ("Writer in the Hyphenated Condition" 82).

2. This list includes Tara L. Masih, Heinz Insu Fenkl, Thaddeus Rutkowski, and Peter Ho Davies, among numerous others. There is, of course, the question of how descent is determined. Here, I have relied on interviews, articles, book reviews, and other print and online sources to determine the status of an Asian American writer as "mixed race."

3. In Jonathan Brennan's edited collection *Mixed Race Literature*, he defines mixed-race literatures as "texts written by authors who represent multiple cultural and literary traditions. These authors are, in many cases, culturally mixed themselves, and in other cases are attempting to represent a mixed race subjectivity in their literary text" (Introduction 6). I differ from Brennan's definition in that the biological descent of the writer must operate in tandem with the construction of the fictional world.

4. In the context of the contemporary period, Trey Ellis theorizes the figure of the cultural mulatto "who can also navigate easily in the white world" (189). Ellis's theorizations, though framed from a different interracial context, could clearly fall in line with Asian American mixed-race subjects as well.

5. I take a different literary approach than Jeffrey J. Santa Ana, who has already critiqued how Asian American mixed-race writers claim an Asian ancestry that is often elided in a late-capitalist era that promotes multiracialism as a celebration (462). Asian Americanist approaches to the topic of mixed race in cultural production have been explored in isolated examples, but no extended monographs within the humanities and literary studies have yet been produced. For some useful articles that explore

Asian American writers and mixed race, see Barringer on Chang's *The Frontiers of Love*; Cutter on Sui Sin Far; Dariotis; and Heise on Ozeki's novel *All Over Creation*.

6. Whereas Elam focuses part of her book on the anti-bildungsroman, I focus on a different form: the fictionalized biography.

7. For an overview of biographical approaches, see Novarr. One particular strain of biographical study has been that of literary biography, focusing on the lives of writers; for more considerations of this specific subtype, see Edel; D. Ellis; Karl; and Gillies, among others. For psychobiographical approaches, see Runyan; Elms; and Carrard, among others. For history and biography, see Ambrosius. There is obviously a close relationship between critical approaches to biography and autobiography, but for the purposes of this chapter, I delineate a fairly rigid boundary between those genres.

8. I do not use the term "fictional biography" to characterize Nunez's work because, as Ina Schabert reminds us, this term refers to work based on a "historical person" (45). The three Nunez novels I analyze cannot be considered fictional biographies because the biographical subjects within them are not based on "historical" personalities but rather are fictively constructed themselves. There can be no prior information regarding these characters.

9. See Middlebrook 5; and Benton 51.

10. Literary critic Reed Whittemore further asserts that "biography has always been, and remains, chiefly dedicated to celebrating individual human success" (6). Literary critic Hermione Lee also emphasizes the importance of the individual biographical subject to the form (*Body Parts* 3).

11. Brenda Wineapple likens biographical writing to the process of mourning (440). In this regard, the question of value immediately emerges as a central concern in the biographies, so that the object of the biography comes under scrutiny. Because the lives archived in Nunez's fictions are not Asian American, their relevance to the field might seem debatable in contrast to studies within the field concerning creative nonfiction; see Rocío Davis's *Begin Here* and Helena Grice's *Asian American Fiction, History, and Life Writing*. Such books focus on Asian American lives as often (if not always) central to the mobilization of the critiques.

12. For other critical approaches to biography, see Colwill 428; Tridgell 17–18; Stout 62; and Nadel 208.

13. Many critics have noted the affiliations between biography and fiction or between biography and representation; see Porterfield 180; and Hibbard 32.

14. According to the literary critic Mary Evans, "The form of the auto/biography carries with it some considerable responsibility for allowing authors to convey the impression that lives are lived in orderly and coherent ways" (134). This desire for order is discarded in Nunez's fictions, precisely as the aporias in the biographical projects suggest that the readers must continually turn their gazes elsewhere to consider one life in a greater, more complicated structure of power relations.

15. For some foundational early critical work on Vietnam War–era literary representation, see Beidler, *American Literature*; Hellman; Lomperis; and Myers, all of which tend to focus on the experience of the male veteran.

16. In a short article, Doreen Spelts provides profiles of the nurses who were killed.

17. Rob Steinman reminds us that "often overlooked are the women who died in Vietnam. Eight have their names on the Wall. Seven were army nurses, including one

killed in action and one air force nurse" (25). For more on the social context relating to women, military service, and the Vietnam War, see Freedman and Rhoads; and Norman.

18. Kathryn Marshall further reveals that "for civilian women, there are no official figures. Independent surveys indicate that the total number of American women, both military and civilian, working in Vietnam during the war years is somewhere between 33,000 and 55,000" (4).

19. See K. Marshall 6.

20. Olga Gruhzit-Hoyt explains, "as women flocked to help in Vietnam, the antiwar feeling in the United States grew by leaps and bounds, until returning veterans were almost universally scorned" (xii).

21. Maureen Ryan contends that the current scholarly archive "ignores a significant component of the creative analysis of the war and the Vietnam era, for, like those combat veterans-authors, women began offering interpretations of the Vietnam experience in the early 1980s and more and more female authors continue to add harmony to the rich polyphony" (62). See also Acton 54, for a similar point.

22. Susan Carter makes a similar point concerning the way nurses were perceived: "Treated by most American soldiers as either lesbians or whores (Why else would they volunteer for Nam?), nurses were torn between their assigned role of nurturer and sustainer of life and the emotional numbing required to survive a year's tour in Vietnam" (292).

23. Literary critic Donald J. Ringnalda has made a similar point in relation to Vietnam War representations in general (20).

24. Here, Nguyen takes some inspiration from Katherine Kinney, who argues that depictions of Vietnamese within cultural production "typically serve as little more than exotic backdrop for the American encounter with 'the heart of darkness' within itself" (5). For William Spanos, the Vietnam War is typified by amnesia at its very heart (ix). Yen Le Espiritu has further noted the ways in which America revises its role in relation to the war through the presence of Vietnamese American refugees ("'We-Win-Even-When-We-Lose' Syndrome" 329).

25. One interesting development in Vietnam War literary criticism has been the emergence of a comparativist approach to the field. Jinim Park's *Narratives of the Vietnam War by Korean and American Writers* explores the importance of Korean literary representations to the field (4). A portion of Philip Jason's *Acts and Shadows* is devoted to exploring thematic similarities between representations of the Korean War and of the Vietnam War.

26. The novel was released to widely positive reviews. Elizabeth Benedict's praise in the *New York Times* offers a common viewpoint: "Into our landscape of multicultural chick lit, blogger novelists, tipping points, blinks, bling, fashionistas and reality television without end comes a remarkable novel for those whose trendiness is in decline." Barbara Fisher, of the *Boston Globe*, is similarly effusive: "This is a brilliant, dazzling, daring novel. Nunez has taken the old American Dream and stood it on its head" ("Short Takes").

27. A number of book reviewers agreed that this section was creatively and aesthetically important to the novel, including Joyce Johnson of the *Washington Post* and Robert Roper of the *San Francisco Chronicle*. Roper specifically reflects that "the novel's best pages come late, in a long section supposedly written by a fellow lifer at

the state prison where Ann, serving a sentence for murder, is wasting away while also inching toward redemption."

28. According to Franklin, "at least from the viewpoint of the people creating these works, America is itself a prison, and the main lines of American literature can be traced from the plantation to the penitentiary" (xxii). The literary critic Kimberly Drake explores how race becomes elided due to the emphasis and construction of the individual as a prisoner, resulting in a "uniform institutional identity" (122). Dana Williams explores the racial minority's narrative of development within the prison system (34). For other studies of and approaches considering racial minorities and prison writings, see Caster 24; Ek; and Rymhs.

29. My approach therefore contrasts to that of the narratologist Monika Fludernik, who argues that "the carceral imaginary remains a fantasy world, an exotic heterotopia that displaces our real-world emotions into the safe and apolitical realm of fiction. Its historical veracity is minimal and so is its immediate impact on our actions" ("Metaphoric (Im)Prison(ment)" 24).

30. Fludernik has published extensively in relation to "carceral topography." Two other useful articles are "The Metaphorics and Metonymics of Carcerality" and "Metaphoric (Im)prison(ment) and the Constitution of a Carceral Imaginary."

31. In *Fugitive Thought*, Michael Hames-Garcia makes a similar point about the ways in which prison intellectuals can theorize their existence (xliv). Because Hames-Garcia's approach is specific to a materialist context, his work is extremely relevant to the way in which Olympia is constructed as an individual aware of the structure of injustice pervading the carceral landscape.

32. For specific statistics on the prison, see Ohio Reformatory for Women, http://www.drc.ohio.gov/Public/orw.htm.

33. In this vein, Jodie Lawston recounts the growing number of women in the prison system (1–2). Despite this gendered shift, there is still much scholarly work to do, as Lorna Rhodes argues (74). Fludernik has made similar claims, more particularly aimed at discussing literary representations ("Carceral Topography" 58).

34. Nicole Hahn Rafter contends that the rise in women's incarceration rates can be attributed to a variety of factors, including "drug offense," "changes in the criminal justice system," and the "feminization of poverty" (178). Jocelyn Pollock echoes this point (5). For more on the social contexts in women's prisons, see E. Freedman; O'Shea; Sudbury; Reynolds; and Schlesinger.

35. In Cusac's exploration of drug crimes, she cites the work of Kuziemko and Levitt; and Tonry 3. According to Meda Chesney-Lind and Lisa Pasko, "given the past history of women in prison, it should come as no surprise that drug use, possession, and, increasingly, drug trafficking are themes in women's imprisonment" (153).

36. Two other important elements to Olympia's narrative include the focus on the AIDS epidemic in prisons and the increasing problem of mentally ill female inmates. Clearly, such issues have also been explored in academic studies of women's prisons; see Banks 88–89; and Flowers 174.

37. For some excoriating and incisive critiques of the prison system, see A. Davis; Dow; D. Rodriguez; Gilmore; and Parenti.

38. Although the reviewer Joyce Johnson of the *Washington Post* does not elaborate on her specific reasoning for denoting Olympia's racial background, she does corroborate the implication that she is African American.

39. Olympia's narrative reveals that Scarecrow is part Native American (355), but she is later described by guards as "Cleopatra" (356), serving to also Africanize her. Toy Babe's background is not clearly delineated or implied.

40. According to prison activist Victoria Law, "women of color are overrepresented in the prison system" (1).

4 / Comparative Colonial Narration

1. In the introduction to an issue of *New Literary History* on the topic of comparison, Rita Felski and Susan Stanford Friedman articulate both the perils and the utilities of comparative approaches to scholarly disciplines. Theorist R. Radhakrishnan further explains that "comparison foregrounds the following philosophical issues: 1) the politics of representation; 2) the intra- and interidentitarian thresholds of recognition and validation" (457). Following Felski, Friedman, and Radhakrishnan, the rubric of comparativity offers much, specifically for the Asian American writer, as a way to investigate the complex web of history, colonialism, and accordant social contexts.

2. To think about the syncretic dynamism in Murray's approach, one need not look beyond the recent study offered by Allan Punzalan Isaac in *Articulating Filipino America*, which considers Filipino colonial history and cultural productions alongside that of its Mexican, Caribbean, and Pacific Island counterparts.

3. The novel is easily relatable in content to Jessica Hagedorn's *Dogeaters* (1990), which was published at a similar historical moment.

4. For more on the debates regarding World War II and Japan's role as victimizer or as victim, see Ivy, "Revenge and Recapitulation"; Jeans; and Tsutsui. The American occupation of Japan in the wake of World War II has often similarly been contested as a narrative of trauma and damage (Harootunian 716). For other studies of Japan and the United States in the context of postwar politics and postwar representations, see Blackburn; Cunningham; Dudden; Hein and Takenaka; C. Hong; Koschmann; Sakai; Schuessler; Totani; Yamazaki; and Yoneyama. For studies specifically concerning war crimes and atrocities during this period, see Francis; Futamura; Hearder; Lie; S. MacKenzie; Maga; Tanaka; and Yoshimi.

5. Some reviewers target this scene, questioning the efficacy and impact of the narrative resolution. See Wolff 4P; and Kakutani.

6. For more on cannibalism in relation to colonialism and indigenous populations of the Caribbean, see Hulme; and Boucher. Budasz explores the discourse of cannibalism as it relates to modern Brazilian identity.

7. Hans Askenasy argues similarly that "culture, in turn, implied a deletion of human flesh from the food inventory, and since Christians, of course, did not devour one another, it became their duty to civilize the mindless savages" (231).

8. Cătălin Avramescu argues more forcefully that even culturally inflected forms of cannibalism that underpin the lives of indigenous peoples are not ultimately tolerated at any level and are considered savage (107). Within the context of a reading of Peter Dillon's adventure narrative, Gananath Obeyesekere advances, "falsification [of cannibal narratives] must be done for the period of European expansion, because these narratives perpetuate derogatory colonial myths and ideologies of the other under the guise of truth" ("Narratives of the Self" 70). Obeyesekere takes on the issue of cannibalism more broadly in *Cannibal Talk*.

9. Anthropologist William E. Engelbrecht contends that "the evidence suggests that in the past the Iroquois practiced cannibalism, at least on ritual occasions. Oral tradition speaks of it" (44).

10. See Noll 20; Keener 786–87; and E. Jones 526.

11. Sanday's larger study explores Iroquois cannibalism as a cultural system ingrained into their way of life rather than as some aberrant form of savagery. This view has been supported by many other scholars. See also Phelps and Burgess; and Snow, for other instances of Iroquois cannibalism as a "cultural system."

12. Abler also cites other sources to support his conclusion, including documents that go beyond the work of the Jesuits in the region. In relation to Iroquois cannibalism, Dean Snow writes, "the Iroquois were not monsters to any greater or lesser degree than any other human beings; they were only acting as many humans have done when faced with a particular set of predilections and stressful conditions" (128). Snow's estimation of this practice can be contrasted with Abler's attitude that the cannibalism practiced by the Iroquois, in fact, could not be labeled as "barbarity," especially in comparison to the genocide perpetrated by European colonialism (315).

13. In relation to bones reputed to be the remnants of an Iroquois man-eating feast, Arens contends, "first, charred human remains do not necessarily imply that the remains were a repast" (128).

14. Lewis Petrinovich corroborates this point: "Arens (1979) considered the claims for cannibalism among the Iroquois to be yet another example of interpretive reporting that exploited preset images the popular media had provided of these tribes" (157).

15. In Merrilee H. Salmon's view, the issue of scientific disputation arises from the problematics of witnessing, precisely because the Jesuits were never eyewitnesses to actual scenes of cannibalism but rather only to "torture and sacrifice" (203).

16. Of Francis Parkman, a prominent historian who charged the Iroquois with cannibalism in his various studies, biographer Wilbur R. Jacobs explains, "we can be reasonably sure he emphasized Jesuit accounts of torture and cannibalism because they could be used so easily to liven his narrative" (65). The question of writerly bias in relation to Jesuit accounts of Iroquois cannibalism is also considered by Gordon Sayre (56). For more on the connection between religious bias and Iroquois cannibalism, see Bitterli 105.

17. The suggestion that intertribal warfare occurred complicates any simplistic notion of pantribal identity politics that can undergird conceptions of American Indian racial formation.

18. For Turner and Turner, evidence for cannibalism "required a minimal signature containing six features of peri-mortem damage (damage that occurred during the brief transitional phase at or around the time of death). The six criteria are (1) high proportion of breakage among the bone samples, (2) cut marks, (3) anvil abrasions, (4) burning, (5) many missing vertebrae, and (6) pot polishing" (Petrinovich 103). Osteological fragments have formed the basis of many studies, including Tim D. White's influential work *Prehistoric Cannibalism at Mancos 5Mtumr-2346*. In a different study, Turner and Turner begin developing their thesis that Anasazi cannibalism appears to have been motivated by the effects of "interpersonal conflict and social pathology" rather than a culturally derived system embedded in the Anasazi way of life ("First Claim for Cannibalism" 679).

19. See Turner, Turner, and Green for a study in which cannibalism is disputed rather than corroborated.

20. See Turner, Turner, and Green 107–08.

21. Building on the "social pathology" thesis, Billman, Lambert, and Leonard contend, "we propose that, faced with severe environmental stress, food scarcity, and sociopolitical upheaval in the mid-AD 1100s, certain groups in the Mesa Verde region used violence to terrorize or even eliminate neighboring villages, and that cannibalism was part of this pattern of violence" (146). By offering up the pressures of environmental stress as a motivating factor for cannibalism, Billman, Lambert, and Leonard provide a vital context to theorize why indigenous populations might have resorted to anthropophagy. For another useful study contending Anasazi cannibalism, see Flinn, Turner, and Brew. The anthropologist Brian Fagan also argues that the Anasazi engaged in "eating human flesh" (126).

22. In a series of articles, including "A Reappraisal of Anasazi Cannibalism" and "A Return to the Question of Cannibalism," anthropologist Peter Y. Bullock has been particularly vocal about his opposition to the possibility that the Anasazi practiced cannibalism. His work is clearly positioned, in part, against the work of the Turners in *Man Corn*. According to John Kantner, there are "no foolproof ways of demonstrating that human flesh was actually eaten" (78).

23. Dongoske, Martin, and Ferguson specifically dispute the human-fecal-matter hypothesis (offered by Billman et al. and others) contending that "without reporting the laboratory techniques and scientific methods used in the study, it is not known whether the analysis was microscope, biochemical, or molecular-genetic, and the validity of the scientific results cannot be evaluated with respects to the known limitations of blood residue analysis" (184). Lambert et al. do offer their rebuttal to Dongoske, Martin, and Ferguson in a published response appearing in 2000.

24. For instance, studies of Anasazi cannibalism directly affect Hopi Pueblo native groups seeking advocacy and legal aid. Larry J. Zimmerman explains that Hopi tribesmen face much difficulty in building coalitions in the political arena due to perceptions that they are part of a culture promoting human-flesh eating; he thus has cautioned scholars and academics to think more deeply about the ramifications of their research (306). Further still, the Native American Graves Protect and Repatriation Act (NAGPRA; 1990) was passed in order to allow indigenous communities the possibility of claiming artifacts and important objects related to ancestral land claims. For more on NAGPRA, see Pensley; Dumont; and Fish.

25. With respect to the work conducted by Christy Turner and a documentary based on Anasazi cannibalism, Jeff Berglund contends that such work ultimately reinforces damaging stereotypes rather than complicating them or placing them in wider context (6).

26. Athanassopoulos adds that "the work of anthropologists and other scholars has made it clear that Greece is viewed somewhere between the familiar and the exotic, the European and the Oriental. The modern Greek state emerged as a cultural construct before its political formation" (280).

27. Along these lines, see Loukaki 29; and Morris 31. For more on the "treasure hunting" aspect of Greece and its classical antiquities from the seventeenth to the nineteenth century, see J. Scott.

28. According to Jusdanis, "archaeologists in the nineteenth century were the ones responsible for discovering, interpreting, and popularizing Greek art, the one realm in which the ancients held superiority over the moderns" (47). Yannis Hamilakis makes clear that Western and colonial archaeological practices must be seen in tandem with the ways in which nationalist projects redefined and rearticulated the notion of Greek identity (16–21). For further studies on the importance of classical artifacts and ruins in the imagination of Greece, see Shanks; and Peckham.

29. See Gummere; Richard, *Golden Age of the Classics* and *Greeks and Romans Bearing Gifts*; Kassel; Roessel; Winterer; and Shalev.

30. These intelligence reports were ultimately wrong or at least overemphasized the geographical importance of Greece to the advancement of communist ideologies (Panourgiá 117).

31. Numerous useful studies of Greece in the postwar period exist; also see Couloumbis; Roubatis; Frazier; and Close.

32. Whether or not American intelligence was correct in the matter of Soviet involvement in Greece, Howard Jones explains, "policymakers believed that the Soviets hoped to strip Greece of its northern territory by encouraging the establishment of an independent Macedonia, which might become part of the Yugoslav Federation, and by facilitating Bulgaria's acquisition of Thrace" (13). See also Frazier 167.

33. See H. Jones 13; and Hatzivassiliou, *Greece and the Cold War* 7–13.

34. See Gantzel and Schwinghammer 221–22; and Clogg 19.

35. For some useful sources on the Greek civil war, see Vlavianos; Sfikas; Close; and Iatrides.

36. This position has been challenged by the historian James Edward Miller, who places some emphasis on the failure of Greek policy administrators (x).

37. For considerations of the tensions between Greece and Turkey, also see Kalaitzaki 106; Moustakis and Sheehan; and Hatzivassiliou.

38. In fact, Amanda gives Tomas the forgery to shift attention to the excavation site's project and away from her whereabouts, as she is later found to be the murderer of her husband, who is killed on the local island of Hydra.

39. Katherine is more a figurative embodiment and reproduction of America's continuing legacy of violence. Her motive, never fully revealed over the course of the narrative, is not as important as the fact that her father is a business magnate and that his single-minded interest in pursuing profits is, however tangentially, connected to his neglected daughter, who seeks to consume the very bodies of the young men who might one day become the foot soldiers of America's new economic empire.

5 / Impossible Narration

1. Though I primarily employ Chu's theory of science fiction, a number of scholars have offered their own approaches to the field; see, e.g., C. Freedman.

2. I employ the literary term "analogy" in contrast to other comparative rubrics such as the allegory precisely because the analogy allows one to explore various juxtapositions. The allegory is understood in its most traditional sense to be a kind of masked narrative functioning in a metaphorical way. That is, the allegory functions with one primary comparison point, but the narratives analyzed in this chapter can be compared in multiple ways against and alongside external referents.

3. The use of analogical practices within literary criticism occurs prominently in the work of Stephen Best in relation to African American literature, law, and racial formation, as well as in Colleen Lye's exploration of African American and Asian American racial formations.

4. In this regard, I follow the cultural critic Isiah Lavender's point that "science fiction often talks about race by not talking about race, makes real aliens, has hidden race dialogues" (7). We can extend Lavender's contention to apply to speculative fiction's broad boundaries to make explicit how the genre speaks to issues of social inequality. See Mark Jerng's "A World of Difference" for an exploration of how to read race within Samuel Delany's fictions. For a book-length study on science fiction and race, see Kilgore.

5. Chiang has received some limited critical attention; see T. Foster; and Huang.

6. See also Salaita 159.

7. Jana Evans Braziel makes a similar claim concerning racial formation and the enemy combatant (139). For more on the category of the enemy combatant, see also Castresana 126–27; and Goodman 26–27.

8. Light also includes intertextual references to four classic Japanese American works: Jeanne Wakatsuki Houston and James D. Houston's *Farewell to Manzanar* (1973), John Okada's *No-No Boy* (1957), Wakako Yamauchi's *And the Soul Shall Dance*, which was later republished in *Songs My Mother Taught Me* (1994), and Monica Sone's *Nisei Daughter* (1953).

9. See Light's web-published essay "Defining and Identifying Cultural Appropriation."

10. See Brown 18; and Dean 54. The Cold War, of course, is also the period that saw the rise of space programs.

11. For other considerations of alien-abduction narratives, see Bynum; Luckhurst; Drysdale.

12. See Sturma; Barbeito; Panay.

13. See Roberts; Eshun; Troy.

14. Techno-orientalism has been described and employed by numerous scholars and critics. See, e.g., Morley and Robins; and Ueno.

15. For some studies of Japanese Americans and agricultural history, see Matsumoto; Neiwert.

16. Greg Forter pushes Cathy Caruth's trauma theories further, articulating a form of "social trauma" that is "so woven into the fabric of our societies, that they cannot count as 'shocks' in the way that Nazi persecution and genocide do in the accounts of Caruth and others" (260). Forter distinguishes what he calls "punctual traumas" from these historically and structurally embedded traumas. In relation to Light's story, we can see that the older brother faces not only the punctual trauma of the internment but also the structural trauma of racial oppression. Though Roberta Culbertson and others such as Caruth are more skeptical about any transparent representation of trauma, the medical doctor Judith Lewis Herman argues that trauma can be addressed, especially through narrative form (177).

17. See W. Ng 91; for more on issues of property, see also Hayashi 193. Yoon Sun Lee provides critical readings of Miné Okubo's *Citizen 13660* and Hisaye Yamamoto's "The Legend of Miss Sasagawara" from *Seventeen Syllables and Other Stories* to show

how the everyday home spaces of internees were uncannily replicated in the camps (*Modern Minority* chap. 2).

18. For some explorations of collective and historical traumas and literary representation, see also Vickroy; Schwab.

19. For two excellent considerations of the Japanese American internment in relation to trauma, see Dass-Brailsford 15; and Roxworthy.

20. Further still, the internment created considerable rifts in the Japanese American community due to certain attitudes toward relocation and evacuation; for some considerations of these issues, see Kurashige 108; Kutulas 101; and Ichioka 6.

21. For example, Nina Revoyr's *Southland* (2003), Julie Shigekuni's *Invisible Gardens* (2003), Julie Otsuka's *When the Emperor Was Divine* (2002), David Mura's *Famous Suicides of the Japanese Empire* (2008), and *History and Memory* (2008; dir. Rea Tajiri).

22. For other critical approaches to issues of representation, trauma, and Japanese American internment literatures, see Teorey; Elliott.

23. While it is not surprising that Japanese American writers would be invested in exploring the issue of internment in their writings, there has been an upsurge of fictional publications dealing with internment from Asian American writers who do not possess Japanese ancestry. See Anis Shivani's "Manzanar" from *Anatolia and Other Stories* (2009), Don Lee's "Widowers" from *Yellow* (2001), Susan Choi's *American Woman* (2003), and Jamie Ford's *Hotel on the Corner of Bitter and Sweet* (2009).

24. Kim clarifies the great political stakes of Asian American literary representation in its earlier phases in her seminal piece "Defining Asian American Realities through Literature."

25. Interestingly enough, Chiang has revealed that he did not seriously consider the contemporary context of Iraq while writing this story. Chiang's focus on the narrative elements does follow what literary critic Betsy Huang has described as Chiang's "fidelity to genre" rather than to any overt political thematics contained in the fictional world (103).

26. For more considerations of the oriental tale as a genre, see Leask; Kamrath; Nussbaum (esp. chaps. 6 and 7); Makdisi (esp. chap. 5); Aravamudan, *Tropicopolitans* (esp. chap. 9); and Topping.

27. For more on the oriental tale in the French context, see Douthwaite 78.

28. In the context of a translation study during the period, Hayrettín Yücesoy explains, "circulation of caravans over land routes and merchant ships in the Indian Ocean expanded the trade network and contributed to drastic changes in human technology, habits, and diet across continents" (527).

29. For discussions of silk and scarves, see Bennison, *Great Caliphs* 45; for silk and linen and other textiles, see Stillman 46–48; for other discussions of relevant textiles, see Kühnel; Onians 125, 129.

30. For someone like Fuwaad, with an intimate knowledge of trade and the merchant industry, this shop presents its own mystery precisely because it reveals such a high level of affluence, even considering Baghdad's centrality in the period. For more on Baghdad during the Islamic Golden Age, see also Guy Le Strange's classic study on the Abbasid Caliphate, first published in 1900, as well as Cooperson; Goodwin 26; Kennedy, *When Baghdad Ruled*; and Bennison, "Muslim City Life" 22.

31. For considerations of alchemy during the Abbasid Caliphate period, see Hill, "Literature of Arabic Alchemy"; Bennison, *Great Caliphs* 590; and Freely 74.

32. For more on the uses of the astrolabe during the Abbasid period, see King, *In Synchrony* 419–33 and "Astronomy"; and Hansen and Curtis 251–52.

33. For more on the uses of the water-clock during the Abbasid period, see Hill, *History* 232 and "Mathematics"; and Freely 108.

34. I do not have the space to fully address the third embedded narrative, "The Tale of the Wife and Her Lover," which focuses on Hassan's wife, Raniya.

35. The historian Courtney Hunt corroborates this point: the caliphs "wielded the power of life and death over their subjects and were the final religious authority" (420). For more on caliphs and their broad powers, see J. Spielvogel 194.

36. For more on governance structures with respect to diwans and viziers, see J. Spielvogel 194; and Burbank and Cooper 77.

37. For more on boon-companions, see C. Robinson 4; Nasrallah 32; and Kennedy, *Great Arab* 16, 20.

38. For more on governance and political hierarchies during the Abbasid caliphate, see Hanne.

39. According to Hugh Kennedy, "The authority of the caliphs in provinces like Mosul and Egypt rested not on military dictatorship but on a careful arrangement of alliances and compromises with local interests. Only by making these arrangements could so vast an empire be held together" (*Byzantine* 38).

40. The historian J. J. Sanders articulates that "the Abbasids were acutely aware of the discontent that had helped to bring down the Umayyads and realized that they must make concessions to the disaffected groups. Even though they were Arabs themselves, their victory ended the old practice of giving Arabs privileged status in the empire" (94).

41. Mohammed Sharafuddin is exemplary of the hard-line stance of orientalism first advocated by Edward Said (Sharafuddin xvi), but since the publication of Said's *Orientalism*, many critics, including Ibn Warraq and Daniel Varisco, have argued against its central thesis. My intent is not to rehash those arguments but rather to explore the ways in which orientalisms proliferate multidirectionally beyond the binary established by Said. My position mirrors that of Ziauddin Sardar, who writes that orientalism is both heterogeneous and a "work of change and continuity" (117).

42. Nance's approach can be considered alongside other American orientalist studies, which have broadened traditional Saidian definitions to include Western conceptions of Asia in general (including the Far East).

43. The legal scholar Richard Falk argues that "there are robust reasons and ample evidence to support the belief that a massive campaign of mystification had been relied upon with respect to Iraq policy as it evolved during the Bush presidency" (49).

44. In this vein, Colleen Elizabeth Kelly contends, "such a large scale deception occurred through protofascist talk, the manipulation of the nation's fear and sense of vulnerability that something worse than 9/11 awaited them" (197).

45. Literary critic Srinivas Aravamudan ("Wake of the Novel" 10) and historian John MacKenzie (211) remind us of the ways that the oriental tale is necessarily related to the project of empire building.

46. See Bowman 78; Brancati 14; Crocker 79; Rivkin and Bartram 101; and Žižek 4.

47. While Christian Spielvogel does not frame the 2003 invasion of Iraq in terms of an orientalist discourse, the binary that structures a radical difference between East, as evil, and West, as good, is made clear in the corresponding argument taken in his article (552).

48. Hamid Dabashi considers the post-9/11 period through the lens of what he calls "post-Orientalism," a period in which "mass deception" is employed (225).

Coda

1. For more on Chang's exploration of the postracial aesthetic, see the conclusion to *Writing the Ghetto*.

2. See Fludernik's *Introduction to Narratology*.

3. For some critical studies of *The Woman Warrior*, see Bella Adams's "Identity-in Difference"; Yu; and Dunick. For a psychoanalytic approach to *The Woman Warrior*, see Diaz; for a scholar's approach to the novel with respect to its postmodern valences, see Hutcheon.

Works Cited

Abelmann, Nancy, and John Lie. *Blue Dreams: Korean Americans and the Los Angeles Riots*. Cambridge: Harvard University Press, 1997.

Abler, Thomas S. "Iroquois Cannibalism: Fact Not Fiction." *Iroquois*. Spec. issue of *Ethnohistory* 27.4 (1980): 309–16.

Acton, Carol. "Diverting the Gaze: The Unseen Text in Women's War Writing." *College Literature* 31.2 (2004): 53–79.

Acuña, Rodolfo. *Anything but Mexican: Chicanos in Contemporary Los Angeles*. New York: Verso, 1996.

Aczel, Richard. "Hearing Voices in Narrative Texts." *New Literary History* 29.3 (1998): 467–500.

Adams, Bella. *Amy Tan*. New York: Manchester University Press, 2005.

———. "Identity-in-Difference: Re-generating Debate about Intergenerational Relationships in Amy Tan's *The Joy Luck Club*." *Studies in the Literary Imagination* 39.2 (Fall): 79–94.

Adolf, Antony. *Peace: A World History*. Malden, MA: Polity, 2009.

Alam, M. Shahid. *Challenging the New Orientalism: Dissenting Essays on the "War against Islam."* North Haledon, NJ: Islamic Publications International, 2006.

Alarcón, Daniel Cooper. *The Aztec Palimpsest: Mexico in the Modern Imagination*. Tucson: University of Arizona Press, 1997.

Alber, Jan. *Narrating the Prison: Role and Representation in Charles Dickens' Novels, Twentieth-Century Fiction, and Film*. Youngstown, NY: Cambria, 2007.

Alcoff, Linda Martín. "What Should White People Do?" *Hypatia* 13.3 (1998): 6–26.

Alexander, Michelle. *The New Jim Cross: Mass Incarceration in the Age of Colorblindness*. 2nd ed. New York: New Press, 2012.
Alexander, Susan K. "The Invisible Veterans: Nurses in the Vietnam War." *Women's Studies Quarterly* 12.2 (1984): 16–17.
Allen, Jon G. *Coping with Depression: From Catch-22 to Hope*. Arlington, VA: American Psychiatric Publishing, 2006.
Allen, Theodore. *The Invention of the White Race: Vol. 1, Racial Oppression and Social Control*. New York: Verso, 1994.
———. *The Invention of the White Race: Vol. 2, The Origin of Racial Oppression in Anglo-America*. New York: Verso, 1997.
Almaguer, Tomás. *Racial Fault Lines: The Historical Origins of White Supremacy in California*. Berkeley: University of California Press, 1994.
Ambrosius, Lloyd E., ed. *Writing Biography: Historians and Their Craft*. Lincoln: University of Nebraska Press, 2004.
Anzaldúa, Gloria. *Borderlands / La Frontera: The New Mestiza*. San Francisco: Aunt Lute Books, 1987.
Aravamudan, Srinivas. "In the Wake of the Novel: The Oriental Tale as National Allegory." *NOVEL: A Forum on Fiction* 33. 1 (1999): 5–31.
———. *Tropicopolitans: Colonialism and Agency, 1688–1804*. Durham: Duke University Press, 1999.
Arens, William. *The Man-Eating Myth: Anthropology and Anthropophagy*. New York: Oxford University Press, 1979.
Armstrong, Karen. *Islam: A Short History*. New York: Modern Library, 2002.
Arreola, Daniel D. *Hispanic Spaces, Latino Places: Community and Cultural Diversity in Contemporary America*. Austin: University of Texas Press, 2004.
Arrizón, Alicia. "Mythical Performativity: Relocating Aztlán in Chicana Feminist Cultural Productions." *Theatre Journal* 52.1 (2000): 23–49.
Askenasy, Hans. *Cannibalism: From Sacrifice to Survival*. Amherst, NY: Prometheus Books, 1994.
Athanassopoulos, Effie-Fotini. "An 'Ancient' Landscape: European Ideals, Archaeology, and Nation Building in Early Modern Greece." *Journal of Modern Greek Studies* 20.2 (2002): 273–305.
Avramescu, Cătălin. *An Intellectual History of Cannibalism*. Trans. Alistair Ian Blyth. Princeton: Princeton University Press, 2009.
Azuma, Eiichiro. *Between Two Empires: Race, History, and Transnationalism In Japanese America*. New York: Oxford University Press, 2005.
Babb, Valerie. *Whiteness Visible: The Meaning of Whiteness in American Literature and Culture*. New York: NYU Press, 1998.
Bacho, Peter. *Entrys*. Honolulu: University of Hawai'i Press, 2005.
Backhaus, Bhira. *Under the Lemon Trees*. New York: St. Martin's, 2009.
Bacon, David. *The Children of NAFTA: Labor Wars on the U.S./Mexico Border*. Berkeley: University of California Press, 2004.

Ballaster, Rosalind. *Fabulous Orients: Fictions of the East in England, 1662–1785.* Oxford: Oxford University Press, 2005.

Banfield, Ann. *Unspeakable Sentences: Narration and Representation in the Language of Fiction.* Boston: Routledge and Kegan Paul, 1982.

Banks, Cyndi. *Women in Prison: A Reference Handbook.* Santa Barbara, CA: ABC-CLIO, 2003.

Banner, Olivia. "The Postracial Imagination: *Gattaca*'s Imperfect Science." *Discourse* 33.2 (2011): 221–24.

Barbeito, Patricia Felisa. "'He's Making Me Feel Things in My Body That I Don't Feel': The Body as Battleground in Accounts of Alien Abduction." *Journal of American Culture* 28.2 (2005): 201–15.

Barringer, Sandra. "'The Hybrids and the Cosmopolitans': Race, Gender, and Masochism in Diana Chang's *The Frontiers of Love*." *Mixed Race Literature.* Ed. Jonathan Brennan. Stanford: Stanford University Press, 2002. 107–21.

Basco, Monica Ramirez, and A. John Rush. *Cognitive-Behavioral Therapy for Bipolar Disorder.* New York: Guilford, 2007.

Bates, Milton J. *The Wars We Took to Vietnam: Cultural Conflict and Storytelling.* Berkeley: University of California Press, 1996.

Bauer, Mark S. "Psychosocial Interventions for Bipolar Disorder: A Review." *Bipolar Disorder.* Ed. Mario Maj, Hagop S. Akiskal, Juan José López-Ibor, and Norman Sartorius. Hoboken, NJ: Wiley, 2007. 281–313.

Baxandall, Rosalyn, and Elizabeth Ewen. *Picture Windows: How the Suburbs Happened.* New York: Basic Books, 2000.

———. "Race Relations in the Suburbs." *Invisible Crises: What Conglomerate Control of Media Means for America and the World.* Ed. George Gerbner, Hamid Mowlana, and Herbert I. Schiller. Boulder, CO: Westview, 1996. 99–119.

Bayoumi, Moustafa. "Racing Religion." *CR: The New Centennial Review* 6.2 (2006): 267–93.

Beauregard, Robert A. *When America Became Suburban.* Minneapolis: University of Minnesota Press, 2006.

Bedolla, Lisa. *Fluid Borders: Latino Power, Identity, and Politics in Los Angeles.* Berkeley: University of California Press, 2005.

Beidler, Philip D. *American Literature and the Experience of Vietnam.* Athens: University of Georgia Press, 1982.

———. "Enlarging the Vietnam Canon: Sigrid Nunez's *For Rouenna*." *Michigan Quarterly Review* 43 (2004): 705–19.

Benedict, Elizabeth. "A Friendship Born in the Turbulent Age of Aquarius." Rev. of *The Last of Her Kind*, by Sigrid Nunez. *New York Times* 17 Jan. 2006. Web. 1 July 2009. http://www.nytimes.com/2006/01/17/books/review/17bene.html.

Bennison, Amira. *The Great Caliphs: The Golden Age of the 'Abbasid Empire.* New York: I. B. Tauris, 2009.

———. "Muslim City Life during the Era of the Great Caliphs." *Historically Speaking* 12.1 (2011): 21–23.
Benton, Michael. "Literary Biography: The Cinderella Story of Literary Studies." *Journal of Aesthetic Education* 39.3 (2005): 44–57.
Berger, Martin A. *Sight Unseen: Whiteness and American Visual Culture*. Berkeley: University of California Press, 2005.
Berglund, Jeff. *Cannibal Fictions: American Explorations of Colonialism, Race, Gender, and Sexuality*. Madison: University of Wisconsin Press, 2006.
Best, Stephen M. *Fugitive's Properties: Law and the Poetics of Possession*. Chicago: University of Chicago Press, 2004.
Billman, Brian R., Patricia M. Lambert, and Banks L. Leonard. "Cannibalism, Warfare, and Drought in the Mesa Verde Region during the Twelfth Century A.D." *American Antiquity* 65.1 (2000): 145–78.
Birchall, Diana. *Onoto Watanna: The Story of Winnifred Eaton*. Urbana: University of Illinois Press, 2001.
Bitterli, Urs. *Cultures in Conflict: Encounters between European and Non-European Cultures, 1492–1800*. Trans. Ritchie Robertson. Stanford: Stanford University Press, 1989.
Blackburn, Kevin. "Recalling War Trauma of the Pacific War and the Japanese Occupation in the Oral History of Malaysia and Singapore." *Oral History Review* 36.2 (2009): 231–52.
Bloom, Harold, ed. *Amy Tan's "The Joy Luck Club."* Philadelphia: Chelsea House, 2002.
Blumenberg, Evelyn, and Paul Ong. "Labor Squeeze and Ethnic/Racial Recomposition in the U.S. Apparel Industry." *Global Production: The Apparel Industry in the Pacific Rim*. Ed. Edna Bonacich. Philadelphia: Temple University Press, 1994. 309–27.
Bobo, Lawrence D. "Somewhere between Jim Crow and Post-Racialism: Reflections on the Racial Divide in America Today." *Daedalus* 140.2 (Spring 2011): 11–36.
Bonacich, Edna, and Richard P. Appelbaum. *Behind the Label: Inequality in the Los Angeles Apparel Industry*. Berkeley: University of California Press, 2000.
Bonastia, Christopher. *Knocking on the Door: The Federal Government's Attempt to Desegregate the Suburbs*. Princeton: Princeton University Press, 2006.
Boucher, Philip P. *Cannibal Encounters: Europeans and Island Caribs, 1492–1763*. Baltimore: John Hopkins University Press, 1992.
Bow, Leslie. *Betrayal and Other Acts of Subversion: Feminism, Sexual Politics, Asian American Women's Literature*. Princeton: Princeton University Press, 2001.
Bowman, Bradley L. "After Iraq: Future U.S. Military Posture in the Middle East." *Washington Quarterly* 31.2 (2008): 77–91.
Brada-Williams, Noelle. "Reading Jhumpa Lahiri's *Interpreter of Maladies* as a Short Story Cycle." *MELUS*. 29.3–4 (Autumn–Winter 2004): 451–64.

Brancati, Dawn. "Can Federalism Stabilize Iraq?" *Washington Quarterly* 27.2 (2004): 7–21.
Braziel, Jana Evans. "Haiti, Guantánamo, and the 'One Indispensable Nation': U.S. Imperialism, 'Apparent States,' and Postcolonial Problematics of Sovereignty." *Cultural Critique* 64 (2006): 127–60.
Brennan, Jonathan. Introduction. *Mixed Race Literature*. Ed. Jonathan Brennan. Stanford: Stanford University Press, 2002. 1–56.
Brown, Bridget. *They Know Us Better than We Know Ourselves: The History and Politics of Alien Abduction*. New York: NYU Press, 2007.
Brysk, Alison. *Globalization and Human Rights*. Berkeley: University of California Press, 2002.
Budasz, Rogério. "Of Cannibals and the Recycling of Otherness." *Music and Letters* 87.1 (2006): 1–15.
Budde, Rebecca. *Mexican and Central American L.A. Garment Workers: Globalized Industries and Their Economic Constraints*. Münster, Germany: Lit, 2005.
Buitron, Richard A. *The Quest for Tejano Identity in San Antonio, Texas, 1913–2000*. New York: Routledge, 2004.
Bullock, Peter Y. "A Reappraisal of Anasazi Cannibalism." *Kiva* 57.1 (1991): 5–16.
———. "A Return to the Question of Cannibalism." *Kiva* 58.2 (1992): 203–05.
Bulosan, Carlos. *America Is in the Heart: A Personal History*. New York: Harcourt, Brace, 1946.
Burbank, Jane, and Frederick Cooper. *Empires in World History: Power and the Politics of Difference*. Princeton: Princeton University Press, 2010.
Burns, Christy L. "Erasure: Alienation, Paranoia, and the Loss of Memory in *The X-Files*." *Camera Obscura* 15.3 45 (2000): 194–225.
Bush, Melanie E. L. *Breaking the Code of Good Intentions: Everyday Forms of Whiteness*. Lanham, MD: Rowman and Littlefield, 2004.
Byman, Daniel. "Constructing a Democratic Iraq: Challenges and Opportunities." *International Security* 28.1 (Summer 2003): 47–78.
Bynum, Joyce. "Kidnapped by an Alien: Tales of UFO Abductions." *ETC: A Review of General Semantics* 50 (1993): 86–95.
Caistor, Nick. *Mexico City: A Cultural and Literary Companion*. Oxford, UK: Signal Books, 2000.
Calotychos, Vangelis. *Modern Greece: A Cultural Poetics*. New York: Berg, 2003.
Camarillo, Albert M. "Cities of Color: The New Racial Frontier in California's Minority-Majority Cities." *Pacific Historical Review* 76.1 (Feb. 2007): 1–28.
Cao, Lan. *Monkey Bridge*. New York: Viking, 1997.
Carrard, Philippe. "Picturing Minds: Biography and the Representation of Consciousness." *Narrative* 5.3 (1997): 287–305.
Carter, Susan. "Creating a Landscape that Never Was: Women's Fictional Interpretations of the Vietnam War Experience." *Midwest Quarterly* 33.3 (1992): 289–303.

Caruth, Cathy. *Unclaimed Experience: Trauma, Narrative, and History.* Baltimore: Johns Hopkins University Press, 1996.
———. "Violence and Time: Traumatic Survivals." *Assemblage* 20 (1993): 24–25.
Caster, Peter. *Prisons, Race, and Masculinity in Twentieth-Century U.S. Literature and Film.* Columbus: Ohio State University Press, 2008.
Castresana, Carlos González. "Torture as a Greater Evil." *South Central Review* 24.1 (2007): 119–30.
Castro-Klarén, Sara. "A Genealogy for the 'Manifesto Antropofago,' or the Struggle between Socrates and the Caraibe." *Nepantla: Views from South* 1.2 (2000): 295–322.
Chae, Youngsuk. *Politicizing Asian American Literature: Towards a Critical Multiculturalism.* New York: Routledge, 2008.
Chang, Diana. *The Frontiers of Love.* New York: Random House, 1956.
———. *A Passion for Life.* New York: Random House, 1961.
———. *A Woman of Thirty.* New York: Random House, 1959.
Chang, Juliana. "'I Cannot Find Her': The Oriental Feminine, Racial Melancholia, and Kimiko Hahn's *The Unbearable Heart*." *Meridians* 4.2 (2004): 637–63.
Chang, Lan Samantha. *Hunger.* New York: Norton, 1998.
Chang, Yoonmee. *Writing the Ghetto: Class, Authorship, and the Asian American Enclave.* New Brunswick: Rutgers University Press, 2011.
Chao, Patricia. *Monkey King.* New York: HarperCollins, 1997.
Chapa, Jorge, and Belinda De La Rosa. "Latino Population Growth, Socioeconomic and Demographic Characteristics, and Implications for Educational Attainment." *Education and Urban Society* 36.2 (Feb. 2004): 130–49.
Chatman, Seymour. *Story and Discourse: Narrative Structure in Fiction and Film.* Ithaca: Cornell University Press, 1978.
Chávez, Ernesto. *"Mi Raza Primero!" (My People First!): Nationalism, Identity, and Insurgency in the Chicano Movement in Los Angeles, 1966–1978.* Berkeley: University of California Press, 2002.
Chávez, John R. *The Lost Land: The Chicano Image of the Southwest.* Albuquerque: University of New Mexico Press, 1984.
Chejne, Anwar G. "The Boon-Companion in Early 'Abbāsid Times." *Journal of the American Oriental Society* 85.3 (1965): 327–35.
Chen, Da. *The Last Empress.* New York: Crown, 2012.
Chen, Tina. *Double Agency: Acts of Impersonation in Asian American Literature and Culture.* Stanford: Stanford University Press, 2005.
Cheng, Anne Anlin. *The Melancholy of Race: Psychoanalysis, Assimilation, and Hidden Grief.* New York: Oxford University Press, 2000.
Cheng, Bill. *Southern Cross the Dog.* New York: Ecco, 2013.
Cheng, Vincent. *Inauthentic: The Anxiety over Culture and Identity.* New Brunswick: Rutgers University Press, 2004.

Chesney-Lind, Meda, and Lisa Pasko. *The Female Offender: Girls, Women, and Crime*. 2nd ed. Thousand Oaks, CA: Sage, 2004.
Cheung, King-Kok. *Articulate Silences: Hisaye Yamamoto, Maxine Hong Kingston, Joy Kogawa*. Ithaca: Cornell University Press, 1993.
Chiang, Mark. *The Cultural Capital of Asian American Studies: Autonomy and Representation in the University*. New York: NYU Press, 2009.
Chiang, Ted. *The Merchant and the Alchemist's Gate*. Burton, MI: Subterranean, 2007.
Chin, Frank, Jeffery Paul Chan, Lawson Fusao Inada, and Shawn Wong. *Aiiieeeee! An Anthology of Asian-American Writers*. Washington, DC: Howard University Press, 1974.
Chirot, Daniel. "The Debacle in Cote d'Ivoire." *Journal of Democracy* 17.2 (2006): 63–77.
Choi, Susan. *American Woman*. New York: HarperCollins, 2003.
Chou, Rosalind S., and Joe R. Feagin. *The Myth of the Model Minority: Asian American Facing Racism*. Boulder, CO: Paradigm, 2008.
Chu, Louis. *Eat a Bowl of Tea*. New York: L. Stuart, 1961.
Chu, Patricia P. *Assimilating Asians: Gendered Strategies of Authorship in Asian America*. Durham: Duke University Press, 2000.
Chu, Seo-Young. *Do Metaphors Dream of Literal Sleep? A Science-Fictional Theory of Representation*. Cambridge: Harvard University Press, 2010.
Chuh, Kandice. *Imagine Otherwise: On Asian Americanist Critique*. Durham: Duke University Press, 2003.
———. "Of Hemispheres and Other Spheres: Navigating Karen Tei Yamashita's Literary World." *American Literary History* 18.3 (2006): 618–37.
Clogg, Richard. *A Concise History of Greece*. 2nd ed. Cambridge: Cambridge University Press, 2002.
Close, David H. *Greece since 1945: Politics, Economy, and Society*. London: Pearson, 2002.
Coe, Sue. *Dead Meat*. New York: Four Walls Eight Windows, 1995.
Cohen, Bruce J. *Theory and Practice of Psychiatry*. New York: Oxford University Press, 2003.
Cohn, Dorrit. *The Distinction of Fiction*. Baltimore: Johns Hopkins University Press, 2000.
———. "Signposts of Fictionality: A Narratological Perspective." *Poetics Today* 11.4 (1990): 775–804.
Cole, Jean Lee. *The Literary Voices of Winnifred Eaton: Redefining Ethnicity and Authenticity*. New Brunswick: Rutgers University Press, 2002.
Colwill, Elizabeth. "Subjectivity, Self-Representation, and the Revealing Twitches of Biography." *French Historical Studies* 24.3 (2001): 421–37.
Comaroff, Jean, and John L. Comaroff. "Millennial Capitalism: First Thoughts on a Second Coming." *Public Culture* 12.2 (2000): 291–343.

Cook-Lynn, Elizabeth. *Anti-Indianism in Modern America: A Voice from Tatekeya's Earth*. Urbana: University of Illinois Press, 2001.
Cooperson, Michael. "Baghdad in Rhetoric and Narrative." *Muqarnas* 13 (1996): 99–113.
Couloumbis, Theodore A. *The United States, Greece, and Turkey: The Troubled Triangle*. Westport, CT: Praeger, 1983.
Crocker, Bathsheba. "Reconstructing Iraq's Economy." *Washington Quarterly* 27.4 (2004): 73–93.
Culbertson, Roberta. "Embodied Memory, Transcendence, and Telling: Recounting Trauma, Re-establishing the Self." *New Literary History* 26.1 (1995): 169–95.
Culler, Jonathan D. "Omniscience." *Narrative* 12.1 (2004): 22–34.
Cunningham, Michael. "Prisoners of the Japanese and the Politics of Apology: A Battle over History and Memory." *Collective Memory*. Spec. issue of *Journal of Contemporary History* 39.4 (2004): 561–74.
Cusac, Anne-Marie. *Cruel and Unusual: The Culture of Punishment in America*. New Haven: Yale University Press, 2009.
Cutter, Martha J. "Smuggling across the Borders of Race, Gender, and Sexuality: Sui Sin Far's *Mrs. Spring Fragrance*." *Mixed Race Literature*. Ed. Jonathan Brennan. Stanford: Stanford University Press, 2002. 137–64.
Dabashi, Hamid. *Post-Orientalism: Knowledge and Power in the Time of Terror*. New Brunswick, NJ: Transaction, 2009.
Dadabhay, Yusuf. "Circuitous Assimilation among Rural Hindustanis in California." *Social Forces* 33.2 (1954): 138–41.
Daniels, Roger. *Prisoners without Trial: Japanese Americans in World War II*. New York: Hill and Wang, 1993.
Dariotis, Wei Ming. "Developing a Kin-Aesthetic: Multiraciality and Kinship in Asian and Native North American Literature." *Mixed Race Literature*. Ed. Jonathan Brennan. Stanford: Stanford University Press, 2002. 177–99.
Darling, J. Andrew. "Mass Inhumation and the Execution of Witches in the American Southwest." *American Anthropologist* 100.3 (1998): 732–52.
Dass-Brailsford, Priscilla. *A Practical Approach to Trauma: Empowering Interventions*. Los Angeles: Sage, 2007.
Davis, Angela Y. *Are Prisons Obsolete?* New York: Seven Stories, 2003.
Davis, N. Ann. "Invisible Disability." *Ethics*. 116.1 (2005): 153–213.
Davis, Rocío G. *Begin Here: Reading Asian North American Autobiographies of Childhood*. Honolulu: University of Hawai'i Press, 2007.
Davis, Rocío G, and Sue-Im Lee, eds. *Literary Gestures: The Aesthetic in Asian American Writing*. Philadelphia: Temple University Press, 2006.
Dawkins, Marcia. "Mixed Messages: Barack Obama and *Post*-Racial Politics." *Spectator* 30.2 (Fall 2010): 9–17.
Dean, Jodi. *Aliens in America: Conspiracy Cultures from Outerspace to Cyberspace*. Ithaca: Cornell University Press, 1998.

De Genova, Nicholas. *Racial Transformations: Latinos and Asians Remaking the United States*. Durham: Duke University Press, 2006.

De Jesús, Melinda L. "Rereading History, Rewriting Desire: Reclaiming Queerness in Carlos Bulosan's *America Is in the Heart* and Bienvenido Santos' *Scent of Apples*." *Journal of Asian American Studies* 5.2 (2002): 91–111.

De León, Arnoldo, and Richard Griswold del Castillo. *North to Aztlán: A History of Mexican Americans in the United States*. 2nd ed. Wheeling, IL: Harlan Davidson, 2006.

Diamond, Jared M. *Collapse: How Societies Choose to Fail or Succeed*. New York: Viking, 2005.

Diaz, Robert G. "Melancholic Maladies: Paranoid Ethics, Reparative Envy, and Asian American Critique." *Women and Performance: A Journal of Feminist Theory* 16.2 (2006): 201–19.

Doležel, Lubomír. *Heterocosmica: Fiction and Possible Worlds*. Baltimore: Johns Hopkins University Press, 1998.

———. "Possible Worlds of Fiction and History." *New Literary History* 29.4 (1998): 785–809.

Donaldson, Elizabeth J. "The Corpus of the Madwoman: Toward a Feminist Disability Studies Theory of Embodiment and Mental Illness." *NWSA Journal* 14.3 (2002): 99–119.

Dong, Lan. "The Joy Luck Club." *The Greenwood Encyclopedia of Multiethnic American Literature*. Ed. Emmanuel Sampath Nelson. Westport, CT: Greenwood, 2005. 1205–06.

Dongoske, Kurt E., Debra L. Martin, and T. J. Ferguson. "Critique of the Claim of Cannibalism at Cowboy Wash." *American Antiquity* 65.1 (2000): 179–90.

Douthwaite, Julia V. *Exotic Women: Literary Heroines and Cultural Strategies in Ancien Régime France*. Philadelphia: University of Pennsylvania Press, 1992.

Dow, Mark. *American Gulag: Inside U.S. Immigration Prisons*. Berkeley: University of California Press, 2004.

Drake, Kimberly. "Doing Time in/as 'The Monster': Abject Identity in African-American Prison Literature." *From the Plantation to the Prison: African-American Confinement Literature*. Ed. Tara T. Green. Macon, GA: Mercer University Press, 2008. 118–53.

Drysdale, David. "Alienated Histories, Alienating Futures: Raciology and Missing Time in *The Interrupted Journey*." *ESC: English Studies in Canada* 34.1 (2008): 103–23.

D'Souza, Tony. *Whiteman*. Boston: Houghton Mifflin, 2006.

Dudden, Alexis. *Troubled Apologies among Japan, Korea, and the United States*. New York: Columbia University Press, 2008.

Dumont, Clayton, W. "The Politics of Scientific Objections to Repatriation." *Wicazo Sa Review* 18.1 (Spring 2003): 109–28.

Duncan, Patti. *Tell This Silence: Asian American Women Writers and the Politics of Speech*. Iowa City: University of Iowa Press, 2004.

Dunick, Lisa M. S. "The Silencing Effect of Canonicity: Authorship and the Written Word in Amy Tan's Novels." *MELUS* 31.2 (2006): 20.
Dyer, Richard. *White*. New York: Routledge, 1997.
Edel, Leon. *Literary Biography*. Bloomington: Indiana University Press, 1973.
Ek, Auli. *Race and Masculinity in Contemporary American Prison Narratives*. New York: Routledge, 2005.
Elam, Michele. *The Souls of Mixed Folk: Race, Politics, and Aesthetics in the New Millennium*. Stanford: Stanford University Press, 2012.
Elliott, Matthew. "Sins of Omission: Hisaye Yamamoto's Vision of History." *MELUS* 34.1 (2009): 47–68.
Ellis, David. *Literary Lives: Biography and the Search for Understanding*. Edinburgh: Edinburgh University Press, 2000.
Ellis, Trey. *Platitudes and "The New Black Aesthetic."* Boston: Northeastern University Press, 2003.
Elms, Alan C. *Uncovering Lives: The Uneasy Alliance of Biography and Psychology*. New York: Oxford University Press, 1994.
Eng, David L. *Racial Castration: Managing Masculinity in Asian America*. Durham: Duke University Press, 2001.
Engelbrecht, William E. *Iroquoia: The Development of a Native World*. Syracuse: Syracuse University Press, 2005.
Eshun, Kodwo. "Further Considerations of Afrofuturism." *CR: The New Centennial Review* 3.2 (2003): 287–302.
Espiritu, Augusto. "Transnationalism and Filipino American Historiography." *Journal of Asian American Studies* 11.2 (2008): 171–84.
Espiritu, Yen Le. *Asian American Women and Men*. Lanham, MD: Rowman and Littlefield, 2007.
———. "The 'We-Win-Even-When-We-Lose' Syndrome: U.S. Press Coverage of the Twenty-Fifth Anniversary of the 'Fall of Saigon.'" *American Quarterly* 58.2 (2006): 329–52.
Evans, Mary. *Missing Persons: The Impossibility of Auto/Biography*. New York: Routledge, 1999.
Eyerman, Ron. "The Past in the Present: Culture and the Transmission of Memory." *Acta Sociologica* 47.2 (2004): 159–69.
Fachinger, Petra. "German Mothers, New World Daughters: Angelika Fremd's *Heartland* and Sigrid Nunez's *A Feather on the Breath of God*." *Critique* 46.3 (2005): 253–66.
Fagan, Andrew. *Human Rights: Confronting Myths and Misunderstandings*. Northampton, MA: Edward Elgar, 2009.
Fagan, Brian. *The Time Detectives*. New York: Simon and Schuster, 1996.
Falk, Richard A. "Demystifying Iraq?" *CR: The New Centennial Review* 5.1 (2005): 43–62.
Feagin, Joe, and Eileen O'Brien. *White Men on Race: Power, Privilege, and the Shaping of Cultural Consciousness*. Beacon: Beacon, 2003.

Feder, Ellen K. *Family Bonds: Genealogies of Race and Gender.* New York: Oxford University Press, 2007.

Felski, Rita, and Susan Stanford Friedman. Introduction. *New Literary History* 40.3 (2009): v–ix.

Ferber, Abby L. *White Man Falling: Race, Gender, and White Supremacy.* New York: Roman and Littlefield, 1998.

Ferens, Dominika. *Edith and Winnifred Eaton: Chinatown Missions and Japanese Romances.* Urbana: University of Illinois Press, 2002.

Fink, Deborah. *Cutting Into the Meatpacking Line: Workers and Change in the Rural Midwest.* Chapel Hill: University of North Carolina Press, 1998.

Fish, Adam. "Indigenous Bodies in Colonial Courts: Anthropological Science and the (Physical) Laws of the Remaining Human." *Wicazo Sa Review* 21.1 (Spring 2006): 77–95.

Fisher, Barbara. "Short Takes." Rev. of *The Last of Her Kind*, by Sigrid Nunez. *Boston Globe* 8 Jan. 2006. Web. 1 July 2009. http://www.boston.com/ae/books/articles/2006/01/08/short_takes_boston_globe.

Fisher, Lloyd H. *The Harvest Labor Market in California.* Cambridge: Harvard University Press, 1953.

Flanagan, Joseph. "The Seduction of History: Trauma, Re-memory, and the Ethics of the Real." *Clio* 31.4 (2002): 387–402.

Flinn, Lynn, Christy G. Turner II, and Alan Brew. "Additional Evidence for Cannibalism in the Southwest: The Case of LA 4528." *American Antiquity* 41.3 (1976): 308–18.

Flowers, Ronald B. *Drugs, Alcohol and Criminality in American Society.* Jefferson, NC: McFarland, 1999.

Fludernik, Monika. "Carceral Topography: Spatiality, Liminality and Corporality in the Literary Prison." *Textual Practice* 13.1 (1999): 43–77.

———. *Introduction to Narratology.* New York: Routledge, 2009.

———. "Metaphoric (Im)Prison(ment) and the Constitution of a Carceral Imaginary." *Anglia—Zeitschrift für englische Philologie* 123.1 (2005): 1–25.

———. "The Metaphorics and Metonymics of Carcerality: Reflections on Imprisonment as Source and Target Domain in Literary Texts." *English Studies* 86.3 (2005): 226–44.

———. "New Wine in Old Bottles? Voice, Focalization and New Writing." *New Literary History* 32.3 (2001): 619–38.

Ford, Jamie. *Hotel on the Corner of Bitter and Sweet.* New York: Ballantine Books, 2009.

Forter, Greg. "Freud, Faulkner, Caruth: Trauma and the Politics of Literary Form." *Narrative* 15.3 (2007): 259–85.

Foster, Sesshu. *Atomik Aztex.* San Francisco: City Lights, 2005.

———. *City Terrace Field Manual.* Los Angeles: Kaya, 1996.

Foster, Thomas. "Faceblindness, Visual Pleasure, and Racial Recognition: Eth-

nicity and Technicity in Ted Chiang's 'Liking What You See: A Documentary.'" *Camera Obscura* 24.1 70 (2009): 135–75.
Fox, John W. "Social Class, Mental Illness, and Social Mobility: The Social Selection-Drift Hypothesis for Serious Mental Illness." *Journal of Health and Social Behavior* 31.4 (1990): 344–53.
Francis, Timothy Lang. "'To Dispose of the Prisoners': The Japanese Executions of American Aircrew at Fukuoka, Japan, during 1945." *Pacific Historical Review* 66.4 (1997): 469–501.
Frankenberg, Ruth. *White Women, Race Matters: The Social Construction of Whiteness*. Minneapolis: University of Minnesota Press, 1993.
Franklin, H. Bruce. *The Victim as Criminal and Artist: Literature from the American Prison*. New York: Oxford University Press, 1978.
Frazier, Robert. *Anglo-American Relations with Greece: The Coming of the Cold War, 1942–47*. New York: St. Martin's, 1991.
Freedman, Carl. *Critical Theory and Science Fiction*. Middletown, CT: Wesleyan University Press, 2000.
Freedman, Dan, and Jacqueline Rhoads. *Nurses in Vietnam: The Forgotten Veterans*. Austin: Texas Monthly Press, 1987.
Freedman, Estelle B. *Their Sisters' Keeper: Women's Prison Reform in America, 1830–1930*. Ann Arbor: University of Michigan Press, 1981.
Freely, John. *Aladdin's Lamp: How Greek Science Came to Europe through the Islamic World*. New York: Vintage Books, 2010.
Freund, David M. P. *Colored Property: State Policy and White Racial Politics in Suburban America*. Chicago: University of Chicago Press, 2007.
Fu, Bennett. "Chang, Diana." *Encyclopedia of Asian-American Literature*. Ed. Seiwoong Oh. New York: Infobase, 2007. 35–37.
Fujita-Rony, Dorothy. "Coalitions, Race, and Labor: Rereading Philip Vera Cruz." *Journal of Asian American Studies* 3.2 (2000): 139–62.
Futamura, Madoka. *War Crimes Tribunals and Transitional Justice: The Tokyo Trial and the Nuremberg Legacy*. London: Routledge, 2008.
Futrell, Alison. *Blood in the Arena: The Spectacle of Roman Power*. Austin: University of Texas Press, 1997.
Galatzer-Levy, Isaac R., and Robert M. Galatzer-Levy. "The Revolution in Psychiatric Diagnosis: Problems at the Foundations." *Perspectives in Biology and Medicine* 50.2 (2007): 161–80.
Gallo, Rubén. "Introduction: Delirious Mexico City." *The Mexico City Reader*. Ed. Rubén Gallo. Trans. Rubén Gallo and Lorna Scott Fox. Madison: University of Wisconsin Press, 2004. 3–32.
Gannon, Charles E. *Rumors of War and Infernal Machines: Technomilitary Agenda-Setting in American and British Speculative Fiction*. New York: Rowman and Littlefield, 2003.
Gans, Herbert J. *The Levittowners: Ways of Life and Politics in a New Suburban Community*. New York: Pantheon Books, 1967.

Gantzel, Klaus Jürgen, and Torsten Schwinghammer. *Warfare since the Second World War.* New Brunswick, NJ: Transaction, 2000.
García, Ignacio M. *Chicanismo: The Forging of a Militant Ethos among Mexican Americans.* Tucson: University of Arizona Press, 1997.
Garner, Dwight. "Adopted Voice." Interview with Chang-rae Lee. *New York Times* 5 Sept. 1999. Web. July 2009. http://www.nytimes.com/books/99/09/05/reviews/990905.05garnet.html.
Garner, Steve. *Whiteness: An Introduction.* New York: Routledge, 2007.
Gaspar de Alba, Alicia. "There's No Place like Aztlán: Embodied Aesthetics in Chicana Art." *CR: The New Centennial Review* 4.2 (2004): 103–40.
Genette, Gerard. *Narrative Discourse: An Essay in Method.* Ithaca: Cornell University Press, 1980.
Geron, Kim. *Latino Political Power.* Boulder, CO: Lynne Rienner, 2005.
Gibson, Andrew. "'And the Wind Wheezing through That Organ Once in a While': Voice, Narrative, Film." *New Literary History* 32.3 (2001): 639–57.
Gillies, Midge. *Writing Lives: Literary Biography.* New York: Cambridge University Press, 2009.
Gilmore, Ruth Wilson. *Golden Gulag: Prisons, Surplus, Crisis, and Opposition in Globalizing California.* Berkeley: University of California Press, 2007.
Ginsburg, Ruth. "Ida Fink's Scraps and Traces: Forms of Space and the Chronotope of Trauma Narratives." *Partial Answers: Journal of Literature and the History of Ideas* 4.2 (2006): 205–18.
Giroux, Henry A. "Dirty Democracy and State Terrorism: The Politics of the New Authoritarianism in the United States." *Comparative Studies of South Asia, Africa and the Middle East* 26.2 (2006): 163–77.
———. "The Emerging Authoritarianism in the United States: Political Culture under the Bush/Cheney Administration." *Symploke* 14.1–2 (2006): 98–151.
Glannon, Walter. "Depression as a Mind-Body Problem." *Philosophy, Psychiatry, and Psychology* 9.3 (2002): 243–54.
Goldberg, Elizabeth Swanson. *Beyond Terror: Gender, Narrative, Human Rights.* New Brunswick: Rutgers University Press, 2007.
Gómez-Quiñones, Juan. *Chicano Politics: Reality and Promise, 1940–1990.* Albuquerque: University of New Mexico Press, 1990.
Gonzales, Juan L., Jr. "Asian Indian Immigration Patterns: The Origins of the Sikh Community in California." *International Migration Review* 20.1 (1986): 40–54.
Good, Byron J. "Studying Mental Illness in Context: Local, Global, or Universal?" *Ethos* 25.2 (1997): 230–48.
Goodman, Robin Truth. "Terrorist Hunter: Walter Mosley, the Urban Plot, and the Terror War." *Cultural Critique* 66 (2007): 21–57.
Goodwin, Jason. "The Glory That Was Baghdad." *Wilson Quarterly* 27.2 (2003): 24–28.

Gordon, Avery F., and Christopher Newfield, eds. *Mapping Multiculturalism*. Minneapolis: University of Minneapolis Press, 1996.

Gordon, Jennifer. *Suburban Sweatshops: The Fight for Immigrant Rights*. Cambridge: Belknap Press of Harvard University Press, 2005.

Green, Ronald Michael. "What Does It Mean to Use Someone as 'A Means Only': Rereading Kant." *Kennedy Institute of Ethics Journal* 11.3 (2001): 247–61.

Greene, Graham. *The Quiet American*. 1955. Reprint, New York: Viking, 1956.

Grey, Mark A. "Meatpacking in Storm Lake, Iowa: A Community in Transition." *Pigs, Profits, and Rural Communities*. Ed. Kendall M. Thu and E. Paul Durrenberger. Albany: SUNY Press, 1998. 57–70.

Grice, Helena. *Asian American Fiction, History and Life Writing: International Encounters*. New York: Routledge, 2009.

Grob, Gerald N. "Psychiatry's Holy Grail: The Search for the Mechanisms of Mental Diseases." *Bulletin of the History of Medicine* 72.2 (1998): 189–219.

Gruhzit-Hoyt, Olga. *A Time Remembered: American Women in the Vietnam War*. Novato, CA: Presidio, 1999.

Guerin-Gonzales, Camille. *Mexican Workers and American Dreams: Immigration, Repatriation, and California Farm Labor, 1900–1939*. New Brunswick: Rutgers University Press, 1994.

Gummere, Richard M. *The American Colonial Mind and the Classical Tradition: Essays in Comparative Culture*. Cambridge: Harvard University Press, 1963.

Gunn, Daniel P. "Free Indirect Discourse and Narrative Authority in 'Emma.'" *Narrative* 12.1 (2004): 35–54.

Hagedorn, Jessica. *Toxicology*. New York: Viking, 2011.

Halle, David. *New York and Los Angeles: Politics, Society, and Culture: A Comparative View*. Chicago: University of Chicago Press, 2003.

Halliwell, Martin. *American Culture in the 1950s*. Edinburgh: Edinburgh University Press, 2007.

Halpern, Rick. *Down on the Killing Floor: Black and White Workers in Chicago's Packinghouses, 1904–54*. Urbana: University of Illinois Press, 1997.

Hames-Garcia, Michael Roy. *Fugitive Thought: Prison Movements, Race, and the Meaning of Justice*. Minneapolis: University of Minnesota Press, 2004.

Hamilakis, Yannis. *The Nation and Its Ruins: Antiquity, Archaeology, and National Imagination in Greece*. Oxford: Oxford University Press, 2007.

Hamilton, Nigel. *Biography: A Brief History*. Cambridge: Harvard University Press, 2007.

Haney-López, Ian F. "Post-Racial Racism: Racial Stratification and Mass Incarceration in the Age of Obama." *California Law Review* 98.3 (2010): 1023–73.

———. "Race on the 2010 Census: Hispanics and the Shrinking White Majority." *Daedalus* 134.1 (Winter 2005): 42–52.

———. *White by Law: The Legal Construction of Race*. New York: NYU Press, 2006.

Hanne, Eric J. *Putting the Caliph in His Place: Power, Authority, and the Late Abbasid Caliphate.* Madison, NJ: Fairleigh Dickinson University Press, 2007.

Hansen, Valerie, and Kenneth R. Curtis. *Voyages in World History.* Boston: Wadsworth, 2010.

Hantke, Steffen H. "The Uses of the Fantastic and the Deferment of Closure in American Literature on the Vietnam War." *Rocky Mountain Review of Language and Literature* 55.1 (2001): 63–82.

Harootunian, Harry D. "Japan's Long Postwar: The Trick of Memory and the Ruse of History." *South Atlantic Quarterly* 99.4 (2000): 715–39.

Harris, Cheryl I. "Whiteness as Property." *Harvard Law Review* 106.8 (1993): 1707–91.

Hartigan, John. *Odd Tribes: Toward a Cultural Analysis of White People.* Durham: Duke University Press, 2005.

Harvey, David. *A Brief History of Neoliberalism.* New York: Oxford University Press, 2007.

Harvey, Jennifer. *Whiteness and Morality: Pursuing Racial Justice through Reparations and Sovereignty.* New York: Palgrave Macmillan, 2007.

Hatzivassiliou, Evanthis. "Cold War Pressures, Regional Strategies, and Relative Decline: British Military and Strategic Planning for Cyprus, 1950–1960." *Journal of Military History* 73.4 (2009): 1143–66.

———. *Greece and the Cold War: Frontline State, 1952–1967.* New York: Routledge, 2006.

Hayashi, Brian Masaru. *Democratizing the Enemy.* Princeton: Princeton University Press, 2008.

Hearder, Rosalind. "More Complex than a Stereotype: Australian POW Doctors and the Japanese in Captivity, 1942–45." *Health and History* 6.2 (2004): 75–91.

Hein, Laura, and Akiko Takenaka. "Exhibiting World War II in Japan and the United States since 1995." *Pacific Historical Review* 76.1 (2007): 61–94.

Heise, Ursula K. "Ecocriticism and the Transnational Turn in American Studies." *American Literary History* 20.1–2 (Spring–Summer 2008): 381–404.

Hellmann, John. *American Myth and the Legacy of Vietnam.* New York: Columbia University Press, 1986.

Herman, Judith Lewis. *Trauma and Recovery.* 1992. Reprint, New York: Basic Books, 1997.

Herzfeld, Michael. "The Absence Presence: Discourses of Crypto-Colonialism." *South Atlantic Quarterly* 101.4 (2002): 899–926.

———. *Portrait of a Greek Imagination: An Ethnographic Biography of Andreas Nenedakis.* Chicago: University of Chicago Press, 1997.

Hesse, Barnor. "Self-Fulfilling Prophecy: The Postracial Horizon." *South Atlantic Quarterly* 110.1 (Winter 2011): 155–78.

Hibbard, Allen. "Biographer and Subject: A Tale of Two Narratives." *South Central Review* 23.3 (2006): 19–36.

Hicks, James Whitney. *Fifty Signs of Mental Illness: A Guide to Understanding Mental Health.* New Haven: Yale University Press, 2005.

Hiday, Virginia. "The Social Context of Mental Illness and Violence." *Journal of Health and Social Behavior* 36.2 (1995): 122–37.

Higonnet, Etelle. *"My Heart Is Cut": Sexual Violence by Rebels and Pro-Government Forces in Côte d'Ivoire.* New York: Human Rights Watch, 2007.

Hill, Donald R. *A History of Engineering in Classical and Medieval Times.* La Salle, IL: Open Court, 1984.

———. "The Literature of Arabic Alchemy." *Religion, Learning and Science in the 'Abbasid Period.* Ed. M. J. L. Young, J. D. Latham, and R. B. Serjeant. Cambridge: Cambridge University Press, 1990. 328–41.

———. "Mathematics and Applied Science." *Religion, Learning and Science in the 'Abbasid Period.* Ed. M. J. L. Young, J. D. Latham, and R. B. Serjeant. Cambridge: Cambridge University Press, 1990. 263–67.

History and Memory. Dir. Rea Tajiri. Akiko Productions, 2008. DVD.

Hofmann, Bettina. *Ahead of Survival: American Women Writers Narrate the Vietnam War.* New York: Peter Lang, 1996.

Homans, John. "Soft Aloft." Rev. of *Aloft,* by Chang-rae Lee. *New York* 8 Mar. 2004. Web. 16 Mar. 2009. http://nymag.com/nymetro/arts/books/reviews/n_9942/.

Hondagneu-Sotelo, Pierrette. *Doméstica: Immigrant Workers Cleaning and Caring in the Shadows of Affluence.* Berkeley: University of California Press, 2007.

Hong, Christine. "Flashforward Democracy: American Exceptionalism and the Atomic Bomb in *Barefoot Gen.*" *Comparative Literature Studies* 46.1 (2009): 125–55.

Hong, Terry. "Flying Aloft with Chang-rae Lee: A Conversation." Interview with Chang-rae Lee. *Bloomsbury Review* 24.5 (2004): 23–24.

———. "Writing from a Different Place: A Profile of 2003 PEN/Faulkner Award Winner Sabina Murray." Interview with Sabina Murray. *Bloomsbury Review* 24.1 (2004): 7.

Horowitz, Roger. *Negro and White, Unite and Fight! A Social History of Industrial Unionism in Meatpacking, 1930–90.* Urbana: University of Illinois Press, 1997.

Houston, Jeanne Wakatsuki, and James D. Houston. *Farewell to Manzanar.* Boston: Houghton Mifflin, 1973.

Hsu, Hsuan L., and Martha Lincoln. "Biopower, Bodies . . . the Exhibition, and the Spectacle of Public Health." *Discourse* 29.1 (2007): 15–34.

Huang, Betsy. *Contesting Genres in Asian American Fiction.* New York: Palgrave Macmillan, 2010.

Hulme, Peter. *Colonial Encounters: Europe and the Native Caribbean, 1492–1797.* New York: Routledge, 1992.

Hunt, Courtney. *The History of Iraq.* Westport, CT: Greenwood, 2005.

Huntley, E. D. *Amy Tan: A Critical Companion.* Westport, CT: Greenwood, 1998.

Hurley, Andrew. *Diners, Bowling Alleys, and Trailer Parks: Chasing the American Dream in the Postwar Consumer Culture.* New York: Basic Books, 2001.

Hutcheon, Linda. *The Politics of Postmodernism.* 2nd ed. New York: Routledge, 2002.

Iatrides, John O. "Revolution or Self-Defense? Communist Goals, Strategy, and Tactics in the Greek Civil War." *Journal of Cold War Studies* 7.3 (2005): 3–33.

Ichioka, Yûji. Introduction. *Before Internment: Essays in Prewar Japanese American History.* Ed. Gordon H. Chang and Eiichirō Azuma. Stanford: Stanford University Press, 2006. 3–9.

Ignatieff, Michael. *Human Rights as Politics and Idolatry.* Princeton: Princeton University Press, 2001.

Isaac, Allan Punzalan. *American Tropics: Articulating Filipino America.* Minneapolis: University of Minnesota Press, 2006.

Ivy, Marilyn. "Revenge and Recapitulation in Recessionary Japan." *South Atlantic Quarterly* 99.4 (2000): 819–40.

———. "Trauma's Two Times: Japanese Wars and Postwars." *Positions: East Asia Cultures Critique* 16.1 (2008): 165–88.

Jacobs, Wilbur R. *Francis Parkman, Historian as Hero: The Formative Years.* Austin: University of Texas Press, 1991.

Jacobson, Matthew Frye. *Whiteness of a Different Color: European Immigrants and the Alchemy of Race.* Cambridge: Harvard University Press, 1999.

Jarrett, Gene Andrew. *Deans and Truants: Race and Realism in African American Literature.* Philadelphia: University of Pennsylvania Press, 2007.

Jason, Philip K. *Acts and Shadows: The Vietnam War in American Literary Culture.* Lanham, MD: Rowman and Littlefield, 2000.

Jaynes, Gerald D. "The Effects of Immigration on the Economic Position of Young Black Males." *Against the Wall: Poor, Young, Black, and Male.* Ed. Elijah Anderson. Philadelphia: University of Pennsylvania Press, 2008. 87–101.

Jeans, Roger B. "Victims or Victimizers? Museums, Textbooks, and the War Debate in Contemporary Japan." *Journal of Military History* 69.1 (2005): 149–95.

Jeffery, Judith S. *Ambiguous Commitments and Uncertain Policies: The Truman Doctrine in Greece, 1947–1952.* Lanham, MD: Lexington Books, 2000.

Jeffords, Susan. *The Remasculinization of America: Gender and the Vietnam War.* Bloomington: Indiana University Press, 1989.

Jerng, Mark C. "Nowhere in Particular: Perceiving Race, Chang-rae Lee's *Aloft*, and the Question of Asian American Fiction." *MFS: Modern Fiction Studies* 56.1 (2010): 183–204.

———. "A World of Difference: Samuel R. Delany's *Dhalgren* and the Protocols of Racial Reading." *American Literature* 83.2 (2011): 251–78.

Jin, Wen. *Pluralist Universalism: An Asian Americanist Critique of U.S. and Chinese Multiculturalisms*. Columbus: Ohio State University Press, 2012.

Johns, Christina Jacqueline. *The Origins of Violence in Mexican Society*. Westport, CT: Praeger, 1995.

Johnson, Dale D., Bonnie Johnson, and Stephen J. Farenga. *Stop High-Stakes Testing: An Appeal to America's Conscience*. Lanham, MD: Rowman and Littlefield, 2007.

Johnson, Joyce. "Rich Girl, Poor Girl." Rev. of *The Last of Her Kind*, by Sigrid Nunez. *Washington Post* 29 Jan. 2006. Web. 1 July 2009. http://www.washingtonpost.com/wp-dyn/content/article/2006/01/26/AR2006012601670_pf.html.

Johnson, Kenneth M., and Daniel T. Lichter. "Natural Increase: A New Source of Population Growth in Emerging Hispanic Destinations in the United States." *Population and Development Review* 34.2 (June 2008): 327–46.

Johnson, Sheri L. "Defining Bipolar Disorder." *Psychological Treatment of Bipolar Disorder*. Ed. Sheri L. Johnson and Robert L. Leahy. New York: Guilford, 2004. 3–16.

Johnson, Sheri L., and Björn Meyer. "Psychosocial Predictors of Symptoms." *Psychological Treatment of Bipolar Disorder*. Ed. Sheri L. Johnson and Robert L. Leahy. New York: Guilford, 2004. 83–105.

Johnson, Sheri L., Ray Winters, and Björn Meyer. "A Polarity-Specific Model of Bipolar Disorder." *The Interpersonal, Cognitive, and Social Nature of Depression*. Ed. Janet Kistner and Jessica S. Brown. New York: Routledge, 2006. 133–72.

Jones, Eric E. "Using Viewshed Analysis to Explore Settlement Choice: A Case Study of the Onondaga Iroquois." *American Antiquity* 71.3 (2006): 523–38.

Jones, Howard. *"A New Kind of War": America's Global Strategy and the Truman Doctrine in Greece*. New York: Oxford University Press, 1989.

Joseph, Gilbert M., Anne Rubenstein, and Eric Zolov. "Writing a Cultural History of Mexico since 1940." *Fragments of a Golden Age: The Politics of Culture in Mexico since 1940*. Ed. Gilbert M. Joseph, Anne Rubenstein, and Eric Zolov. Durham: Duke University Press, 2001. 3–22.

Joyce, Patrick D. *No Fire Next Time: Black-Korean Conflicts and the Future of America's Cities*. Ithaca: Cornell University Press, 2003.

Jurca, Catherine. *White Diaspora: The Suburb and the Twentieth-Century American Novel*. Princeton: Princeton University Press, 2001.

Jusdanis, Gregory. "Farewell to the Classical: Excavations in Modernism. *Modernism/Modernity* 11.1 (2004): 37–53.

Kagy, Tom. "Chang-rae Lee: An Artist of the Floating World." *Goldsea* n.d. Web. 16 Mar. 2009. http://www.goldsea.com/Innovators/Leecr/leecr.html.

Kakutani, Michiko. "How an Appetite for Horror Can Get Out of Hand." Rev. of *A Carnivore's Inquiry*, by Sabina Murray. *New York Times* 17 Aug. 2004. Web. July 2009. http://www.nytimes.com/2004/08/17/books/17kaku.html.

Kalaitzaki, Theodora. "US Mediation in the Greek-Turkish Disputes since 1954." *Mediterranean Quarterly* 16.2 (2005): 106–24.
Kalat, David. *A Critical History and Filmography of Toho's Godzilla Series.* Jefferson, NC: McFarland, 1997.
Kamrath, Mark. "An 'Inconceivable Pleasure' and the Philadelphia Minerva: Erotic Liberalism, Oriental Tales, and the Female Subject in Periodicals of the Early Republic." *American Periodicals: A Journal of History, Criticism, and Bibliography* 14.1 (2004): 3–34.
Kantner, John. "Anasazi Mutilation and Cannibalism in the American Southwest." *The Anthropology of Cannibalism.* Ed. Laurence Goldman. Westport, CT: Greenwood, 1999. 75–104.
Kaplan, Amy. "Where Is Guantanamo?" *American Quarterly* 57.3 (2005): 831–58.
Karl, Frederick R. *Art into Life: The Craft of Literary Biography.* Youngstown, OH: Etruscan, 2005.
Kassell, Nancy. *The Pythia on Ellis Island: Rethinking the Greco-Roman Legacy in America.* Lanham, MD: University Press of America, 1998.
Kaufmann, Chaim. "Threat Inflation and the Failure of the Marketplace of Ideas: The Selling of the Iraq War." *International Security* 29.1 (2004): 5–48.
Keener, Craig S. "An Ethnohistorical Analysis of Iroquois Assault Tactics Used against Fortified Settlements of the Northeast in the Seventeenth Century." *Ethnohistory* 46.4 (1999): 777–807.
Keller, Nora Okja. *Comfort Woman.* New York: Viking, 1997.
Kelley, Colleen Elizabeth. *Post-9/11 American Presidential Rhetoric: A Study of Protofascist Discourse.* Lanham, MD: Lexington Books, 2007.
Kelly, Barbara M. *Expanding the American Dream: Building and Rebuilding Levittown.* Albany: SUNY Press, 1999.
Kendall, Frances E. *Understanding White Privilege: Creating Pathways to Authentic Relationships across Race.* New York: Routledge, 2006.
Kennedy, Hugh. *Byzantine and Early Islamic Near East.* Burlington, VT: Ashgate.
———. *The Great Arab Conquests: How the Spread of Islam Changed the World We Live In.* Cambridge, MA: Da Capo, 2007.
———. *When Baghdad Ruled the Muslim World: The Rise and Fall of Islam's Greatest Dynasty.* Cambridge, MA: Da Capo, 2005.
Kenny, Lorraine Delia. *Daughters of Suburbia: Growing Up White, Middle Class, and Female.* New Brunswick: Rutgers University Press, 2000.
Kidwai, Abdur Raheem. *Orientalism in Lord Byron's "Turkish Tales."* Lewiston, NY: Edwin Mellen, 1995.
Kilgore, De Witt Douglas. *Astrofuturism: Science, Race, and Visions of Utopia in Space.* Philadelphia: University of Pennsylvania Press, 2003.
Kim, Claire Jean. *Bitter Fruit: The Politics of Black-Korean Conflict in New York City.* New Haven: Yale University Press, 2000.
Kim, Daniel Y. *Writing Manhood in Black and Yellow: Ralph Ellison, Frank*

Chin, and the Literary Politics of Identity. Stanford: Stanford University Press, 2005.

Kim, Elaine H. "Asian American Literature and the Importance of Social Context." *ADE Bulletin* 80 (1985): 34–41.

———. *Asian American Literature: An Introduction to the Writings and Their Social Context*. Philadelphia: Temple University Press, 1982.

———. "Defining Asian American Realities through Literature." *The Nature and Context of Minority Discourse*. Spec. issue of *Cultural Critique* 6 (1987): 87–111.

Kim, Jodi. *Ends of Empire: Asian American Critique and the Cold War*. Minneapolis: University of Minnesota Press, 2010.

Kim, Sue. "Beyond Black and White: Race and Postmodernism in *The Lord of the Rings* Films." *MFS: Modern Fiction Studies* 50.4 (2004): 875–907.

———. "Narrator, Author, Reader: Equivocation in Theresa Hak Kyung Cha's *Dictee*." *Narrative* 16.2 (May 2008): 163–77.

King, David A. "Astronomy." *Religion, Learning and Science in the 'Abbasid Period*. Ed. M. J. L. Young, J. D. Latham, and R. B. Serjeant. Cambridge: Cambridge University Press, 1990. 274–89.

———. *In Synchrony with the Heavens: Studies in Astronomical Timekeeping and Instrumentation in Medieval Islamic Civilization*. Leiden: Brill, 2004–05.

Kingston, Maxine Hong. *The Woman Warrior*. New York: Knopf, 1975.

Kinney, Katherine. *Friendly Fire: American Images of the Vietnam War*. Oxford: Oxford University Press, 2000.

Klaas, Brian. "From Miracle to Nightmare: An Institutional Analysis of Development Failures in Côte d'Ivoire." *Africa Today* 55.1 (2008): 109–26.

Klein, Christina. *Cold War Orientalism: Asia in the Middlebrow Imagination, 1945–1961*. Berkeley: University of California Press, 2003.

Knadler, Stephen P. *The Fugitive Race: Minority Writers Resisting Whiteness*. Jackson: University Press of Mississippi, 2002.

Knight, Alan. *Mexico: From the Beginning to the Spanish Conquest*. New York: Cambridge University Press, 2002.

Knox, Paul. *Metroburbia, USA*. New Brunswick: Rutgers University Press, 2008.

Koch, Peter O. *The Aztecs, the Conquistadors, and the Making of Mexican Culture*. Jefferson, NC: McFarland, 2006.

Kofas, Jon V. *Under the Eagle's Claw: Exceptionalism in Postwar U.S.-Greek Relations*. Westport, CT: Praeger, 2003.

Koschmann, J. Victor. "National Subjectivity and the Uses of Atonement in the Age of Recession." *South Atlantic Quarterly* 99.4 (2000): 741–61.

Koshy, Susan. "The Fiction of Asian American Literature." *Yale Journal of Criticism* 9.2 (1996): 315–46.

———. "Morphing Race into Ethnicity: Asian Americans and Critical Transformations of Whiteness." *boundary 2* 28.1 (2001): 153–94.

Kruse, Kevin M., and Thomas J. Sugrue. *The New Suburban History*. Chicago: University of Chicago Press, 2006.

Kudlick, Catherine J. "Disability History: Why We Need Another 'Other.'" *American Historical Review* 108.3 (2003): 763–93.

Kühnel, Ernst. "Abbasid Silks of the Ninth Century." *Ars Orientalis* 2 (1957): 367–71.

Kurashige, Scott. *The Shifting Grounds of Race: Black and Japanese Americans in the Making of Multiethnic Los Angeles*. Princeton: Princeton University Press, 2008.

Kutulas, Judy. *The American Civil Liberties Union and the Making of Modern Liberalism, 1930–1960*. Chapel Hill: University of North Carolina Press, 2006.

Kuziemko, Ilyana, and Steven D. Levitt. "An Empirical Analysis of Imprisoning Drug Offenders." National Bureau of Economic Research Working Paper No. 8489. Sept. 2001.

Kymlicka, Will. *Multicultural Citizenship: A Liberal Theory of Minority Rights*. New York: Oxford University Press, 1995.

LaBrack, Bruce, and Karen Leonard. "Conflict and Compatibility in Punjabi-Mexican Immigrant Families in Rural California, 1915–1965." *Journal of Marriage and the Family* 46.3 (1984): 527–37.

LaCapra, Dominick. "Trauma, Absence, Loss." *Critical Inquiry* 25.4 (1999): 696–727.

———. *Writing History, Writing Trauma*. Baltimore: Johns Hopkins University Press, 2001.

Lahiri, Jhumpa. *Interpreter of Maladies: Stories*. Boston: Houghton Mifflin, 1999.

———. *Unaccustomed Earth*. New York: Knopf, 2008.

Lamb, Charles M. *Housing Segregation in Suburban America since 1960*. New York: Cambridge University Press, 2005.

Lambert, Bruce. "Long Island Has Failed to Stem Segregation, A Group Charges." *New York Times* 19 Apr. 2005. Web. 16 Mar. 2009. http://www.nytimes.com/2005/04/19/nyregion/19race.html.

———. "Study Calls L.I. Most Segregated Suburb." *New York Times* 5 Jun. 2002. Web. 16 Mar. 2009. http://www.nytimes.com/2002/06/05/nyregion/study-calls-li-most-segregated-suburb.html.

Lambert, Patricia M., Banks L. Leonard, Brian R. Billman, Richard A. Marlar, Margaret E. Newman, and Karl J. Reinhard. "Response to Critique of the Claim of Cannibalism at Cowboy Wash." *American Antiquity* 65.2 (2000): 397–406.

Landman, Todd. *Studying Human Rights*. New York: Routledge, 2006.

Lanser, Susan S. *Fictions of Authority: Women Writers and Narrative Voice*. Ithaca: Cornell University Press, 1992.

———. "The 'I' of the Beholder: Equivocal Attachments and the Limits of Structuralist Narratology." *A Companion to Narrative Theory*. Ed. James Phelan and Peter J. Rabinowitz. Malden, MA: Blackwell, 2005.

Lapcharoensap, Rattawut. *Sightseeing: Stories*. New York: Grove, 2005.

Laub, Dori. "Bearing Witness or the Vicissitudes of Listening." *Testimony: Crises of Witnessing in Literature, Psychoanalysis, and History*. Ed. Shoshana Felman and Dori Laub. New York: Routledge, 1992. 57–71.

Laungani, Pittu. "Cultural Influences on Mental Illness." *Economic and Political Weekly* 24.43 (1989): 2427–30.

Lavender, Isiah, III. *Race in American Science Fiction*. Bloomington: Indiana University Press, 2011.

Law, Victoria. *Resistance behind Bars: The Struggles of Incarcerated Women*. Oakland, CA: PM, 2009.

Lawston, Jodie Michelle. "Women, the Criminal Justice System, and Incarceration: Processes of Power, Silence, and Resistance." *NWSA Journal* 20.2 (2008): 1–18.

Le, Nam. *The Boat*. New York: Knopf, 2008.

Leask, Nigel. *Anxieties of Empire: British Romantic Writers and the East*. New York: Cambridge University Press, 1992.

Lee, Chang-rae. *Aloft*. New York: Riverhead Books, 2004.

———. *A Gesture Life*. New York: Riverhead, 1999.

———. *Native Speaker*. New York: Riverhead, 1995.

Lee, Don. *Yellow: Stories*. New York: Norton, 2001.

Lee, Erika. "Orientalisms in the Americas: A Hemispheric Approach to Asian American History." *Journal of Asian American Studies* 8.3 (2005): 235–56.

Lee, Fred I. "The Japanese Internment and the Racial State of Exception." *Theory & Event* 10.1 (2007). Web. 20 May 2009.

Lee, Hermione. *Biography: A Very Short Introduction*. New York: Oxford University Press, 2009.

———. *Body Parts: Essays in Life-Writing*. London: Chatto and Windus, 2005.

Lee, James Kyung-Jin. *Urban Triage: Race and the Fictions of Multiculturalism*. Minneapolis: University of Minnesota Press, 2004.

Lee, Jennifer. *Civility in the City: Blacks, Jews, and Koreans in Urban America*. Cambridge: Harvard University Press, 2002.

Lee, Josephine D. *Performing Asian America: Race and Ethnicity on the Contemporary Stage*. Philadelphia: Temple University Press, 1997.

———. Rev. of *A Feather on the Breath of God*, by Sigrid Nunez. *Journal of Asian American Studies* (1998): 109–12.

Lee, Julia H. "Estrangement on a Train: Race and Narratives of American Identity." *ELH* 75.2 (2008): 345–65.

Lee, Sky. *Disappearing Moon Café*. Chicago: Howard E. Seals, 1991.

Lee, Stacey J. *Unraveling the "Model Minority" Stereotype: Listening to Asian American Youth*. New York: Teachers College Press, 1996.

Lee, Sue-Im. Introduction. *Literary Gestures: The Aesthetic in Asian American*

Writing. Ed. Rocío G. Davis and Sue-Im Lee. Philadelphia: Temple University Press, 2006.

Lee, Tosca. *Iscariot*. Brentwood, TN: Howard Books, 2013.

Lee, Yoon Sun. *Modern Minority: Asian American Literature and Everyday Life*. New York: Oxford University Press, 2013.

Lejeune, Philippe. *On Autobiography*. Ed. Paul John Eakin. Trans. Katherine Leary. Minneapolis: University of Minnesota Press, 1989.

Leonard, Karen Isaksen. *Making Ethnic Choices: California's Punjabi Mexican Americans*. Philadelphia: Temple University Press, 1992.

Le Strange, Guy. *Baghdad during the Abbasid Caliphate: From Contemporary Arabic and Persian Sources*. Oxford, UK: Clarendon, 1900.

Lestringant, Frank. *Cannibals: The Discovery and Representation of the Cannibal from Columbus to Jules Verne*. Trans. Rosemary Morris. Berkeley: University of California Press, 1997.

lê thi diem thúy. *The Gangster We Are All Looking For*. New York: Knopf, 2003.

Levander, Caroline F., and Robert S. Levine, eds. *Hemispheric American Studies*. New Brunswick: Rutgers University Press, 2008.

Lewiecki-Wilson, Cynthia. "Rethinking Rhetoric through Mental Disabilities." *Rhetoric Review* 22.2 (2003): 156–67.

Li, David Leiwei. *Imagining the Nation: Asian American Literature and Cultural Consent*. Stanford: Stanford University Press, 1998.

Li, Guofang. "Other People's Success: Impact of the 'Model Minority' Myth on Underachieving Asian Students in North America." *KEDI: Journal of Educational Policy* 2.1 (2005): 69–86.

Lie, John. "The State as Pimp: Prostitution and the Patriarchal State in Japan in the 1940s." *Sociological Quarterly* 38.2 (1997): 251–63.

Light, Claire. "Abducted by Aliens!" *Slightly Behind and to the Left: Four Stories and Three Drabbles*. Seattle: Aqueduct, 2009. 64–83.

———. Afterword. *Slightly Behind and to the Left: Four Stories and Three Drabbles*. Seattle: Aqueduct, 2009. 84–87.

———. "Defining and Identifying Cultural Appropriation." Home page. 15 Jan. 2009. Web. 1 Oct. 2011. http://www.clairelight.typepad.com/seelight/2009/01/defining-cultural-appropriation.html.

Light, Ivan. *Deflecting Immigration: Networks, Markets, and Regulation in Los Angeles*. New York: Russell Sage Foundation, 2008

Lim, Shirley Geok-lin. "Assaying the Gold: Or, Contesting the Ground of Asian American Literature." *New Literary History* 24.1 (Winter 1993): 147–69.

Ling, Amy. "Asian American Literature: A Brief Introduction and Selected Bibliography." *ADE Bulletin* 80 (1985): 29–33.

———. *Between Worlds: Women Writers of Chinese Ancestry*. New York: Pergamon, 1990.

———. "Winnifred Eaton: Ethnic Chameleon and Popular Success." *MELUS* 11.3 (Autumn 1984): 5–15.

———. "Writer in the Hyphenated Condition: Diana Chang." *MELUS* 7.4 (Winter 1980): 69–83.
Ling, Jinqi. "Forging a North-South Perspective: Nikkei Migration in Karen Tei Yamashita's Novels." *Amerasia Journal* 32.3 (2006): 1–22.
———. *Narrating Nationalisms: Ideology and Form in Asian American Literature.* New York: Oxford University Press, 1998.
Ling, L. H. M. "The Monster Within: What Fu Manchu and Hannibal Lecter Can Tell Us about Terror and Desire in a Post-9/11 World." *Positions: East Asia Cultures Critique* 12.2 (2004): 377–400.
Lipsitz, George. *Dangerous Crossroads: Popular Music, Postmodernism, and the Poetics of Place.* London: Verso, 1994.
———. *The Possessive Investment in Whiteness: How White People Profit from Identity Politics.* Philadelphia: Temple University Press, 1998.
———. "The Possessive Investment in Whiteness: Racialized Social Democracy and the 'White' Problem in American Studies." *American Quarterly* 47.3 (1995): 369–87.
Little, Douglas. *American Orientalism: The United States and the Middle East since 1945.* Chapel Hill: University of North Carolina Press, 2008.
Liu, Aimee. *Face.* New York: Warner Books, 1994.
Liu, Amy. "Unraveling the Myth of Meritocracy within the Context of US Higher Education." *Higher Education* 62 (2011): 383–97.
Lockman, Zachary. *Contending Visions of the Middle East: The History and Politics of Orientalism.* 2nd ed. New York: Cambridge University Press, 2010.
Lomperis, Timothy J. *"Reading the Wind": The Literature of the Vietnam War.* Durham: Duke University Press, 1987.
Loukaki, Argyro. *Living Ruins, Value Conflicts.* Aldershot, UK: Ashgate, 2008.
Lowe, Lisa. *Immigrant Acts: On Asian American Cultural Politics.* Durham: Duke University Press, 1996.
Luckhurst, Roger. "The Science-Fictionalization of Trauma: Remarks on Narratives of Alien Abduction." *Science Fiction Studies* 25.1 (1998): 29–52.
Lumpkins, Charles L. *American Pogrom: The East St. Louis Race Riot and Black Politics.* Athens: Ohio University Press, 2008.
Lundrigan, Margaret, Tova Navarra, and Margaret L. Ferrer. *Levittown: The First Fifty Years.* Charleston, SC: Arcadia, 1999.
Lye, Colleen. "The Afro-Asian Analogy." *PMLA* 123.5 (2008): 1732–36.
———. *America's Asia: Racial Form and American Literature, 1893–1945.* Princeton: Princeton University Press, 2005.
———. "Introduction: In Dialogue with Asian American Studies." *Representations* 99 (2007): 1–12.
MacKenzie, John M. *Orientalism: History, Theory and the Arts.* New York: Manchester University Press, 1995.
MacKenzie, S. P. "The Treatment of Prisoners of War in World War II." *Journal of Modern History* 66.3 (1994): 487–520.

Maeda, Daryl J. "Black Panthers, Red Guards, and Chinamen: Constructing Asian American Identity through Performing Blackness, 1969–1972." *American Quarterly* 57.4 (Dec. 2005): 1079–1103.

———. *Chains of Babylon: The Rise of Asian America*. Minneapolis: University of Minnesota Press, 2009.

Maga, Timothy P. *Judgment at Tokyo: The Japanese War Crimes Trials*. Lexington: University Press of Kentucky, 2001.

Mahler, Sarah J. *Salvadorans in Suburbia: Symbiosis and Conflict*. Boston: Allyn and Bacon, 1995.

Mahoney, Rob. *Côte d'Ivoire, Country on a Precipice: The Precarious State of Human Rights and Civilian Protection in Côte d'Ivoire*. New York: Human Rights Watch, 2005.

Makdisi, Saree. *Romantic Imperialism: Universal Empire and the Culture of Modernity*. New York: Cambridge University Press, 1998.

Makdisi, Saree, and Felicity Nussbaum. Introduction. *The "Arabian Nights" in Historical Context: Between East and West*. Ed. Saree Makdisi and Felicity Nussbaum. New York: Oxford University Press, 2008. 1–24.

Marez, Curtis. "Signifying Spain, Becoming Comanche, Making Mexicans: Indian Captivity and the History of Chicana/o Popular Performance." *American Quarterly* 53.2 (2001): 267–307.

Marshall, Kathryn. *In the Combat Zone: An Oral History of American Women in Vietnam, 1966–1975*. Boston: Little, Brown, 1987.

Marshall, Megan. "Something Happening Here." Rev. of *The Last of Her Kind*, by Sigrid Nunez. *New York Times* 5 Feb. 2006. Web. 1 July 2009. http://www.nytimes.com/2006/02/05/books/review/05marshall.html?_r=1.

Marshall-Fratani, Ruth. "The War of 'Who Is Who': Autochthony, Nationalism, and Citizenship in the Ivoirian Crisis." *African Studies Review* 49.2 (2006): 9–43.

Martin, Philip. "Mexican Workers and U.S. Agriculture: The Revolving Door." *International Migration Review* 36.4 (2002): 1124–42.

Massey, Dennis. *Doing Time in American Prisons: A Study of Modern Novels*. Westport, CT: Greenwood, 1989.

Matsumoto, Valerie J. *Farming the Home Place: A Japanese American Community in California, 1919–1982*. Ithaca: Cornell University Press, 1993.

Maxey, Ruth. "'Who Wants Pale, Thin, Pink Flesh?': Bharati Mukherjee, Whiteness, and South Asian American Writing." *Textual Practice* 20.3 (2006): 529–47.

May, Elaine Tyler. *Homeward Bound: American Families in the Cold War Era*. New York: Basic Books, 1990.

Mbembe, Achille. "Necropolitics." *Public Culture* 15.1 (2003): 11–40.

McCarthy, Kevin F., and Georges Vernez. *Immigration in a Changing Economy: California's Experience*. Santa Monica, CA: Rand, 1997.

McGowan, Miranda Oshige, and James Lindgren. "Testing the 'Model Minority Myth.'" *Northwestern University Law Review* 100.1 (2006): 331–78.

McNamee, Stephen J., and Robert K. Miller, Jr. *The Meritocracy Myth*. 2nd ed. Lanham, MD: Rowman and Littlefield, 2009.

Messud, Claire. "The Way We Lived Then." Rev. of *The Last of Her Kind*, by Sigrid Nunez. *New York Review of Books* 11 May 2006. Web. 1 July 2009. http://www.nybooks.com/articles/article-preview?article_id=18975.

Middlebrook, Diane Wood. "The Role of the Narrator in Literary Biography." *South Central Review* 23.3 (2006): 5–18.

Miklowitz, David Jay. *The Bipolar Disorder Survival Guide: What You and Your Family Need to Know*. New York: Guilford, 2002.

Miklowitz, David Jay, and Sheri L. Johnson. "Bipolar Disorder." *Adult Psychopathology and Diagnosis*. Ed. Michel Hersen, Samuel M. Turner, and Deborah C. Beidel. Hoboken, NJ: Wiley, 2007. 317–48.

Millard, Ann V., Jorge Chapa, and Catalina Burillo. *Apple Pie and Enchiladas: Latino Newcomers in the Rural Midwest*. Austin: University of Texas Press, 2004.

Miller, James Edward. *The United States and the Making of Modern Greece: History and Power, 1950–1974*. Chapel Hill: University of North Carolina Press, 2009.

Min, Pyong Gap. *Caught in the Middle: Korean Communities in New York and Los Angeles*. Berkeley: University of California Press, 1996.

Mizruchi, Susan L. *The Science of Sacrifice: American Literature and Modern Social Theory*. Princeton: Princeton University Press, 1998.

Mollow, Anna. "'When Black Women Start Going on Prozac': Race, Gender, and Mental Illness in Meri Nana-Ama Danquah's *Willow Weep for Me*." *MELUS* 31.3 (2006): 67–99.

Moraga, Cherríe, and Irma Mayorga. *The Hungry Woman*. Albuquerque, NM: West End, 2001.

Morley, David, and Kevin Robins. "Techno-Orientalism: Japan Panic." *Spaces of Identity: Global Media, Electronic Landscapes, and Cultural Boundaries*. New York: Routledge, 1995. 147–43.

Morris, Ian. *Archaeology as Cultural History: Words and Things in Iron Age Greece*. Malden, MA: Blackwell, 2000.

Moustakis, Fotios, and Michael Sheehan. "Democratic Peace and the European Security Community: The Paradox of Greece and Turkey." *Mediterranean Quarterly* 13.1 (2002): 69–85.

Moy, James S. *Marginal Sights: Staging the Chinese in America*. Iowa City: University of Iowa Press, 1993.

Moya, Paula. Introduction. *Reclaiming Identity: Realist Theory and the Predicament of Postmodernism*. Ed. Paula M. L. Moya and Michael Roy Hames-Garcia. Berkeley: University of California Press, 2000. 1–28.

———. *Learning from Experience: Minority Identities, Multicultural Struggles.* Berkeley: University of California Press, 2002.
Mukherjee, Bharati. *Jasmine.* New York: Grove Weidenfeld, 1989.
Mura, David. *Famous Suicides of the Japanese Empire.* Minneapolis: Coffee House, 2008.
Murray, Sabina. *The Caprices.* 2002. Reprint, New York: Grove, 2007.
———. *A Carnivore's Inquiry.* New York: Grove, 2004.
———. *Forgery.* New York: Grove, 2007.
———. *Slow Burn.* New York: Ballantine Books, 1990.
———. *Tales of the New World.* New York: Grove, 2011.
Myers, Thomas. *Walking Point: American Narratives of Vietnam.* New York: Oxford University Press, 1988.
Naber, Nadine C. "So Our History Doesn't Become Your Future: The Local and Global Politics of Coalition Building Post September 11th." *Journal of Asian American Studies* 5.3 (2002): 217–42.
Nadel, Ira Bruce. *Biography: Fiction, Fact, and Form.* New York: St. Martin's, 1984.
Nance, Susan. *How the "Arabian Nights" Inspired the American Dream, 1790–1935.* Chapel Hill: University of North Carolina Press, 2009.
Nasrallah, Nawal. *Annals of the Caliphs' Kitchens: Ibn Sayyār al-Warrāq's Tenth-Century Baghdadi Cookbook.* Leiden: Brill, 2007.
Navarro, Armando. *Mexicano Political Experience in Occupied Aztlán: Struggles and Change.* Walnut Creek, CA: Altamira, 2005.
Neiwert, David A. *Strawberry Days: How Internment Destroyed a Japanese American Community.* New York: Palgrave Macmillan, 2005.
Nemade, Rashmi, and Mark Dombeck. "Evolution of Bipolar Disorder Classification and the DSM." *MentalHelp.net* 13 Dec. 2006. Web. 16 Mar. 2009. http://www.mentalhelp.net/poc/view_doc.php?type=doc&id=11202&cn=4.
Nevels, Cynthia Skove. *Lynching to Belong: Claiming Whiteness through Racial Violence.* College Station: Texas A&M Press, 2007.
Newman, Corey E. "Bipolar Disorder." *Comprehensive Handbook of Personality and Psychopathology.* Ed. Michel Hersen and Jay C. Thomas. Hoboken, NJ: Wiley, 2006. 244–61.
Ng, Fae Myenne. *Bone.* New York: Hyperion, 1993.
Ng, Wendy L. *Japanese American Internment during World War II: A History and Reference Guide.* Santa Barbara, CA: ABC-CLIO, 2001.
Ngai, Mae M. *Impossible Subjects: Illegal Aliens and the Making of Modern America.* Princeton: Princeton University Press, 2004.
Nguyen, Bich Minh. *Short Girls.* New York: Viking, 2009.
Nguyen, Viet Thanh. *Race and Resistance: Literature and Politics in Asian America.* New York: Oxford University Press, 2002.
———. "Speak of the Dead: Speak of Viet Nam: The Ethics and Aesthetics of Minority Discourse." *CR: The New Centennial Review* 6.2 (Fall 2006): 7–37.

Nicki, Andrea. "The Abused Mind: Feminist Theory, Psychiatric Disability, and Trauma." *Hypatia* 16.4 (2001): 80–104.

Nielson, Henrik Skov. "The Impersonal Voice in First-Person Narrative Fiction." *Narrative* 12.2 (2004): 133–50.

Noll, Mark A. *A History of Christianity in the United States and Canada*. Grand Rapids, MI: Eerdmans, 1992.

Nomura, Gail M. "Significant Lives: Asia and Asian Americans in the History of the U.S. West." *Western Historical Quarterly* 25.1 (1994): 69–88.

Noriega, Chon A. *Shot in America: Television, the State, and the Rise of Chicano Cinema*. Minneapolis: University of Minnesota Press, 2000.

Norman, Elizabeth M. *Women at War: The Story of Fifty Military Nurses Who Served in Vietnam*. Philadelphia: University of Pennsylvania Press, 1990.

Novarr, David. *The Lines of Life: Theories of Biography, 1870–1970*. West Lafayette, IN: Purdue University Press, 1986.

Nunez, Sigrid. *A Feather on the Breath of God*. New York: HarperCollins, 1995.

———. *For Rouenna*. New York: Farrar, Straus and Giroux, 2001.

———. *The Last of Her Kind*. New York: Farrar, Straus and Giroux, 2006.

———. *Mitz: The Marmoset of Bloomsbury*. New York: Harper, 1998.

———. *Naked Sleeper: A Novel*. New York: HarperCollins, 1996.

———. *Salvation City*. New York: Riverhead, 2010.

Nussbaum, Felicity. *Torrid Zones: Maternity, Sexuality, and Empire in Eighteenth-Century English Narratives*. Baltimore: Johns Hopkins University Press, 1995.

Obeyesekere, Gananath. *Cannibal Talk: The Man-Eating Myth and Human Sacrifice in the South Seas*. Berkeley: University of California Press, 2005.

———. "Narratives of the Self: Chevalier Peter Dillon's Fijian Cannibal Adventures." *Body Trade: Captivity, Cannibalism and Colonialism in the Pacific*. Ed. Barbara Creed and Jeanette Hoorn. New York: Routledge, 2001. 69–111.

Obourn, Megan. *Reconstituting Americans: Liberal Multiculturalism and Identity Difference in Post-1960s Literature*. New York: Palgrave Macmillan, 2011.

Okada, John. *No-No Boy*. 1957. Reprint, Tokyo: Charles E. Tuttle, 1975.

Okubo, Miné. *Citizen 13660*. 1946. Reprint, Seattle: University of Washington Press, 1983.

Oliver, J. Eric. *Democracy in Suburbia*. Princeton: Princeton University Press, 2001.

Oliver, Melvin L., and Thomas M. Shapiro. *Black Wealth / White Wealth: A New Perspective on Racial Inequality*. 10th ann. ed. New York: Routledge, 2006.

Olson, Joel. *The Abolition of White Democracy*. Minneapolis: University Minneapolis Press, 2004.

Omi, Michael, and Howard Winant. *Racial Formation in the United States*. 2nd ed. New York: Routledge, 1994.

Ong, Aihwa. *Flexible Citizenship: The Cultural Logics of Transnationality*. Durham: Duke University Press, 1999.

Onians, John. *Atlas of World Art*. New York: Oxford University Press, 2004.
O'Shea, Kathleen. *Women and the Death Penalty in the United States, 1900–1998*. Westport, CT: Praeger, 1999.
Otano, Alicia. *Speaking the Past: Child Perspective in the Asian American Bildungsroman*. Münster, Germany: Lit, 2004.
Pagedas, Constantine A. "Ellis O. Briggs and the US Embassy in Greece, 1959 to 1962: A 'Relentless Struggle.'" *Mediterranean Quarterly* 17.4 (2006): 91–120.
Pak, Sang. *Wait until Twilight*. New York: Harper, 2009.
Palmer, Alan. *Fictional Minds*. Lincoln: University of Nebraska Press, 2004.
Panay, Andrew. "From Little Big Man to Little Green Men: The Captivity Scenario in American Culture." *European Journal of American Culture* 23.3 (2004): 201–16.
Panourgiá, Neni. *Dangerous Citizens: The Greek Left and the Terror of the State*. New York: Fordham University Press, 2009.
Parenti, Christian. *Lockdown America: Police and Prisons In the Age of Crisis*. New York: Verso, 1999.
Parikh, Crystal. *An Ethics of Betrayal: The Politics of Otherness in Emergent U.S. Literatures and Culture*. New York: Fordham University Press, 2009.
Park, Ed. "Drastic Alterations." Rev. of *Aloft*, by Chang-rae Lee. *Village Voice* 2 Mar. 2004. Web. 16 Mar. 2009. http://www.villagevoice.com/2004-03-02/books/drastic-alterations/.
Park, Edward J. W., and John S. W. Park. "A New American Dilemma? Asian Americans and Latinos in Race Theorizing." *Journal of Asian American Studies* 2.3 (Oct. 1999): 289–309.
Park, Jinim. *Narratives of the Vietnam War by Korean and American Writers*. New York: Peter Lang, 2007.
Parks, Virginia. *The Geography of Immigrant Labor Markets: Space, Networks, and Gender*. New York: LFB, 2005.
Parreñas, Rhacel Salazar. *The Force of Domesticity: Filipina Migrants and Globalization*. New York: NYU Press, 2008.
———. *Servants of Globalization: Women, Migration, and Domestic Work*. Stanford: Stanford University Press, 2001.
Partridge, Jeffrey F. L. *Beyond Literary Chinatown*. Seattle: University of Washington Press, 2007.
Pavel, Thomas G. "Fiction and Imitation." *Poetics Today* 21.3 (2000): 521–41.
Peckham, Robert Shannan. *National Histories, Natural States: Nationalism and the Politics of Place in Greece*. London: I. B. Tauris, 2001.
Pennock, Caroline Dodds. *Bonds of Blood: Gender, Lifecycle and Sacrifice in Aztec Culture*. New York: Palgrave Macmillan, 2008.
Pensley, D. S. "The Native American Graves Protection and Repatriation Act (1990): Where the Native Voice Is Missing." *Wicazo Sa Review* 20.2 (Fall 2005): 37–64.

Pérez, Emma. *The Decolonial Imaginary: Writing Chicanas into History*. Bloomington: Indiana University Press, 1999.
Pérez, Laura Elisa. "El Desorden, Nationalism, and Chicana/o Aesthetics." *Between Woman and Nation: Nationalisms, Transnational Feminisms, and the State*. Ed. Caren Kaplan, Norma Alarcón, and Minoo Moallem. Durham: Duke University Press, 1999. 19–46.
Pérez-Torres, Rafael. "Refiguring Aztlán." *Postcolonial Theory and the United States: Race, Ethnicity, and Literature*. Ed. Amritjit Singh and Peter Schmidt. Jackson: University Press of Mississippi, 2000. 103–21.
Perry, Pamela. "White University Identity as a 'Sense of Group Position.'" *Symbolic Interaction* 30.3 (2007): 375–93.
Petrinovich, Lewis F. *The Cannibal Within*. New York: Aldine de Gruyter, 2000.
Phan, Aimee. *We Should Never Meet: Stories*. New York: St. Martin's, 2004.
Phelan, James. *Experiencing Fiction: Judgments, Progressions, and the Rhetorical Theory of Narrative*. Columbus: Ohio State University Press, 2007.
Phelps, David Sutton, and Rebekah Burgess. "A Possible Case of Cannibalism in the Early Woodland Period of Eastern Georgia." *American Antiquity* 30.2 (1964): 199–202.
Pihlainen, Kalle. "The Moral of the Historical Story: Textual Differences in Fact and Fiction." *New Literary History* 33.1 (2002): 39 60.
Pollock, Jocelyn M. *Women, Prison, and Crime*. 2nd ed. Belmont, CA: Wadsworth Thomson Learning, 2002.
Polo, "Never Coming Down." Rev. of *Aloft*, by Chang-rae Lee. *Asian Reporter* 4 Sept. 2004. Web. 16 Mar. 2009. http://www.asianreporter.com/reviews/2004/09-04aloft.htm.
Porterfield, Nolan. "Telling the Whole Story: Biography and Representation." *Issues in Collaboration and Representation*. Spec. double issue of *Journal of Folklore Research* 37.2–3 (2000): 175–83.
Prasad, Chandra. *On Borrowed Wings*. New York: Atria, 2007.
Prashad, Vijay. "Bruce Lee and the Anti-imperialism of Kung Fu: A Polycultural Adventure." *Positions: East Asia Cultures Critique* 11.1 (2003): 51–90.
———. "Ethnic Studies Inside Out." *Journal of Asian American Studies* 9.2 (June 2006): 157–76.
Price, Patricia L. *Dry Place: Landscapes of Belonging and Exclusion*. Minneapolis: University of Minnesota Press, 2004.
Puar, Jasbir K., and Amit S. Rai. "The Remaking of a Model Minority: Perverse Projectiles under the Specter of (Counter)Terrorism." *Social Text* 22.3 80 (2004): 75–104.
Quan, Kenneth. Interview with Chang-rae Lee. *Asia Pacific Arts* (UCLA Asia Institute) 12 Apr. 2004. Web. 16 Mar. 2009. http://www.asiaarts.ucla.edu/article.asp?parentid=11432.
Rachlinski, Jeffrey J., and Gregory S. Parks. "Implicit Bias, Election '08, and the

Myth of a Post-Racial America." *Cornell Law Faculty Publications* (2010): 659–716.

Radhakrishnan, R. "Why Compare?" *New Literary History* 40.3 (2009): 453–71.

Rafter, Nicole Hahn. *Partial Justice: Women, Prisons, and Social Control*. 2nd ed. New Brunswick, NJ: Transaction, 1990.

Read, Kay Almere. *Time and Sacrifice in the Aztec Cosmos*. Bloomington: Indiana University Press, 1998.

"Reading Guide: *Aloft*." *Penguin.com* n.d. Web. 16 Mar. 2009. http://us.penguingroup.com/static/rguides/us/aloft.html.

Revoyr, Nina. *Southland*. New York: Akashic Books, 2003.

Reynolds, Marylee. "The War on Drugs, Prison Building, and Globalization: Catalysts for the Global Incarceration of Women." *NWSA Journal* 20.2 (2008): 72–95.

Rhodes, Lorna A. "Toward an Anthropology of Prisons." *Annual Review of Anthropology* 30 (2001): 65–83.

Richard, Carl J. *The Golden Age of the Classics in America: Greece, Rome, and the Antebellum United States*. Cambridge: Harvard University Press, 2009.

———. *Greeks and Romans Bearing Gifts: How the Ancients Inspired the Founding Fathers*. Lanham, MD: Rowman and Littlefield, 2008.

Richardson, Alan. Introduction. *Three Oriental Tales*. Ed. Alan Richardson. Boston: Houghton Mifflin, 2002. 1–13.

Richardson, Brian. *Unnatural Voices: Extreme Narration in Modern and Contemporary Fiction*. Columbus: Ohio State University Press, 2006.

Richardson, Michael. *Georges Bataille*. London: Routledge, 1994.

Richter, Allan. "Black and White on Long Island: Like Oil and Water." *New York Times* 16 June 2002. Web. 16 Mar. 2009. http://www.nytimes.com/2002/06/16/nyregion/black-and-white-on-long-island-like-oil-and-water.html?pagewanted=1.

Rimmon-Kenan, Shlomith. *Narrative Fiction: Contemporary Poetics*. London: Methuen, 1983.

Ringnalda, Don. *Fighting and Writing the Vietnam War*. Jackson: University Press of Mississippi, 1994.

Rivkin, David B., and Darin R. Bartram. "Military Occupation: Legally Ensuring a Lasting Peace." *Washington Quarterly* 26.3 (2003): 87–103.

Roberts, Adam. *Science Fiction*. London: Routledge, 2000.

Robinson, Chase F. *Islamic Historiography*. Cambridge: Cambridge University Press, 2003.

Robinson, Greg. *By Order of the President: FDR and the Internment of Japanese Americans*. Cambridge: Harvard University Press, 2001.

Rodriguez, Dylan. *Forced Passages: Imprisoned Radical Intellectuals and the U.S. Prison Regime*. Minneapolis: University of Minnesota Press, 2004.

Rody, Caroline. *The Interethnic Imagination: Roots and Passages in Contemporary Asian American Fiction*. Oxford: Oxford University Press, 2009.

Roediger, David. *Toward the Abolition of Whiteness*. New York: Verso, 1994.

———. *The Wages of Whiteness: Race and the Making of the American Working Class*. 3rd rev. ed. New York: Verso, 2007.

———. *Working toward Whiteness: How America's Immigrants Became White: The Strange Journey from Ellis Island to the Suburbs*. New York: Basic Books, 2005.

Roessel, David E. *In Byron's Shadow: Modern Greece in the English and American Imagination*. New York: Oxford University Press, 2002.

Roley, Brian Ascalon. *American Son: A Novel*. New York: Norton, 2001.

Roos, Patricia A., and Joyce F. Hennessy. "Assimilation or Exclusion? Japanese and Mexican Americans in California." *Sociological Forum* 2.2 (1987): 278–304.

Roper, Robert. "Class Struggles in the 60s." Rev. of *The Last of Her Kind*, by Sigrid Nunez. *San Francisco Gate* 22 Jan. 2006. Web. 1 July 2009. http://sfgate.com/cgi-bin/article.cgi?f=/c/a/2006/01/22/RVG4OGLRDB1.DTL.

Rosales, Francisco A. *Chicano! The History of the Mexican American Civil Rights Movement*. Houston: Arte Público, 1996.

Rosenberg, Charles E. "Contested Boundaries: Psychiatry, Disease, and Diagnosis." *Perspectives in Biology and Medicine* 49.3 (2006): 407–24.

Roubatis, Yiannis P. *Tangled Webs: The U.S. in Greece, 1947–1967*. New York: Pella, 1989.

Roxworthy, Emily. *The Spectacle of Japanese American Trauma*. Honolulu: University of Hawai'i Press, 2008.

Roy-Bhattacharya, Joydeep. *The Watch*. New York: Hogarth, 2012.

Ruíz, Vicki. *From Out of the Shadows: Mexican Women in Twentieth-Century America*. New York: Oxford University Press, 1998.

Runyan, William McKinley. *Life Histories and Psychobiography: Explorations in Theory and Method*. New York: Oxford University Press, 1982.

Ryan, Marie-Laure. "Postmodernism and the Doctrine of Panfictionality." *Narrative* 5.2 (1997): 165–87.

Ryan, Maureen. *The Other Side of Grief: The Home Front and the Aftermath in American Narratives of the Vietnam War*. Amherst: University of Massachusetts Press, 2008.

Ryan, Valerie. "There's No Escaping Messy Lives in Lee's Inspired *Aloft*." Rev. of *Aloft*, by Chang-rae Lee. *Seattle Times* 12 Mar. 2004. Web. 16 Mar. 2009. http://community.seattletimes.nwsource.com/archive/?date=20040312&slug=aloft12.

Rymhs, Deena. *From the Iron House: Imprisonment in First Nations Writing*. Waterloo, ON: Wilfrid Laurier University Press, 2008.

Sadock, Benjamin J., Harold I. Kaplan, and Virginia A. Sadock. *Kaplan and Sadock's Synopsis of Psychiatry: Behavioral Sciences / Clinical Psychiatry*. 10th ed. Philadelphia: Lippincott Williams & Wilkins, 2007.

Saenz, Rogelio. "Latinos and the Changing Face of America." *Population Refer-

ence Bureau Aug. 2004. Web. Sept. 2010. http://www.prb.org/Articles/2004/LatinosandtheChangingFaceofAmerica.aspx.

Saito, Natsu Taylor. "Reflections on Homeland and Security." *CR: The New Centennial Review* 6.1 (2006): 239–67.

Sakai, Naoki. "Imperial Nationalism and the Comparative Perspective." *Positions: East Asia Cultures Critique* 17.1 (2009): 159–205.

Salaita, Steven George. "Ethnic Identity and Imperative Patriotism: Arab Americans before and after 9/11." *College Literature* 32.2 (2005): 146–68.

Salmon, Merrilee H. "Anthropology: Art or Science? A Controversy about the Evidence of Cannibalism." *Scientific Controversies: Philosophical and Historical Perspectives.* Ed. Peter K. Machamer, Marcello Pera, and Aristides Baltas. New York: Oxford University Press, 2000. 199–212.

Sanday, Peggy Reeves. *Divine Hunger: Cannibalism as a Cultural System.* New York: Cambridge University Press, 1986.

Sanders, J. J. *History of Medieval Islam.* London: Routledge, 1978.

Sandoval, Chela. *Methodology of the Oppressed.* Minneapolis: University of Minneapolis Press, 2000.

San Juan, E., Jr. "In Search of Filipino Writing: Reclaiming Whose 'America'?" *The Ethnic Canon: Histories, Institutions, and Interventions.* Ed. David Palumbo-Liu. Minneapolis: University of Minnesota Press, 1995. 213–40.

Santa Ana, Jeffrey J. "Feeling Ancestral: The Emotions of Mixed Race and Memory in Asian American Cultural Productions." *Positions: East Asia Cultures Critique* 16.2 (Fall 2008): 457–82.

Sardar, Ziauddin. *Orientalism.* Philadelphia: Open University Press, 1999.

Sassen, Saskia. *The Global City.* 2nd ed. Princeton: Princeton University Press, 2001.

Satz, Debra. *Why Some Things Should Not Be for Sale: The Moral Limits of Markets.* New York: Oxford University Press, 2010.

Saxton, Alexander. *The Rise and Fall of the White Republic: Class Politics and Mass Culture in Nineteenth-Century America.* New York: Verso, 1990.

Sayre, Gordon M. "Communion in Captivity: Torture, Martyrdom, and Gender in New France and New England." *Finding Colonial Americas: Essays Honoring J. A. Leo Lamay.* Ed. Carla Mulford and David S. Shields. Newark: University of Delaware Press, 2001. 50–78.

Schabert, Ina. *In Quest of the Other Person: Fiction as Biography.* Tübingen, Germany: Francke Verlag, 1990.

Scheper-Hughes, Nancy. "The Ends of the Body: Commodity Fetishism and the Global Traffic in Organs." *SAIS Review* 22.1 (2002): 61–80.

Schlesinger, Traci. "Equality at the Price of Justice." *NWSA Journal* 20.2 (2008): 27–47.

Schlosser, Eric. *Fast Food Nation: The Dark Side of the All-American Meal.* Boston: Houghton Mifflin, 2001.

Schuessler, John M. "The Deception Dividend: FDR's Undeclared War." *International Security* 34.4 (2010): 133–65.

Schwab, Gabriele. *Haunting Legacies: Violent Histories and Transgenerational Trauma*. New York: Columbia University Press, 2010.

Scott, A. O. "Above It All." Rev. of *Aloft*, by Chang-rae Lee. *New York Times* 14 Mar. 2004. Web. 16 Mar. 2009. http://www.nytimes.com/2004/03/14/books/above-it-all.html.

Scott, Jonathan. *The Pleasures of Antiquity: British Collections of Greece of Rome*. New Haven: Yale University Press for the Paul Mellon Centre for Studies in British Art, 2003.

See, Lisa. *Dreams of Joy*. New York: Random House, 2011.

———. *Shanghai Girls*. New York: Random House, 2009.

Sellers, Christopher. "Nature and Blackness in Suburban Passage." *To Love the Wind and the Rain: African Americans and Environmental History*. Ed. Dianne D. Glave and Mark Stoll. Pittsburgh: University of Pittsburgh Press, 2005. 93–119.

Serfaty, Simon. *Architects of Delusion: Europe, America, and the Iraq War*. Philadelphia: University of Pennsylvania Press, 2008.

Seshadri-Cooks, Kalpana. *Desiring Whiteness: A Lacanian Analysis of Race*. New York: Routledge, 2000.

Sfikas, Thanasis D. *The British Labour Government and the Greek Civil War, 1945–1949: The Imperialism of "Non-Intervention."* Keele, UK: Ryburn, 1994.

Shalev, Eran. *Rome Reborn on Western Shores: Historical Imagination and the Creation of the American Republic*. Charlottesville: University of Virginia Press, 2009.

Shanks, Michael. *Classical Archaeology of Greece: Experiences of the Discipline*. London: Routledge, 1996.

Sharafuddin, Mohammed. *Islam and Romantic Orientalism: Literary Encounters with the Orient*. New York: I. B. Tauris, 1994.

Shigekuni, Julie. *A Bridge between Us*. New York: Doubleday, 1995.

———. *Invisible Gardens*. New York: Thomas Dunne Books, 2003.

Shih, Shu-mei. "Comparative Racialization: An Introduction." *PMLA* 123.5 (Oct. 2008): 1347–62.

Shimakawa, Karen. *National Abjection: The Asian American Body on Stage*. Durham: Duke University Press, 2002.

Shivani, Anis. *Anatolis and Other Stories*. Theresa, NY: Black Lawrence, 2009.

Sickels, Robert. *The 1940s*. Westport, CT: Greenwood, 2004.

Sinclair, Upton. *The Jungle*. New York: Doubleday, Jabber, 1906.

Slaughter, Joseph R. *Human Rights, Inc.: The World Novel, Narrative Form, and International Law*. New York: Fordham University Press, 2007.

Smith, Michael Ernest. *The Aztecs*. 2nd ed. Malden, MA: Blackwell, 2003.

Snow, Dean R. *The Iroquois*. Oxford, UK: Blackwell, 1996.

Somtow, S. P. *The Darker Angels*. New York: Tor Books, 1998.

Sone, Monica. *Nisei Daughter*. New York: Little, Brown, 1953.
Song, Min Hyoung. *Strange Future: Pessimism and the 1992 Los Angeles Race Riots*. Durham: Duke University Press, 2005.
Spanos, William V. *American Exceptionalism in the Age of Globalization: The Specter of Vietnam*. Albany: SUNY Press, 2008.
Spelts, Doreen. "Nurses Who Served: And Did Not Return." *American Journal of Nursing* 86.9 (1986): 1037–39.
Spickard, Paul. *Mixed Blood: Intermarriage and Ethnic Identity in Twentieth-Century America*. Madison: University of Wisconsin Press, 1989.
Spielvogel, Christian. "'You Know Where I Stand': Moral Framing of the War on Terrorism and the Iraq War in the 2004 Presidential Campaign." *Rhetoric and Public Affairs* 8.4 (2005): 549–69.
Spielvogel, Jackson J. *World History to 1800*. Cincinnati: West, 1999.
Spivak, Gayatri Chakravorty. 1987. *In Other Worlds: Essays in Cultural Politics*. New York: Routledge.
Srikanth, Rajini. *The World Next Door: South Asian American Literature and the Idea of America*. Philadelphia: Temple University Press, 2004.
Starr, Kevin. *California: A History*. New York: Modern Library, 2005.
Steinman, Rob. *Women in Vietnam*. New York: TV Books, 2000.
Stillman, Yedida Kalfon. *Arab Dress: A Short History: From the Dawn of Islam to Modern Times*. Ed. Norman A. Stillman. Leiden: Brill, 2003.
Stokes, Mason. *The Color of Sex: Whiteness, Heterosexuality, and the Fictions of White Supremacy*. Durham: Duke University Press, 2001.
Stout, Janis P. "Writing on the Margins of Biography." *South Central Review* 23.3 (2006): 60–75.
Strom, Dao. *Grass Roof, Tin Roof*. New York: Mariner Books, 2003.
Strong, Pauline Turner. "Representational Practices." *A Companion to the Anthropology of North American Indians*. Ed. Thomas Biolsi. Malden, MA: Blackwell, 2004. 341–59.
Stull, Donald D. "Knock 'Em Dead: Work on the Kill Floor of a Modern Beef-packing Plant." *Newcomers in the Workplace: Immigrants and the Restructuring of the U.S. Economy*. Ed. Louise Lamphere, Alex Stepick, and Guillermo J. Grenier. Philadelphia: Temple University Press, 1994. 44–77.
Sturma, Michael. "Aliens and Indians: A Comparison of Abduction and Captivity Narratives." *Journal of Popular Culture* 36.2 (Fall 2002): 318–34.
Sudbury, Julia. "Celling Black Bodies: Black Women in the Global Prison Industrial Complex." *Feminist Review* 70 (2002): 57–74.
Suvin, Darko. *Metamorphoses of Science Fiction*. New Haven: Yale University Press, 1979.
———. *Positions and Presuppositions in Science Fiction*. Kent, OH: Kent State University Press, 1988.
Tabios, Eileen. *Black Lightning: Poetry-in-Progress*. New York: Asian American Writers Workshop, 1998.

Takezawa, Yasuko I. *Breaking the Silence: Redress and Japanese American Ethnicity*. Ithaca: Cornell University Press, 1995.
Tan, Amy. *The Bonesetter's Daughter*. New York: Putnam, 2000.
———. *The Hundred Secret Senses*. New York: Putnam, 1995.
———. *The Joy Luck Club*. New York: Putnam, 1989.
———. *The Kitchen God's Wife*. New York: Putnam, 1991.
Tanaka, Toshiyuki. *Hidden Horrors: Japanese War Crimes in World War II*. Boulder, CO: Westview, 1996.
Tate, Claudia. *Psychoanalysis and Black Novels: Desire and the Protocols of Race*. New York: Oxford University Press, 1998.
Tchen, Jack. *New York before Chinatown: Orientalism and the Shaping of American Culture, 1776–1882*. Baltimore: Johns Hopkins University Press, 2001.
Teorey, Matthew. "Untangling Barbed Wire Attitudes: Internment Literature for Young Adults." *Children's Literature Association Quarterly* 33.3 (2008): 227–45.
Thagard, Paul. "Mental Illness from the Perspective of Theoretical Neuroscience." *Perspectives in Biology and Medicine* 51.3 (2008): 335–52.
Thaler, Ingrid. *Black Atlantic Speculative Fictions: Octavia Butler, Jewelle Gomez, and Nalo Hopkinson*. New York: Routledge, 2010.
Tobias, James. "The Vampire and the Cyborg Embrace: Affect beyond Fantasy in Virtual Materialism." *Vampires: Myths and Metaphors of Enduring Evil*. Ed. Peter Day. New York: Rodopi, 2006. 159–76.
Tonry, Michael. *Thinking about Crime: Sense and Sensibility in American Penal Culture*. New York: Oxford University Press, 2006.
Topping, Margaret, ed. *Eastern Voyages, Western Visions: French Writing and Painting of the Orient*. New York: Peter Lang, 2004.
Totani, Yuma. *The Tokyo War Crimes Trial: The Pursuit of Justice in the Wake of World War II*. Cambridge: Harvard University Asia Center, 2008.
Toungara, Jeanne Maddox. "Ethnicity and Political Crisis in Cote d'Ivoire." *Journal of Democracy* 12.3 (2001): 63–72.
Tridgell, Susan. *Understanding Our Selves: The Dangerous Art of Biography*. New York: Peter Lang, 2004.
Trillin, Calvin. "The Color of Blood: Race, Memory, and a Killing in the Suburbs." *New Yorker* 3 Mar. 2008. Web. 16 Mar. 2009. http://www.newyorker.com/reporting/2008/03/03/080303fa_fact_trillin.
Troy, Maria Holmgren. "Negotiating Genre and Captivity: Octavia Butler's *Survivor*." *Callaloo* 33.4 (2010): 1116–31.
Trumpbour, John, and Elaine Bernard. "Unions and Latinos: Mutual Transformations." *Latinos: Remaking America*. Ed. Marcelo M. Suárez-Orozco and Mariela Páez. 2nd ed. Berkeley: University of California Press, 2009. 126–45.
Trytten, Deborah A., Anna Wong Lowe, and Susan E. Walden. "'Asians Are Good at Math. What an Awful Stereotype': The Model Minority Stereotype's

Impact on Asian American Engineering Students." *Journal of Engineering Education* 101.3 (July 2012): 439–68.
Tsutsui, Kiyoteru. "The Trajectory of Perpetrators' Trauma: Mnemonic Politics around the Asia-Pacific War in Japan." *Social Forces* 87.3 (2009): 1389–1422.
Tuan, Mia. *Forever Foreigners or Honorary Whites?* New Brunswick: Rutgers University Press, 1999.
Turner, Christy G., II, and Jacqueline A. Turner. "The First Claim for Cannibalism in the Southwest: Walter Hough's 1901 Discovery at Canyon Butte Ruin 3, Northeastern Arizona." *American Antiquity* 57.4 (1992): 661–82.
———. *Man Corn: Cannibalism and Violence in the Prehistoric American Southwest.* Salt Lake City: University of Utah Press, 1999.
Turner, Christy G., II, Jacqueline A. Turner, and Roger C. Green. "Taphonomic Analysis of Anasazi Skeletal Remains from Largo-Gallina Sites in Northwestern New Mexico." *Journal of Anthropological Research* 49.2 (1993): 83–110.
Ueno, Toshiya. "Techno-Orientalism and Media Tribalism: On Japanese Animation and Rave Culture." *Third Text* 47 (1999): 95–106.
United Nations, General Assembly. *The Universal Declaration of Human Rights.* 10 Dec. 1948. Web. 1 July 2010. http://www.un.org/Overview/rights.html.
Urbanski, Heather. *Plagues, Apocalypses, and Bug-Eyed Monsters: How Speculative Fiction Shows us Our Nightmares.* Jefferson, NC: McFarland, 2007.
Valdés, Dennis Nodín. *Barrios Norteños: St. Paul and Midwestern Mexican Communities in the Twentieth Century.* Austin: University of Texas Press, 2000.
Varisco, Daniel Martin. *Reading Orientalism: Said and the Unsaid.* Seattle: University of Washington Press, 2007.
Verghese, Abraham. *Cutting for Stone.* New York: Knopf, 2009.
Vickroy, Laurie. *Trauma and Survival in Contemporary Fiction.* Charlottesville: University of Virginia Press, 2002.
Vlavianos, Haris. *Greece, 1941–49: From Resistance to Civil War: The Strategy of the Greek Communist Party.* London: Palgrave Macmillan, 1992.
Võ, Linda Trinh. "Beyond Color-Blind Universalism: Asians in a 'Postracial America.'" *Journal of Asian American Studies* 13.3 (2010): 327–42.
Waldinger, Roger David, and Michael Ira Lichter. *How the Other Half Works: Immigration and the Social Organization of Labor.* Berkeley: University of California Press, 2003.
Walker, Keith. *A Piece of My Heart: The Stories of 26 American Women Who Served in Vietnam.* Novato, CA: Presidio, 1985.
Walsh, Richard. "Fictionality and Mimesis: Between Narrativity and Fictional Worlds." *Narrative* 11.1 (2003): 110–21.
———. "Who Is the Narrator?" *Poetics Today* 18.4 (1997): 495–513.
Warhol, Robyn. "How Narration Produces Gender: Femininity as Affect and Effect in Alice Walker's *The Color Purple.*" *Narrative* 9.2 (May 2001): 182–87.

Warraq, Ibn. *Defending the West: A Critique of Edward Said's "Orientalism."* Amherst, NY: Prometheus Books, 2007.

Warren, Wilson J. *Tied to the Great Packing Machine: The Midwest and Meatpacking.* Iowa City: University of Iowa Press, 2007.

Weir, Robert E. "Levittown." *Class in America.* Ed. Robert E. Weir. Vol. 2. Westport, CT: Greenwood, 2007. 453–54.

Wendell, Susan. "Unhealthy Disabled: Treating Chronic Illnesses as Disabilities." *Hypatia* 16.4 (2001): 17–33.

Whitaker, Beth Elise. "Citizens and Foreigners: Democratization and the Politics of Exclusion in Africa." *African Studies Review* 48.1 (2005): 109–26.

White, Tim D. *Prehistoric Cannibalism at Mancos 5Mtumr-2346.* Princeton: Princeton University Press, 1992.

Whittemore, Reed. *Whole Lives: Shapers of Modern Biography.* Baltimore: Johns Hopkins University Press, 1989.

Wiegman, Robyn. "Whiteness Studies and the Paradox of Particularity." *boundary 2* 26.3 (1999): 115–50.

Wiese, Andrew. *Places of Their Own: African American Suburbanization in the Twentieth Century.* Chicago: University of Chicago Press, 2004.

———. "Racial Cleansing in the Suburbs: Suburban Government, Urban Renewal, and Segregation on Long Island, New York, 1945–1960." *Contested Terrain: Power, Politics, and Participation in Suburbia.* Ed. Marc L. Silver and Martin Melkonian. Westport, CT: Greenwood, 1995. 61–70.

Williams, Dana A. "Lessons before Dying. The Contemporary Confined Character-in-Process." *From the Plantation to the Prison: African-American Confinement Literature.* Ed. Tara T. Green. Macon, GA: Mercer University Press, 2008. 32–57.

Williams, Laura Anh. "Foodways and Subjectivity in Jhumpa Lahiri's *Interpreter of Maladies.*" *MELUS* 32.4 (Winter 2007): 69–79.

Williams, Linda Faye. *The Constraint of Race: Legacies of White Skin Privilege in America.* University Park: Pennsylvania State University Press, 2003.

Williams-León, Teresa, and Cynthia Nakashima Brock, eds. *The Sum of Our Parts: Mixed-Heritage Asian Americans.* Philadelphia: Temple University Press, 2001.

Wineapple, Brenda. "Mourning Becomes Biography." *American Imago* 54.4 (1997): 437–51.

Wing, Jean Yonemura. "Beyond Black and White: The Model Minority Myth and the Invisibility of Asian American Students." *Urban Review* 39.4 (Nov. 2007): 455–87.

Winterer, Caroline. *The Mirror of Antiquity: American Women and the Classical Tradition, 1750–1900.* Ithaca: Cornell University Press, 2007.

Wise, Tim. J. *Colorblind: The Rise of Post-racial Politics and the Retreat from Racial Equity.* San Francisco: City Lights Books, 2010.

Wolff, Carlo. "What's Eating You?" Rev. of *A Carnivore's Inquiry*, by Sabina Murray. *St. Petersburg Times* 18 July 2004: 4P.
Woloch, Alex. *The One vs. the Many*. Princeton: Princeton University Press, 2003.
Wong, Sau-ling C. "Denationalization Reconsidered: Asian American Cultural Criticism at a Theoretical Crossroads." *Amerasia Journal* 21.1–2 (1995): 1–27.
———. Introduction. *Maxine Hong Kingston's "The Woman Warrior": A Casebook*. Ed. Sau-ling C. Wong. New York: Oxford University Press, 1999. 3–16.
———. *Reading Asian American Literature: From Necessity to Extravagance*. Princeton: Princeton University Press.
———. "'Sugar Sisterhood': Situating the Amy Tan Phenomenon." *The Ethnic Canon: Histories, Institutions, and Interventions*. Ed. David Palumbo-Liu. Minneapolis: University of Minnesota Press, 1997. 174–210.
Wong, Sunn Shelley. "Unnaming the Same: Theresa Hak Kyung Cha's *Dictee*." *Feminist Measures: Soundings in Poetry and Theory*. Ed. Cristanne Miller and Lynn Keller. Ann Arbor: University of Michigan Press, 1995. 43–68.
Wood, Jeffrey C. *Getting Help: The Complete and Authoritative Guide to Self-Assessment and Treatment of Mental Health Problems*. Oakland, CA: New Harbinger, 2007.
Wood, Mary Elene. "'I've Found Him!': Diagnostic Narrative in the DSM-IV Casebook." *Narrative* 12.2 (2004): 195–220.
Wu, Frank H. *Yellow: Race in America beyond Black and White*. New York: Basic Books, 2002.
Yamauchi, Wakako. *Songs My Mother Taught Me*. New York: Feminist Press, 1994.
Yamazaki, Jane W. *Japanese Apologies for World War II: A Rhetorical Study*. London: Routledge, 2006.
Yancey, George. *Who Is White? Latinos, Asians, and the New Black/Nonblack Divide*. Boulder, CO: Lynne Rienner, 2003.
Yoneyama, Lisa. *Hiroshima Traces: Time, Space, and the Dialectics of Memory*. Berkeley: University of California Press, 1999.
Yoshihara, Mari. *Embracing the East: White Women and American Orientalism*. New York: Oxford University Press, 2002.
Yoshimi, Yoshiaki. *Comfort Women: Sexual Slavery in the Japanese Military during World War II*. Trans. Suzanne O'Brien. New York: Columbia University Press, 2000.
Yu, Su-lin. "Sisterhood as Cultural Difference in Amy Tan's *The Hundred Secret Senses* and Cristina Garcia's *The Aguero Sisters*." *Critique: Studies in Contemporary Fiction* 47.4 (2006): 345–61.
Yücesoy, Hayrettín. "Translation as Self-Consciousness: Ancient Sciences, Antediluvian Wisdom, and the 'Abbāsid Translation Movement." *Journal of World History* 20.4 (2009): 523–57.

Zachar, Peter. "Psychiatric Disorders Are Not Natural Kinds." *Philosophy, Psychiatry, and Psychology* 7.3 (2000): 167–82.

Zentgraf, Kristine M. "Through Economic Restructuring, Recession, and Rebound: The Continuing Importance of Latina Immigrant Labor in the Los Angeles Economy." *Asian and Latino Immigrants in a Restructuring Economy: The Metamorphosis of Southern California*. Ed. Marta López-Garza and David R. Diaz. Stanford: Stanford University Press, 2001. 46–74.

Zhou, Xiaojing, and Samina Najmi, eds. *Form and Transformation in Asian American Literature*. Seattle: University of Washington Press, 2005.

Zieger, Robert H. *For Jobs and Freedom: Race and Labor in America since 1865*. Lexington: University Press of Kentucky, 2007.

Zimmerman, Larry J. "First, Be Humble: Working with Indigenous Peoples and Other Descendant Communities." *Indigenous Archaeologies: Decolonizing Theory and Practice*. Ed. Claire Smith and Hans Martin Wobst. London: Routledge, 2005. 301–14.

Žižek, Slavoj. *Iraq: The Borrowed Kettle*. New York: Verso Books, 2004.

Zunshine, Lisa. *Why We Read Fiction: Theory of Mind and the Novel*. Columbus: Ohio State University Press, 2006.

Index

Ted Chiang's *The Merchant and the Alchemist's Gate* is abbreviated in the subheadings as *TMATAG*.

Abbasid Caliphate period, 193–94, 199, 232n28, 232n30, 233n35, 233nn39–40
"Abducted by Aliens!." *See under* Light, Claire
Abler, Thomas, 147, 228n12
A Carnivore's Inquiry. *See under* Murray, Sabina
activism: Chicano cultural nationalism, 76–77, 80, 87, 89–90, 93, 98–99; in Foster's *Atomik Aztex*, 82–89; importance of, 81; limits of white, 131–33
Acuña, Rodolfo, 66
Adolf, Antony, 200
African American literature: and alien-abduction narratives, 178–79; criticism, 215n28
African Americans: in segregated Long Island suburbs, 47–48
agricultural industry, 64, 66, 69–73, 220n4
Aiiieeeee! An Anthology of Asian-American Writers, 17, 215n25
Alam, M. Shahid, 204
Alarcón, Daniel Cooper, 98
Alber, Jan, 124
Alcoff, Linda Martín, 66
Alexander, Susan K., 111
alienation: various subject positions, 31–32, 33
Almaguer, Tomás, 64

Aloft. *See under* Lee, Chang-rae
American identity: and cannibalism, 145, 157–58; gradation of racialization, 28; immigrants' names changed, 50–51; jettisoning hazardous past, 15; shift in US racial makeup (Chicanos and Latinos), 80–81; whiteness as ultimate criterion, 63. *See also* whiteness and white identity
American indigenous captivity narrative, 178
American Studies, 22, 217n38
analogy: racial, 179, 181–84, 191–92, 207; speculative fictions, 172; time-traveling cultural document, 193, 207; use of term, 230n2, 231n3
Anasazi and cannibalism, 148–51, 228n18–25
anthropophagy, 146, 147, 155, 169. *See also* cannibalism
appropriation, ethnoracial and cultural: by Asian American writers, 29, 65, 89, 191, 233n35; by characters in Chiang's *TMATAG*, 207; by characters in Light's "Abducted by Aliens!," 190, 207; by characters in Nunez's *The Last of Her Kind*, 130–33; classical art acquisitions, 158, 162, 165, 169; dangers of, 75, 76, 92, 100; of storytelling, 177
Aravamudan, Srinivas, 233n45

Arens, William, 147, 228nn13–14
Armstrong, Karen, 199
Arrizón, Alicia, 76, 221n17
Asian American literature: author, narrator and storyteller, 216–17n36; constitution and narrative perspective, 4–6; genre fiction and young adult fiction, 213n4; on Japanese American internment, 190, 232n23 (*see also* Light, Claire: "Abducted by Aliens!"); language of, 213n1; literary craft, 12; mixed race writers, 102; multifocal, 18, 215n27; polycultural critique, 66; rise of criticism, 17–20, 215–16nn25–30; severing link between author and narrator, 20–22; traditional understanding of, 1–2. *See also* Asian American speculative fictions; criticism and critical trends; *individual* authors
Asian Americans: versus Asian-Americans (hyphenated), 49; distinctions among populations, 220n5; importance of fictional minor characters, 130; term as metaphor, 105; use of term, 48–49
Asian American speculative fictions: alien-abduction narratives, 177–79, 181, 187, 207–8; analogy and allegory, 172, 230n2; as cautionary tales, 81, 221n14; and cultural criticism, 171–72; Japanese American internment as, 188–92; race in, 201, 231n4; racial asymmetries in, 173; time travel, 196. *See also* Chiang, Ted; Foster, Sesshu; Light, Claire
Asian American studies: and Foster's *Atomik Aztex*, 65; intersectional, need for, 22, 103, 212; and Lee's *Aloft*, 25; and Light's "Abducted by Aliens!," 191, 201; and mixed race studies, 12; and Murray's fictions, 152, 155, 157; and Murray's *Forgery*, 159, 169; and Nunez's fictions, 105, 109–10, 120, 131, 224n11; programs, 6; and speculative fictions, 171–72. *See also* criticism and critical trends
Asian Reporter: Polo, 36
Asiatic Barred Zone law (1917), 66
Askenasy, Hans, 227n7
Athanassopoulos, Effie-Fotini, 160, 229n26
authenticity. *See* ethnoracial authenticity
authoritarianism, 202

autobiographic/ethnographic readings: and ethnoracial appropriation, 130, 223n35; glimpses of (in Foster's *Atomik Aztex*), 93–94; and minor characters, 72–73; mixed race and function of fictionalized biography, 103–4; and mixed race writers, 102–3, 120, 155–56; and model minority paradigm, 11–12 (*see also* model minority paradigm); and myths of postrace discourse, 136–37; narrator/author ethnicity differs, 27–28; not paralleled in writing, 2–4, 213n3, 214nn11–12; resisted and complicated, 19–20, 64, 70–71, 76, 89–90, 120, 210–12; severing link between author and narrator, 20–22; and speculative fictions, 173, 207–8. *See also* biography and fictional form of; ethnoracial authenticity; narrative perspective
autobiography/memoir: author and narrator-character, 20; and model minority myth, 11–12; use of literary form, 4–5, 13–14, 213n7. *See also* bildungsroman and anti-bildungsroman
Avramescu, Cătălin, 227n8
Aztec Empire, 78–79. *See also* Foster, Sesshu: *Atomik Aztex*
Aztlán, 76, 98–99, 221nn16–18. *See also* Chicanos and Asian Americans

Bacho, Peter: V. Nguyen's critique of *Entrys*, 112–13, 119
Backhaus, Bhira: *Under the Lemon Trees*, 64–65, 70–73, 99
Ballaster, Rosalind, 198–99, 201, 203
Bataille, Georges, 79
Bates, Milton J., 119
Baxandall, Rosalyn, 218n15
Bedolla, Lisa, 80–81
Benedict, Elizabeth, 225n26
Benton, Michael, 107
Berglund, Jeff, 229n25
Bernard, Elaine, 222n25
bildungsroman and anti-bildungsroman, 5, 10, 13, 101, 139, 213n7, 216n30, 224n6. *See also* autobiography/memoir
Billman, Brian R., 229n21

binary of East and West: in American identity, 15. *See also* orientalism
biography and fictional form of: biography as life-writing, 106–7; choice of biographical life, 120–21, 127, 224nn10–11; mixed race and function of, 103–4; narrator/writer's role, 107–9; terminology, 224n8, 224n13. *See also* Nunez, Sigrid
bipolar disorder: in *Aloft* (Lee), 51–55; DSM description, 51, 218n21, 219n23; genetic component, 53, 219n25
Birchall, Diana, 214n11
Blade Runner (film), 179
Blumenberg, Evelyn, 220n7
Boston Globe, 225n26
Bowman, Bradley L., 203
Brada-Williams, Noelle, 31–32
Brancati, Dawn, 203
Braziel, Jana Evans, 231n7
Brennan, Jonathan, 223n3
Budde, Rebecca, 220n8
Bullock, Peter Y., 229n22
Bulosan, Carlos: *America Is in the Heart*, 2, 64, 67–69, 73
Burns, Christy L., 178
Bush, Melanie E. L., 39
Butler, Robert Olen, 113
Byman, Daniel, 205–6

California: agricultural industry, 64, 66, 69–73; Asian migrants, 66; garment industry, 67; labor force historic context, 64, 66, 89, 222n30; literary presentations, 70; literary racial asymmetries, 99–100; minority laborers, 65; multiracial labor force, 94 (*see also under* slaughterhouse work); shift in demographics (Chicanos and Latinos), 81
Calotychos, Vangelis, 168
Camarillo, Albert M., 81
Cambodian American writers, 13–14
cannibalism: Goya's *Scenes of Cannibalism*, 146–47, 148; of indigenous subject, 146–55, 228nn11–25; in Murray's *A Carnivore's Inquiry*, 145, 227n5; origin of term, 146; scholarship on, 151, 229nn24–25. *See also* consumption

canonical status: Bulosan's *America Is in the Heart*, 67–68; literary commodification, 14; Nunez's *A Feather in the Breath of God*, 106; understanding of Asian American literature, 1–2; and women in war literature, 111
Cao, Lan: *Monkey Bridge*, 15
capitalism, global: black market in organs, 95–96, 223nn32–33; California's garment industry, 67; and cannibalism, 157–58, 230n39; Chicano underclass and, 65; and classical antiquities, 162–63; and emergent oppositional consciousness, 82–89; in Foster's *Atomik Aztex*, 79–80, 89, 95–96; globalization, 22, 222n30; meatpacking industry, 91, 222n27; monstrous appetite of, 96–97; and sacrificial system, 82
The Caprices. See under Murray, Sabina
Caputo, Philip, 113
carceral topography, 126, 226n29, 226n31
Carter, Susan, 225n22
Caruth, Cathy, 182, 231n16
Caster, Peter, 125
Castillo, Richard Griswold del, 221n16
Castro-Klarén, Sara, 146
Cha, Theresa Hak Kyung: *Dictee*, 18, 215n27
Chan, Jeffery Paul, 17
Chang, Diana, 6; *The Frontiers of Love*, 102–3, 138; mixed-race Asian American writer, 102
Chang, Yoonmee, 7–8, 210
character construction: versus discerning authenticity, 38–39
Chávez, John, 221n15
Chejne, Anwar G., 199
Chen, Tina: *Double Agency*, 18
Chan, Sucheng, 63
Chiang, Mark, 215n26
Chiang, Ted, and *The Merchant and the Alchemist's Gate*, 192–207: didactic purpose, 201, 202, 204; fables, 196; ink sketches, 194; orientalist tale subverted, 193–96, 203–7; plot summary, 192–93; political context, 173, 174; racial asymmetries (overview), 3, 23–24; sociohistorical context, 200–201, 206–7, 207–8, 232n25; temporal frames, 201–7; "The Tale of the Fortunate Rope-Maker," 196–97; "The Tale of the Weaver Who Stole from Himself," 197–98

Chicanos and Asian Americans,
  64–73; class and interracial
  tensions, 68–70, 72–73; interracial
  influences, 75; interracial romance,
  70, 73, 221n13; linked migration
  history, 66–67; narrative cross-
  minority hybridity, 65; yellow
  Chicanismo, 89–94
Chicanos, Latinos, and Latin Americans,
  67, 73–89; cultural nationalism,
  76–77, 80–81, 221n16; importance of
  fictional minor characters, 72, 89; in
  slaughterhouse work, 65; status as a
  group, 222n22; use of term, 220n6,
  221n11, 221n15
Chin, Frank, 17
Chinatowns, 90, 92–93
Chinese American writers: in early
  anthology, 17; effect of Tan's *The
  Joy Luck Club,* 14–15, 215n23; of
  mixed race, 177; Nunez differs from
  traditional, 106; tour guide function,
  14–17. *See also* Asian American
  literature; Chiang, Ted; Kingston,
  Maxine Hong; Light, Claire; Nunez,
  Sigrid; Tan, Amy
Chinese expatriate authors, 14
Chu, Louis: *Eat a Bowl of Tea,* 17
Chu, Seo-Young, 171–72
Chuh, Kandice, 105, 131; *Imagine
  Otherwise,* 18
chupacabras, 97
class: Asian and Latino working classes,
  67, 220n8; in *Atomik Aztex*'s socialism,
  78, 89; in Chiang's *TMATAG,* 197, 198;
  in Murray's *Forgery,* 166–67; suburban
  erasure, 55–60; and suburbia,
  40–43, 54, 218n15; tensions among
  Asian American and Latino, 69–70;
  whiteness and upper-middle-class,
  40–41; and white privilege, 133–34
Cohn, Dorrit, 20, 216n34
Cold War: and alien-abduction narrative,
  178–79; role of Greece, 160–61, 169,
  230nn30–32
colonialism, postcolonialism, and
  neocolonialism: of Asia and America
  compared, 144; and cannibalism,
  146, 148, 151–52, 155–56, 159,
  227nn7–8; comparative colonialisms,
  137–38, 152, 155–56, 170, 227nn1–2;
  crypto-colonialism (Greece), 159–61,
  162, 169; and enemy combatant, 174;
  Filipino-Mexican connection, 68; in
  Foster's *Atomik Aztex,* 78; ideologies
  of race in Côte d'Ivoire, 9–10; and
  Iraq, 205–6; multinational scope, 156;
  in Murray's *A Carnivore's Inquiry,*
  144–58; and oriental tales, 203, 204;
  palace of Hernán Cortés, 156; and
  scholarship on cannibalism, 151–52; of
  Spanish and Aztecs, 79; transnational
  appropriation of classical art, 158;
  in Vietnamese fictional characters,
  114–15
color-blindness, 7, 49, 62, 218n10
Columbus, Christopher, 144–46
Comaroff, Jean and John, 96
commodification, literary, 6; Asian
  American as native informant, 5–6, 8;
  imperiling fictionality, 21; marketing
  strategies, 14–16, 27, 35–36, 215n24;
  touristing Asian America, 14–17. *See
  also* consumption
community: interracial influences, 75
consumption: American gaze in Chiang's
  TMATAG, 203–4; of antiquities
  market, 162–63. *See also* cannibalism;
  commodification, literary
Cook-Lynn, Elizabeth, 150
Cortés, Hernán: palace of, 156
Côte d'Ivoire, 9–10
criticism and critical trends: analogy and
  allegory, 230n2, 231n3; biography, 108,
  224nn10–11, 224nn13–14; comparative
  race methodology, 66, 220n2;
  consideration of minor characters,
  72, 130; critical race theories, 40, 41;
  cross-disciplinary approaches, 211–12;
  and interracial elements (Bulosan's
  America Is in the Heart), 67–68,
  221n10; mixed-race writers, 102–3, 120,
  138–39, 170, 223nn1–5; orientalism,
  233n41; oriental tale, 194; on prison
  writings, 124, 126, 226nn28–29; in
  relation to Asian American writers, 6;
  responsibility of minority writers, 112–
  13 (*see also* Nguyen, Viet Thanh); rise
  of Asian American literature criticism,
  17–20, 215n26; and speculative fictions,
  171–72; subjectless discourse, 105; use
  of phenomenology, 40–41; of Vietnam

War literature, 114–15, 225nn24–25; whiteness studies, 39, 217n5, 217n9. *See also* Asian American studies; politics (social); reception and reviewers' commentary
Crocker, Bathsheba, 203
cuisine: of Chinatowns, 93–94; food-specific humor (Nunez's *For Rouenna*), 114; sushi versus *gimbap*, 55–56
Culbertson, Roberta, 231n16
Culler, Jonathan, 216n33
cultural geography: Mexican American sites, 67–68, 88, 222n24; race and space, 217n37. *See also* politics (social)
cultural studies, 22
Cusac, Anne-Marie, 128

Daniels, Roger, 186
Darling, J. Andrew, 150
The Day the Earth Stood Still (film), 95
De Genova, Nicholas, 66
De Jesús, Melinda, 221n10
De León, Arnoldo, 221n16
Dickens, Charles, 124
Doležel, Lubomír, 216n32
Dongoske, Kurt E., 150, 229n23
Drake, Kimberly, 226n28
D'Souza, Tony: *Whiteman*, 8–11, 13, 214n14, 217n2
Duncan, Patti, 189

Eaton, Winnifred, 6, 214n11
Elam, Michele, 103
Ellis, Trey, 223n4
Encyclopedia of Asian-American Literature, 102–3
enemy combatant, 174
Engelbrecht, William E., 228n9
The English Patient (film), 118–19
Espiritu, Augusto, 137
Espiritu, Yen Le, 67, 225n24
ethnic literature, 215n21
ethnoracial authenticity: assumptions of, 5, 214n9; in book marketing, 27 (*see also* commodification, literary); ghostly narratorial presence, 37–39; and mixed-race writer, 170; and myths of postrace discourse, 136–37; narrative perspective erasing, 26; and postrace aesthetic, 8; reviewers' commentary of (*Aloft*/Lee), 26, 36–39,

217n8; tour-guide role of author, 14–17. *See also* autobiographic/ethnographic readings
ethnoracial bildungsroman, 4–5, 13–14, 213n7. *See also* bildungsroman and anti-bildungsroman
Evans, Mary, 224n14
Ewan, Elizabeth, 218n15

Fachinger, Petra, 106
Falk, Richard, 233n43
Farenga, Stephen J., 218n20
Farmingville, Long Island, 46
Feagin, Joe, 62
A Feather on the Breath of God. *See under* Nunez, Sigrid
fecal matter, 150
Federal Housing Administration (FHA), 46, 218n18
Felski, Rita, 227n1
feminism: second-wave feminism, 110. *See also* gender
Ferber, Abby L., 40
Ferguson, T. J., 150, 229n23
fetishization: and alienation, 56–57
fictionalized biography. *See* biography and fictional form of
fictional narration: compared to historical, 20, 216n32; nature of narration, 216nn35–36. *See also* narrative perspective
Filipino American writers: canonical status, 2, 67; in early anthology, 17. *See also* Bacho, Peter; Bulosan, Carlos; Hagedorn, Jessica; Murray, Sabina; Philippines
Filipino migrants: restrictions on, 66
first person. *See under* narrative perspective
Fisher, Barbara, 225n26
Fisher, Lloyd H., 220n4
Fludernik, Monika, 126, 211, 226n29
Ford, Jamie Ford: *Hotel on the Corner of Bitter and Sweet*, 16
Forgery. *See under* Murray, Sabina
For Rouenna. *See under* Nunez, Sigrid
Forter, Greg, 231n16
Foster, Sesshu: *City Terrace Field Manual*, 75; interracial aesthetic and influence, 75; politics of narrative perspective, 89–90

– *Atomik Aztex*, 73–99; and Chicano cultural nationalism, 98–99, 100; Chicano studies subject, 212; emergent oppositional consciousness, 82–89; organ harvesting, 95–96; plot summary, 73–75; political vision behind, 64–65; race, class, and power, 82–83; racial asymmetries (overview), 3, 22–23, 102; racial order, 81, 94–95; sacrifice, critique of, 84–85, 87; sacrifice and massacre, 79–80; speculative hybridities, 94–99, 171, 221n14; yellow Chicanismo, 89–94
Franklin, H. Bruce, 124, 226n28
Friedman, Susan Stanford, 227n1
Fu, Bennett, 102
Futrell, Alison, 78–79

garment industry, 67, 220nn7–8
gender: Chicana feminism, 76; equity and military service, 104, 110–21; exploitation of Asian women, 90; immigration imbalance, 68, 70; masculinist bias in Vietnam War representations, 111, 120, 224nn17–18, 225n21; rates of women's incarceration, 127–28, 226nn34–35
geography. *See* cultural geography
Geron, Kim, 80–81
G.I. Bill of Rights, 46
Giroux, Henry A., 202
global capitalism. *See* capitalism, global
globalization, 22, 222n30
Godzilla, 97
Good, Byron J., 219n27
Goya: *Scenes of Cannibalism*, 146–47, 148
Greece: ancient and contemporary, 163–64, 168; ancient art and culture, 159–60, 230n28; and Cold War, 169, 230nn30–32; postwar politics, 160–62; relationship to colonialism, 159–60, 229n26
Greene, Graham: *The Quiet American*, 114–15
Grob, Gerald, 53, 219n28
Gruhzit-Hoyt, Olga, 225n20
Guantanamo Bay, 202
Guerin-Gonzales, Camille, 220n4

Hagedorn, Jessica: *Dogeaters*, 227n3; *Toxicology*, 2–3, 13

Halle, David, 218n20
Hames-Garcia, Michael, 226n31
Hamilakis, Yannis, 230n28
Hamilton, Nigel, 108
Haney-López, Ian F., 39, 48, 81
Hantke, Steffen, 119
Harris, Cheryl I., 39, 48
Harvey, David, 202, 203
Hatzivassiliou, Evanthis, 161
Hawai'i, 66
Hayashi, Brian Masaru, 182–83, 186
Heath American literature anthology, 213n1
Heinemann, Larry, 113
Herman, Judith Lewis, 231n16
Herzfeld, Michael, 159–60, 161
Hicks, James Whitney, 219n30
Hiroshima: post–World War II, 142–43
historical framework: assumption of Asian American literature, 16; of Chicano and Asian American relationship, 66–67; juncture between fiction and nonfiction, 21–22. *See also* ethnoracial authenticity; politics (social)
historical narration: compared to fictional, 20, 216n32
Hofmann, Bettina, 111
Homans, John (*New York* magazine), 217n8
Hong, Terry, 138, 139; interview with Lee, 38
Huang, Betsy, 232n25
Hunt, Courtney, 233n35
hybridity, cultural, 69, 73, 98–99, 104

identity: complicated subject position, 85–86; crisis in prison writing, 126; Greek national, 168. *See also* American identity; whiteness and white identity
Immigration Act: 1924, 68; 1965, 6
immigration and migration: acculturation difficulties, 29–31, 31–32; alien abductions and illegal aliens, 178; and California labor, 66–67, 87–88, 91, 220n7, 222n30; and demonized culture, 191; gender imbalance, 68, 70; mental health and stress of, 53–55; migration in Foster's *Atomik Aztex*, 83–84, 87–88; name changes, 50–51; Punjabi, 70, 73; of

Vietnamese post war, 119–20. *See also* transnationalism
Inada, Lawson Fusao, 17
Indian American writers: canonical status, 2. *See also* Backhaus, Bhira; D'Souza, Tony; Lahiri, Jhumpa; Mukherjee, Bharati
individualism. *See* Backhaus, Bhira; D'Souza, Tony; Lahiri, Jhumpa; liberal individualism
Iraq: setting for Chiang's *TMATAG*, 192–93; and US authoritarianism, 202–3; US invasion, 205–7, 233nn43–44, 234n47
Iroquois and cannibalism, 146–48, 228n9, 228nn11–16
Isaac, Allan Punzalan, 227n2
Ishiguro, Kazuo: referenced in *Aloft* (Lee) reviews, 36
Ivy, Marilyn, 143

Jacobs, Wilbur R., 228n16
Japan: post–World War II, 142–43, 227n4
Japanese Americans: and Aztlán, 98–99; internment, 90, 93–94, 94–95, 173–74, 179–85, 182–83, 232n20, 232n23; internment as cultural trauma, 187–92; internment as speculative fiction, 188–92 (*see also* Light, Claire: "Abducted by Aliens!"); internment rationale, 186; internment "relocation centers," 184; migrant workers and farmers, 180. *See also* Foster, Sesshu
Japanese American writers: canonical status, 2; in early anthology, 17; sansei, 188. *See also* Okada, John
Jeffery, Judith S., 160
Jeffords, Susan, 111
Jerng, Mark, 40–41, 231n4
Jesuits and Brebeuf, 146–47, 228n12
Johns, Christina Jacqueline, 78–79
Johnson, Bonnie, 218n20
Johnson, Dale D., 218n20
Johnson, Joyce, 225n27, 226n38
Johnson, Kenneth M., 81
Johnson, Sheri L., 51, 54, 219n31
Jones, Howard, 161, 230n30
Jurca, Catherine, 60
Jusdanis, Gregory, 160, 230n28

Kagy, Tom, 36

Kakutani, Michiko, 157
Kang, Younghill, 5
Kantner, John, 229n22
Kaplan, Amy, 174
Kaplan, Harold I., 51, 54
Kaufmann, Chaim, 202
Kelly, Colleen Elizabeth, 233n44
Kennedy, Hugh, 233n39
Kenny, Lorraine Delia, 47
Kidwai, Abdur Raheem, 204
Kim, Claire Jean: *Bitter Fruit*, 81
Kim, Elaine H., 191; *Asian American Literature*, 18
Kim, Jodi, 169
Kim, Sue J., 176, 215n27
Kingston, Maxine Hong: *The Woman Warrior*, 1, 5, 211, 214n20
Kinney, Katherine, 225n24
kinship systems, 82
Knox, Paul, 46
Kofas, Jon V., 161
Korean American culture: cuisine, 55–56; immigration experience, 53–55, 57–58; names, 50–51; suburban erasure of, 55–60
Korean American writers: canonical status, 2; in early anthologies, 18. *See also* Lee, Chang-rae
Koshy, Susan, 217n5; "The Fiction of Asian American Literature," 18

LaBrack, Bruce, 221n13
LaCapra, Dominick, 189, 190, 191
Lahiri, Jhumpa: *Interpreter of Maladies*, 31; "Mrs. Sens," 31–34; *Unaccustomed Earth*, 215n22
Lambert, Bruce, 47
Lambert, Patricia M., 229n21
language: and alienation, 56; coded racial discourses (doublespeak), 48; Filipino-Mexican colonial connection, 68; and gradation of racialization, 28–29; Lee's construction of Italian American character, 38; racial terminology, 48–50
Lapcharoensap, Rattawut: "Don't Let Me Die in This Place," 27–31, 217n4; "Farangs," 29–30; *Sightseeing*, 27–28; white narrator's perspective, 27–31
Latin Americans, 67. *See also* Chicanos
Latinos: use of term, 220n6. *See also* Chicanos and Asian Americans

Laub, Dori, 190
Lavender, Isiah, 231n4
Law, Victoria, 128, 227n40
Le, Nam: "Love and Honor and Pity and Pride and Compassion and Sacrifice," 7; *The Boat*, 8, 13
Lee, Chang-rae
- *A Gesture Life*, 25
- *Aloft*, 34–62; Korean American housewife (Daisy), 55–60; Lee comment on Jerry Battle (character), 38; Lee comment on Paul Pyun (character), 38; Long Island's sociohistorical conditions, 46–47; madness and suburbia (Daisy), 50–55; marketing strategies, 35–36; narrator, Italian American (Jerry Battle), 25; plot summary, 34–35; racial asymmetries, 3, 22, 25–26, 101, 133; racialized thought bomb (Jerry re Hal), 43–45, 47–48, 60; reception, 26, 34–39, 217n8; refracting whiteness, 39–50; uses of whiteness, 25–27
- *Native Speaker*, 2, 25
Lee, Christopher: *The Semblance of Identity*, 18
Lee, C. Y., 5
Lee, Fred, 173
Lee, Hermione, 108, 224n10
Lee, Josephine D., 105–6
Lee, Sue-Im, 215n29
Lejeune, Philippe, 20
Leonard, Banks L., 229n21
Leonard, Karen Isaksen, 70, 220n5, 221n13
Lestringant, Frank, 146
lê thi diem thúy: *The Gangster We Are All Looking For*, 120
Levittown, Long Island, 46–47, 218n17, 218n20
Levittown, Pennsylvania, 47
Li, Guofang, 12
liberal individualism: as advancing racial inequality, 41, 218n10; and authoritarianism, 202; and Foster's *Atomik Aztex*'s socialism, 77–78, 82–89; misreadings of, 53; neoliberal state and oil, 203–4; whiteness at center, 26–27; and white privilege, 40, 62
Lichter, Daniel T., 81

Light, Claire: "Abducted by Aliens!," 175–92; blinded by the light episode, 180; choice of narrator, 189–90; episodic structure, 179–80; hybrid narrative, 185; identity of aliens, 185–88; internment afterword, 175–77, 179, 180, 189, 191, 192; intertextual references, 231n8; mixed-race writer, 176–77, 191; plot summary, 175; political context, 173, 174, 207–8; racial analogy, 179, 181–84, 191–92, 201, 207; racial asymmetries (overview), 3, 23–24; racial background, 177; *Slightly Behind and to the Left*, 173; spaceship becomes internment camp, 181–83; temporal and spatial disturbance, 181, 184, 188–92; tourist trap planet, 183–84; trauma narrative, 182–83, 188–92; voice appropriation, 177
Lim, Shirley Geok-lin, 18
Lindgren, James, 11–12
Ling, Amy, 18, 102–3, 223n1
Ling, Jinqi, 216n30
Ling, L. H. M., 204
Lipsitz, George, 4, 39, 48, 218n10
"literary Chinatown" (Partridge), 16
literary commodification. *See* commodification, literary
literary criticism. *See* Asian American literature; criticism and critical trends
Little, Douglas, 206
Lockman, Zachary, 206
Long Island suburbia: class and race, 58–59, 218n15; race and sociohistorical conditions, 46–47, 218n20; whiteness and multiculturalism, 40–50. *See also* suburbia
Look magazine, 47
Lord of the Rings (film), 176
Los Angeles, 65, 67. *See also* California; Foster, Sesshu: *Atomik Aztex*
Lowe, Anna Wong, 12
Lowe, Lisa, 18, 63, 106, 215n27
Lye, Colleen, 1, 5, 231n3

MacArthur Field, Long Island, 46
MacKenzie, John, 233n45
Makdisi, Saree, 204
Marshall, Kathryn, 110, 225n18

Marshall, Megan, 133
Marshall-Fratani, Ruth, 9
Martin, Debra L., 150, 229n23
Martin, P., 220n4
Maryland, Ohio Reformatory for Women (ORW), 127
Massey, Dennis, 126
The Matrix (film), 179
Maxey, Ruth, 32, 33
May, Elaine Tyler, 218n17
Mbembe, Achille, 142
McCarthy, Kevin F., 222n30
McGowan, Miranda Oshige, 11–12
meatpacking industry. *See* slaughterhouse work
medicalization, 219n24
mental health: bipolar disorder, 51–54; environmental factors, 53–55, 57–58, 219n26; treatment of (Daisy in *Aloft*), 60–61, 219n31, 219nn27–28
The Merchant and the Alchemist's Gate (Chiang). *See under* Chiang, Ted
Messud, Claire, 134
Mexican American, 67–68; use of term, 221n11. *See also* Chicanos and Asian Americans
Mexico: economic crisis, 97
Meyer, Björn, 54, 219n31
Michael, Ronald, 223n33
Middlebrook, Diane Wood, 107
Middle East: American gaze in Chiang's *TMATAG*, 203–4; setting for Chiang's *TMATAG*, 193
migration. *See* immigration and migration
Miklowitz, David Jay, 53
military (US): gender equity for women, 104, 110–21
mixed-race Asian American writers: asymmetrically read, 134–35; collective experience of discrimination, 191; critical reception, 102–3, 138–39, 223nn1–2; use of term, 103, 223nn2–4. *See also* Foster, Sesshu; Light, Claire; Murray, Sabina; Nunez, Sigrid; Roley, Brian Ascalon
mixed-race studies, 12, 214n18
Mizruchi, Susan, 82
model minority paradigm: in postracial era, 7, 11–12; and racial exclusion, 25; resisted and complicated, 210
Moraga, Cherríe, 221nn17–18
Moya, Paula, 213n5
Mukherjee, Bharati: *Jasmine*, 2
multiculturalism: and postrace discourse, 13; shift in US racial makeup (Chicanos and Latinos), 80–81; suburban assimilation, 59–60; use of term Asian American, 48–49; and whiteness, 40–50
Murray, Sabina: comparative colonialisms, 137–44, 155–56, 170; mixed-race writer, 138, 139; racial asymmetries, 137–38, 143–44, 155–56, 159; reception, 138–39; *Slow Burn*, 138, 139–40; *Tales of the New World*, 138
Murray, Sabina: *A Carnivore's Inquiry*, 144–58; Anasazi and cannibalism, 148–54, 228n18–25; consumption of indigenous populations, 170; Goya's *Scenes of Cannibalism*, 146–47, 148; Iroquois and cannibalism, 146–48; mixed-race writer, 138; palace of Hernán Cortés, 156; plot summary, 144–45; postcolonialism, 143–44; racial asymmetries (overview), 3, 23; racial identity of subject, 145, 150, 155–56
Murray, Sabina: *Forgery*, 158–69; aesthetics discussion, 163; American intelligence agencies narrative, 166–67; crypto-colonialism, 169; forger as cultural producer, 169–70; forgers as artists, 167–68; Greek working-class locals, 166–67; Lincoln's pencil (provenance and provenience), 164–65; mixed-race writer, 138; plot summary, 158–59, 230n38; postcolonialism, 143–44; racial asymmetries (overview), 3, 23
Murray, Sabina: *The Caprices*, 138; "Colossus," 140–41; "Folly," 140; "Intramuros," 141; "Order of Preference," 140; "Position," 141–43, 170; shifting narrative perspectives, 170; "The Caprices," 140, 141; "Walkabout," 140; "Yamashita's Gold," 141
Muslim Americans: and Japanese-American internment, 174

284 / INDEX

Myers, William and Mary, 47

names and names changed: American identity, 50–51
Nance, Susan, 194, 202, 233n42
narration. *See* narrative perspective
narrative perspective: American indigenous captivity narrative, 178; and authorial descent, 4–6, 25–26, 89–90, 130, 215n28; and authorial descent, severing link, 20–22; in biography, 107–8; and comparative colonialisms, 141–44; as distant *(Aloft)*, 41–43; elision between narration and perspective, 116; embedded narratives, 179–80, 192, 196, 199–200, 202, 204; emphatic imagination and telepathic, 216nn33–34; extradiegetic narrators, 20, 216n31, 216n33, 217n4; first-person as "we," 77, 88, 92; first-person to third-person shifts, 71–72; and historical malleability, 145; and mixed-race writers, 103; nature of narration, 216nn35–36; racism revealed, 60–62; resisting autobiographical, 211; shift of the narrative "I," 124; and speculative fictions, 207–8; use of "you," invoking an audience, 117; various subject positions, 31–34; and voice appropriation, 177 *(see also* appropriation, ethnoracial and cultural); white narrator constructing whiteness, 28, 32, 44–50, 217n2. *See also* autobiographic/ethnographic readings; biography and fictional form of; racial asymmetries
Nassau-Suffolk, Long Island, 46
Native American Graves Protect and Repatriation Act (1990), 229n24
native informant, 5–6, 8, 29, 38
neoliberalism, 203
New Criticism, 36, 38
New York Times, 36, 38, 133, 225n26; best-seller list, 14, 215n22
Nguyen, Bich Minh: *Short Girls,* 120
Nguyen, Viet Thanh: critique of Peter Bacho's *Entrys,* 112–13, 119; *Race and Resistance,* 18
Nicki, Andrea, 219n28
Nunez, Sigrid, 101–35; biographer's control over subject, 106–7; choice of biographical life, 127; ethnoracial variations, 105–6; fictional form of biography, 224n8, 224n14; importance of fictional minor characters, 130; mixed-race writer, 105; racial asymmetries, 131, 134–35; *A Feather on the Breath of God,* 105–7, 134; autobiographical valences, 23; *Mitz: The Marmoset of Bloomsbury,* 106; *Naked Sleeper,* 106; *Salvation City,* 106
Nunez, Sigrid: *For Rouenna,* 109–21; asymmetries in fictionalized biography, 110, 114; function of fictionalized biography, 103–5, 134–35; Luther's role, 135; plot summary, 109; racial asymmetries (overview), 3, 23, 121; role of narrator-biographer, 107–8, 109–12, 114–16, 117–18, 120–21; treating Vietcong, 115–16; Vietnamese characters in, 113–17, 119; Vietnamese children, 116–18
Nunez, Sigrid: *The Last of Her Kind,* 121–34; biographical content, 123–24; Chinese Lucy, 129–30, 133; function of fictionalized biography, 103–5, 134; Olympia's prison biography, 123–34, 225n27, 226n31, 227n39; Olympia's racial identity, 129, 226n38; plot summary, 122–23; race and Kwame, 131–33; racial asymmetries (overview), 3, 23; reception, 225nn26–27
nurses in Vietnam War, 110–21, 224nn16–18, 225n22
Nussbaum, Felicity, 204

Obeyesekere, Gananath, 227n8
O'Brien, Eileen, 62
O'Brien, Tim, 113
Ohio Reformatory for Women (ORW), 127
Okada, John: *No-No Boy,* 2, 17
Old Westbury, Long Island, 46, 48
Oliver, Melvin L., 46
Omi, Michael, 211
Ong, Paul, 220n7
oppositional consciousness, 85
organ harvesting, 95–96, 223nn32–33
orientalism: American orientalism, 193, 202, 234nn47–48; criticism, 233n41; oriental tales, 194, 198–99, 201–2, 202–7, 233n45; techno-orientalism, 179, 231n14; use of term Oriental, 48–49

Pagedas, Constantine A., 162
Papandreou, George, 161–62
Parikh, Crystal, 66
Park, Ed, 36
Parkman, Francis, 228n16
Partridge, Jeffrey F. L., 14–15, 16
Patriot Act, 202
Pavel, Thomas, 216n34
Penguin Books: *Aloft* (Lee) reading guide, 35
Pérez-Torres, Rafael, 76
Perry, Pamela, 39
Petrinovich, Lewis, 228n14
Phan, Aimee: *We Should Never Meet: Stories,* 120
Phelan, James, 216n36
Philippines: multiple colonial histories, 137–38. *See also* Filipino American writers
Pihlainen, Kalle, 20, 216n31
PMLA: Shu-mei Shih, 64
politics (social): of biographical form, 108–9; of Chiang's *TMATAG,* 196–201, 200–201, 202–7; of difference, 18; fictional worlds linked to, 65; Filipino-Mexican labor connection, 68–70; ignored in reviews, 39; juncture between fiction and nonfiction, 21–22, 67; of Murray's *A Carnivore's Inquiry,* 152, 170; necropolitics of colonialism, 142; of Nunez's *For Rouenna,* 119–20; progressivism in Foster's *Atomik Aztex,* 87; self-effacement and biography, 127; shift in US demographics (Chicanos and Latinos), 81; socially conscious fictions, 210–11; trauma of Japanese American internment, 190–92; of white exclusion, 40; of white narrative perspective, 27. *See also* criticism and critical trends; postrace discourse
Polo *(Asian Reporter),* 36–37
post-9/11 era: and American orientalism, 204–5, 234nn47–48; context for Asian American writing, 13–14, 174; context for Chiang's *TMATAG,* 174, 193, 202; context for Light's "Abducted by Aliens!," 174. *See also* terrorism
post–civil rights moment: legislative inclusion of Asian Americans, 17; pessimism in, 121–34; race and race consciousness, 40, 48; second-wave feminism, 104; societal hybridity, 104; visions of Aztlán, 76

postpositivist realism, 213n5
postrace discourse: and comparative colonialisms, 136–38; development of, 214n13; fallacy of, 13–14; and mixed-race writers, 103; model minority era, 6–7; not supported, 65, 210; postrace aesthetic, 7–11, 173, 210; social context of fictional world (Lee), 26–27. *See also* politics (social)
power: and community ideals, 54; and need to justify violence, 80; and nurses in Vietnam War, 111; of the word and racism, 49–50
Prashad, Vijay, 66
Price, Patricia L., 98
prison system (American): AIDS epidemic, 226n36; critique of, 122, 133, 135; effect on multiracial community beyond, 104; racial injustice in prisons, 128–29; rates of drug crime and women's incarceration, 127–28, 226nn34–35; women from minority backgrounds, 129, 227nn39–40
prison writings genre, 124; carceral topography, 126
provenance and provenience, 164–65
Puar, Jasbir K., 205
publishing market. *See* commodification, literary

Quan, Kenneth: interview with Lee, 38

race and racism: and alien-abduction narratives, 178–79, 181–84, 191; blurring racial identity, 75; in Chicano cultural nationalism, 98–99; and comparative colonialisms, 139; in context of Vietnam War, 115–18; encoded in speculative fictions, 172–73; in Foster's *Atomik Aztex,* 78; gradation of racialization, 28–29; inequality advanced through liberal individualism, 41; inferential racism exposed, 29, 39–50; interracial connections, 66, 220n3, 221n9, 221nn12–13; interracial tensions (Asian American and Latino), 69–70, 72–73; interracial unions and cultural hybridity, 69, 73, 99; and Japanese Americans, 173–74; in Long Island suburban development, 46–47; multiracial laboring force, 73,

286 / INDEX

race and racism (*continued*)
90–92; and narration, 60–62; race as construct, 211; racial essentialization, 130; racial injustice in prisons, 128–29, 226n28; racial orders, 81, 94–95; racial profiling, 132; in speculative fictions, 176, 231n4; suburban erasure, 55–60; in sugar beet industry, 68–69; of white consciousness, 26 (*see also* whiteness and white identity); and white political activism, 131–33
race and space: cultural geography, 217n37; Long Island's sociohistorical conditions, 46–47; whiteness mapped, 27
racial asymmetries: of Asian American literary California, 99–100; and authorial descent, 213n3 (*see also* ethnoracial authenticity); challenge to narrative perspectives, 2–4; and comparative colonialisms, 137–38, 143–44, 155–56, 159; cross-disciplinary criticism, 212; double levels in Lee's *Aloft*, 25–26; exposed in Nunez's fictionalized biographies, 121, 131; at juncture between fiction and nonfiction, 21–22; in mixed-race Asian American writers, 102, 133–35, 177; outline of study, 22–24; of speculative fictions, 173. *See also* narrative perspective
racial deviance: and constructions of whiteness, 34
racial exclusion: historical background, 25
racial profiling, 13–14, 132
Radhakrishnan, R., 227n1
Rafter, Nicole Hahn, 226n34
Rai, Amit S., 205
real estate: discrimination, 47–48, 218n18, 218n20; white identity, 40
reception and reviewers' commentary: *Aloft* (Lee), 26, 35–39, 217n8; *A Carnivore's Inquiry* (Murray), 157; *The Last of Her Kind* (Nunez), 225nn26–27; mixed-race Asian American writers, 102–3, 223nn1–2; political ramifications ignored, 39. *See also* criticism and critical trends
refractive narration, 27, 31, 34, 39–50. *See also* narrative perspective
Richardson, Alan, 201–2

Richardson, Michael, 79
Ringnalda, Donald J., 225n23
Roberts, Adam, 178
Robinson, Greg, 186
Roley, Brian Ascalon: *American Son*, 64–65, 69–70, 73
Roper, Robert, 225n27
Roxworthy, Emily, 187–88
Ryan, Marie-Laure, 216n35
Ryan, Maureen, 225n21
Ryan, Valerie, 37

sacrifice and sacrificial systems: compared to massacre, 79–80; critique of, 84–85, 87
Sadock, Benjamin J., 51, 54
Sadock, Virginia A., 51, 54
Saenz, Rogelio, 80
Said, Edward, 233n41
Saito, Natsu Taylor, 174
Salmon, Merrilee H., 228n15
Sanday, Peggy Reeves, 147, 228n11
Sanders, J. J., 233n40
Sandoval, Chela, 85
San Francisco Chronicle, 225n27
San Juan, E., Jr., 221n10
Santa Ana, Jeffrey J., 223n5
Sardar, Ziauddin, 233n41
Sassen, Saskia, 97
Satz, Debra, 223n32
Schabert, Ina, 224n8
Scheper-Hughes, Nancy, 96
Schlosser, Eric, 90
Scott, A. O., 36, 38
See, Lisa: *Shanghai Girls*, 16
September 11. *See* post-9/11 era
Serfaty, Simon, 206
Shapiro, Thomas M., 46
Sharafuddin, Mohammed, 233n41
Shelly v. Kraemer, 218n18
Shih, Shu-mei, 64
Sickels, Robert, 46
Sinclair, Upton: *The Jungle*, 91
slaughterhouse work: Chicanos in, 65; danger of work, 90; in Foster's *Atomik Aztex*, 74, 82–89, 90, 96, 100; global reach, 91, 222n27; labor recruitment, 91, 222nn25–28; multiracial laborers, 90–92, 223n31
Slightly Behind and to the Left. See under Light, Claire

Snow, Dean, 228n12
social difference and inequalities: literary cross-cultural engagement, 13
social inequality theme in Asian American literature: and model minority myth, 11–12
South Asian immigration, 70, 73
Spanos, William, 225n24
Spelts, Doreen, 224n16
Spielvogel, Christian, 234n47
Spivak, Gayatri, 213n6
Srikanth, Rajini, 19
Starr, Kevin, 64
Steinman, Rob, 224n17
strategic antiessentialism, 4
strategic essentialism: marginalizing influence, 19–20
Strom, Dao: *Grass Roof, Tin Roof*, 120
Strong, Pauline Turner, 148
Stull, Donald, 223n31
subjectless discourse, 105, 131
suburbia: ethnic, racial, and cultural erasure, 55–60; Long Island suburbia, 40–50, 46–47, 58–59, 218n15, 218n20; and madness (Daisy in *Aloft*), 50, 53–55, 57–58, 62; segregated suburbs, 46–47; urban dispersal, 218n17
sugar beet industry, 68
Sugimoto, Etsu Inagaki, 5
suicide: by Daisy in *Aloft*, 26, 35, 52–53, 60–61
Suvin, Darko, 171, 172

Tabios, Eileen: interview of Foster, 75
Takaki, Ronald, 63
Takezawa, Yasuko I., 191
Tan, Amy: *The Joy Luck Club*, 6, 14, 214n10, 214n20, 215n21. *See also* Chinese American writers
techno-orientalism, 179
terrorism: state sponsored, 202; US and Iraq relationship, 204–5; and War on Terror, 173–74, 193, 207, 210. *See also* post-9/11 era
Thagard, Paul, 219n26
Thailand (in fictional narrative), 27–31
The Last of Her Kind. See under Nunez, Sigrid
Tiananmen Square massacre, 14
time travel, 196, 199–200, 201–7
Tobias, James, 97

Todorov, Tzvetan, 79
touristing Asian America, 14–17
transnationalism: and academic discourses on cannibalism, 153; and appropriation, 158, 162; and capitalism, 97, 100; and the Cold War, 121; and elitism, 165, 169; of migrant labor, 64, 66, 83–84, 96; myths of postracial discourse, 137; and orientalism, 115, 194; and racial formation, 173–74; of racial asymmetries (overview), 23, 214n14; reverse assimilation and white, 28–29, 30; and spatial formulations, 217n37; and speculative fictions, 178. *See also* immigration and migration
trauma narratives, 182–83, 187–88, 188–92, 211, 231n16
Truman Doctrine, 160–61, 169
Trumpbour, John, 222n25
Trytten, Debora A., 12
Tuan, Mia, 25
Turner, Christy G., 149, 228n18, 229n25
Turner, Jacqueline, 149, 228n18

unionization: in fiction, 74; in Foster's *Atomik Aztex*, 85–89, 92, 100; meatpacking industry, 222n28; of sugar beet industry, 68–69
universal themes: and specific social contexts, 8–11; universal human rights in D'Souza's *Whiteman*, 8–11, 214n15
Urbanski, Heather, 221n14
US–Greek relations, 160–62

Valdés, Dennis Nodín, 91
Verghese, Abraham: *Cutting for Stone*, 16
Vernez, George, 222n30
Veterans' Administration (VA), 46
victimhood: vicarious, 191
Vietnamese American writers: Lan Cao, 15; Nam Le, 7–8; postwar fictions by, 120
Vietnam War: civilian casualties, 104; critique of veterans' fictionalized stories, 112–14; female veteran in Nunez's *For Rouenna*, 110–21; literature and criticism, 114–15, 225nn24–25; number of active American women, 110, 224nn17–18; in Nunez's *The Last of Her Kind*, 133, 135; women veterans, 111, 225n20, 225n22

violence: in Foster's *Atomik Aztex*, 77, 82; human sacrifice versus massacre, 79–80; in Murray's *A Carnivore's Inquiry*, 230n39
Võ, Linda Trinh, 7

Walden, Susan E., 12
Walker, Keith, 110
Walsh, Richard, 21
Walt Whitman Mall, Long Island, 46
Wang, Wayne, 14
War on Terror, 173–74, 193, 207, 210. *See also* terrorism
Washington Post, 225n27
Weir, Robert E., 47
whiteness and white identity, 40; and alien-abduction narrative, 178–79; assumptions exposed, 25–26; baseball, 217n3; constructed through white narrator, 27–34, 28–31, 31–34; definitions of white identity, 39–40, 218nn10–11; elitism and multiculturalism, 40–50; limits to white activism, 131–33; not a monolithic concept, 217n1; in refracted narration, 39–50; sentimental dispossession and, 60; studies in nation-state model, 217n5; white privilege, 62. *See also* American identity

Whittemore, Reed, 224n10
Wiegman, Robyn, 218n10
Wiese, Andrew, 46
Williams, Dana, 226n28
Williams, Laura Anh, 31–32
Wilson, Warren J., 222n25
Winant, Howard, 211
Wineapple, Brenda, 224n11
Wing, Jean Yonemura, 12
Winters, Ray, 54
Wolff, Carlo, 157
Woloch, Alex, 72
The Woman Warrior (Kingston), 1, 5, 211, 214n20
women. *See under* gender
Wong, Jade Snow, 5
Wong, Sau-ling C., 184, 214n20
Wong, Shawn, 17
Wong, Sunn Shelley, 18, 213n7
Wood, Jeffrey C., 219n25
Wu, Frank, 12

yellow peril, 4, 15, 26, 173
Yücesoy, Hayrettin, 232n28
Yutang, Lin, 5

Zieger, Robert, 222n28
Zimmerman, Larry J., 229n24
Žižek, Slavoj, 203, 205

About the Author

Stephen Hong Sohn is Assistant Professor of English at Stanford University. He is the coeditor of *Transnational Asian American Literature: Sites and Transits*.